DATE DUE

D0070635

PQ 149 .M54 1988
Miller, Nancy K., 1941-
Subject to change

.DEMCO.

Subject to Change

GENDER AND CULTURE

Carolyn G. Heilbrun and Nancy K. Miller, *editors*

GENDER AND CULTURE
A SERIES OF COLUMBIA UNIVERSITY PRESS
Edited by Carolyn G. Heilbrun and Nancy K. Miller

In Dora's Case: Freud, Hysteria, Feminism
Edited by Charles Bernheimer and Claire Kahane

Breaking the Chain: Women, Theory, and French Realist Fiction
Naomi Schor

Between Men: English Literature and Male Homosocial Desire
Eve Kosofsky Sedgwick

Romantic Imprisonment: Women and Other Glorified Outcasts
Nina Auerbach

The Poetics of Gender
Edited by Nancy K. Miller

Reading Woman: Essays in Feminist Criticism
Mary Jacobus

Honey-Mad Women: Emancipatory Strategies in Women's Writing
Patricia Yaeger

Thinking Through the Body
Jane Gallop

Gender and the Politics of History
Joan Wallach Scott

Nancy K. Miller

SUBJECT TO CHANGE

READING FEMINIST WRITING

COLUMBIA UNIVERSITY PRESS

New York   1988

Columbia University Press
New York   Guildford, Surrey
Copyright © 1988 Columbia University Press
All rights reserved
Printed in the United States of America

LIBRARY OF CONGRESS
LIBRARY OF CONGRESS CATALOGING-IN-PUBLICATION DATA

Miller, Nancy K.
Subject to change.

(Gender and culture)
Bibliography: p.
Includes index.
1. French literature—Women authors—History and criticism.
2. Feminism and literature—France.
3. Women and literature—France.   4. Feminist criticism—France.
I. Title.   II. Series.
PQ149.M54   1988   843'.009'352042   88-4341 CIP
ISBN 0-231-06660-0 (alk. paper)

Book design by Jennifer Dossin
Hardback editions of Columbia University Press books are Smyth-sewn
and are printed on permanent and durable acid-free paper.

For Carolyn

Contents

Acknowledgments

THIS BOOK has been a long time in the making, and it would never have been finished without two crucial moments of very special support: a Non-Tenured Faculty Fellowship at the Mary Ingraham Bunting Institute in Cambridge in the fall of 1980 and the spring of 1984, and a Rockefeller Foundation Humanities Fellowship in 1985–86. For these gifts of time I am much indebted.

Other debts, accumulated more diffusely and more personally over the years, are less easy to account for. When I first encountered feminist criticism I was struck by what seemed to me *lists* of acknowledgment, whole paragraphs of people feminist critics would thank for reading their work and talking about it with them. I thought this was either pretentious or implausible (or both): who *were* all these people so generous with their time and counsel? Perhaps this proliferation of readers was part of the poetics of sisterhood (about sharing—something, growing up as an older sister, I always hated). Now I have come to see this implication of others as part of the feminist project itself; or rather, though writing tends of course to remain a lonely affair, there is, I think, an equally real sense in which the practice of feminist criticism by virtue of its status as a *collective* project necessarily involves a map of acknowledgment and recognition. The writing of other feminist critics, the responsiveness of readers, the efforts of colleagues who through conferences, journals, and institutes produce scenes in which to work (*for* which to work) finally seems to relocate any criticism "of one's own" beyond the borders of personal investment.

Given the nature of this book (its interventionist fantasies), I am particularly grateful to the organizers of conferences and panels who got me to produce this writing in the first place, to try out new material in public, to rehearse and perform it in context. To Nelly Furman at Cornell University; Patricia Spacks at the English Institute; Nancy Huston at Urbino; Susan Lanser and Michael

Ragussis at Georgetown University; Michael Riffaterre at Columbia University; Elizabeth Weed and Joan Scott at the Pembroke Center, Brown University; Teresa de Lauretis at the University of Wisconsin-Milwaukee; Nancy Rabinowitz and Patricia Cholakian at Hamilton College; Frederick Keener and Susan Lorsch at Hofstra University; Virginia Swain at Dartmouth College. I also want to thank here Myra Dinnerstein and the remarkable group of feminist colleagues at the University of Arizona who brought me to Tuscon to present my work on women's writing under the auspices of an NEH Curriculum Integration Project.

I am equally grateful to the audiences at colleges and universities where I was invited to read this work while it was still in progress for their questions, suggestions, resistances, all of which (especially, perhaps, the last), in different ways, have helped me to reformulate my positions or reform my views. I am pleased to be able to thank here all the friends and colleagues who, over the years, have graciously brought me to lecture at their campuses. I list here in (more or less) chronological order the places to which I traveled: the University of Michigan (at Ann Arbor), Harvard University, New York University, Miami University (Oxford), the Ohio State University, Dartmouth College, Hamilton College, the University of Arizona at Tuscon, Tulsa University, Princeton University, Amherst College, the University of Toronto, MacMaster University, the University of North Carolina (Chapel Hill), Emory University, Drew University, Rutgers University, Stanford University, the University of California (at Berkeley and Irvine), Mount Holyoke College, Boston University, Pomona College.

There of course have been less formal but often more elaborate exchanges. Nina Auerbach, Barbara Babcock, Jane Bennett, Peggy Brawer, Rachel Brownstein, Terry Castle, Joan DeJean, Helene Foley, Christine Froula, Carolyn Heilbrun, Marianne Hirsch, Myra Jehlen, Alice Kaplan, Susan Lanser, Christie McDonald, Sandy Petrey, Naomi Schor, English Showalter, Brenda Silver, Catharine Stimpson, Margaret Waller, and Carolyn Williams have at different but always (it seemed) desperate stages of various chapters given me generous feedback and sharp criticism. Ellen Bassuk, Caroline Bynum, Linda Gordon, Marilyn Massey, and Eve Sedgwick in the spring of 1984 at Cambridge provided me with a context of critical thinking that helped me to move on to the final stages of the book.

My feminist students at Barnard and Columbia have honored me by the patience with which they allowed me in our seminars to elaborate this material before it became writing. For the chance to practice and to think aloud I am deeply in their debt. I want especially to tell Peggy Waller and Kate Jensen how much their inimitable way of being there mattered to me.

Donald Petrey and Jane Bennett relieved me of much of the burden of word-processing; Jane invented ways to be helpful; Peggy Brawer and Simone Kahn mercifully supplied local research assistance; the Barnard Faculty Grants Committee provided stipends that financed most of that work. I have appreciated the support.

There are, finally, three people whose belief in my work has sustained me in various modes throughout what had to seem to them the endless amount of time I have taken to let go of this book; who willy-nilly have had to live with this project in one way or another from its writing to the always penultimate revision of "finishing." To Carolyn Heilbrun, with whom I have taught and edited, gossiped and soul-searched, done Barnard/Columbia business over innumerable dinners in our neighborhood for almost a decade, and to whom, in the end, the magnitude of my debt is condensed in the dedication to this book; to Naomi Schor with whom I have perfected the art of the feminist literary phone date in our twice weekly incarnation as "les parleuses" between Providence and New York; to Sandy Petrey *with* whom I wrote most of these chapters, and who has complicated their writing by his presence in my life, I am, as they say, eternally grateful.

VERSIONS OF a number of chapters in this book have been previously published, in some cases with slightly different titles, in the following journals and essay collections. "Emphasis Added: Plots and Plausibilities in Women's Fiction," in *PMLA* (January 1981), vol. 96, no. 1, and in *The New Feminist Criticism* (New York: Pantheon, 1985); "For a Dialectics of Identification: Women's Autobiography in France," in *Women and Language in Literature and Society,* edited by Sally McConnell-Ginet, Ruth Borker, and Nelly Furman, copyright © 1980 by Praeger Publishers (New York: Praeger, 1980); "The Text's Heroine: A Feminist Critic and her Fictions," in *Diacritics* (Summer 1982), vol. 12, no. 2; "Writing (from) the Feminine: George Sand and the Novel of Female Pastoral" in *The Representation of Women in Fiction* (Baltimore: Johns Hopkins University Press, 1983); "Arachnologies: The Woman, the Text, and the Critic," in *The Poetics of Gender* (New York: Columbia University Press, 1986); and "Changing the Subject: Authorship, Writing, and the Reader," in *Feminist Studies/Critical Studies* (Bloomington: Indiana University Press, 1986).

I am grateful for permission to reprint these essays here.

NOTE: I have on the whole made use of published translations where convenient, available, or practical. In the case of the *Peruvian Letters*, I have slightly modernized the translation throughout. If no English translation is listed in the bibliography, the translation is mine. Where two sets of page references are included in the text, the first reference is to the English translation; the referencing for chapter 2 constitutes an exception to this practice.

Subject to Change

INTRODUCTION

Writing Feminist Criticism

And it is but a twin fact with this, that in France alone woman
has had a vital influence on the development of literature; in
France alone the mind of woman has passed like an electric
current through the language, making crisp and definite what
is elsewhere heavy and blurred; in France alone, if the writings
of women were swept away, a serious gap would be made in
the national history.

George Eliot, "Woman in France: Madame de Sablé"

The custom among the ancients—
as Priscian testifies—
was to speak quite obscurely
in the books they wrote,
so that those who were to come after
and study them
might gloss the letter and supply its significance
from their own wisdom.

Marie de France, Prologue to the *Lais*

THE WRITING of this book has from the beginning been bound
up with two separate but for me always interrelated scenes,
the seminar and the academic conference. In that very particular
sense of a work's location, this book began to take shape in the
fall of 1977 when I taught for the first time a course on women's
writing I then called (daringly, I thought) "French Women Writers: Toward a Definition of the Feminine Text." In 1977 Elaine
Showalter's study of British women novelists, *A Literature of Their
Own,* had just appeared; Ellen Moers's *Literary Women: The Great
Writers,* the previous year. Although Moers's book included discussions of Staël, Sand, and Colette, and indeed as early as 1973
Germaine Brée had brought out a collection of public lectures on
a tradition of French feminist literature, on the whole it would be
fair to say that those of us working "in French" felt ourselves to
be without a critical tradition.

No course on women writers had ever been offered in the French Department at Columbia, and at the time I knew of no others to draw upon. This did not, however, seem an altogether bad thing: we might not have known just what it was, but we had the sense of doing something. From my admittedly apocalyptic point of view on things, moreover, it seemed almost subversive (a good thing) for an assistant professor to offer a course on the "feminine text" in the seminar room in which I had been a graduate student (and in which the subject, needless to say, had never come up). Looking back now after ten years, I run the risk of mythologizing the moment, but I think the students in the seminar took as much pleasure as I did in the complicities of a slightly dangerous (at the very least, we thought, professionally radical) experience behind closed doors in the paranoid corridors of the fifth floor of Philosophy Hall.[1]

It was in the spirit of that adventure that I accepted an invitation to speak on a panel at the 1978 annual Barnard "Scholar and Feminist" conference, whose theme that year was called "Creating Feminist Works." The lone scholar's voice between those of a painter and a poet, I spoke in terms I hoped might be both personal (not too academic) and representative (not too personal) about what I thought was at stake in the study of women's writing (an academic's idea of being creative).[2] What bothered me then and still bothers me now was a double problem of theory and language: on what grounds was it possible to locate the question of female authorship? In what metaphors could one figure the discussion? At the time I played around with a vegetarian tropology: I compared artichokes to onions. Following out the implications of an opposition which distinguished as separate critical activities the critique of men's writing (sexual politics) and the analysis of women's writing,[3] I contrasted in this account of my own work the stripping away of leaves in order to get—past the choke—to the heart of the matter, the (male) text's ideological core (textual politics), with the peeling away of layers that ends somehow without closure, without ever arriving at a discernible (somehow feminist) center. I opposed the excitement that comes from an emphasis on product, meaning unveiled, to a more diffuse and ambiguous erotics of process.

In the opposition of two modes of textual pleasure, I was of course reinventing Roland Barthes's theoretical wheel; even his metaphors, though I was blithely unaware of it at the time.[4] In an essay called "Style and Its Image," Barthes compares an *already* superannuated view of the text as a "fruit with a kernel (an apricot, for example)" with a more current critical perspective on literary acts: "an onion, a construction of layers (or levels, or systems) whose body contains, finally, no heart, no kernel, no irreducible principle, nothing except the unit of its own surfaces" (10). As I review this history of my critical moves, I am struck by the fact that from the beginning I have cast the issues of a predominantly Anglo/American feminist discussion of female authorship in terms that rehearse French post-structuralist paradigms of textuality, by way of a Barthesian poetics (this is especially true of "Arachnologies" and "Changing the Subject"). At the same time, if, over the years, Barthes has seduced me with an attractive point of departure, I invariably part company with him at a crucial moment in the journey. My difference typically takes the form of a resistance to the end point of the argument. Thus, though in this occasional piece for the Barnard conference I entertain the possibility that women's writing might not have an identifiable core or center, I do not draw Barthes's conclusion that therefore *nothing* is to be found beyond "the unit of its own surfaces," that the body of women's (onion) writing contains nothing but signifiers to gloss. In my homelier (kitchen) expansion of the onion metaphor, I argue, for instance, that the layers of an onion are perceived only by a cut through its body. For me, a supplement of experience comes to check a critical politics dependent for its practice on the free-play of signifiers. The question of experience requires a theorization that refuses to scrap the material of its formation.

Despite the inadvertent but implicit support offered by Roland Barthes, onions and artichokes did not finally seem specific enough to support a poetics of women's writing. But by the fall of 1978, when I began to take the question of women's writing on the road, I had arrived at a language in which to begin to talk about a poetics of reading women's writing: plots and plausibilities.[5] In a way, each of the chapters in this book constitutes a similar effort to find working metaphors for the problems involved in creating a critical discourse in which to talk about women's writing both within the field of feminist studies, and within the critical debates that have dominated literary studies in the United States over the past twenty years. (These have not usually been the same discussion.) Emphasis added, tropes and sensible shoes, female pastoral, coming to writing, performance, arachnologies, overreading the underread, changing the subject: these formulations have all been part of my desire to theorize female authorship and put on the table the textual and political stakes of female signature in the production, reception, and circulation of women's writing.

More locally, I have tried to articulate through a variety of critical modes and strategies the possibility of elaborating a feminist literary theory and practice that emerges from working at the junctures where French literature, theory, and the realities of American institutions intersect.[6] Put another way, this book is about *coming* "from French" and *being* in Women's Studies. It has mattered to me, for instance, in symbolic and material ways not always easy to define, but that I know have played a shaping role in my critical positioning, that most of the essays in this book were written while I was running the Women's Studies Program at Barnard, and teaching, some of the time, in a French department—across the street at Columbia—of which I was not a voting member.

IN *Subject to Change* I explore ways of reading women as writing subjects, of tracking the erratic relations between female authorship and literary history in a particular cultural context. Of the writers whose work is most centrally the focus of this book— Lafayette, Graffigny, Staël, Sand, Colette—only Graffigny's name is likely to be unknown to many readers. But if these writers, and especially Sand and Colette, function to some extent as figures in a national literary landscape, this does not mean that their work (with the exception of *The Princess of Clèves*) belongs to the history of rereadings that have come to constitute that literature's canon of self-reference. One of the aims of this book, then, is implicitly to call the canon of exclusions into question by repopulating the landscape, and at a closer focus, to display the writing of these figures and the figures of their writing.

At stake, however, is not simply the reconstruction of another feminist literature. To the extent that all critical models exist and operate in a dialogical relation with the literature they account for, to change literatures is to change the subject of their criticism. If I want to add to the repertory of feminist criticism the performances of *other writing subjects,* it is also in order to articulate other models, other metaphorics. Building more narrowly on Adrienne Rich's notion of a "politics of location," I'm proposing a "poetics of location" that would acknowledge both the geographics of the writing it reads and the limits of its own project. (In this sense, I'm working toward a more historicized poetics, which, in an emphasis on local specificities—comparative bodies of writing?—works against the temptations of a feminist reuniversalization.)

Despite the national emphasis and the focus on feminist writing, this is not a book about "new French feminisms" (or "French feminist theory") except to the extent that these imports to the U.S. scene emerge from the critical upheaval produced by the political events of May 1968 in France, and whose discourses operate now in complicated ways within both feminist theory and literary studies. Although the argument I will make here is deeply (if ambivalently) indebted to the kind of thinking that this movement has engendered, this is not the French connection I'm after. I'm interested in another kind of "traffic in women," the circulation throughout literary history of French feminist writing.

THE FIRST five chapters deal with the issues I see as central to the question of women's writing and feminist critical theory, foregrounding as exemplary instances for constructing the subjects of criticism—*The Princess of Clèves, The Mill on the Floss, The Portuguese Letters, Indiana,* and *Villette,* in addition to the autobiographical writings (writing fictions) of Sand, Daniel Stern, Colette, and Beauvoir. In chapters 6–9, under the thematics of "coming to writing," I take four novels of feminist signature to expose and work through a certain number of problems in contemporary critical theory, notably the question of (female) authorship itself. In the discussions of individual novels, *The Peruvian Letters, Corinne, Valentine,* and *The Vagabond,* which like "Emphasis Added" grew out of teaching situations and are structured as readings, I am especially concerned with articulating both a general critical matrix—women's writing as a feminist literature of dissent—and specific strategies of figuration: the revision of female plot and the reappropriation of cultural space by a challenge to the male gaze I call "writing from the pavilion." Unlike "The Text's Heroine," "Arachnologies," and "Changing the Subject," which, as I indicate in the frames that precede them, were all originally written for conferences that carried their own agendas, polemics, and cast of characters, these chapters were written as a return to the work of the seminar, by which I mean primarily a scene of novel reading. Taken together in this uneven weave of textures and origins, the chapters, I hope, will point to the ways in which the intersecting claims of pedagogy, literary history, and theory coexist materially in feminist practice.

Although the novels I take up are "representative" in the conventional sense of reflecting a recognizable historical spectrum of a national literature—1678–1910—choices have of course been made. Why these and not others? For the beginning of an answer I will turn briefly here to Gail Godwin's account of the *Norton Anthology of Literature by Women* (entitled in the *New York Times Book Review*), "One Woman Leads to Another." In Godwin's view the anthology's greatest flaw is that it is "organized to bear out Virginia Woolf's opinion that women's 'books continue each other' " (13). Godwin goes on to object that "the editors might more appropriately have subtitled their anthology "The Feminist Tradition in English . . ." (14). Presumably the recourse to Woolf is meant to invalidate the whole project. But when one returns to the context of Woolf's remark in *A Room of One's Own,* it is not at all clear that her discussion either supports Godwin's opinion or explains the absence of aesthetic criteria in the anthology that Godwin deplores.

Reading the first novel of Mary Carmichael, the novelist Woolf has invented to speak of a future of women's writing, Woolf's feminist subject reflects upon the critical approach to a work that may be concerned with "writing as an art, not as a method of self-expression" (83). Confronted with this new novel, she wonders how best to read:

> It seems to be her first book, I said to myself, but one must read it as if it were the last volume in a fairly long series, continuing all those other books that I have been glancing at— Lady Winchilsea's poems and Aphra Behn's plays and the novels of the four great novelists. *For books continue each other, in spite of our habit of judging them separately.* And I must also consider her—this unknown woman—as the descendant of all those other women whose circumstances I have been glancing at and see what she inherits of their characteristics and restrictions. (84; emphasis added)

While it is clear that Woolf is indeed talking about a tradition of women writers, the part of the sentence Godwin quotes—"books continue each other"—does not itself bear the "mark of gender" (Wittig, 63). Rather, Woolf makes a statement about reading and about what today we might want to call intertextuality: books are not individually authored works of art but textual productions caught up in a web of quotation and rewriting.

Woolf here speaks the universal from the woman writer. More

than fifty years later, the possibility of women engendering the universal has yet to become an operative critical reality, for as we see, Godwin assumes that Woolf's generalization refers only to women writers (more typically, the gender of generalizations goes the other way).[7] Thus, for Godwin to say with recourse to Woolf that the anthology should have been called one of *feminist* literature does not really carry the point (her anxiety about Authorship notwithstanding). Woolf's poetics neither legislates a particular thematics for a literature written by women nor distinguishes feminist writing from (women's) art.

If I have taken the time to rehearse the terms of this polemic as it has come to attach itself to the question of the *Norton,* it is not to defend the anthology as an object (this others have done elsewhere), but to object quite self-interestedly on theoretical grounds to the terms in which its *project* is attacked. Woolf's notion that "books continue each other" (just as do feminist critics) is central to the question of women's writing and to the critique of canon-formation feminist literary history performs by its very existence ("masterpieces are not single and solitary births" [68]). In France that history turns, not surprisingly, around questions of identity and difference. In *Women Writers in France: Variations on a Theme,* Germaine Brée organizes her discussions around the "querelle des femmes," a debate about woman's nature and women's rights that began in the early modern period and that in many ways remains a subject of serious controversy today (between feminists and the forces of the new right; between women, but also, between feminists). In part because this has always been a feminist question, and in part because the network of associations that attach themselves to the terms "feminine" and "female" create other problems of connotation, Brée chooses to call the women's writing she discusses "feminist literature," which she defines "as referring merely to literature written by women" (5). I will follow Brée's lead here, though I will say a little more about what I mean by feminist, and argue that the novels I take up here indeed supply examples of (another) French feminism.[8]

Brée takes Christine de Pisan as the first in a small group of early modern French women writers she calls "initiators" (16). Although in certain historical perspectives Christine has been seen to occupy the place of "*first* author" (Poirion, in Brée, 21), for the development of the novel as I see it, I want to reframe the inaugural moments of feminist authorship. In a gesture meant to blur the moment of origins, I prefer to evoke Marie de France on one side

of Christine's writing while placing Lafayette on the other, both
before and after.

In "Lafayette's Ellipses: The Privileges of Anonymity," Joan
DeJean, connecting Marie de France's (twelfth-century) poetics of
gender to Lafayette's, and placing Lafayette in a tradition of seventeenth-century women writers who precede her, argues that "the
complex relation that Lafayette engineered between author and
text provoked a new type of reading for women's fiction and may
thus have altered the course of criticism in France" (887). Although
DeJean does not make a historical claim for Lafayette's originary
status, she identifies a moment of text production that will come
to give the French novel and French women writers' relation to it
a very particular alignment and coloration. In a variety of ways
all the novels I study in this book rewrite the effects of Lafayette's
signature: "the trace of her authority that must simultaneously
assert her power and protect her person" (887). While only
Graffigny, after Lafayette, literally withholds her name from the
title page of her fiction, all the writers whose work is in question
here understand and stage the drama of female signature for their
heroines and their authors. The *Peruvian Letters* (1747), *Corinne,
or Italy* (1807), *Valentine* (1832), and *The Vagabond* (1910) all may
be said to "continue" *The Princess of Clèves* as *feminist texts.*[9]

As a poetics derived from a specific cultural production, the de-
scription of feminist writing that follows is not meant to bear the
weight of a universal authorship. If it sketches a horizon of writing
that will enable other cartographies and other scenes, it will have
served its purpose. At a first level, then, feminist writing articulates
as and in a discourse a self-consciousness about woman's identity.
I mean by this both an inherited cultural fiction and a process of
social construction. Second, feminist writing makes a claim for the
heroine's singularity by staging the difficulty of her relation as a
woman in fiction to Woman. Third, it contests the available plots
of female development or *Bildung* and embodies dissent from the
dominant tradition in a certain number of recurrent narrative gestures, especially in the modalities of closure that Rachel DuPlessis
has called "writing beyond the ending."[10] Finally, through an insistence on singularity, feminist writing figures the existence of other
subjective economies, other styles of identity.

In its attack on the fathers *Corinne* thematizes most explicitly
an indictment of patriarchy (Colette's Renée Néré refers to the
regime of "patriarchal laundry"). But from *The Princess of Clèves*
to *The Vagabond* in a variety of tones the protest can be heard.

In these novels, for instance, we can read as feminist writing the princess of Clèves's celebrated "refusal of love" repeated in Zilia's decision not to marry Déterville and Renée's not to marry Maxime, and even (perversely, perhaps) reenacted in Corinne's choice of Oswald as the man *least* likely to marry her. The "refusal of love," of course, more pointedly seen as the critique of marriage as a political institution, is also at work in the clearly overdetermined failure of Bénédict and Valentine's love to culminate in proper marriage.

In another set of intertextual relations, the princess's forest pavilion as a representation of female-controlled space that would exist outside the demands of plot is reappointed in Valentine's pavilion on the estate of her patrimony, in Zilia's library, Corinne's Italy, and Renée's borrowed "Elysian refuge." These *places* all mark, to different degrees, a form of resistance to the plausibilities of patriarchal plot. On still another level of continuity, Zilia's refusal of marriage, which coincides with the literal mastery of writing itself, throws into relief the sense in which the princess of Clèves's most singular gestures—the confession, the rejection of Nemours, the final retirement to female spaces—speak a desire to control story by refusing its plots that constitutes the trope of the woman writer in France par excellence.

If the Inca princess's "writing lessons" in the language of the dominant culture by their insistence on the costs of "coming to writing" supply a metaphorics for all of these novels as instances of feminist revision—*rewriting* conventional expectations for female protagonists—that metaphorics must at the same time be understood as the effect (or language) of the critique of the ideology of a woman's identity that I have called "changing the subject." Under this attention to the *possibilities of cultural resistance* I emphasize the deconstruction of the gaze and the reconstruction of the scene of writing itself. Thus, if at one end of the scale the princess of Clèves chooses to desire the duke of Nemours in a representation she controls, looking at his portrait within the walls of her pavilion, and removing herself (or trying to) from the empire of his gaze, the better to inhabit her desire; at the other, Corinne represents herself theatrically in public, offering herself to her lover's gaze the better to bring him into a mode of pleasure outside the specular regime of patriarchy. The captive Peruvian princess, the anthropologist's exotic object, becomes the writing subject of an ethnography on colonial culture that challenges the universal claims of the Enlightenment subject. Renée, the star of ambiguous vaudeville shows, returns to a writing of which she is the visionary. In Valentine's short-lived feminist utopia, the woman, forgetting convention, and wanting to see for herself, fantasizes herself briefly as a painter. *Corinne* and *The Vagabond* boldly display in their texts the relations between writing and the gaze, the gaze and performance, performance and the scene of writing. But in both novels the attempt to change the subject through performance proves to be vulnerable to the cultural power of the dominant male gaze observing; in both cases, only the production of writing—an authored text—offers an escape from the surveillance of masculine regard. Writing gives form to the vision of an imaginary elsewhere.

In a way, however, the difficulty of imagining a beyond-the-male-gaze may be inherent to the plots of heterosexual fiction. If all the novels dissent from an ideal of love, suffering, and conformity to female plot, each ending suggests nonetheless that the daughter's destiny is somehow fatally blocked: the daughters all thus come to mark the end of the line, of a certain line, a refusal to circulate. It is not only that they do not marry: they will not become mothers. They are final daughters. Is this bypassing of maternity the ultimate effect of the indictment of patriarchy? The fate of the daughters who appear at the end of Corinne and Valentine's novels raises (without solving) real problems of interpretation. Is little Juliette or little Valentine the signature of a difference *as yet* to come to writing? It may be that after the great period of novel writing for women in France, these new daughters come to embody a way of imagining another tradition. It may be also be that the difference of another coming to writing requires an outside to heterosexual economies. At best we can say that the value of the new daughters' signs, like the currency of a new country, remains subject to change.

IF *The Princess of Clèves* is the new novel of 1680, seen by the critics of its time as a rupture with the idea of the novel itself (Rousset, 17–19), what about *The Vagabond* and the novel in 1910? If the conventions of literary history that grant *The Princess of Clèves* inaugural status as the first psychological novel add justification for that position in this partial account of women's writing, what of Colette in last place? Why end here, in 1910?

Woolf, in her 1924 essay "Mr. Bennett and Mrs. Brown," asserts famously and flamboyantly that "in or about December, 1910, human character changed" (320). In this reflection about " 'charac-

ter' in fiction" and "the question of reality" (319), the change Woolf
is interested in identifying is a shift in human relations, a shift
accompanied by "a change in religion, conduct, politics, and literature" (321). Much in the style of *A Room of One's Own*, Woolf
concretizes her argument in a story she tells about observing a man
(Mr. Smith) and a woman (Mrs. Brown) in a railway carriage. The
interactions of Mr. Smith and Mrs. Brown take Woolf to the question of representation—how to make Mrs. Brown "seem real" (326),
and how Mr. (Arnold) Bennett would have one do it. (Woolf's
essay may also be read as a parable about sexism and feminism
and what that means for the production and reception of women's
writing [Daugherty, 269]).[11] The problem for the "men and women
who began writing novels in 1910 or thereabouts," Woolf writes,
was that "there was no English novelist from whom they could
learn their business" (326). Concluding that to render Mrs. Brown
will require "tools" and "conventions" different from the dated
ones of earlier periods, Woolf recommends patience: "But do not
expect just at present a complete and satisfactory presentment of
her. Tolerate the spasmodic, the obscure, the fragmentary, the failure" (337). If we recall the language she uses to imagine Mary
Carmichael's imaginary novel, we see the extent to which Woolf's
vision of a future of women's writing is bound up with new forms
and practices of literature; practices already visible in Colette's
writing, even before 1910.

The question of 1910 is not only a matter of the continuities and
discontinuities of feminist writing and women's texts. Animated
by a rather different agenda, Alain Robbe-Grillet, in the opening
essay of his 1963 revisionary poetics *Pour un nouveau roman*, also
identifies 1910 as a watershed year in the history of the novel in
France: "Flaubert was writing the new novel of 1860, Proust of
1910. The writer must accept to bear his date, knowing that there
are no masterpieces in eternity, only works in history; and that
they survive only to the extent that they have left the past behind
them and announced the future" (10). Although Robbe-Grillet, one
knows, has remained unregenerately indifferent to questions of
women's writing, the language in which he makes his choice
of Proust in 1910 returns us to the question we raised earlier of
Colette's date and place in the conventions of French literary history. For if I have been arguing that books continue each other as
feminist rewritings in the verticality of a female affiliation, it is no
less the case that in the lateral positionings of a national literature
women's books exist alongside men's: what happens, for instance,

to Colette's date seen together with Proust's? Proust's with Colette's?
To the extent that the study of canon formation is a question of
locatable instances of reading, it also becomes important to take
the signatures together: reading at the intersections.[12]

Colette's new woman writer in 1910, before Mary Carmichael,
casts her gaze on the "infinitely obscure lives" of the "majority of
women" whose stories remain unrecorded, and adds to the human
comedy, portraits "of the other sex," like those of Mr. Woodhouse
and Mr. Casaubon, which reveal "that spot the size of a shilling
at the back of the head" (94). But if Colette's novel thus anticipates
Woolf's poetics, does this mean that her work comes after "1910"?
Yes and no. In *The Vagabond* Colette both continues and breaks
with the traditions of writing from which she emerges. She clearly
belongs to a line of feminist writers and yet begins to unravel its
pact with the conventions of representation; her novel marks a
shift in location.[13]

It might, finally, be more useful to place Colette like her heroine-
writer, as a liminal figure in the history of women's writing;
on the edge of another kind of literary production. Thus, while
Beauvoir produces after Colette feminist novels that formally and
thematically follow the lines of a pre "1910" novel, Duras, Sarraute,
Wittig, Cixous—the list is both incomplete and arbitrary—produce works that radically break with the old plot and the very
notion of "character" in fiction. In that spirit I would now propose
Wittig's *Les Guérillères* (1969) as an emblematic "after" to that
tradition. Wittig's revisionary epic replaces closure with circular-
ity, and female subjectivity at radically oblique angles to compul-
sory heterosexual structures. In *Les Guérillères* the signifiers of
women's names march across the pages in a textual adventure that
leaves the women beyond both men and the representation of
women; freed from the sign of Woman, the particular female subject becomes plural and potentially universal: *elles*.

I WANT TO return now to my retrospective of writing feminist
criticism. When I began working on women's writing I felt, as I
said then, that I somehow had to justify this act, by which I meant
theorizing it. This is how I put it in 1978 (parodying myself through
Woolf):

> But why, you might ask, does reading women's writing im-
> mediately translate into a compulsion to make theory?
> If a person whose function in this world is not to be a lit-

erary critic decides to read a woman writer, that person only has to decide after the fact whether she or he likes the work in question. If, however, the reader, not having Virginia Woolf's recommended income of 500 pounds a year, earns her living by writing and talking about texts in an institution (of higher learning), that reader has a rather more arduous task to perform. That reader, as she inscribes the critical act within the academy, must not only justify the choice of the work in the first place (because most women's writing has no obvious, i.e., canonical claim to consideration), but, if she is to survive, she must also for political and intellectual reasons say something about the writing *qua* women's writing. ("Creating Feminist Works," 19)

But to whom was this justification of the need for justification addressed? Since that study was on the face of it highly, even unambiguously valued within the precincts of a dominant feminist scholarship, whose authorization was I worried about? To the extent that I was vividly untenured, I of course worried at all times about everyone. But it seems to me today that my concern was really both more and less disembodied.

Having worked for years on male authors within an intellectual climate that took itself for the scene of theory and imagined no outside to its language, it was inevitable that good daughter that I was, leaving men's writing for women's would make me anxious. Reading male-authored texts for the ways in which ideology constructed Woman was one thing; seeing the ideology of a dominant tradition through its exclusion of women writers as the construction of literary history itself was another. Was that a subject of theory, subject to theory? I now wanted questions of women's writing to "count" as theory; I wanted my (feminist) theory to be persuasive to "them"; I wanted the discussion of women's writing to reveal to them that their theories of text, subjectivity, poetics, the canon, etc. were in need of revision (not the other way around!). I wanted these things, but at the same time I continued to worry about the grounds of my own position in *their* terms. (This is part of what is going on in "The Text's Heroine," "Arachnologies," and "Changing the Subject.")

But if the problems between "us" and "them" loomed large in institutional terms—tenure, promotions, journals, fellowships, etc.— the question over female authorship—how to authorize it—for me was equally bound up with another problem of alignment: the

borders and range of positions structuring (and fracturing) the field
of feminist literary studies, the famous "Franco-American Dis-
Connection" that characterized so much of the rhetoric of the late
1970s and which is still with us.[14] In other words, from the beginning my desire to justify the question of female authorship was
knotted from within internal tensions of feminist debate.

Debate is probably not the right word to describe the profound
differences in assumptions about language, identity, sexual difference, and politics that underlie unevenly and freight asymmetri-
cally the discussions of this period. On the whole this has been
coded as a polarization between Anglo-American and French approaches to literature. It more accurately has had to do with one's
relation to "theory"—construed as deconstruction, psychoanalysis, and neo-Marxism—and to a profound ambivalence within a
certain feminist analysis to those bodies of theory as "male." (We
could also see this as a problem of signature: a tension between
the cultural and political force of unitary theory grounded by proper
names as an effect of the "already read" and the attempt to theorize from a multiplicity of underread perspectives. Put another way,
what seemed to some as "untheorized" may also be understood
as the not-yet-theorized.) Since I analyze these issues at length in
both "Arachnologies" and "Changing the Subject," for now I simply want to point to the crucial thematics of the debate over theory
as it played itself out in the study of women writers. This is the
reflection on textuality that may be summarized in the title of
Barthes's famous 1968 essay "The Death of the Author."

As someone "in French" I had two specific problems in coming
to women's writing, a field whose outlines had been defined by
critics working in English and American studies, or in Women's
Studies. On the one hand, as someone who had (as theory) read
Lévi-Strauss and Barthes *before* Virginia Woolf and Adrienne Rich
(as feminism), it was no easy matter to invent a way to reembody
the author (who had never been alive for me in the first place).
On the other, the *women* "in French" (this of course includes some
women "from English") whose work I most admired *because* it
was theoretical were not interested in women's writing as a challenge to the Dead Author in the ways that I was—as a politics
of signature located in institutional pedagogies of exclusion.
They, like the theorists with whom they engaged—Freud, Lacan,
Derrida—insisted on the complexity of a feminine not necessarily
attached to women's bodies, but as bound up in stories of sexual
difference. I thus found myself caught between two conflicting at-

tractions. I also found myself in an oscillation of my own ambivalence inhabiting two positions: a "formalist" to certain feminists, a certain feminist to my friends "in theory."

In 1977, for example (though the essay was published in 1980), Peggy Kamuf was already arguing that to reduce a "literary work to its signature" will "produce only tautological statements of dubious value: women's writing is writing signed by women" ("Writing Like a Woman," 285–86). Mary Jacobus, after Kamuf, writing in "Is There a Woman in This Text?" (1982), also sketches out the implications of such a position, naming it and placing it within Anglo-American positions on the woman writer, in contrast to a "French insistence on *écriture féminine*—on woman as writing-effect instead of an origin" (109). Jacobus holds (as do Showalter and Gilbert and Gubar on this), that "the category of 'women's writing' remains as strategically important in classroom, curriculum or interpretive community as the specificity of women's oppression is to the women's movement," but like Kamuf she draws the line at the question of signature: "And yet to leave the question there, with an easy recourse to the female signature or to female being, is either to beg it or to biologize it" (108). Like Kamuf, Jacobus refuses "to posit the woman author as origin and her life as the primary locus of meaning" (108). While Kamuf was taking as her example of "a certain feminist criticism" remarks by Patricia Meyer Spacks in *The Female Imagination* (1975), for most mainstream feminist critics the question of signature itself simply was not perceived as a matter of philosophical debate. For them the question was not so much on what theoretical grounds to place the discussion, as what claims could one make for the body of writing one had assembled: the various "heroinisms" of Moers's "literary women" (1976); Showalter's "literature of their own" (1977); Gilbert and Gubar's figure of "the madwoman in the attic" (1979). In those volumes, female authorship poses itself as a set of problems within a politics of literature that is *already* a grounded context.

If the challenge to the signature from deconstructive and psychoanalytic positions has not on the whole been picked up directly by the feminist critics working on women's writing to whom it seemed addressed, it has, however, continued to surface in other quarters, coming from other places. On the one hand, as we have just seen, a wariness about signature is central to the attack from the traditionalists on the Gilbert and Gubar Norton Anthology (1985) for its principles of inclusion or exclusion—the worry being that "literary art and individual talent" are sacrificed to feminist values (Godwin, 12; Donoghue, 147). Or, as another disgruntled critic of the volume put it: "Why might a woman writer prefer not to be a Woman Writer? Perhaps for the same reason a frog dislikes to be used as a demonstration of the nervous system. It's afraid that might be all there is to life" (Rose, 89). On the other hand, at the other extreme of the critical spectrum, we find the philosophical questioning of identity that engenders Kamuf's analysis of the trope "a woman writing as a woman" enlisted in Jonathan Culler's discussion of feminist criticism in *On Deconstruction,* "Reading as a Woman."

Thus we observe this curious situation in which the study of women's writing is put into question both by the believers in art, origin, meaning, intention, and the individual talent and by those who believe in none of the above. Is this necessarily what the alternatives boil down to? Essentialism or theory? Artichokes (apricots) *or* onions?

It seems to me that the study of women's literature has made it possible to unhook signature from the interpretive securities of Authorship by rematerializing the relations of subjectivity, writing, and literary theory in very specific ways. In the critical turns I have made since writing *The Heroine's Text* (artichokes), I have tried to imagine authorship as a more complexly contextual activity than I had dreamed of in my original training and incarnation as a hardline structuralist: as a matter of writing that includes the problem of agency—the marks of a producing subject; and as a question of reading that includes the gendered effects of critical and institutional ideologies.

In "Writing Fictions: Women's Autobiography in France" I suggest that locating the signature of a woman's writing across the body of writing allows feminist critics to reproblematize the question of authorship and biography as interpretive ground. It is in part for this reason that I have included that essay in the argument I am making here. The stories of Sand, Stern, Colette, and Beauvoir are accounts of coming to writing in a historical real. In this sense they provide a social field of contrast to the metaphorical accounts of coming to writing that I read in the novels of feminist writers.[15] But that relation of course is too simple, since it is as clear that becoming a writer for a writer is also about making texts. Seen together in fiction and autographics, the scenes of authorization layer our understanding of the writing project as a negotiation between the subject and the social.

For me, the signature of the woman writer who is also a feminist writer is the mark of a resistance to dominant ideologies; for the feminist critic, the signature is the site of a possible political disruption. To insist on a meaning that attaches to signature is to value the challenge it can bring to the institutional arrangements based on its exclusion. This is not to say that I ignore the dangers of the claim or the appeal of a headier (sexier, as these things go) destabilization from deconstructive, psychoanalytic, and neo-Marxist perspectives. On the contrary. The chapters of this book all testify to my awareness of their seductions. But in the end, the critical theory I am looking for goes other ways.

At the Pembroke conference (1985) at which I first presented "Changing the Subject," Naomi Schor addressed the problem of viewing feminine specificity (what I talk about as female signature) from the bridge of French post-structuralist theory. Articulating her own resistance as a feminist to the "discourse of sexual indifference/pure difference," Schor wondered whether the insistence on indifferentiation in Barthes and Foucault wasn't perhaps the "latest ruse of phallocentrism," and observed that a significant number of feminist theorists have adopted other strategies for "subverting the unitary subject," strategies that take the form of a *doubling* more complex than the simple erasure of the tell-tale marks of sexual difference. Like Myra Jehlen, whose argument for "the claim of difference" (the understanding that "the other will have to live as other") as the crucial piece in a critique of the "male universal norm" Schor enlists in her own polemic, Schor concludes that only the dissymmetry of difference can undermine the grounds of repetition; providing "perhaps the only chance we have to construct a post-deconstructionist society which will not simply reduplicate our own" (110).

When I say, then, that I want to make claims for the female signature but not in the name of a biocritics of intention, I am saying in part that I want to have it two ways (tropes *and* sensible shoes)—French *and* (North) American. I am also saying that those terms themselves give us false dilemmas and equally false choices.[16] While I myself have continued to invoke those two positionings as if this outline constituted a reliable map of the territory, that is to a great extent because I have had a role to play in it (it is part of my history), and because I have been located in it by others. At the same time I have come to find this relentless redrawing of the boundaries a narrowing process rather than a gesture of complication. I long to see a more international geo-graphics in feminist writing. It seems to me that as feminist critics we do ourselves in by playing the old Franco-American game of binary oppositions (theory and empiricism, indifference and identity) as though it were the only game in town, as though we knew all the rules by which it could be played, as though layers were all there is to an onion, a pit to an apricot, or a heart to an artichoke; as though there weren't also Italians, for instance.[17]

I ORIGINALLY WANTED to call my book *Changing the Subject.* By this I meant to evoke both a voluntaristic desire for change— let's change the subject (this is boring), let's talk about something else (women writers, feminist criticism), let's make the subject different (refigure the universal, change the canon), etc. But when I learned to my chagrin that a book with that title had already been announced for publication, I decided to change my title to a phrase that had appealed to me earlier.[18] Now, "subject to change," of course, typically is followed by "without notice," and for a while, I resisted the new title precisely because of a certain programmatic arbitrariness (and a certain resulting annoyance from its effects— higher prices, cancelled trains) implicit in it. It was close to the original, but did it take me too far? It seems to me now that a dose of the arbitrary is not a bad thing; that the phrase nicely reappropriates clichés of femininity (*la donna e mobile*) while announcing a resistance to closure and readiness for revolution: this is all vulnerable; it all can go.

Finally, I have come to feel that "subject to change" suits the gamble of this book; that I could bring together pieces from my critical history and let them inhabit a space with newer ones that while not perhaps presenting radical contradictions, at the very least contain their own reworking of the earlier formulations (I argue the same cases with different emphases). I have revised the essays in varying degrees, changing titles, playing with epigraphs, adding and deleting notes, intervening to clarify points now lost even on me, but it is certain that publishing as one goes builds in very real problems. The most obvious one, of course, is the constraint involved in reprinting pieces already taken up in dialogue, or anthologized. As much as I might have wanted to in places, I wasn't able to rewrite the history of the past ten years. It has also seemed to me that at a moment when writing *on* feminist criticism is tending to draw up positions (battle lines?) as if they couldn't change, as if no one's thinking evolved, as if nothing overflowed the neat paradigms we have been tempted to construct in order to have a history "of our own," it was worth running the risk of leaving in the traces of the difficulty and embarrassment of doing the work (its scenes, in all senses of the word) in the hope that we not—playing Athena to Arachne—cut ourselves off from a possible future of subjects to change.

NOTES

1. The students in that graduate seminar, whom I thank collectively here for helping me begin, were: Louise Adler, Elvire Borenstein, Theresa Bowers, Mary Jane Ciccarello, Marie-Claude Hays, Claude Holland, Alice Jardine, Judith A. Low, Carol V. Richards, Sylvia Richards, Paulette Rose, Françoise Thybulle, Margaret Waller.

2. My contribution was published as an edited record of the proceedings in pamphlet form by the Barnard Women's Center, 1978.

3. This was the distinction betwen feminist critique and feminist criticism that Elaine Showalter had elaborated informally at an earlier "Scholar and Feminist" conference at Barnard, and that became the unevenly valued opposition of critique and "gynocritics" of "Toward a Feminist Poetics."

4. After the conference, Margaret Waller, then one of the students from the seminar on French women writers, gracefully brought Barthes's onion metaphor to my attention.

5. As it turned out, it was largely from the work of that first seminar that "Emphasis Added: Plots and Plausibilities in Women's Fiction" emerged. I wrote "Emphasis Added" for a public lecture at the University of Michigan at Ann Arbor (Fall 1978) where I had been invited by the French department to spend a week visiting and teaching in Michel Pierssens's seminar on criticism and theory. This was my first public lecture, and I had been asked to speak to an audience who would not necessarily be "in French." At the time, that request seemed daunting, and I smoked through the entire lecture. Looking back, I am grateful that I was asked to address myself to a more "general" public. Otherwise, I might still be in French.

6. This intersection of concerns is close in spirit to the configuration of relations mapped in the title of the important 1981 special—collectively edited at Dartmouth—issue of *Yale French Studies*, "Feminist Readings: French Texts/American Contexts."

7. I'm thinking of Elaine Showalter's remarks in "Women Who Write Are Women": "The female witness, sensitive or not, is still not accepted as first-person universal" (33).

8. On the history of Feminisms in France see *New French Feminisms*, edited by Elaine Marks and Isabelle de Courtivron, and Maïté Albistur and Daniel Armogathe's *Histoire du féminisme français*.

9. In the tradition I describe I would include before Sand works by Villedieu, Tencin, Riccoboni, and Claire de Duras. The writing that takes place in what appears to be a gap between Sand and Colette remains to be explored as a history. Some individual names are known—Louise Colet, Daniel Stern, Gyp, Rachilde, Juliette Adam—but for now their literary relations have

not been traced. Cheryl Morgan, a doctoral candidate in the French department at Columbia, has begun to explore the reasons for the feminist critical blank.

10. Despite the very different corpus with which she works, Rachel DuPlessis and I have quite similar ideas about a poetics of feminist writing. Thus, DuPlessis says of the writers she discusses: "These authors are 'feminist' because they construct a variety of oppositional strategies to the depiction of gender institutions in narrative" (34). I develop our contiguities more explicitly throughout the individual readings, especially in my chapter on Graffigny's *Peruvian Letters.*

In part because of these kinds of intertextual connections, in part because of the theoretical complications it raises (about reading literature in history), despite my sense that a poetics (even of gender) needs to be grounded, I have not sought to tie a definition of feminist writing to the historical moments of feminist movements or currents. In *A Literature of Their Own,* for instance, Elaine Showalter identifies feminist writing (as opposed to what she calls feminine and female literature) with the period 1880 to 1920 and women's right to vote (although she also reserves the possibility of a more fluid use of the term). And most recently, in the introduction to her new book, "Mothers, Daughters, and Narrative," Marianne Hirsch chooses to restrict the use of the term "feminist" to the feminist movement of the 1970s and 1980s, "an aesthetic connected to a movement of active social resistance."

11. Beth Rigel Daugherty's "The Whole Contention Between Mr. Bennett and Mrs. Woolf, Revisited," offers enormously useful detail about the actual exchange. I thank Brenda Silver for bringing the essay to my attention. "Mr. Bennett and Mrs. Brown" is the central fable of Mary Ann Caws's moving "Centennial Presidential Address 1983: Realizing Fictions"; and the writing fiction of a thoughtful position paper by Shari Benstock, "Reading the Signs of Women's Writing."

12. By this I mean that we have to find new ways to get at the weave of writing at a given historical moment in order to see what has been retained, and why. In *French Novelists of Today* (a book first published in 1955 and reprinted in 1967), for example, Henri Peyre, following Woolf's chronology, also locates a "revolution in French fiction" in 1910. In his survey, which is meant to appraise, Peyre, in passing, places Colette (whom he sees as "antedeluvian"). While he acknowledges her "skilled workmanship" and compares her use of the adjective to Proust's, he judges her qualities as a novelist to be "grossly overrated and . . . responsible for the sad plight of feminine writing in France up to the fourth decade of the present century" (276–77). Although a look at these moments of canon formation has not been my project here, I think now that the study of women's writing in the future will need to focus on these intergendered occasions in literary history.

13. To point to an area I have left underdeveloped in this discussion: before the twentieth century, the imaginary of French women writers under the sign of Lafayette is generally aristocratic. Although the question of money and productive activity for women subtly punctuates most of these novels, only in *The Vagabond* does the issue become a central feature of woman's identity as it is bound up with a scene of work. The attention to money, class, and work comes much earlier in the novels of English women writers.

14. I'm alluding to the arguments articulated in Domna Stanton's essay in

The Future of Difference, and indeed the premises of the conference ("The Scholar and the Feminist VI"), conceived and orchestrated by Alice Jardine, that took place at Barnard in 1979, and that led to the volume. This is the moment when French theory as a powerful intervention begins to have its day in feminist and nonfeminist contexts. Mary Jacobus identifies a similar chronology, and its importance to her own evolution in the preface to *Reading Woman.* Margaret Homans, who has rehearsed these issues in several essays, seeks in *Bearing the Word* to elaborate a productive practice through the "critical contradictions" (xiii) posed by Anglo/American and French positionings.

15. It is also the case that the essay on autobiography was my first attempt to come to terms with women's writing, and that to the extent that I am reconstructing my own history as a feminist critic I wanted to include it. In the notion of "a dialectics of identification" that constituted the first part of the essay's original title, I was rehearsing the notion of "overreading" that I develop in "Arachnologies." In the shift now to "Writing Fictions," I am concerned with promoting the attrition of genre. That I began working on women's writing by writing on autobiography has something to do with good fortune—in 1977 Domna Stanton invited me to speak at a panel she was chairing on women's autobiography at the meetings of the Northeast Modern Language Association—and something to do with the status of this material in the French tradition: the autobiographical writings of Sand, Colette, and Beauvoir are well known (and in print—Sand's autobiography in a Pléiade edition) and they provided me with an accessible point of departure (given the status of women writers in France as figures, this is not surprising). I needed more of an education to discover the texts of women's fiction.

16. I'm thinking about the reification of this polarization operated by Toril Moi in *Sexual/Textual Politics.* Moi manages to collapse each side of the American/French divide with an astonishing lack of concern for the bodies (and positions) under erasure. On the one hand, she declares: "So far, lesbian and/or black feminist criticism have presented exactly the same *methodological* and *theoretical* problems as the rest of Anglo/American feminist criticism" (86). On the other, she makes Julia Kristeva (whose reluctance to be identified with feminism is well documented) the heroine of French feminism and ends her book *in* Derrida's words. It would be the subject of another book to restore the complexities to "French" and "American" eradicated here, but more crucially to redefine the "*textual theory*" that supplies Moi's categories. Naomi Schor acutely reviews Moi's moves in "Introducing Feminism."

17. This is of course playful and serious. I'm thinking specifically of Teresa de Lauretis and Rosi Braidotti's critical projects, and the voices of Italian feminism. But I'm also thinking more generally of the necessity to look elsewhere, beyond the inevitable metropolitan references, for different locations and material, beyond the exclusions of another, feminist "already read."

18. When I then learned from Carolyn Heilbrun that Lois Gould had just completed a novel called *Subject to Change,* I had to acknowledge the futility of trying not to bear one's date.

I
Reading Women's Writing

Vüe des deux pavillons français à Monceau. After Carmontelle. Engraving, Musée Carnavalet. © Musées de la Ville de Paris by SPADEM 1987.

Emphasis Added: Plots and Plausibilities in Women's Fiction

> Nothing came down the street; nobody passed. A single leaf
> detached itself from the plane tree at the end of the street, and
> in that pause and suspension fell. Somehow it was like a signal
> falling, a signal pointing to a force in things which one had
> overlooked.
>
> Virginia Woolf, *A Room of One's Own*[1]

IF WE TAKE *The Princess of Clèves* as the first text of women's
fiction in France, then we may observe that French women's fiction has from its beginnings been *discredited*.[2] By this I mean literally and literarily denied credibility: "Mme de Clèves's confession to her husband," writes Bussy-Rabutin to his cousin Mme de
Sévigné, "is extravagant, and can only occur in a true story; but
when one makes up a story it is ridiculous to ascribe such extraordinary feelings to one's heroine. The author in so doing was more
concerned with not resembling other novels than with using common sense."[3] Without dwelling on the local fact that a similarly
"singular" confession had appeared in Villedieu's *Les Désordres
de l'amour* some three years before the publication of Lafayette's
novel, and bracketing the more general fact that the novel as a
genre has from its beginnings labored under charges of *invrai-
semblance*,[4] let us reread Bussy-Rabutin's complaint. In a true story,
as in "true confessions," the avowal would be believable because
in life, unlike art, anything can happen; hence the constraints of
likeliness do not apply. In a made-up story, however, the confession offends because it violates our readerly expectations about
fiction. In other words, art should not imitate life but *reinscribe*
received ideas about the presentation of life in art. To depart from
the limits of common sense (tautologically, to be extravagant) is
to risk exclusion from the canon.[5] Because—as Genette, glossing

this same document in "Vraisemblance et motivation," puts it—
"extravagance is a privilege of the real" (74), to produce a work
not like other novels, an original rather than a copy, means par-
adoxically that its literariness will be sniffed out: "The first adventure of the Coulommiers gardens is not plausible," Bussy-Rabutin
observes later in his letter, "and smells of the novel [*sent le roman*]."

Genette begins his essay with an analysis of contemporary reactions to *The Princess of Clèves*. Reviewing the writings of seventeenth-century poeticians, Genette shows that *vraisemblance* and
bienséance, "plausibility" and "propriety," are wedded to each
other; and the precondition of plausibility is the stamp of approval
affixed by *public opinion*:[6] "Read or assumed, this 'opinion' is
quite close to what today would be called an ideology, that is, a
body of maxims and prejudices which constitute both a vision of
the world and a system of values" (73). What this statement means
is that the critical reaction to any given text is hermeneutically
bound to another and preexistent text: the *doxa* of socialities.
Plausibility then is an effect of reading through a grid of
concordance:

> What defines plausibility is the formal principle of respect for
> the norm, that is, the existence of a relation of implication
> between the particular conduct attributed to a given charac-
> ter, and a given, general, received and implicit maxim. . . .
> To understand the behavior of a character (for example), is
> to be able to refer it back to an approved maxim, and this
> reference is perceived as a demonstration of cause and effect.
> (174–75)

If no maxim is available to account for a particular piece of
behavior, that behavior is read as unmotivated and unconvincing.
Mme de Clèves's confession makes no sense in the seventeenth-
century sociolect because it is, Genette argues, *"an action without
a maxim"* (75). A heroine without a maxim, like a rebel without
a cause, is destined to be misunderstood. And she is.

To build a narrative around a character whose behavior is deliberately idiopathic, however, is not merely to create a puzzling
fiction but to fly in the face of a certain ideology (of the text and
its context), to violate a grammar of motives that describes while
prescribing, in this instance, what wives, not to say women, should
or should not do. The question one might then ask is whether this
crucial barbarism is in any way connected to the gender of its author. If we were to uncover a feminine "tradition"—diachronic

recurrences—of such ungrammaticalities, would we have the basis for a poetics of women's fiction? And what do I mean by women's fiction?

Working backward, I should say first that I do not mean what in a certain French feminism is called *écriture féminine,* which can be described roughly as a process or a practice by which the female *body,* with its peculiar drives and rhythms, inscribes itself as text.[7] "Feminine writing" is an important theoretical formulation; but it privileges a textuality of the avant-garde, a literary production of the late twentieth century, and it is therefore fundamentally a hope, if not a blueprint for the future. In what is perhaps the best-known statement of contemporary French feminist thinking about women's writing, "The Laugh of the Medusa," Hélène Cixous states that, "with a few rare exceptions, there has not yet been any writing that inscribes femininity" (878). On the contrary, what she finds historically in the texts of the "immense majority" of female writers is "workmanship [which is] . . . in no way different from male writing, and which either obscures women or reproduces the classic representations of women (as sensitive—intuitive—dreamy, etc.)" (878). I think this assertion is both true and untrue. It is true if one is looking for a radical difference in women's writing and locates that difference in an insurgence of the body, in what Julia Kristeva has called the irruption of the semiotic.[8] And it is true again if difference is sought on the level of the sentence. If, however, we situate difference in the insistence of a certain thematic structuration, in the form of content, then it is not true that women's writing has been in no way different from male writing. I consider the "demaximization" wrought by Lafayette's novel to be one example of how difference can be read.

Before I proceed to other manifestations of difference, let me make a few general remarks about the status of women's literature—about its existence, in my view, as a viable corpus for critical inquiry. Whether one believes, as does Cixous, that there is "male writing," "*marked* writing . . . run by a libidinal and cultural—hence political, typically masculine economy" ("Laugh of the Medusa," 879), or that (great) literature has no sex because a "great mind must be androgynous," literary *history* remains a male preserve, a history of writing by men.[9] In England the history of the novel admits the names of Jane Austen, the Brontës, George Eliot, and Virginia Woolf. In France it includes Lafayette, although only for *The Princess of Clèves* and always with the nagging insinuation that La Rochefoucauld had a hand in that. Staël,

George Sand, and Colette figure in the national record, although
mainly as the scandalous heroines of their times. Nevertheless, there
have always been women writing. What is one to do with them?
One can leave them where they are, like so many sleeping dogs,
and mention them only in passing as epiphenomena in every period, despite the incontrovertible evidence that most were successful and even literarily influential in their day. One can continue, then, a politics of benign neglect that reads difference, not
to say popularity, as inferiority.[10] Or one can perform two simul-
taneous and compensatory gestures: the archaeological act of re-
covering "lost" women writers and the reconstructive act of establishing a parallel tradition, as Elaine Showalter has done in *A
Literature of Their Own* and Ellen Moers in *Literary Women: The
Great Writers*. The advantage of these moves is that they make
visible an otherwise invisible intertext: a reconstituted record of
predecession and prefiguration, debts acknowledged and unac-
knowledged, anxieties and enthusiasms.[11]

Elizabeth Janeway, by way of T. S. Eliot, has suggested another
way of thinking about women's literature. She cites the evolution
in Eliot's attitude toward that body of texts we know as American
literature. At first he held, as many critics have about women's
literature, that it does not exist: "There can only be one English
literature. . . . There cannot be British or American literature."
Later, however, he was to acknowledge "what has never, I think,
been found before, two literatures in the same language" (344).
That reformulation, as Janeway adapts it to delineate the continent of women's literature, is useful because it locates the problem
of identity and difference not on the level of the sentence—not as
a question of another language—but on the level of the text in all
its complexities: a culturally bound, and I would even say, culturally overdetermined production. This new mapping of a parallel
geography does not, of course, resolve the oxymoron of margin-
ality: how is it that women, a statistical majority in our culture,
perform as a "literary subculture" (Showalter, *A Literature*, 14–
15)? But it does provide a body of writing from which to begin to
identify specificities that derive from that relation. Because women
are both of the culture and out of it (or under it), written by it
and remaining a largely silent though literate majority, to look for
uniquely "feminine" textual indexes that can be deciphered in
"blind" readings is pointless. (Documentation on the critical reception of *Jane Eyre* and *Adam Bede*, for example, has shown how

silly such pretensions can be.)[12] There are no infallible signs, no failsafe technique by which to determine the gender of an author. But that is not the point of the *post*-compensatory gesture that follows what I call the new literary history. At stake instead is a reading that *consciously* recreates the object it describes, attentive always to a difference—what T. S. Eliot calls "strong local flavor" (in Janeway, 344) not dependent on the discovery of an exclusive alterity.

The difficulty of the reading comes from the irreducibly complicated relationship women have historically had to the language of the dominant culture, a playful relationship that Luce Irigaray has described as "mimeticism":

> To play with mimesis is, thus, for a woman to try to recover the place of her exploitation by discourse, without allowing herself to be simply reduced to it. It means to resubmit herself . . . to "ideas," in particular to ideas about herself, that are elaborated in/by a masculine logic, but so as to make "visible," by an effect of playful repetition what was supposed to remain invisible: the cover-up of a possible operation of the feminine in language. It also means "to unveil" the fact that if women are such good mimics, it is because they are not simply reabsorbed in this function. *They also remain else where.* . . . (76/74)

This "elsewhere"—which, needless to say, is not so easily pinpointed—is, she adds, an "insistence" of "matter" and "sexual pleasure" ("jouissance").[13] I prefer to think of the insistence Irigaray posits as a form of emphasis: an italicized version of what passes for the neutral or standard face. Spoken or written, italics are a modality of intensity and stress; a way of marking what has always already been said, of making a common text one's own.[14] Italics are also a form of intonation, "the tunes," McConnell-Ginet writes, "to which we set the text of our talk." "Intonation," she continues, "serves to underscore the gender identification of the participants in certain contexts of communication," and because of differences in intonation, "women's tunes will be interpreted and evaluated from an androcentric perspective" (542). When I speak of italics, then, I mean the emphasis added by registering a certain quality of voice. And this expanded metaphor brings me back to my point of departure.

Genette codes the perception of plausibility in terms of silence:

> The relationship between a plausible narrative and the system
> of plausibility to which it subjects itself is . . . essentially mute:
> the conventions of genre function like a system of natural forces
> and constraints which the narrative obeys as if without no-
> ticing them, and a fortiori without naming them. (76)

By fulfilling the "tacit contract between a work and its public"
(77) this silence both gives pleasure and signifies conformity with
the dominant ideology. The text emancipated from this collusion,
however, is also silent, in that it refuses to justify its infractions,
the "motives and maxims of the actions" (78). Here Genette cites
the silence surrounding Julien Sorel's attempted murder of Mme
de Rênal and the confession of Mme de Clèves. In the first instance, the ideologically complicitous text, the silence is a function
of what Genette calls "plausible narrative"; in the second it is a
function of "arbitrary narrative" (79). And the *sounds* of silence?
They are heard in a third type of narrative, one with a motivated
and *"artificial plausibility"*; this literature, exemplified by the
"endless chatting" of a Balzacian novel, we might call "other-di-
rected," for here authorial commentary justifies its story to society
by providing the missing maxims, or by inventing them. In the
arbitrary narrative Genette sees a rejection of the ideology of a
certain plausibility—an ideology, let us say, of accountability. This
"inner-directed" posture would proclaim instead "that rugged in-
dividuality which makes for the unpredictability of great actions—
and great works" (77).

Two remarks are in order here. Arbitrariness can be taken as
an ideology in itself, that is, as the irreducible freedom and orig-
inality of the author (Bussy-Rabutin's complaint, *en somme*). But
more specifically, the refusal of the demands of one economy may
mask the inscription of another. This inscription may seem silent,
or *unarticulated* in/as *authorial commentary (discours)*, without
being absent. (It may simply be inaudible to the dominant mode
of reception.) In *The Princess of Clèves*, for example, "extravagance" is in fact accounted for, I would argue, both by maxims
and by a decipherable effect of italicization. The maxims I refer
to are not direct commentary; and it is true, as Genette writes,
that "nothing is more foreign to the style [of the novel] than sen-
tentious epiphrasis: as if the actions were always either beyond or
beneath all commentary" (78). It is also true that within the narrative the characters do comment on the actions; and although
Genette does not "count" such comments as "chatting," I would

suggest that they constitute an internally motivating discourse: an artificial plausibility *en abyme*. This intratext is maternal discourse; and its *performance* through the "extraordinary feelings" of Mme de Clèves is an instance of italicization. The confession, to state the obvious, makes perfect sense in terms of the idiolect spoken by Mme de Chartres: "Be brave and strong, my daughter; withdraw from the court, force your husband to take you away; do not fear the most brutal and difficult measures; however awful they may seem at first, in the end they will be milder in their effects than the misery of a love affair" (69/68).[15] Moreover, the confession qua confession is set up by reference to a "real life" precedent and is presented by the prince himself as a model of desirable behavior: "Sincerity is so important to me that I think that if my mistress, and even my wife, confessed to me that she was attracted by another . . . I would cast off the role of lover or husband to advise and sympathize with her" (76/76). Seen from this perspective the behavior of the princess is both motivated within the narrative and supplied with a pre-text: the conditions of imitation.

But the confession, which I may already have overemphasized, is not an isolated extravagance in the novel. It is a link in the chain of events that lead to Mme de Clèves's decision not to marry Nemours, even though in this instance, the maxims of the sociolect might support, even expect, the marriage. As Bussy-Rabutin again observes, "And if, against all appearances and custom, this combat between love and virtue were to last in her heart until the death of her husband, then she would be delighted to be able to bring love and virtue together by marrying a man of quality, the finest and the most handsome gentleman of his time." Mme de Lafayette clearly rejects this delightful denouement. Now, Stendhal has speculated that if Mme de Clèves had lived a long life she would have regretted her decision and would have wanted to live like Mme de Lafayette (111). We shall never know, of course, but his comment raises an interesting question: why should Mme de Lafayette keep Mme de Clèves from living in fiction the life she herself had led? The answer to that question would be an essay in itself, but let us tackle the question here from another angle: what do Mme de Clèves's "renunciation" and, before that, her confession tell us about the relation of women writers to fiction, to the heroines of their fiction? Should the heroine's so-called "refusal of love" be read as a defeat and an end to passion—a "suicide," or "the delirium of a *précieuse*" (Doubrovsky, 48; Rousset, 25)? Or is it, rather, a *bypassing* of the dialectics of desire, and in that sense, a pecul-

iarly feminine "act of victory" (Varga, 524)?[16] To understand the
refusal as a victory and as, I believe, a rewriting of eroticism (an
emphasis placed "elsewhere"—as both Irigaray and Woolf say),
from which we might generalize about the economy of representation regulating the heroine and her authors, let us shift critical
gears for a while.

Claudine Herrmann describes the princess as a heroine "written
in a language of dream, dreamt by Mme de Lafayette" (77). What
is the language of that dream, and what is the dream of that language? In the essay called "The Relation of the Poet to Daydreaming" (1908), Freud wonders how that "strange being, the poet, comes
by his material" (44). He goes on to answer his question by considering the processes at work in children's play and then moves
to daydreams and fantasies in adults. When he begins to describe
the characteristics of the mode of creativity, he makes a blanket
generalization about its impulses that should immediately make
clear the usefulness of his essay for our purposes: "Unsatisfied wishes
are the driving power behind phantasies; every separate phantasy
contains the fulfillment of a wish, and improves upon unsatisfactory reality" (47). What then is the nature of these wishes and,
more to our point, does the sex of the dreamer affect the shaping
of the daydream's text? Freud writes:

> The impelling wishes vary according to the sex, character and
> circumstances of the creator; they may easily be divided, how-
> ever, into two principal groups. Either they are ambitious
> wishes, serving to exalt the person creating them, or they are
> erotic. In young women erotic wishes dominate the phantasies
> *almost exclusively,* for their ambition is *generally comprised*
> in their erotic longings; in young men egoistic and ambitious
> wishes assert themselves plainly enough alongside their erotic
> desires. (47–48; emphasis added)

Here we see that the either/or antinomy, ambitious/erotic, is immediately collapsed to make coexistence possible in masculine fantasies: "in the greater number of ambitious daydreams . . . we
can discover a woman in some corner, for whom the daydreamer
performs all his heroic deeds and at whose feet all his triumphs
are to be laid" (48).

But is this observation reversible? If, to make the logical ex-
trapolation, romance dominates the female daydream and constitutes its primary heroism, is there a *place* in which the ambitious
wish of a young woman asserts itself? Has she an egoistic desire

to be discovered "in some corner"? Freud elides the issue—while leaving the door open (for us) by his modifiers, "almost exclusively" and "generally comprised"—presumably because he is on his way to establishing the relationship between daydreaming and literary creation. The pertinence of differences there is moot, of course, because he conjures up only a male creator: not the great poet, however, but "the less pretentious writers of romances, novels and stories, who are read all the same by the widest circles of men and women" (50). Freud then proceeds to identify the key "marked characteristic" of these fictions: "They all have a hero who is the centre of interest, for whom the author tries to win our sympathy by every possible means, and whom he places under the protection of a special providence" (50). The hero in this literature is continually exposed to danger, but we follow his perilous adventures with a sense of security, because we know that at each turn he will triumph. According to Freud, the basis for this armchair security, for our tranquil contemplation, is the hero's own conviction of invincibility, best rendered by the expression "Nothing can happen to me!" And Freud comments, "It seems to me . . . that this significant mark of invulnerability very clearly betrays—His Majesty the Ego, the hero of *all daydreams* and *all novels*" (51; emphasis added).

Now, if the plots of male fiction chart the daydreams of an ego that would be invulnerable, what do the plots of female fiction reveal? Among French women writers, it would seem at first blush to be the obverse of "nothing can happen to me." The phrase that characterizes the heroine's posture might well be a variant of Murphy's law: if anything can go wrong, it will. And the reader's sense of security, itself dependent on the heroine's, comes from feeling not that the heroine will triumph in some conventionally positive way but that she will transcend the perils of plot with a self-exalting dignity. Here national constraints on the imagination, or what in this essay Freud calls "racial psychology," do seem to matter: the second-chance rerouting of disaster typical of Jane Austen's fiction, for example, is exceedingly rare in France. To the extent that we can speak of a triumph of Her Majesty the Ego in France, it lies in being beyond vulnerability, indeed beyond it all. On the whole, French women writers prefer what Peter Brooks has described as "the melodramatic imagination," a dreamlike and metaphorical drama of the "moral occult" (20). There are recurrent melodramatic plots about women unhappy in love because men are men and women are women. As I said earlier, however, the suffering seems to have its own rewards in the economy of the female unconscious. The heroine proves to be better than her victimizers; and perhaps this ultimate superiority, which is to be read in the choice to go beyond love, beyond "erotic longings," is the figure that the "ambitious wishes" of women writers (dreamers) takes.

In the economy of Freud's plot, as we all know, fantasy scenarios are generated by consciously repressed content; and so he naturally assumes a motive for the "concealment" of "ambitious wishes": "the overweening self-regard" that a young man "acquires in the indulgent atmosphere surrounding his childhood" must be suppressed "so that he may find his proper place in a society that is full of other persons making similar claims" (48)—hence the daydreams in which the hero conquers all to occupy victoriously center stage. The content that a young woman represses comes out in erotic daydreams because "a well-brought-up woman is, indeed, credited with only a minimum of erotic desire" (48). Now, there is a class of novels by women that "maximizes" that minimum, a type of fiction that George Eliot attacks as "Silly Novels by Lady Novelists": "The heroine is usually an heiress . . . with perhaps a vicious baronet, an amiable duke, and an irresistible younger son of a marquis as lovers in the foreground, a clergyman and a poet sighing for her in the middle distance, and a crowd of undefined adorers dimly indicated beyond" (*Essays*, 301–2). After sketching out the variations of plot that punctuate the heroine's " 'starring' expedition through life," Eliot comments on the security with which we await the inevitably happy end:

> Before matters arrive at this desirable issue our feelings are tried by seeing the noble, lovely and gifted heroine pass through many *mauvais moments*, but we have the satisfaction of knowing that her sorrows are wept into embroidered pocket-handkerchiefs . . . and that whatever vicissitudes she may undergo . . . she comes out of them all with a complexion more blooming and locks more redundant than ever. (303)

The plots of these "silly novels" bring grist to Freud's mill—or rather, the grist I bring to his mill—in an almost uncanny way; and they would seem to undermine the argument I am on the verge of elaborating. But as Eliot says:

> Happily, we are not dependent on argument to prove that Fiction is a department of literature in which women can, after

their kind, fully equal men. A cluster of great names, both living and dead, rush to our memories in evidence that women can produce novels not only fine, but among the very finest;—novels too, that have a precious speciality, lying quite apart from masculine aptitudes and experience. (324)

(Let me work through her essay to my own.) What Eliot is attacking here is not only the relationship of certain women writers to literature but the critical reception given women's fiction. We might also say that she is attacking, the better to separate herself from, those women writers whose language is structured exactly like the unconscious that Freud has assigned to them, those writers (and their heroines) whose ambitious wishes are contained *entirely* in their erotic longings. And she is attacking these novelists the better to defend not those women who write *like* men (for she posits a "precious speciality" to women's productions), but those women who write in their own way, "after their kind," and implicitly about something else. Silly novels are that popular artifact which has always been and still is known as "women's literature"—a term, I should add, applied to such fiction by those who do not read it.[17]

Women writers then, in contrast to lady novelists, are writers whose texts would be "among the finest" (to stay with Eliot's terminology) and for whom the "ambitious wish" (to stay with Freud's) manifests itself as fantasy within another economy. In this economy, egoistic desires would assert themselves paratactically alongside erotic ones. The repressed content, I think, would be not erotic impulses but an impulse to power: a fantasy of power that would revise the social grammar in which women are never defined as subjects; a fantasy of power that disdains a sexual exchange in which women can participate only as objects of circulation. The daydreams or fictions of women writers would then, like those of men, say, "Nothing can happen to me!" But the modalities of that invulnerability would be marked in an essentially different way. I am talking, of course, about the power of the weak.[18] The inscription of this power is not always easy to decipher, because "the most essential form of accommodation for the weak is to conceal what power they do have" (Watson, 113). Moreover, to pick up a lost thread, when these modalities of difference are perceived, they are generally called implausibilities. They are not perceived, or are misperceived, because the scripting of this fantasy does not bring the aesthetic "forepleasure" Freud says fantasy scenarios

inevitably bring: pleasure bound to recognition and *identification*
(54), the "agrément" Genette assigns to plausible narrative. (Perhaps we shall not have a poetics of women's literature until we
have more weak readers.)

In *Les Voleuses de langue,* Claudine Herrmann takes up what
I call the politics of dreams, or the ideology of daydreaming, in
The Princess of Clèves:

> A daydream is perpetuated when it loses all chance of coming
> true, when the woman dreaming [*la rêveuse*] cannot make it
> pass into reality. If women did not generally experience the
> love they desire as a repeated impossibility, they would dream
> about it less. They would dream of other, perhaps more in-
> teresting things. Nevertheless, written in a language of dream,
> dreamt by Mme de Lafayette, the Princess of Clèves never
> dreams . . . for she knows that *love as she imagines it* is not
> realizable. What is realizable is a counterfeit she does not want.
> Her education permits her to glimpse this fact: men and women
> exchange feelings that are not equivalent. . . . Woman's
> "daydreaming" is a function of a world in which nothing comes
> true on her terms. (77–79)

"Men and women exchange feelings that are not equivalent." Mme
de Clèves's brief experience of the court confirms the principle of
difference at the heart of her mother's maxims. Mme de Clèves's
rejection of Nemours on his terms, however, derives its necessity
not only from the logic of maternal discourse (Nemours's love, like
his name, is negative and plural: *ne/amours*) but also from the
demands of Mme de Lafayette's dream. In this dream nothing can
happen to the heroine, because she understands that the power
and pleasure of the weak derive from circumventing the laws of
contingency and circulation. She withdraws then and confesses not
merely to resist possession, as her mother would have wished, but
to improve on it: to *rescript* possession.

The plausibility of this novel lies in the structuration of its fantasy. For if, to continue spinning out Herrmann's metaphor, the
heroine does not dream, she does daydream. And perhaps the most
significant confession in the novel is neither the first (to her husband, that she is vulnerable to desire) nor the third (to Nemours,
that she desires him) but the second, which is silent and entirely
telling: I refer, of course, to her nocturnal reverie at Coulommiers.
Although all three confessions prefigure by their extravagance the
heroine's retreat from the eyes of the world, it is this dreamlike

event that is least ambiguous in underlining the erotic valence of the ambitious scenario.

At Coulommiers, her country retreat, Mme de Clèves sits one warm evening, secretly observed by Nemours, winding ribbons of his colors around an India cane. (I take her surreptitious acquisition of his cane to be the counterpart of his theft of her miniature, in this crisscrossing of desires by metonymy.) As Michel Butor observes in his famous reading of this scene, "the mind of the princess is operating at this moment in a zone obscure to herself; it is as if she is knotting the ribbons around the cane in a dream, and her dream becomes clear little by little; the one she is thinking of begins to take on a face, and she goes to look for it" (76–77). Thus, having finished her handiwork, she places herself in front of a painting, a historical tableau of members of the court that she has had transported to her retreat, a painting including a likeness of Nemours: "She sat down and gazed at this portrait with an intensity and dreaminess [*rêverie*] that only passion can inspire" (168/155). And Butor comments, "One hardly needs a diploma in psychoanalysis to detect and appreciate the symbolism of this whole scene" (76). Indeed, it is quite clear that the princess is seen here in a moment of solitary pleasure, in a daydream of "fetishistic sublimation" (Grossvogel, 134). This autoeroticism would seem to be the only sexual performance she can afford in an economy regulated by dispossession.

Her retreat to Coulommiers, though, must be thought of not as a flight from sexuality but as a movement *into* it. As Sylvère Lotringer has observed, Mme de Clèves leaves the court not to flee passion but to preserve it (517). To preserve it, moreover, on her own terms. Unlike Nemours—who is not content to possess the object of his desire in representation (the purloined portrait) and who pleads silently after this scene, "Only look at me the way I saw you look at my portrait tonight; how could you look so gently at my portrait and then so cruelly fly from my presence?" (171/157)—the princess chooses "the duke of the portrait, not the man who seeks to step out of the frame" (519). Here she differs from Austen's heroine Elizabeth Bennet, who stands gazing before her lover's portrait and feels "a more gentle sensation towards the original than she had ever felt in the height of their acquaintance" (272). Elizabeth can accept the hand of the man who steps out of the frame; the princess cannot. For if, in the world of *Pride and Prejudice*, "between the picture's eyes and Elizabeth's hangs what will be given shape when the marriage of the lovers is formalized"

(Brownstein, 130–31), in the world of the court the princess's response to Nemours must remain specular. Her desire cannot be framed by marriage—à l'anglaise. If, however, as I believe, the withdrawal to Coulommiers is homologous to the final withdrawal, then there is no reason to imagine that at a remove from the world—or, rather, in the company of the world contained by representation in painting—the princess does not continue to experience her "erotic longings." But the fulfillment of the wish is to be realized in the daydream itself.

The daydream, then, is both the stuff of fairy tales ("Someday my prince will come") and their rewriting ("Someday my prince will come, but we will not live happily ever after"). The princess refuses to marry the duke, however, not because she doesn't want to live happily after but because she does. And by choosing not to act on that desire but to preserve it in and as fantasy, she both performs maternal discourse and italicizes it as repossession. Her choice is therefore not the simple reinscription of the seventeenth-century convention of feminine renunciation, dependent on the logic of either/or, but the sign of both/and, concretized by her final dual residence: in the convent *and* at home. "Perverted convention," as Peggy Kamuf names it, writing of another literary fetishist (Saint-Preux in Julie's closet): "The scene of optimal pleasure is within the prohibition which forms the walls of the house. Just on this side of the transgressive act, the fetishist's pleasure . . . is still in the closet" (203–4). This form of possession by metonymy both acknowledges the law and short-circuits it. Nobody, least of all the duke of Nemours, believes in her renunciation (just as her husband never fully believed her confession):

> Do you think that your resolutions can hold against a man who adores you and who is fortunate enough to attract you? It is more difficult than you think, Madame, to resist the attraction of love. You have done it *by an austere virtue which has almost no example;* but that virtue is no longer opposed to our feelings and I hope that you will follow them despite yourself. (191/174–75; emphasis added)

Mme de Clèves will not be deterred by sheer difficulty, by mere plausibility, by Nemour's *maxims*. She knows herself to be without a text. "No woman but you in the world," she has been told earlier in the novel, "would confide everything she knows in her husband" (123/116). "The singularity of such a confession," the narrator comments after the fait accompli, "for which she could find no example, made her see all the danger of it" (134/125). The danger of singularity precisely is sociolinguistic: the attempt to *communicate* in a language, an idiolect, that would nonetheless break with the coded rules of communication. An impossibility, as Jakobson has seen: "Private property, in the domain of language does not exist: everything is socialized. The verbal exchange, like every form of human relation, requires at least two interlocutors; an idiolect, in the final analysis, therefore can only be a *slightly perverse fiction*" (33; emphasis added). Thus in the end Mme de Clèves herself becomes both the impossibility of an example for others "in life" and its possibility in fiction. "Her life," the last line of the novel tells us, which "was rather short, left inimitable examples of virtue" (198/180). The last word in French is the challenge to reiteration—*inimitables,* the mark of the writer's ambitious wish.

I hope it is understood that I am not suggesting we read a heroine as her author's double—a biographical conflation that from the beginning has dominated and distorted the literary criticism of women's writing.[19] Rather, I am arguing that the peculiar shape of a heroine's destiny in novels by women, the implausible twists of plot so common in these novels, is a form of insistence about the relation of women to writing: a comment on the stakes of difference within the theoretical indifference of literature itself.

Woolf begins her essay on Eliot in the *Common Reader* by saying, "To read George Eliot attentively is to become aware how little one knows about her" (166). But then, a few pages later, she comments:

> For long she preferred not to think of herself at all. Then, when the first flush of creative energy was exhausted and self-confidence had come to her, she wrote more and more from the personal standpoint, but she did so without the unhesitating abandonment of the young. *Her self-consciousness is always marked when her heroines say what she herself would have said.* She disguised them in every possible way. She granted them beauty and wealth into the bargain; she invented more improbably, a taste for brandy. The disconcerting and stimulating fact remained that she was compelled by the very power of her genius to step forth in person upon the quiet bucolic scene. (173; emphasis added)

What interests me here is the "marking" Woolf identifies, an underlining of what she later describes as Eliot's heroines' "demand

for something—they scarcely know what—for something that is
perhaps incompatible with the facts of human existence" (175).
This demand of the heroine for something else is in part what I
mean by "italicization": the extravagant wish for a *story* that would
turn out differently.

In the fourth chapter of book 5 of *The Mill on the Floss* Maggie
Tulliver, talking with Philip Wakem in the "Red Deeps," returns
a novel he has lent her:

> "Take back your *Corinne*," said Maggie. . . . "You were
> right in telling me she would do me no good, but you were
> wrong in thinking I should wish to be like her."
>
> "Wouldn't you really like to be a tenth muse, then, Mag-
> gie?" . . .
>
> "Not at all," said Maggie laughing. "The muses were un-
> comfortable goddesses, I think—obliged always to carry rolls
> and musical instruments about with them . . ."
>
> "You agree with me in not liking Corinne, then?"
>
> "I didn't finish the book," said Maggie. "As soon as I came
> to the blond-haired young lady reading in the park, I shut it
> up and determined to read no further. I foresaw that light-
> complexioned girl would win away all the love from Corinne
> and make her miserable. I'm determined to read no more books
> where the blond-haired women carry away all the happiness.
> I should begin to have a prejudice against them. If you could
> give me some story, now, where the dark woman triumphs,
> it would restore the balance. I want to avenge Rebecca, and
> Flora MacIvor, and Minna, and all the rest of the dark un-
> happy ones. . . ."
>
> "Well, perhaps you will avenge the dark women in your
> own person and carry away all the love from your cousin Lucy.
> She is sure to have some handsome young man of St. Ogg's
> at her feet now, and you have only to shine upon him—your
> fair little cousin will be quite quenched in your beams."
>
> "Philip, that is not pretty of you, to apply my nonsense to
> anything real," said Maggie looking hurt. (348–49)

Maggie's literary instincts were correct. True to the laws of genre,
Corinne—despite, or rather because of her genius and exceptionality—is made miserable and the blond Lucile, her half-sister, car-
ries the day, although she is deprived of a perfectly happy end. But
whatever Eliot's, or Maggie's, "prejudices" against the destinies
of Scott's heroines, Maggie no more than Corinne avenges the

dark woman in her own person. Even though, as Philip predicts, Maggie's inner radiance momentarily quenches her fairhaired cousin Lucy, "reality"—that is to say, Eliot's novel—proves to be as hard on darkhaired women as literature is. What is important in this deliberate intertextuality, which has not gone unnoted (Moers, 174), is that both heroines revolt against the text of a certain "happily ever after." As Madelyn Gutwirth observes in her book on Germaine de Staël, Corinne prefers "her genius to the . . . bonds of marriage, but that is not to say she thereby renounces happiness. On the contrary, it is her wish to be happy, that is to be herself *and* to love, that kills her" (225). Maggie Tulliver, too, would be herself and love, but the price for *that* unscriptable wish proves again to be the deferral of conventional erotic longings, what Maggie calls "earthly happiness." Almost two hundred years after the challenge to the maxim wrought by the blond (as it turns out) princess of Clèves, George Eliot, through the scenario of definitive postponement, "imitates" Lafayette.

The last two books of *The Mill on the Floss* are called, respectively, "The Great Temptation" and "The Final Rescue." As the plot moves toward closure, the chapter headings of these books— "First Impressions," "Illustrating the Laws of Attraction," "Borne Along by the Tide," "Waking," "St. Ogg's Passes Judgement," "The Last Conflict"—further emphasize the sexual struggle at the heart of the novel. For, as Philip had anticipated, Maggie dazzles blond Lucy's fiancé, Stephen Guest, in "First Impressions," but then, surely what Philip had not dreamt of, the pair is swept away. Maggie, previously unawakened by her own fiancé, *Wakem,* awakens both to her desire and to what she calls her duty, only to fulfill both by drowning, attaining at last that "wondrous happiness that is one with pain" (545). Though I do some violence to the scope of Eliot's narrative by carving a novel out of a novel, the last two books taken together as they chart the culmination of a heroine's erotic destiny have a plot of their own—a plot, moreover, with elective affinities to the conclusion of *The Princess of Clèves,* and to the conclusion of my argument.

Like Mme de Clèves after her husband's death, Maggie knows herself to be technically free to marry her lover but feels bound, though not for the same reasons, to another script. And Stephen Guest, who like Nemours does not believe in "mere resolution" (499), finds Maggie's refusal to follow her passions "unnatural" and "horrible": "If you loved me as I love you, we should throw everything else to the winds for the sake of belonging to each other"

(447). Maggie does love him, just as the princess loves the duke, passionately; and she is tempted: part of her longs to be transported by the exquisite currents of desire. But her awakening, like that of the princess, though again not for the same reasons, is double. She falls asleep on the boatride down the river. When she awakens and disentangles her mind "from the confused web of dreams" (494), like Mme de Clèves after her own brush with death, Maggie pulls away from the man who has briefly but deeply tempted her. She will not build her happiness on the unhappiness of others:

> It is not force that ought to rule us—this that we feel for each other; it would rend me away from all that my past life has made dear and holy to me. I can't set out on a fresh life and forget that; I must go back to it, and cling to it, else I shall feel as if there were nothing firm beneath my feet. (502)

What is the content of this sacred past? Earlier, before the waking on the river, when Maggie was tempted only by the "fantasy" of a "life filled with all luxuries, with daily incense of adoration near and distant, and with all possibilities of culture at her command," the narrator had commented on the pull of that erotic scenario:

> But there were things in her stronger than vanity—passion, and affection, and long deep memories of early discipline and effort, of early claims on her love and pity; and the stream of vanity was soon swept along and mingled imperceptibly with that wider current which was at its highest force today. . . .
> (457)

Maggie's renunciation of Stephen Guest, then, is not so simple as I have made it out to be, for the text of these "early claims" this archaic wish has a power both erotic and ambitious in its own right. That "wider current" is, of course, the broken bond with her brother. And the epigraph to the novel, "In their death they were not divided," is the telos toward which the novel tends; for it is also the last line of the novel, the epitaph on the tombstone of the brother and sister who drown in each other's arms.

Maggie, obeying what Stephen called her "perverted notion of right," her passion for a "mere idea" (538), drowns finally in an implausible flood. Maggie, no more than Mme de Clèves, could be *persuaded* (to invoke Jane Austen's last novel); for neither regarded a second chance as an alternative to be embraced. Maggie's return home sans husband is not understood by the community. And the narrator explains that "public opinion in these cases is always of the feminine gender—not the world, but the world's wife" (512–13). Despite the phrase, Eliot does not locate the inadequacy of received social ideas in gender per se; her attack on the notion of a "master-key that will fit all cases" is in fact directed at the "men of maxims": "The mysterious complexity of our life is not to be embraced by maxims" (521). This commentary seeks to justify Maggie's choice, her turning away from the maxim, and thus inscribes an internal "artificial plausibility": the text within the text, as we saw that function in *The Princess of Clèves*. The commentary constitutes another reading, a reading by "reference," as Eliot puts it, to the "special circumstances that mark the individual lot" (521). Like Mme de Clèves, Maggie has been given extraordinary feelings, and those feelings engender another and extravagant narrative logic.

There is a feminist criticism today that laments Eliot's ultimate refusal to satisfy her heroine's longing for that "something . . . incompatible with the facts of human existence":

> Sadly, and it is a radical criticism of George Eliot, she does not commit herself fully to the energies and aspirations she lets loose in these women. Does she not cheat them, and cheat us, ultimately, in allowing them so little? Does she not excite our interest through the breadth and the challenge of the implications of her fiction, and then deftly dam up and fence round the momentum she has so powerfully created? She diagnoses so brilliantly "the common yearning of womanhood," and then cures it, sometimes drastically, as if it were indeed a disease. (Calder, 158)

It is as though these critics, somewhat like Stendhal disbelieving the conviction of Mme de Clèves, would have Maggie live George Eliot's life. The point is, it seems to me, that the plots of women's literature are not about "life" and solutions in any therapeutic sense, nor should they be. They are about the plots of literature itself, about the constraints the maxim places on rendering a female life in fiction. Lafayette quietly, George Eliot less silently, both italicize by the demaximization of their heroines' texts the difficulty of curing plot of life, and life of certain plots.[20]

In her essay "On Women and Fiction," Lynn Sukenick describes the uncomfortable posture of all women writers in our culture, within and without the text: what I would call a posture of imposture. And she says of the role of gender in relation to the literary project: "Like the minority writer, the female writer exists

within an inescapable condition of identity which distances her
from the mainstream of the culture and forces her either to stress
her separation from the masculine literary tradition or to pursue
her resemblance to it" (28). Were she to forget her double bind,
the "phallic critics" (as Mary Ellman named them) would remind
her that she is dreaming: "Lady novelists," Hugh Kenner wrote
not so long ago, "have always claimed the privilege of transcending *mere plausibilities*. It's up to men to arrange such things. . . .
Your bag is sensitivity, which means knowing what to put into
this year's novels" (in Sukenick, 30; emphasis added). And a re-
viewer (in 1978) of a woman's novel in *Newsweek:*

> Like most feminist novels [this one] represents a triumph of
> sensibility over plot. Why a strong, credible narrative line that
> leads to a satisfactory resolution of conflicts should visit these
> stories so infrequently, I do not know. Because the ability to
> tell a good story is unrelated to gender, I sometimes suspect
> that the authors of these novels are simply indifferent to the
> rigors of narrative. (Prescott, 112)

The second gentleman is slightly more generous than the first. He
at least thinks women capable of telling a good—that is, credi-
ble—story. The fault lies in their *in*difference. The magazine re-
viewer echoes, with curious persistence, the objections of Bussy-
Rabutin's correspondence.

The attack on female plots and plausibilities assume that women
writers cannot or will not obey the rules of fiction. It also assumes
that the truth devolving from *veri*similitude is male. For sensibility,
sensitivity, "extravagance"—so many code words for feminine in
our culture that the attack is in fact tautological—are taken to be
not merely inferior modalities of production but deviations from
some obvious truth. The blind spot here is both political (or philosophical) and literary. It does not see, nor does it want to, that
the fictions of desire behind the desiderata of fiction are masculine
and not universal constructs. It does not see that the maxims that
pass for the truth of human experience and the encoding of that
experience, in literature, are organizations, when they are not fantasies, of the dominant culture. To read women's literature is to
see and hear repeatedly a chafing against the "unsatisfactory reality" contained in the maxim. Everywhere in *The Mill on the Floss*
one can read a protest against the division of labor that grants
men the world and women love. Saying no to Philip Wakem and
then to Stephen Guest, Maggie refuses the hospitality of the happy

end: "But I begin to think there can never come much happiness to me from loving; I have always had so much pain mingled with it. I wish I could make myself a world outside it, as men do" (430). But as in so much women's fiction a world outside love proves to be out of the world altogether. The protest against that topographical imperative is more or less muted from novel to novel. Still, the emphasis is always there to be read, and it points to another text. To continue to deny the credibility of women's literature is to adopt the posture of the philosopher of phallogocentrism's "credulous man who, in support of his testimony, offers truth and his phallus as his own proper credentials" (Derrida, "Becoming Woman," 113). Those credentials are more than suspect.

NOTES

1. Although what is being pointed to ultimately is an "elsewhere" under the sign of an androgyny I resist, I respond here to the implicit invitation to look again. The quotation should be replaced both in its original context and within Carolyn Heilbrun's concluding argument in *Toward a Recognition of Androgyny*, which is where I found it (again). There is an interesting discussion of this passage in Jane Marcus's *Virginia Woolf and the Languages of Patriarchy* (160–62). Marcus reads the falling of the leaf as a textual maternal legacy, which in my argument oddly refigures the fate of the final daughter in Lafayette's novel.

2. If one must have a less arbitrary origin—and why not?—the properly inaugural fiction would be Hélisenne de Crenne's *Les Angoysses douloureuses qui procèdent d'amours*, 1538. But *The Princess of Clèves* has this critical advantage: it also marks the beginning of the modern French novel.

3. Bussy-Rabutin's oft-cited remarks on the novel are most easily found in Maurice Laugaa's volume of critical responses, *Lectures de Mme de Lafayette*, pp. 18–19. The translation is mine unless otherwise indicated.

4. On the function and status of the confession in Mme de Villedieu's novel and on the problems of predecession, see Micheline Cuénin's introduction to her critical edition of *Les Désordres de l'amour*. The best account of the attack on the novel and the problem of *vraisemblance* remains Georges May's *Le Dilemme du roman au XVIIIᵉ siècle*, especially his first chapter.

5. I allude here (playfully) to the first definition of "extravagant" in *Le Petit Robert:* "S'est dit de textes non incorporés dans les recueils canoniques" [Used to refer to texts not included in the canon].

6. In my translation-adaptation of Genette's analysis I have chosen to render *vraisemblance* by "plausibility," a term with a richer semantic field of connotations than "versimilitude."

7. The best overview of the discussion about women's writing in France remains Elaine Marks's 1978 "Women and Literature in France."

8. For Kristeva's (1977) position on a possible specificity to women's writing, see "Questions à Julia Kristeva."

9. The opposition between these positions is, I think, more rhetorical than actual, as Woolf's gloss on Coleridge in *A Room of One's Own* shows.

10. I understate the stakes of an apparently passive indifference. As Edward Said has written in another context: "Any philosophy or critical theory exists and is maintained in order not merely *to be there, passively around everyone and everything,* but in order to be taught and diffused, to be absorbed decisively into the institutions of society or to be instrumental in maintaining or changing or perhaps upsetting these institutions and that society" (682).

11. When I wrote "Emphasis Added" in the fall of 1978, I was unaware of Sandra Gilbert and Susan Gubar's groundbreaking work. Obviously *Madwoman in the Attic* has radically transformed our understanding of women's writing. To the extent that my book records its own history, I have preferred simply to place in a note here my esteem for their accomplishment.

12. See, for instance, Showalter's chapter "The Double Critical Standard and the Feminine Novel," pp. 73–99.

13. Mary Jacobus has written interestingly about Irigaray's and Eliot's metaphorics of women and language in "The Question of Language: Men of Maxims and *The Mill on the Floss.*"

14. Eliot herself has commented on the use of italics by lady novelists: "We imagine the double-refined accent and profusion of chin which are feebly represented by the italics in this lady's sentences!" ("Silly Novels," 315)

15. My translations from *The Princess of Clèves* are deliberately literal; page references to the French are from the readily available Garnier-Flammarion edition (Paris, 1966) and are incorporated within the text. The published English translation is Penguin (New York, 1978) and I have included page references to it.

16. Jules Brody, in "*La Princesse de Clèves* and the Myth of Courtly Love" (1969), Domna C. Stanton, in "The Ideal of *Repos* in Seventeenth-Century French Literature" (1975), and Joan DeJean in "Lafayette's Ellipses" (1984) also interpret the princess's final refusal of Nemours and her renunciation as heroic and self-preserving actions within a certain seventeenth-century discourse.

17. On the content of popular women's literature and its relationship to high culture, see Lillian Robinson's "On Reading Trash."

18. See Elizabeth Janeway's discussion of this notion in her essay "On the Power of the Weak."

19. On this desperately unimaginative hermeneutics, see my discussion of Jean Larnac in "Writing Fictions."

20. I'm playing here with the terms of Peter Brooks's analysis of the relations between "plot" and "life" in his illuminating essay "Freud's Masterplot."

[2]

Writing Fictions: Women's Autobiography in France

Were I a writer and dead, how I would love it if my life, through the pains of some friendly and detached biographer, were to reduce itself to a few details, a few preferences, a few inflections, let us say to "biographemes."

Roland Barthes, *Sade, Fourier, Loyola*

Is there, for me, no other haven than this commonplace room? Must I stay forever before this impenetrable mirror where I come up against myself, face to face?

Colette, *The Vagabond*

THE OFT-CITED and apparently transparent epigraph to Colette's *Break of Day*—"Do you imagine in reading my books that I am drawing my portrait? Patience: it's only my model"[1]—challenges the reader's competence in distinguishing life from art, nature from imitation, autobiography from fiction. Although this inaugural gesture, anticipating both our misreading and our improper labeling of the text, will prove to be more than a simple inveighing against the fallacy of reference, let us, for the moment, proceed as docile and linear readers. The novel opens with a letter, and the author's first words ostensibly authenticate the document: "This note, signed 'Sidonie Colette, née Landoy,' was written by my mother to one of my husbands, the second. A year later she died at the age of seventy-seven" (5). The invitation thus extended to seal the identity gap between the "I" of narration and Sidonie Gabrielle Colette is reissued in the second chapter. Defending herself against "one of my husband's" claims that she could write nothing but love stories, the narrator (a novelist) reviews the history of her fictional heroines and the genealogy of her *name*:

In them I called myself Renée Néré or else, prophetically, I
introduced a Léa. So it came about that both legally and fa-
miliarly as well as in my books, I now have only one name,
which is my own. Did it take only thirty years of my life to
reach that point, or rather to get back to it? I shall end by
thinking that it wasn't too high a price to pay.[2] (19)

Who is speaking? And in whose name? The liminary warning op-
erates like a free-floating anxiety, already there at the very threshold of the text to prevent the foreclosure of identification. The "I"
of narration may, like Colette, have "only one name" but her project is no less ambiguous for that symmetry.[3] To bypass the am-
biguity would be to assume, for example, that the fiction of *Break
of Day* is a page from Colette's autobiography, and hence to perform a "masculine" reading:

Why do men—writers or so-called writers—still show surprise that a woman should so easily reveal to the public love-
secrets and amorous lies and half-truths? *By divulging these,
she manages to hide other important and obscure secrets which
she herself does not understand very well . . .* Man, my friend,
you willingly make fun of women's writings because they can't
help being autobiographical. On whom then were you relying
to paint women for you? . . . On yourself? (62; emphasis
added)

"Colette" would have her critics not confuse "the illuminated zone"
of the feminine sector, love's brilliant disasters, with the darker,
shadowy text of the female self, "the true intimate life of a woman"
(62–63). But that intimacy, that maskless self, has to do with
"*preference,*" and here, we are told, she will "keep silent" (45).
    Shall we take "Colette" at her word then? That what we have
are deliberate *fictions* of self-representation, "rearranged frag-
ments of . . . emotional life" (45) as she calls them, and not autobiography after all? Philippe Lejeune, whose *L'Autobiographie
en France* constitutes the first attempt to define and classify autobiography in the French tradition as a genre, would have it so.
He excludes Colette from his repertory, citing her own reluctance
to talk about herself; but more to the point, the absence of what
he poses as a necessary condition of autobiography: the "autobiographical pact" (72–73). This pact is a declaration of autobiographical intention, an explicit project of sincere truth telling; a
promise to the *reader* that the textual and referential "I" are one.

For Lejeune, however confessional a text may seem, without that covenant of good faith, we remain in the realm of fiction.

It seems, perhaps, perverse that despite the caveat implicit in "Colette's" jibe at the male reader expecting to find autobiography seeping through the pages of women's literature, we so reluctantly accept her exclusion from the French autobiographical canon.[4] This resistance comes not so much from doubts about Lejeune's criteria (as they do or do not apply to Colette) as from a hesitation about embracing wholeheartedly any theoretical model *indifferent to a problematics of genre as inflected by gender*. With this hesitation in mind, let us consider instances of those female autobiographers included by Lejeune—George Sand, Daniel Stern (Marie d'Agoult), and Simone de Beauvoir. Taking his criteria as a point of departure, and moving dialectically between the points of textual production and reception, of authorship and readership, we will return in closing—with some stops along the way—to Colette. Thus by virtue of her undecidable relation to the androcentric paradigm, Colette will serve as the fiction, the pretext really, which allows us to play with the theory.

LEJEUNE'S DEFINITION of autobiography as the "retrospective narrative in prose that someone makes of his existence, when he places the main emphasis on his individual life, especially on the history of his personality" (14), provides a point of departure from which to ask the question: is there a specificity to a female retrospective; how and where in the narrative will it make itself felt? To the extent that autobiography, as Diane Johnson has put it, "requires some strategy of self-dramatization" and "contains, as in fiction, a crisis and a denouement" (19), what conventions govern the production of a female self as *theater*?[5] How does a woman writer perform on the stage of her text?

Historically, the French autobiographer, male or female, has had to come to terms with the exhibitionist performer that is Jean-Jacques Rousseau.[6] Both George Sand and her contemporary Daniel Stern take a certain distance from the *Confessions* because of the inclusive quality of his rememorations. Sand, for example, asks in the "pact" to *Histoire de ma vie*: "Who can forgive him for having confessed Mme de Warens while confessing himself?"[7] (2:13). Daniel Stern takes up the same point in her *Mémoires*, rejecting Rousseau's promiscuous gesture, and concluding that for herself, "I felt neither the right nor the desire, in recalling my own memories, to mix in, inappropriately, those of others" (11). And both issue warnings that the reader hoping for scandalous revelations will be disappointed; their truth, if not their memory, will be selective. Now the problem of selectivity is of course not a problem for women only. Every autobiographer must deal with it. Chateaubriand, for one, writes in the preface to the *Mémoires d'outre-tombe* that he will "include no name other than his own in everything that concerns his private life" (1:547). To some extent, then, this reticence about naming names is a matter of historical context: the nineteenth-century backlash to the tell-all stance of Rousseau—especially in the area of the sexual connection, the erogenous zones of the self. But not entirely. The decision to go public is particularly charged for the woman writer.

In the preface to her second volume of memoirs, *The Prime of Life,* Simone de Beauvoir too goes back to Rousseau: "It may be objected that such an inquiry concerns no one but myself. Not so; if any individual—a Pepys or a Rousseau, an exceptional or a run-of-the-mill character—reveals himself honestly, everyone, more or less, becomes involved. It is impossible for him to shed light on his own life without at some point illuminating the lives of others." (10) But then, following this relative indifference to the inevitable contiguity of other lives, a familiar caveat:

> At the same time I must warn [my readers] that I have no intention of telling them everything. I described my childhood and adolescence without any omissions. . . . I cannot treat the years of my maturity in the same detached way—nor do I enjoy a similar freedom when discussing them. I have no intention of filling these pages with spiteful gossip about myself and my friends; I lack the instincts of the scandal monger. There are many things which I firmly intend to *leave in obscurity.* (10; emphasis added)

And she adds (in the next sentence): "On the other hand, my life has been closely linked with that of Jean-Paul Sartre. As he intends to write his own life story, I shall not attempt to perform the task for him." It is fair, I think, to assume that while for all autobiographers already figures of public fiction there is a strong sense of responsibility about speaking out, because being known, they expect their words to have an impact within a clearly defined readers' circle, the female autobiographers know that they are being read as *women;* women, in the case of Sand, Stern, and Beauvoir (and this is no less true for Colette), known for (or even through) their liaisons with famous men. The concern with notoriety, then, functions as an additional grid or constraint placed upon the truth, upon "the shaping of the past" as truth (Pascal, 5).

Daniel Stern articulates with the greatest insistence the role played by a feminine identity in the autobiographical venture, and the *gender* of sincerity. She asks a friend in 1850, years before actually writing the first volume of her memoirs: "How do you think a work of this sort written by a woman, by a mother, should be composed? . . . I would favor a grave confession, narrow in scope, disengaged from detail, rather moral and intellectual than real. But I am told that that would be without charm" (in Vier, 4:250). And thirteen years later, in a diary entry (but by this time, it would seem, she has already begun writing): "No, my friend, I won't write my *Mémoires*. . . . My instinctive repugnance has conquered . . . I had conceived of a daring book. Feminine confessions as sincere as and consequently more daring (because of public opinion) than those of Jean-Jacques. Once I thought this book was going to come about: *L'Histoire de ma vie* was announced. *I cannot do it*" (in Vier, 4:255).[8] The book does get written, however, and in the preface to *Mes Souvenirs*, Stern traces the logic of her hesitations: "I was a woman, and as such, not bound to a virile sincerity"; but when a woman's life is not governed "by the common rule . . . she becomes responsible, more responsible than a man, in the eyes of all. When this woman, because of some chance or talent, comes out of obscurity she instantly contracts virile duties" (viii–ix). Thus an exceptional woman, by virtue of that exceptionality, becomes subject to a double constraint: masculine responsibilities and feminine sensitivity. For whatever is wrong in the world, Stern contends, "woman has felt it more completely in her whole being"; if a woman is an instrument more sensitive than a man in picking up the "discordances" of society, however, she must nevertheless be more discreet than a man in rendering those vibrations: "My persuasion being . . . that a woman's pen was more constrained than another's by choice within the truth" (*Mémoires*, 11).

Although, as Georges Gusdorf has written in his well-known essay on autobiography, "the man who tells his story . . . is not involved in an objective and disinterested occupation, but in a work of personal justification," and although such self-justification in the eyes of the world may well constitute "the most secret intention" (115) of any autobiographical undertaking, for Stern (as is true in varying degrees of intensity for Sand and Beauvoir) the self being justified is indelibly marked by what Beauvoir calls *féminitude*:

a culturally determined status of difference and oppression (in *L'Arc*, 12). Thus Stern would show (and surely this is the not-so-very-hidden agenda for Sand and Beauvoir) that while a woman may fly in the face of tradition, that is, of traditional expectations for women, particularly in regard to the institution of marriage, she is no less a *human being* of merit; that while on the face of it she is an outlaw, the real fault lies with society and its laws. To justify an unorthodox life by writing about it, however, is to *reinscribe* the original violation, to reviolate masculine turf: hence Stern's defensiveness about the range of her pen. The drama of the self (to return to the histrionic metaphor proposed earlier) is staged in a public theater, and it is *thesis* drama. The autobiographies of these women, to invoke another literary genre, are a defense and illustration, at once a treatise on overcoming received notions of femininity and a poetics calling for another, freer text. These autobiographies, then, belong to that type of women's writing Elaine Showalter in *A Literature of Their Own* has described as "feminist": "*protest* against [the] standards of art and its views of social roles," and "*advocacy* of minority rights and values, including a demand for autonomy" (13). The subject of women's autobiography here is a self both occulted and overexposed by the fact of her femininity as a social reality.

It should come as no surprise that for women determined to go beyond the strictures of convention, conventionally female moments are not assigned privileged status. One does not find even metaphorical traces of what Hélène Cixous calls for in her "feminine future"; "the gestation drive—just like the desire to write: a desire to live self from within, a desire for the swollen belly, for language, for blood" (891). Autobiology is not the subtext of autobio*graphy*. It is not, however, entirely repressed. George Sand, for example, who gives birth nine months after her marriage, embraces her pregnancy with pleasure and female solidarity: "I spent the winter of 1822–23 at Nohant, rather ill, but absorbed by the feeling of maternal love that was revealing itself to me through the sweetest dreams and the liveliest aspirations. The transformation that comes about at that moment in the life and thoughts of a woman is, in general, complete and sudden. It was so for me as for the great majority" (2:32). Forced by her doctor to remain in bed and perfectly still for six weeks, Sand comments: "The order . . . was severe, but what wouldn't I have done to maintain the hope of being a mother?" (2:35) And the account of childbirth itself, if abbreviated and discreet, is no less positive: "My son

Maurice came into the world June 30, 1823, without mishap and very hardy. It was the most beautiful moment of my life, that moment when after an hour of deep sleep which followed upon the terrible pains of that paroxysm, I saw, on waking up, that tiny being asleep on my pillow. I had dreamed of him so much ahead of time, and I was so weak, I wasn't sure I wasn't still dreaming" (2:37).

Colette, in that slim volume of reminiscences called *The Evening Star,* also gives pregnancy a few pages of retrospective attention. Colette, taken by surprise at age 40, is, in the beginning, less sanguine and more anxious than (the younger and at that point in her life more conventional) Sand: "I was simply afraid that at my age I would not know how to give a child the proper love and care, devotion and understanding. Love—so I believed—had already hurt me a great deal by monopolizing me for the past twenty years" (in Phelps, 199/132).[9] This concern results in secrecy about her condition, which when finally revealed to a male friend leads him to say: "You're behaving as a man would, you're having a masculine pregnancy!" The "masculine" pregnancy, however, temporarily gives way to a slightly ironic but no less "feminine" text:

> Insidiously, unhurriedly, the beatitude of pregnant females spread through me. I was no longer subject to any discomfort, any unease. This purring contentment, this euphoria—how give a name either scientific or familiar to this state of preservation?—must certainly have penetrated me, since I have not forgotten it and am recalling it now, when life can never again bring me plentitude. . . . One gets tired of keeping to oneself all the unsaid things—in the present case my feeling of pride, of banal magnificence, as I ripened my fruit. (Phelps, 200/132–33)

Despite the euphoria, Colette continued to write: "The 'masculine pregnancy' did not lose all its rights; I was working on the last part of *The Shackle.* The child and the novel were both rushing me, and the *Vie Parisienne,* which was serializing my unfinished novel, was catching up with me. The baby showed signs that it would win the race, and I screwed on the cap of my fountain pen" (Phelps, 203/135). The account of childbirth itself is characterized less by benign irony and humorous reticence than by a brutal distancing from the female lot: "What followed . . . doesn't matter and I will give it no place here. What followed was the prolonged

scream that issues from all women in childbed. . . . What followed was a restorative sleep and selfish appetite" (Phelps, 203/
136). But the anaphora already perceptible in the passage cited above
("What followed"/*la suite*) continues to structure insistently the
narrative of this *hapax,* this unique moment in the writer's life,
connecting an undifferentiating and hence (for Colette) negative
female bond to a singular and bittersweet experience, her post-
partum response to her daughter: "But what followed was also,
once, an effort to crawl toward me made by my bundled up little
larva that had been laid down for a moment on my bed. What
animal perfection! The little creature guessed, she sensed the presence of my forbidden milk, and blindly struggled toward that
blocked source. Never did I cry more brokenheartedly. Dreadful
it is to ask in vain, but small is that hurt when compared with the
pain of not giving . . ." (Phelps, 203–4/136).

Colette accords a few more paragraphs to her passage into
motherhood, but she returns quickly to the "competition between
the book and the birth," the saving grace—for her writing—of
her "jot of virility," to conclude with speculation about her own
mother's probable reaction to this improbable maternity: "When
I was a young girl, if I ever happened to occupy myself with some
needlework, Sido always shook her soothsayer's head and commented, 'You will never look like anything but a boy who is sew-
ing!' She would now have said, 'You will never be anything but
a writer who gave birth to a child,' for she would not have failed
to see the accidental character of my maternity" (Phelps, 205–6/
137).

A writer who gave birth to a child, this *hierarchization* of roles
has everything to do with the shape of the autobiographies under
consideration here: mothers by accident of nature, writers by design. While marriage (and for Beauvoir the decision not to marry),
and childbearing (and again for Beauvoir the decision not to bear
children) sharply punctuate the female retrospective, they are not
self-evidently *signifying* moments. They shape lives rather in coun-
terpoint to the valorized trajectory: the transcendence of the feminine condition through writing. If there is, to return to the language of theatricality invoked earlier, crisis and drama and
denouement in the staging of the autobiographical self, it takes
place around the act of writing. Although Beauvoir is the only
autobiographer of this group to oppose in mutually exclusive categories writing and maternity, her assumption of writing as a vo-

cation and as locus of identity is emblematic: "I knew that in order to become a writer I needed a great measure of time and freedom. I had no rooted objection to playing at long odds, but this was not a game: the whole value and direction of my life lay at stake. The risk of compromising it could only have been justified had I regarded a child as no less vital a creative task than a work of art, which I did not" (67). Mothers or not, maternal or not, destiny is not tributary of anatomy in these texts.[10]

Sand, who is the least ambivalent of the three about her maternity, in the autobiographical account of her apprenticeship to writing in Paris tells (with great relish) the following anecdote about writing and children. As a young woman, already a mother (Sand comes to live in her Parisian mansard with her little daughter), she ponders the ways of the world of letters and wonders whether she has what it takes to make it as a writer in Paris. On the recommendation of a friend, she pays a visit to a certain M. de Kératry, the successful author of *Le Dernier des Beaumanoir* (a story in which a woman, thought to be dead, is raped by the priest whose task it is to bury her), and seeks his advice about her project. The man is terse: "I'm going to be frank with you. A woman shouldn't write." Sand decides to see herself out, but the man suddenly becomes loquacious. He wants to expose his theory on women's inferiority, "on the impossibility for even the most intelligent among them to write a good book." Finally, seeing Sand about to make her exit, he utters his parting shot (that Sand characterizes as an example of Napoleonic wit): "Believe me, don't make books, make babies" (2:150).

The cogito for Sand, Stern, and Beauvoir would seem to be, I write, therefore I am. Writing—for publication—represents entrance into the world of others, and by means of that passage a rebirth: the access through writing to the status of an autonomous subjectivity beyond the limits of feminine propriety established by a Kératry.[11] The meaningful trajectory is thus literary and intellectual.[12] The life of the mind is not, however, coolly cerebral. It is vivid and impassioned. Thus Stern describes her motivation in becoming a writer: "I needed to get outside myself, to put into my life a new interest that was not love for a man, but an intellectual relationship with those who felt, thought, and suffered as I did. I published therefore . . ." (*Mémoires*, 215). The textualization of a female "I" means escape from the sphere inhabited by those "relative beings" (as Beauvoir has characterized women) who experience the world only through the mediation of men. To write is to come out of the wings, and to appear, however briefly, center stage.

It is in those terms that Beauvoir describes the publication of her first novel: "So through the medium of my book I aroused curiosity, irritation, even sympathy: there were people who actually liked it. Now at last I was fulfilling the promises I had made myself when I was fifteen. . . . For a moment it was sufficient that I had crossed the threshold: *She Came to Stay* existed for other people, and I had entered public life" (441). One arrives, then, at this curious but finally not very surprising paradox: these autobiographies are the stories of women who succeeded in becoming more than *just women,* and by their own negative definition of that condition.

Sand, for example, reflecting on Montaigne's exclusion of women from the chapter on friendship by virtue of their inferior moral nature, protests and would exempt herself—at least partially— from that category by virtue of her education:

> I could see that an education rendered somewhat different from that of other women by fortuitous circumstances had modified my being. . . . I was not, therefore, entirely a woman like those whom the moralists censure and mock; in my soul I had enthusiasm for the beautiful, thirst for the true, and yet I was indeed a woman like all the others, sickly, highly strung, dominated by my imagination, childishly vulnerable to the tender emotions and anxieties of maternity. (2:126–27)

While Sand in this reflection concludes that "the heart and the mind have a sex," and that "a woman will always be more of an artist and a poet in her life, a man always more in his work" (but objects to an interpretation of that difference as a definition of "moral inferiority"), she no less aspires to transcendence, dreaming of those "male virtues to which women can raise themselves" (2:127). The question one must now ask is whether the story of a woman who sees conventional female self-definition as a text to be rewritten, who refuses the inscription of her body as the ultimate truth of her self, to become, if not a man, an exceptional woman (hence like a man), is a story significantly different from that of a man who becomes an exceptional man (particularly in this instance of figures who became exceptional by virtue of their writing).[13]

The difference of gender *as genre* is there to be read only if one

accepts the terms of another sort of "pact": the pact of commitment to decipher what women have said (or, more important, left
unsaid) about the pattern of their lives, over and above what any
person might say about his, through genre. I say "his" deliberately.
Not because men in fact lead genderless lives, but because the fact
of their gender is given and received literarily as a mere donnée of
personhood; because the canon of the autobiographical text, like
the literary canon, self-defined as it is by the notion of a human
universal, in general fails to interrogate gender as a meaningful
category of reference or of interpretation. This is not to say, of
course, that the male autobiographer does not inscribe his *sexuality*. And Rousseau is hardly silent on the matter. But when, for
example, Rousseau writes at the beginning of his *Confessions*, "I
want to show my fellow men [*mes semblables*] a man in all nature's truth," he conflates in perfect conformity with the linguistic
economy of the West maleness and humanity, as do most of the
readers of autobiography cited in these pages.

To read for difference, therefore, is to perform a diacritical gesture; to refuse a politics of reading that depends on the fiction of
a neutral (neuter) economy of textual production and reception.
This refusal of a degendered reading fiction is a movement of oscillation which locates difference in the negotiation between writer
and reader. The difference of which I speak here, however, is located in the "I" of the beholder, in the *reader's* perception. I would
propose, then, the notion of gender-marked reading: a practice of
the text that would recognize the status of the reader as a differ-
entiated subject, a reading subject named by gender and committed in a dialectics of identification to deciphering the inscription
of a female subject. (This move is what in "Arachnologies" I will
call "overreading.")

Let us now engage a less docile reading of our autobiographers,
and especially of Colette. Toward the end of the *The Evening Star*,
Colette imagines a publisher asking her: "When will you make up
your mind to give us your memoirs?" And has herself answer:
"Dear Publisher, I will write them neither more, nor better nor
less than today" (141). She thus rejects the specifically autobiographical project in its generic specificity. But then she suddenly
wonders about an earlier female writer and autobiographer:

How the devil did George Sand manage? Robust laborer of
letters that she was, she was able to finish off one novel and
begin another within the hour. She never lost either a lover

or a puff of her hookah by it, produced a twenty volume *His-toire de ma vie* into the bargain and I am completely staggered when I think of it. Pell-mell, and with ferocious energy she piled up her work, her passing griefs, her limited felicities. I could never have done so much, and at the moment when she was thinking forward to her full barns I was still lingering to gaze at the green, flowering wheat. (Phelps, 502/141)

Colette, reading Sand, wonders about that life: the weave of writing, love, happiness, unhappiness. And makes the comparison to her own: she/I. If, as Gusdorf suggests, the "essence of autobiography" is its "anthropological significance" (119), Colette is a good *reader* of autobiography because the text of another's life sends her back to her own (which has been the challenge of autobiography since Augustine). Why Sand, and how does Colette think back to Sand? Having introduced, as we have just seen, the question of memoirs, and having rejected the undertaking, Colette then imagines her image in a publisher's eyes: "God forgive me! They must expect a kind of 'Secret Journal' in the style of the Goncourt brothers!" (141) By ellipsis Colette rejects this negative and implicitly masculine dirty-secrets model. Instead, thinking about how much time and what sacrifices were involved in the elaboration of her own life's work—"It has taken me a great deal of time to scratch out forty or so books. So many hours that could have been used for travel, for idle strolls, for reading, even for indulging a feminine and healthy coquetry" (Phelps, 502/141)—Colette makes a feminist connection: how did Sand manage?[14]

This structure of kinship through which readers as women perceive bonds relating them to writers as women would seem to be a "natural" feature of the autobiographical text. But is it? Are these autobiographies the place par excellence in which the self inscribed and the self deciphering perform the ultimate face to face? I don't think so. Despite the identity between the "I" of authorship and the "I" of narration, and the pacts of sincerity, reading these lives is rather like shaking hands with one's gloves on.[15] Is this decorum a feature of gender? To the extent that autobiography, like any narrative, requires a shaping of the past, a making *sense* of a life, it tends to cast out the parts that don't add up (what we might think of as the flip side of the official, reconstructed personality). Still, autobiography can incorporate what Roy Pascal has called the "cone of darkness at the center"; indeed, as he comments, "it seems to be required of the autobiographer that he should

recognize that there is something unknowable in him" (184–85).
One has the impression reading Stern,[16] Sand, and Beauvoir that
the determination to have their lives make sense and thus be sus-
ceptible to *universal* reception blinds them, as it were, to their own
darkness: the "submerged core," "the sexual mystery that would
make a drama" (Kael, 100–1).[17] It is as though the anxiety of gender identity, of a culturally devalued femininity, veiled its inscription in strategies of representation.

But should we give up so easily? We are, after all, given clues
in the autobiographies telling us where to look (or not to look)
for what Colette calls the "unsaid things." When Beauvoir, for
example, describes the stakes of her fiction writing, how she wanted
to be read, she tells us something important about her other self:

> I passionately wanted the public to like my work; therefore
> like George Eliot, who had become identified in my mind with
> Maggie Tulliver, I would myself become an imaginary char-
> acter, endowed with beauty, desirability, and a sort of shim-
> mering transparent loveliness. It was this metamorphosis that
> my ambition sought . . . I dreamed of splitting into two selves,
> and of having a shadowy alter ego that would pierce and haunt
> people's hearts. It would have been no good if this phantom
> had had overt connections with a person of flesh and blood;
> anonymity would have suited me perfectly. (291)

Sand points us in the same direction:

> It was inevitably said that *Indiana* was my person and my
> story. It is nothing of the sort. I have presented many types
> of women, and I think that after reading this account of the
> impressions and reflections of my life, it will be clear that I
> have never portrayed myself [*mise en scène*] as a woman [*sous
> des traits féminins*]. I am too much of a romantic [*trop ro-
> manesque*] to have seen the heroine of a novel in my mirror.
> . . . Even if I had tried to make myself beautiful and dram-
> atize my life, I would never have succeeded. My *self*, con-
> fronting me face to face would have dampened my enthusi-
> asm. (2:160)

By suggesting, as I am, that a *double* reading—of the autobiography with the fiction—would provide a more sensitive measure
for deciphering a female self, I am not proposing a return to the
kind of biographical "hermeneutics" that characterizes a Jean Larnac
(in his 1929 *Histoire de la littérature féminine*). Like Colette's in-

terpellated male reader in *Break of Day*, Larnac reads all women's
fiction as autobiography: "In the center of every feminine novel,
one discovers the author. . . . Incapable of abstracting a fragment
of themselves to constitute a whole, [women writers] have to put
all of themselves into their work" (253–54). (It is not, of course,
a question of saying, as he does, Indiana is George Sand—in female drag.)

I am proposing instead an intratextual practice of interpretation
which, in articulation with the gendered overreading I have just
proposed, would privilege neither the autobiography nor the fiction, but take the two writings together in their status as text.[18]
Germaine Brée has performed such a reading. In an essay on George
Sand entitled "The Fictions of Autobiography," Brée isolates what
she calls the "matrix of fabulation" (121) and analyzes its function
in both the autobiography and the fiction. The matrix is that structure through which Sand deals with the problem of origins and
identity. Brée decodes the Sandian inscription of the self, allowing
the "fictional fiction" and the "fictions of autobiography" to il-
luminate each other (446). Because of the literary protocol and cultural constraints that historically have governed women's writing,
and the problems of imagining public female identities, not to perform an expanded reading—in this instance, not to read the fiction *with* the autobiography—is to remain prisoner of a canon
that bars women from their own texts.

And Colette?

Let us return briefly to the epigraph from *Break of Day*. Early
in the novel, the narrator gives us a portrait of her mother taking
stock at the end of her life. The metaphor used for this putting-
into-perspective of the past is that of a painter before a canvas:
"She stands back, and returns, and stands back again, pushing
some scandalous detail into place, bringing into the light of day a
memory drowned in shadow. By some unhoped-for art she becomes—equitable. Is anyone imagining as he reads me, that I'm
portraying myself? *Have patience: this is merely my model*" (34–
35; emphasis added). In context, then, the epigraph seems to narrow its focus. Indeed, it has been taken to mean that the model
in question is "the model of the mother," and that this "affiliation,
recognized and reclaimed" constitutes the deep structure of the
novel (Mercier, 46); painter of her mother, and through her mother,
herself. This is no less, however, the portrait of the writer in this
same novel as autobiographer: "No other fear, not even that of
ridicule, prevents me from writing these lines which I am willing

to risk will be published. Why should I stop my hand from gliding over this paper to which for so many years I've confided what I know about myself, what I've tried to hide, what I've invented and what I've guessed?" (62) Every inscription of the self is an approximation and a projection; a matter of details, shadows, adjustment, and proportion—an *arrangement* of truths. Still, does the collection of self-portraits make an autobiography? Robert Phelps tried to construct one in a volume called *Earthly Paradise: An Autobiography* in which he strings together moments in Colette's life through passages from her works in a thematic and roughly chronological continuum. Lejeune rejects Phelps's construction as just that: one does not ghostwrite an autobiography; the "pact" cannot be concluded by a third party.

How then to conclude?

At the end of an article published two years after *L'Autobiographie en France,* Lejeune renounces his previous attempts to find a definition of autobiography that would be coherent and exhaustive. Having decided that autobiography is as much a *mode of reading* as a mode of writing, he looks instead to a history (as yet to be written) of autobiography that would be the history of the way in which autobiography is read. To be sure, Lejeune is not concerned with female autobiography. But his notion of a contractual genre dependent upon codes of transmission and reception joins our purposes, because it relocates the problematics of autobiography as genre in an interaction between reader and text.

And Colette?

To read Colette is not, perhaps, in the final analysis (*pace* Lejeune), to read (generically) a woman's *autobiography.*[19] It is, however, to read the inscription of a female signature: a cultural fabrication that names itself as such, and that we can identify through the patient negotiation we ourselves make with the neither/nor of "memoirs mixed with fiction, fictions compounded of fact" (Gass, 12). Colette's textual "I" is not bound by genre. For Sand, Stern, and Beauvoir, despite their pact, the locus of identification, I would suggest, is no different. The historical truth of a woman writer's life lies in the reader's grasp of her intratext: the body of her writing and not the writing of her body.

NOTES

1. See, for example, Elaine Marks in her critical study *Colette*, p. 213; translation is hers. All future references to *Break of Day*, however, will be drawn from the Enid McLeod translation.

2. Christiane Makward has pointed out the importance of this evolution in her analysis of patronyms and their relationship both to women's writing and the representation of femininity: "not only is the father's name feminized and stripped of its function (to signify descendence) but it takes the place of a first name. 'Colette' is no longer a first name, a patronym or a pseudonym but *the name* that a free woman took fifty years to make for herself." "Le Nom du père: Ecritures féminines d'un siècle à l'autre," paper delivered at the Third Annual Colloquium in Nineteenth-Century French Studies, October 1977, Columbus, Ohio.

3. Elaine Marks comments, citing the same passage: if the narrator is "no longer wearing an obvious mask . . . she is, however, wearing the mask of 'Colette'." And this "Colette" only exposes a self protected by inverted commas. *Colette*, pp. 212–13.

4. It is a nice paradox that Colette is always read biographically, and at the same time excluded from the corpus of autobiographical writing. Perhaps this is a useful way to think about the place of women's writing.

5. In Lejeune's terms, autobiographical writing itself is an act of "staging": *l'écriture y est mise en scène* (73). In a way, the theatricality of female subjectivity is central to feminist writing, thematically autobiographical or not. I deal with this notion more fully in chapters 7 and 9.

6. For Lejeune, French autobiography begins officially with Rousseau; and he dates the genre as beginning around 1760. As for the response to Rousseau, Lejeune writes: "Rousseau is the only one to say aloud what everyone thinks in private. All the autobiographical pacts that follow are written against Rousseau's disastrous frankness" (82).

7. Béatrice Didier, in "Femme/Identité/Ecriture: A propos de *l'Histoire de ma vie* de George Sand," begins her article with an excerpt from Sand's correspondence: "I confess that I am neither humble enough to write confessions like Jean-Jacques nor impertinent enough to praise myself like the literary lights of the century. Furthermore, I don't believe that private life falls within the purview of the critics" (561).

8. Thus Stern distances herself from Sand's *Histoire de ma vie* as well as Rousseau's *Confessions*. Stern comments on Sand's work—based on an incomplete reading—in the following manner: "It seems to me that [the work] is true or not true enough, and that is not how I would conceive of Confessions"; letter to Hortense Allart, dated 1855, cited by Vier, 4:307, n. 727.

9. Colette's *Evening Star* (*L'Etoile Vesper*) has been translated by David LeVay. His translation, however, often misses Colette in spirit and style and I have chosen instead to use those passages cited from this volume of recollections as anthologized by Robert Phelps in *Earthly Paradise*. Phelps's translator, Herma Briffault, seems closer to Colette's rhythms. For those who might wish to consult the passages cited in context, I have provided the page

references to the complete translation; if only one page reference appears, it is to LeVay.

10. The contrast between Sand and Stern is important to note. Sand writes, for example, about maternal feelings: "I wasn't deluded by passion. I had for the artist [Chopin] a kind of very intense, very true maternal adoration, but which could not for an instant compete with maternal love [*l'amour des entrailles*], the only chaste feeling that can be passionate" (2:433). Stern, for her part, reverses the hierarchy: "Let [women] say and repeat that maternal love surpasses all other forms of love, while they cling to it as a last resort [*un pis-aller*], and because they have been too cowardly, too vain, too demanding, to experience love and to understand friendship, those two exceptional feelings which can only germinate in strong souls" (*Mémoires*, 82).

11. This emphasis on intellectual pursuits is not restricted to women writers in France. In "Female Identities," Patricia Spacks comments on the autobiographical works of four eighteenth-century English writers, Mrs. Thrale, Mrs. Pilkington, Mrs. Clarke, and Lady Mary Wortley Montagu: "With an almost mythic insistence all four of these women reiterate a theme common in the century's fiction: the female apology, heavily tinged with resentment, for the life of the mind. Men think, therefore exist; women, who—men believed—hardly think at all, have, therefore, perhaps a questionable hold on their own existences" (78–79).

12. Sand's *Histoire de ma vie*, Béatrice Didier maintains, "is especially and in the end the story of a birth to writing—a difficult birth deferred, sometimes occulted, of which the narrative traverses the entire text . . . this birth becomes . . . the very object of the book" (567–68).

13. Historically, for example, for women writers in France, artistic activity must seem to be economically motivated to be socially justified, to justify the violation of gendered identity. In this sense, Claudine Herrmann argues in *Les Voleuses de langue* that George Sand "sought in every way to convince her readers that she was writing to earn a living." This (alibi?) is placed in the context of Stendhal's discussion of female authorship in *De l'amour*. Stendhal (who, Herrmann comments, audaciously compares women's condition to that of black slaves in nineteenth-century America, and who further observes that "all geniuses born as women are lost to the public good") remarks: "For a woman under the age of fifty to publish a book, is to subject her happiness to the most terrible of lotteries; if she is fortunate enough to have a lover, the first thing that will happen is that she will lose him. I see one exception only: a woman who writes books [*fait des livres*] to feed and raise her family" (31–33).

14. This is oddly close in language to Woolf's remarks on Colette's writing. In a letter to Ethel Smythe about an article of Colette's on Anna de Noailles, Woolf says: "I'm almost floored by the extreme dexterity insight and beauty of Colette. How does she do it? No one in England could do a thing like that. If a copy is ever going I should like to have one to read it again. and see how its done: or guess. And to think I scarcely know her books! Are they all novels? Is it the great French tradition that lifts her so serenely, and yet with such a flare, down, down to what she's saying? I'm green with envy . . ." June 25, 1936 (49). I am grateful to Brenda Silver for finding this reference for me.

15. I am tempted, though the context is radically different, by the passage

in Morrison's *Sula* where we read this contrast between "that version of herself . . . she sought to reach out to and touch with an ungloved hand" and "the naked hand" (121) as a way of talking about degrees of intimate contact.

16. I must here, somewhat belatedly, distinguish between Stern's *Mes Souvenirs* (1806–1833) and her *Mémoires* (1833–1854). Both were published posthumously, in 1880 and 1927, respectively. The later text, which is an account of her love affair with Liszt, is extraordinarily moving. However, the volume itself is a construction, a compilation made by the editor, Daniel Ollivier. It includes journal entries (hers and Liszt's), notes, and fragmentary chapters of the unfinished *Mémoires*. (As one might imagine, the journal is the more passionate, disturbed and disturbing document.) Stern herself seems to have favored this installment of her life's story. In a letter dated 1867, cited by Vier (262), Marie d'Agoult writes: "I am just finishing the second volume of the *Mémoires:* the story of passion that will not be a masterpiece, but *my* masterpiece;" italicized in the text. As I will argue, if one is reading to discover, uncover, a female self, the corpus must be expanded by breaking down the barriers of genre; or rather the hierarchies of the canon: fiction, autobiography, correspondence, diaries, and so on. Here, Vier's remarks on reading the *Mémoires* with the correspondence are very much to the point: "It is Marie whom the *Mémoires* portray; the letters give us glimpses of the Countess d'Agoult; the former is fragile and passive, the latter chatelaine and suzeraine; the former belongs completely to the man she loves and admires, the latter knows herself to be an original mind and senses in herself a literary vocation" (1:175).

17. Pauline Kael, reviewing Lillian Hellman's *Julia* with *Pentimento,* the filmic fiction with the autobiography. Not surprisingly, Hellman's conclusion to the volume of her memoirs called *An Unfinished Woman* points to the dangers lurking in the passion for a coherent self: "I do regret that I have spent too much of my life trying to find what I called 'truth,' trying to find what I called 'sense'. I never knew what I meant by truth, never made the sense I hoped for. All I mean is that I left too much of me unfinished because I wasted too much time. However." (244)

18. Gusdorf himself seems to make a case for a double reading when he remarks: "There would therefore be two versions, or two instances of autobiography: on the one hand, the confession strictly speaking, on the other, the entire work of the artist which takes up the same subject matter in complete freedom and with the protection of incognito" (121).

19. Reading this essay over and revising it for this book ten years after I wrote it, I am struck and slightly dismayed by the dogged way I follow through and worry about Lejeune's moves. (Particularly since I know how profoundly irreversible the interest is!) And yet am I today cured of the gesture to revise, to begin by turning to the male model to see how and where it doesn't work? When will there be an end to the double work of revision, I wonder.

BEST STORIES
OF THE AMERICAN WEST

VOLUME ONE

BEST

STORIES

OF

THE AMERICAN

WEST

VOLUME ONE

MAUD PRESTON PALENSKE
MEMORIAL LIBRARY
500 Market St.
St. Joseph, MI 49085

APR 2 6 2007

EDITED BY

MARC JAFFE

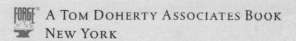
FORGE® A Tom Doherty Associates Book
New York

This is a work of fiction. All the characters and events portrayed
in these stories are either fictitious or are used fictitiously.

BEST STORIES OF THE AMERICAN WEST, VOLUME ONE

Copyright © 2007 by Marc Jaffe

Editor's Note Copyright © 2007 by Marc Jaffe

All rights reserved, including the right to reproduce this book,
or portions thereof, in any form.

This book is printed on acid-free paper.

A Forge Book
Published by Tom Doherty Associates, LLC
175 Fifth Avenue
New York, NY 10010

www.tor.com

Forge® is a registered trademark of Tom Doherty Associates, LLC.

ISBN-13: 978-0-765-31089-7
ISBN-10: 0-765-31089-9

First Edition: April 2007

Printed in the United States of America

0 9 8 7 6 5 4 3 2 1

COPYRIGHT ACKNOWLEDGMENTS

"What Ever Happened to Frank Snake Church?," by Sherman Alexie, copyright © 2003 by Sherman Alexie.

"Red River Crossing," by Johnny D. Boggs, copyright © 2007 by Johnny D. Boggs.

"Come Back," by Richard Cass, copyright © 2005 by Richard Cass.

"Once a Cowboy," by Max Evans, copyright © 2002 by Max Evans.

"Snow Cave," by Pete Fromm, copyright © 2006 by Pete Fromm.

"The Last Running," by John Graves, copyright © 1959 by John Graves.

"The Teachings of Bronc Buster Billy Brown," by Drum Hadley, copyright © 2005 by Drum Hadley. First published in *Voice of the Borderlands* by Rio Nuevo Publishers.

"Continuity," by Elmer Kelton, copyright © 2000 by Elmer Kelton.

"Looking Glass," by William Kittredge, copyright © 1993 by William Kittredge.

"The Hard Way," by Elmore Leonard, copyright © 2004 by Elmore Leonard, Inc. Reprinted by permission of HarperCollins Publishers.

"Among the Living Amidst the Trees," by Bruce Machart, copyright © 2004 by Bruce Machart. Reprinted by permission of Irene Skolnick Literary Agency.

"Vital Signs," by Valerie Miner, copyright © 2004 by Valerie Miner. Published with permission of Michigan State University Press from *Abundant Light* by Valerie Miner (2004).

"Aground and Aloft," by Steven Patterson, copyright © 2004 by Stephen Patterson. First published in *The Iowa Review*.

"Sudden Death, Over Time," by John Rember, copyright © 2007 by John Rember.

"Dillinger in Hollywood," by John Sayles, copyright © 2004 by John Sayles.

"Preserves," by Robert Stubblefield, copyright © 2007 by Robert Stubblefield.

"Stretched Toward Him Like a Dark Wake," by Geronimo Tagatac, copyright © 2003 by Geronimo Tagatac.

"Confession for Raymond Good Bird," by Melanie Rae Thon, copyright © 2006 by Melanie Rae Thon. Reprinted by permission of Irene Skolnick Literary Agency. First published in *AGNI* #63, 2006.

"Bid Farewell to Her Many Horses," by Luis Alberto Urrea, copyright © 2002 by Luis Alberto Urrea, from *Six Kinds of Sky*, published by Cinco Puntos Press. www.cincopuntos.com

"Hearts," by Richard S. Wheeler, copyright © 2003 by Richard S. Wheeler.

To VSJ,
full-time partner in love and literature—
of the West and beyond

ACKNOWLEDGMENTS

THIS BOOK AND its successor volume (or volumes if all goes well) represent yet another step along the trail of my dedication to the writing of the West. It also provides me with an opportunity to thank a number of people who have given me a hand along the way. First, there was my Uncle Lou, a devotee of the pulp magazines of the thirties and forties who introduced me to the world of Tom Blackburn, William McLeod Raine, Charles Alden Seltzer, Walt Coburn, W. R. Cox, and the king of them all, Max Brand, among many others. Next, the late Victor Weybright who not only hired me as western and mystery editor at New American Library (I think mainly on the strength of my apprenticeship at the also late men's magazine *Argosy*), but also encouraged me to travel to the West in support of my neophyte condition as an acquiring editor in a specialized genre. Thanks many times over to Oscar Dystel, then president of Bantam Books, who in 1961 offered me the opportunity to join him as the company's editorial director, succeeding the Hollywood-bound Saul David. From Saul, I inherited a relationship from which we both prospered greatly over the years, though in different ways. Thanks, also, to that network of many, many friends among writers of the West—from members of the professional organization The Western Writers of America (WWA) to the literary contingent at the Fishtrap Gathering, which meets annually at Wallowa Lake, the old Nez Perce homeland in southeastern Oregon, which continually enriched my knowledge of what I still consider the most vibrant of all subsets of American literature.

Finally, and more specifically, thanks to Nat Sobel, literary agent par excellence, who brought me the idea for this series then brought me to the publisher; and the two editors, Natasha Panza and Eric Raab, who shepherded me, with patience and diligence, through the complex process of publishing this collection of twenty examples of the best in short fiction of the West.

CONTENTS

EDITOR'S NOTE

THE WORD "BEST" is, at best, a moving target. The "Ten Best Dressed" and "Ten Worst Dressed" lists are clearly in the eye of the beholder. The "Ten Best Movies of All Time" can be a pure numbers game, the result of a vote by the experts or a nonselective group of average fans. This collection, the first of a series, is the result of a reading of hundreds of stories, conversations with friends and colleagues over the years, and a good deal of brooding about literature, people, and place.

Before launching a search for the "best" short stories of the West, guidelines need to be set and a question or two answered.

First, what *is* the West in the context of fiction? Is it the West of John Ford and John Wayne? Of *Red River* and *Gunsmoke*? Of Denver suburbs and Glacier National Park? Of Hollywood and Vine or the ranchettes of Oregon and Montana? The simple answer, for my purpose, is geographical—namely the eleven western states as drawn on the map.

Next, need the chosen writers be Westerners by birth, or even residence? Again, I think a simple answer is the best—"no" to each part of the question. We are after subject matter here, these are stories "of the West."

Third, and perhaps most important: How wide a net should one cast? Stories by writers living and dead? Stories unpublished heretofore in book form? Stories only with a contemporary setting? And finally, can the best of popular, or so-called "traditional," Western writing live between the same covers as the work of the best of the "literary" world of the West? In the end, this collector wove his own net. The writers are all alive and working at the craft (at least at the time of selection). The work might have been published—in book form, in magazines—or here for the first time (in fact the collection includes examples of all three).

SEVERAL THEMES COMMON to much of Western literature emerge from a reading of these stories. In Steven Patterson's "Aground and Aloft," in which the central character is a woman bush pilot, terrain functions as an adversary over which she must exert control, while at the same time contending with the tragic deaths of her husband and son, and her own adulterous relationship. The terrain is the victor in the man-against-nature conflict in the tragic denouement of Pete Fromm's "Snow Cave."

History, the glue that holds the Western consciousness together, plays a significant role in Richard S. Wheeler's "Hearts," which approaches the iconic world of nineteenth-century Tombstone, Arizona, from an altogether fresh perspective in the person of a fictional female Pinkerton employee dealing (in more ways than one) with Johnny Behan and the Earp brothers. And inevitably, the American cowboy, perhaps the most potent of Western icons, plays his part as written by the ex-cowboys Elmer Kelton, Max Evans, and William Kittredge, and rancher/poet Drum Hadley. The "now" in the West is as forceful as elsewhere in these United States, to be sure, and Valerie Miner goes to the heart of it with the ensemble cast of her California story, "Vital Signs." In a story set against a small town and small farm background, a man reflects on his personal growth, love, and family while building a fence—a potent metaphor—in John Rember's narrative, "Sudden Death, Over Time."

The great black hole in American historiography and in the conscience of American society for more than two centuries has been the genocidal impact of white Euro-American culture and the drive for economic growth and power over Indian nationhood. This hole is just now beginning to be filled by historians and journalists. So it is perhaps not an accident that so much of the best writing of the West grows from such bloody earth. Sherman Alexie, one of the best-known Indian writers and a filmmaker as well, of Spokane/Coeur d'Alene heritage, was born and raised on the Spokane reservation in Washington state. Melanie Rae Thon, a Caucasian, and Luis Alberto Urrea, of mixed blood, each bring a highly sharpened perspective to a complex and explosive subject.

TAKEN TOGETHER, THESE twenty stories set out a powerful literary statement, especially characteristic of writing of the American West. Heady themes, strong characters, and, above all, storytelling, storytelling. In succeeding volumes, more of the "best" is yet to come.

MARC JAFFE
February 2006

BEST STORIES
OF THE AMERICAN WEST

VOLUME ONE

What Ever Happened to Frank Snake Church?

SHERMAN ALEXIE

Sherman Alexie is the author of novels, story collections, and the award-winning screenplay for Smoke Signals, *a film based on his short-story collection* The Lone Ranger and Tonto Fistfight in Heaven, *as well as several books of poetry. He both wrote and directed the feature film,* The Business of Fancydancing.

Sherman Alexie's books have won the Pen/Faulkner Foundation's Malamud Award for Excellence in Short Fiction and the Lila Wallace–Reader's Digest Writers' Award, among others.

He lives in Seattle with his wife and two sons.

FRANK'S HEART FIBRILLATED as he walked along a tree-line trail on the northern slope of Mount Rainier. He staggered, leaned against a small pine tree for balance, but tumbled over it instead, rolled for twenty or thirty yards down the slope, and fell over a small cliff onto the scree below. A moment later, Frank's arrhythmic heart corrected itself and resumed beating normally, but he wondered if he was going to die on the mountain. He was only thirty-nine years old and weighed only eleven more pounds than he had when he graduated from high school, but he'd been smoking too many unfiltered Camels, and his cholesterol level was a dangerous 344, exactly the same as Ted Williams's career batting average. But damn it, Frank thought, he was a Spokane Indian, and Indians are supposed to die young. Thirty-nine years is old for a Spokane. Old enough to join the American Association of Retired Indians. Frank laughed. Bloody and hurt on this mountain, his heart maybe scarred and twisted beyond repair, and he was still making jokes. How indigenous, Frank thought, how wonderfully aboriginal, applause, applause, applause, applause for me and my people. Still laughing, Frank pushed himself to his hands and knees and sat on a flat rock. His heart beat slow and steady. He breathed easily. He felt no tingling pain in his chest, arms, or legs. He wasn't lightheaded or nauseated. He seemed to be fine. Maybe his heart was okay; maybe it had missed only one dance step in a lifetime of otherwise lovely coronary waltzes. He was cut and scraped, a nasty gash on his arm would probably need stitches, but none of his wounds seemed to be too serious. He didn't have any broken bones or sprains. So there was the diagnosis: His heart had played a practical joke on him—how terribly amusing, ha, ha, ha, ha, ha, ha, ha, ha—and he was bruised and battered and had one hell of a headache, but he'd live.

Carefully, painfully, Frank crawled back up the slope to the trail. Once there, while still on his hands and knees, he took a few deep breaths and promised himself that he'd visit a superhero cardiologist as soon as he got off the mountain. He'd promise to see an organic nutritionist, aromatherapist, deep-tissue masseuse, feng shui consultant, yoga master, and Mormon stand-up comedian if those promises would help him get off this mountain. Frank stood, tested his balance, and found it to be true enough, so he resumed his rough trek along the trail. He felt stronger with each step. He was now convinced he was going to be okay. Yes, he was going to be fine. But after a few more steps, an electrical charge jolted him. Damn, Frank thought, I have a heart attack, fall down a damn mountain, and then I crawl back only to get struck by lightning. Frank imagined the newspaper headline: HEART-DISEASED FOREST RANGER STRUCK BY LIGHTNING. Frank was imagining the idiot readers laughing at the idiot park ranger when another electrical bolt knocked him back ten feet and dropped him to the ground, where a third lightning strike shocked him again. Damn, Frank thought, this lightning has a personal vendetta against me. He felt a fourth electrical charge shoot up his spine and into his brain. He convulsed and vomited. He kicked and punched at the air, and then he couldn't move at all. As he lay paralyzed on the trail, Frank thought: This is it, now I'm really dead, and I have crapped my pants; I'm going to die with half-digested pieces of mushroom and sausage pizza stuck to my ass; humiliation, degradation, sin, and mortal shame. But Frank didn't die. Instead, as the electricity fired inside his brain, Frank saw an image of his father, Harrison Snake Church, as the old man lay faceup on the floor of his kitchen in Seattle. Harrison's eyes were open, but there was no light behind them; blood dripped from his nose and ears. In great pain, Frank understood that he hadn't suffered a heart attack or been struck by lightning. No, he'd been gifted and cursed with the first real vision of his life, and though Frank was one of the very few Indian agnostics in the world, he accepted this vision as a simple and secular truth: His father was dead.

How much can one son love one father? Frank loved his father enough to stand and stagger five miles to the logging road where he'd parked his truck. He knew he should get on the radio and call for help. He was exhausted and in no safe shape to drive. But he also knew that his father was lying dead on the kitchen floor. Covered with blood and food, half naked in a ratty bathrobe that his father called a valuable antique, Jerry Springer or Dr. Phil lecturing on the television. Frank needed to be the first on the scene. He needed to restore his father's dignity before the proper authorities were called. Perhaps his father's spirit was waiting for him. But Frank didn't believe in spirits, in souls, in the afterlife. Why was he thinking about his father's soul? Mr. Death, Frank thought, you have entered my house and rearranged the furniture. But it didn't matter what Frank believed. With or without soul and spirit, Harrison was lying dead on the kitchen floor and should be lifted, cleaned, and covered with old quilts. Frank needed to perform burial ceremonies. Harrison needed to have his honor restored, and Frank was the only one who could, or should, do the restoration.

So Frank drove his truck dangerously fast along fifteen miles of logging and undeveloped roads. He didn't need a map; he'd been a forest ranger at Mount Rainier for ten years and had driven thousands of miles on these roads. As he drove, Frank thought of his father and wondered how the old man should be remembered. As he traveled toward his father's dead body, Frank composed the eulogy: "Thank you all for coming here today to say good-bye to my father. For those of you who know me, you know I'm not a man of words. But I do have a few things I'd like to say about my father. Harrison was a beloved man. Beloved. I guess you're supposed to use words like that at a funeral. Fancy words. But I guess I should just say it simple. Most people liked my dad, and quite a few loved him. He was an active member of St. Therese Church. He was always a good Catholic, maybe the only Indian of his generation who went to Catholic boarding school on purpose. That was a joke. I don't know if it was funny or not. But I'm an Indian, and Indians are supposed to be funny at funerals. At least that's what it says in the *Indian Funeral Handbook*. That was another joke.

"Here at St. Therese, my dad volunteered for the youth programs, and he was one of the most dependable readers and Eucharistic ministers. He read the gospels with more passion and pride than the Jesuits. Ay, jokes. Sorry about that, Father Terry, but you know it's true. Ay, jokes.

"My dad, Harry, he was fond of telling people how he would've become a priest if he hadn't loved the ladies so much. And there were always a few ladies who would have loved him back, and you know who you are. You're the ones crying the most. Ay, jokes. But of course my loyal dad has been chaste since his wife, my mother, Helen, died of brain cancer twenty-one years ago. So maybe my dad was like a Jesuit, except he didn't have sex, unlike most of the Jesuits. Ay, jokes.

"My mom died only three days after I graduated from high school. It was a terrible, ugly death. And my dad was never really happy again and never looked to be loved again by another woman, but he stayed active like a shark: *Don't stop moving or you die.* Ha, he was the Great Red Whale, my dad. Ay, jokes. Maybe my dad and I were the Great Red Whale together. We were always together. I've lived in the same house with him all of my life. I guess, in some real way, my father became my mother. Harrison was Helen. He adopted some of her mannerisms, you know, like he scratches his head whenever he's frustrated, just like she does.

"Listen to me. I keep talking about them in the present tense. And then I talk about them in the past tense. And I was never any good at English grammar anyway. So you can blame my high school English teacher for that. Sorry about that, Ms. Balum. Ay, jokes.

"After he got old, my dad was the crossing guard at Thirty-fourth and Union and knew the names of all of his kids. Since they were all Catholic kids, they only had twelve names. Or maybe eleven. Since nobody has named their kid Judas since Judas was named Judas by his folks. Ay, jokes.

"My old man was strong for an old man, you know, and he could still hit ten or twelve of those long-range set shots in a row. Basketball was always my dad's passion. He was Idaho State High School Basketball Player of the Year in 1952. He loved the Lakers when they played in Minneapolis, and he loved them more after they moved to Los Angeles. Elgin Baylor. Gail Goodrich. Jerry West. Wilt Chamberlain. Happy Hairston. Those guys won thirty-three in a row in 1973.

"After my mother died, my dad and I watched thousands of basketball games on television and in person. Sometimes, on cold Saturday nights, he and I would drive for hours to watch small-town high school teams, not because we knew any of the players but because they were playing a small-town version of basketball, and it was ragged and beautiful and passionate and clumsy and perfect. Davenport Gorillas. Darrington Loggers. Selkirk Rangers. Neah Bay Red Devils. Toutle Lake Fighting Ducks.

"And now my father is gone, and my mother is gone, and they're gone together, and I'm a thirty-nine-year-old orphan. I didn't even say good-bye to my father before I left the house on the day he died. I never really said good-bye to my mother before she died. I will have to live the rest of my life with a failed son's regrets. I don't even know what I'm going to do now."

As he drove off Mount Rainier and through the park, Frank knew his eulogy was inadequate, incomplete, and improvisational. He knew he would have to sit and write a real eulogy. He would fill a dozen notebooks with draft after draft. Every word would perfectly capture how much love and pain he felt for his father and mother. Harrison and Helen Snake Church deserved poetry, not the opening monologue of an indigenous talk show. Mr. Death, Frank thought, you are a funnyman, but I will not laugh. Frank sped out of the park. Ignoring the risk of speeding tickets, he drove west on two-lane highways, north on Interstate 5 through Tacoma into Seattle, east off the James Street exit, and ran red lights twenty blocks into the Central District, where he and Harrison lived on Thirty-seventh Avenue. Frank drove his government truck onto the front lawn, leaped out and raced up the front steps, struggled with the front door, threw it open, rushed into the kitchen, and saw his father sitting at the table. Harrison was drinking coffee and eating Grape-Nuts. He ate breakfast for every meal.

"You're alive," said Frank, completely surprised by the fact.

"Yes, I am," Harrison said as he studied his bloody, panicked son. "But you look half dead."

"I had a vision," Frank said.

Harrison sipped his coffee.

"I saw you in my head," Frank said. "You're supposed to be dead. I saw you dead."

"You have blurry vision," said Harrison.

ONE YEAR AND four days later, Harrison died of a heart attack in the QFC supermarket on Broadway and Pike. When he heard the news,

Frank wondered if his previous year's vision had been accurate, if he'd foreseen his father's death. But there must be a statute of limitations for visions, Frank thought, there must be an expiration date for ESP. Beyond all that, Frank didn't believe anyone could predict the future. His supposedly psychic vision of his father's death bore some general resemblance to his real death, but the details were different. Harrison was shopping in the produce department when he coughed once, rubbed his tingling left arm, and died. "Probably dead before he hit the floor," the coroner had said. When Harrison fell, he knocked over an artfully arranged display of bananas, which was appropriate and funny, since Harrison had always hated the taste of what he called "the devil's evil yellow penis." Frank buried his father beside his mother's grave in the same Seattle graveyard where Bruce and Brandon Lee were also buried. So, hey, Frank figured his father was lying with damn good company, and if there was an afterlife, then Harrison was probably learning jeet kune do and making love to his wife, Helen, for all of eternity.

At his father's graveside, overlooking Lake Washington, Frank stood to give the eulogy he'd carefully written but found he couldn't read the words on the page. Grief turned him into an illiterate. He tried to remember what he'd written so he could recite his eulogy by memory, but he discovered he couldn't speak at all. Grief turned him into a mute. Finally, after five minutes of silence, as the assembled mourners shook with collective embarrassment, Frank finally remembered how to say four words: "I love my father."

Afterward, Frank shook the hands and accepted the hugs of dozens of his father's friends and family. He couldn't remember any of their names. Grief turned him into a stranger in his own tribe. Finally, Frank recognized an older woman, his mother's aunt Margaret Marie, who kissed him hard on the lips. She tasted like salt.

"Your father was a ballplayer," she said. "He could have played in college, you know? You should have said something about that."

Frank laughed. What kind of person offered constructive criticism at a funeral? What kind of literate mourner had the nerve to deconstruct a eulogy?

Harrison had been a very good basketball player, but he'd never been good enough to play college hoops, not even at the community-college level. He'd been a great shooter but was never much of an athlete—too short and slow and tentative—but Frank, a genetic freak at six feet six (making him the seventeenth tallest Spokane Indian in tribal history), had always been a truly supernatural baller, the kind of jumper and runner who ignored physics when he played. He'd averaged forty-one points a game during his senior year at Seattle's Garfield High School and had received 114 scholarship offers from colleges all over the country. He'd signed a letter of intent with the University of Washington and had planned to major in environmental science. But then his mother died. To honor her and keep her memory sacred, Frank knew he had to give up something valuable. He had to bury with her one of his most important treasures. So he buried his basketball dreams. On the morning of her funeral, Frank walked to the local park and shot one hundred jump shots and made eighty-five of them. He left the ball at the park, helped bury his mother that afternoon, and had not played the game since. For the first few years, Frank had almost died whenever he thought about basketball, but the acute pain turned chronic, and then it was a dull and distant ache, and then it was the phantom itch of an amputated limb, and then it was gone.

Now he was forty years old, and his life could be divided into two almost equal halves: He'd been a star basketball player for eighteen years—he was a hooper right out of the womb—and a non–basketball player for twenty-two years.

After his father's burial, Frank went home alone and stood in the quiet house. He had not yet cried for his father, and he wondered if he would ever cry, but his grief grew so suddenly huge that it pushed him to the floor. He lay on the living room carpet and wept huge and gasping tears. He screamed and wailed for ten minutes or more. He didn't know how to sing and drum, but he pounded the floor and wailed tribal vocals: *Father, way, ya, way, ha Father, way, ya, way, ha, Father, way, ya, way, ha.* He sang himself hoarse and fell asleep on the carpet. When he woke, he crawled upstairs to his father's bedroom and lay in his father's bed. The sheets still smelled like Harrison. Frank pressed his face into the pillow and breathed in his father's scent. And then Frank gathered his father's hair, so different than Frank's graying crew cut. His father's hair was still black and two feet long on the day he died. Frank found long black hair on the pillow, in the sheets, tangled in a comb, stuck to the bathtub porcelain, clumped into a wet ball in the drain stops, and scattered in every corner of the house. Frank gathered all of the hair, rolled it into a ball, and ate it. He felt split in two, one crazy man eating hair and one rational man watching a crazy man eat hair. He chewed and swallowed the last pieces of his father's life. He felt like he was building a museum of pain, a freak show, where he was the only visitor viewing the only mutant screaming the only prayer he knew: *Come back, Daddy. Come back, Daddy.*

Frank howled. He slept. Woke and howled again. Slept again. Woke and howled until his lips and tongue were bloody. Slept again. Woke and wondered if his grief would ever end. He didn't know what to do, but he needed to love and be loved, so he opened his father's closet and stared at the basketball waiting inside. A couple times a week for many years, Harrison had gone alone to the neighborhood park to shoot baskets, so the ball was worn and comfortable, low on air. Trying to move exactly like his father, to honor his father through muscle memory, Frank picked up the ball, dribbled it around his back, between his legs, bobbled it, and knocked over a chair. Clumsy and stupid with grief, he grabbed the ball, left the house, and walked then ran to the neighborhood park. Once there, he stood at the free-throw line on the northern end of the basketball court. He stared at the iron rim with its chain net. He had not taken a shot in over two decades. He'd given up this game to honor his mother, and now he was reclaiming it to honor his father. He wanted both of them to rise from the dead. Frank dribbled the ball once, twice, three times, stepped back to the three-point line, and rose into the air for a jump shot. He missed the basket completely. Frank watched the sacrilegious air ball bounce away from him and roll quickly across the manicured grass, until it finally slowed to a stop at the tennis court on the other side of the park.

A WEEK AFTER he buried his father, Frank quit his job as a forest ranger. He'd saved tens of thousands of dollars over the years, and the house was completely paid for, so he wasn't worried about money. But he was worried about being alone. For most of his life, he'd loved solitude. Walking through the deep woods, he often imagined he was the only person left in the world, the only survivor of a nuclear war or a smallpox epidemic. During these fantasies, Frank lived alone for fifty years until the day when he curled into a ball at the base of a beautiful pine and died like an old dog, whereby the human race ceased to exist. Inside and outside of this fantasy, Frank knew he was guilty of arrogance and misanthropy, but he compensated by being kind to strangers and tipping really well at restaurants. He didn't have any close friends and had probably shared more conversations with the redheaded clerk at the university bookstore and the blond cashier at the QFC supermarket than he did with anyone other than his father. As for romance, Frank had dated a few women over the years but found them to be too inconsistent and illogical, so he dated a few men and found them to be even more random and frightening. For a while, he had paid for sex with men and women, then women only, but he eventually grew disgusted with the desperation of such acts and, for many years, had lived as chastely as his father had lived. All along, Frank understood that he was suffering from a quiet sickness, a sort of emotional tumor that never grew or diminished but prevented him from living a full and messy life. At the end of every day, Frank thoroughly washed away the human funk of the world, but now, with his father's death, he worried that he would never feel clean again. He needed to take control of his life. He needed to organize his grief; he needed to compose a mournful to-do list: *Bury your father, visit your mother's grave, cry, eat hair, play basketball again, lose weight.* Of course he felt banal. In a time of extraordinary pain, why was he worried about something as ordinary as his body-fat percentage? He only knew for sure that he needed to keep moving, get stronger, build, and connect.

So he picked up the Yellow Pages, looked up personal trainers, and dialed the first one on the list.

"Athletes, Incorporated, this is Russell."

The next day, he walked thirty blocks into downtown Seattle (why not start training immediately?) and met with Russell, a thin and muscular black man who looked more like a long-distance runner than a weight lifter.

"So," said Russell as he sat across the desk from Frank.

"So," Frank said.

"What can we do for you?"

"I'm not sure. I've never done this before."

"Well, why don't we start with your name."

"I'm Frank Snake Church."

"Damn, that's impressive. A man with a name like that is destined for greatness."

"If my name was John Smith, you'd tell me I was destined for greatness, right?"

"Well, I'm supposed to help you be great. That's my job. Stronger body, stronger mind, stronger spirit. That's our motto."

Frank stared at Russell. Silently studied him. A confident man, Russell was comfortable with the silence.

"Are you a serious man?" Frank asked him.

"I'm not sure I understand your question."

Frank stood and walked around the desk. He knelt beside Russell and spoke to him from inches away. Russell didn't mind this closeness.

"Listen," Frank said, "I know this is your job, and I know you need to make money. And I know a large part of what you do here is sales. You're a salesman. And that's okay. You need to make a living. We all need to make a living. And hey, this job you have is a great way to make money, right? You get to wear T-shirts and shorts all year long. And you've probably helped a lot of people get healthy, right?"

Russell could feel Frank's desperation and sense of purpose, the religious fervor that needed to be directed. Russell had met a thousand desperate people, all looking to rescue or be rescued, but this Indian man was especially radiant with need.

"I keep a scrapbook of the clients who've meant the most to me," Russell said. He'd never told anybody about that scrapbook and how he studied it. If exercise was his religion, then the scrapbook was his bible, and every one of his clients was a prophet. Russell never spoke aloud of how proud he was of the woman who lost five hundred pounds and kept it off, of the man who recovered from a triple bypass and now ran marathons, of the teenager paralyzed in a car wreck who now played professional wheelchair basketball. Russell fixed broken people, and sometimes the repairs lasted a lifetime. But he could not say these things aloud. In order to be taken seriously, Russell knew he had to pretend to be less than serious about his job, his *calling*. He could not tell his clients that he thought his gym was a church. He'd sound like a crazy fundamentalist, an idiot parody of a personal trainer. He couldn't express sentiment or commitment; he was forced to be ironic and cynical. He couldn't tell people he cried whenever clients failed or quit or trained too inconsistently for the work to make a difference. So he simply repeated the tired and misleading mantra whenever asked about his work: *It's better than having a real job.* But now, after all these years, Russell somehow understood that he could tell the truth to this sad and desperate stranger.

"I remember everybody I've worked with," Russell said. "I remember their names, their weights, their goals. I remember the exact day when the quitters quit. I keep a running count of the total weight my clients have lost."

"What is it?"

"I can't tell you that. It's just for me. It's a sacred number."

"Okay," Frank said. "I think it's good to remember things that way. Very good. I admire that. So, with my admiration clearly expressed, I want you to answer my question. Are you a serious man?"

"If I said this aloud to most of the world, they'd laugh at me," said Russell. "But I think I have one of the most important jobs in the world. That's how serious I am about what I do. So yes, in answer to your question, when it comes to this work, I am a very serious man."

Frank stood and looked out the window at the Seattle skyline. With his back to Russell, he spoke. It was the only way he could say what he needed to say.

"My father died a week ago," Frank said.

Russell had often heard these grief stories before. He knew five people who'd come directly to the gym from funerals and immediately signed up for full memberships.

"What about your mother?" Russell asked.

"She died when I was eighteen."

"My mother died of sickle cell last year," Russell said. "My father was killed when I was twelve. He was a taxi driver. Guy held him up and shot him in the head."

Frank honored that story—those tragic deaths—with his silence.

"How did your father die?" Russell asked.

"Heart attack."

Frank and Russell were priests and confessors.

"Listen to me," Frank said. "I used to be a basketball player, a really good basketball player, the best in the city and maybe the best in the state, and maybe I could have become one of the best in the country. But I haven't played in a long, long time."

"What do you need from me?" Russell asked.

Frank turned from the window. "I want to be good again," he said.

Russell studied the man and his body, visually estimated his fitness levels, and emotionally guessed at his self-discipline and dedication.

"Give me a year," Russell said.

FOR THE NEXT twelve months, Frank trained five days a week. He lifted free weights, ran miles on the treadmill, climbed hundreds of stories on the stair stepper, jumped boxes until he vomited from the lactic-acid buildup, and climbed ropes until his hands bled. He quit smoking. He measured his food, kept track of all of the calories and the fat, protein, and carbohydrate grams. He drank twelve glasses of water a day. Mr. Death, Frank thought, I am going to drown you before you drown me. Frank's body-fat percentage, heart rate, and blood pressure all lowered. Every three months, he bought new clothes to fit his new body.

During the course of the year, Frank also cleaned his house. He removed the art from the walls and sold it through want ads and garage sales. Without ceremony, he piled up all of the old blankets and quilts, a few of them over eighty years old, and gave them one by one to the neighbors. He gathered financial records, wills, tax returns, old magazines, photograph albums, and scrapbooks, and stored them in a large safe-deposit box at the bank. After that, he scooped all of the various knickknacks and sentimental souvenirs into cardboard boxes and left them on the corner for others to cart away. One day after the movers carried away all of the old-fashioned and overstuffed furniture, other movers brought in the new, sleek, and simple pieces, so there was only one bed, one dresser, one coffee table, one dining table, one wardrobe, one stove, one refrigerator freezer, and four chairs in the entire house. He pulled up the rugs, hired a local teenager to haul them to the dump, and sanded the hardwood until the floors glowed golden and sepia. Near the end of the year, he found enough courage to give away his father's clothes and the boxes of his mother's clothes his father had saved. Frank gave away most of his clothes as well, until he owned only black T-shirts, blue jeans, black socks, black boxers, and black basketball shoes.

Frank kept all of the books, three thousand novels, histories, biographies, and essays, and neatly organized them on bookshelves he built into the walls. He read one book a day. After he disconnected the telephone and permanently stopped the mail, his family and friends worried about him and came to see him, but he turned away all visitors, treating loved ones, strangers, salespeople, religious crusaders, and political activists as if they were all the same.

Frank knew his behavior was obsessive and compulsive, and perhaps he was seriously disturbed, in need of medical care and strong prescriptions, but he didn't want to stop. He needed to perform this ceremony, to disappear into the ritual, to methodically change into something new and better, into someone stronger.

"Make me hurt," he said to Russell before every training session.

"All right," said Russell every few weeks. "I want one thousand sit-ups and one thousand push-ups, and you're not leaving here until I get them."

Sometimes Frank overtrained, ran too many miles or lifted too much weight, and injured himself. Russell would chase him out of the gym, tell him to lay off for a week or even two or three, give his body a chance to recover, to heal, but Frank kept pushing, tore muscles and dislocated joints, broke fingers and twisted vertebrae. He stopped training only when he couldn't get out of bed, and if he found the strength to crawl into a hot shower, he'd warm his muscles enough to lift what he could. At his strongest, he bench-pressed 350 and leg-pressed a thousand pounds. At his weakest, when he was injured, he could lift only paperbacks or pencils, but he'd still do three sets of ten repetitions.

"You can't keep doing this to yourself," Russell said to him again and again. "I can't keep doing this to you. It's malpractice, man. If you get hurt again, I'm quitting. I'm banning you from the gym forever."

But Russell never quit on him, and Frank never quit on Russell. Joined, they were not twins or friends; they were not lovers or brothers; they were not teachers or students; they were not mentors or apprentices; they were not monks or sinners. They remained mutable and variable, sacred and profane. Mr. Death, Frank thought, we are your contraries, your opposites and contradictions, your X factors and missing links, your self-canceling saints and self-flagellating monks, your Saint Francis and the other Saint Francis, and we have come to blaspheme your name.

Away from Russell and the gym, Frank played basketball.

Seven days a week, Frank drove the city and searched for games. He traveled from the manicured intramural courts at the University of Washington to the broken-asphalt courts of the Central District; from the violent and verbose games in Green Lake Park to the genial and clumsy games at the YMCA; from the gladiator battles under the I-5 freeway to the hyperorganized leagues at Sound Mind & Body Gym. He played against black men who believed it was their tribal right to dominate the court. He played against white men who wanted to be black men. He played against brown men who hated black and white men. He played against black, brown, and white men who didn't care about any color other than the green-money bets placed on every point and game. He played against Basketball Democrats who came to the court alone and ran with anybody, and Basketball Republicans who traveled in groups of five and ran only with one another. He played against women who endured endless variations of the same dumb joke: *Hey, girl, you can play, but it's shirts and skins, and you're running skins.* He played against former football players who still wanted to play football, and former wrestlers who wanted only to wrestle. He played against undisciplined young men who couldn't run a basic pick-and-roll, and against elderly men who never missed their two-handed set shots. He played against trash talkers and polite gentlemen. He played against sociopathic ball hogs, wild gunners, rebound hounds, and assist-happy magicians. He played games to seven, nine, eleven, and twenty-one points. He played winner-keeps-ball and alternate possessions. He played one-on-one, two-on-two, three-on-three, four-on-four, five-on-five, and mob rules, improvisational, every-baller-for-himself, anarchist, free-for-all, death-cage matches. He played against cheaters who constantly changed the score, and honest freaks who called fouls on themselves. He played against liars who bragged about how good they used to be, and dreamers who would never be as good as they wanted to be. He played against Basketball Presbyterians who refused to fast-break, and Basketball Pagans who refused to slow down. He played against the vain Allen-Iverson-wanna-be punks who dribbled between their legs, around their backs, and missed 99 percent of the ridiculous, driving, triple-pump, reverse-scoop shots they hoisted up but talked endless and pornographic trash whenever they happened to make even one shot. He played against the vain Larry-Bird-wanna-be court lawyers who argued every foul call and planted themselves at three-point lines and constantly called for the ball because they were open, damn it, more open than any outsider shooter in the history of the damn game, so pass the freaking rock!

Frank played so well that he earned (and re-earned) a playground reputation and was known by a variety of nicknames: Shooter, Old Man, Chief, and Three. Frank's favorite nickname was Oh Shit, given to him in July by a teenage Chicano kid in MLK, Jr. Park.

"Every time the old Indio shoots and makes one of those crazy thirty-footers," the Chicano kid had said, "his man be yelling, 'Oh shit, oh shit, oh shit!'"

Frank was making a comeback, though he hated that word as much as Norma Desmond had hated it, and just like her, he preferred to call it his return. After all, over the course of the year, a few older players had recognized Frank and remembered him as the supernatural Indian kid who'd disappeared from the basketball world two decades ago.

On the basketball courts of Seattle, Frank was the love child of Sasquatch and D. B. Cooper; he was the murder of Charles Lindbergh's baby, the building of Noah's Ark, and the flooding of Atlantis; he was the mystery and the religion and the outright lies.

During one legendary game at the University of Washington Intra-mural Activities Building, Frank caught the ball in the low post and turned to face Double O, the Huskies' power forward. He was a Division I stud slumming among the gym rats, a future second-round draft pick destined to be eleventh man for the Cleveland Cavaliers, which didn't sound glamorous but still made him one of the thousand best basket-ball players in the world.

"Oh Shit, you better give up the rock," Double O taunted. "I ain't let-ting you win this game."

Frank faked the jumper and dribbled right, but Double O, five inches taller and seventy-five pounds heavier, easily pushed Frank away from the key.

"Oh Shit, you're an old man," taunted Double O. "Why you coming after me? I ain't got your social security check."

Frank dribbled the ball between his legs, behind his back, then be-tween his legs again. He didn't know why he was bouncing the ball like a madman. There was no point to it, but he wanted to challenge the trash-talking black kid.

"Oh Shit, you got yourself some skills!" shouted Double O. "Come on, come on, show me the triple-threat position. That's it. That's it. I am so bedazzled, I cannot tell if you're going to shoot, pass, or drive. Oh man, you got them fun-da-men-tals. Bet you learned those with the Original Celtics!"

Distracted by the insulting rant, by its brilliant and racist poetry, Frank laughed and almost lost the ball.

"Better make your move, Old Milk," taunted Double O. "Your expiration date is long past due."

Frank faked right, dribbled left, and scored the game-winning hoop on an archaic rolling left-handed hook shot that barely made it over Double O's outstretched hands.

Frank screamed in triumph and relief as Double O howled with disbelief and fell backward to the floor. All the other players in the gym—the eyewitnesses to a little miracle—shouted curses and promises, screamed in harmony with Frank, slapped one another's hands and backs and butts, and spun in delirious circles. People laughed until they were nauseated. Nobody held anything back. Because he had no idea what else to do with his excitement, one skinny black kid nicknamed Skinny, a sophomore in electrical engineering, ran out of the gym and twenty-four blocks to his house to tell his father and younger brother what he had just seen. Skinny's father and little brother never once asked why he'd run so far to tell the story of one hoop in one meaningless game. They understood why the story had to be immediately told. In basketball, there is no such thing as "too much" or "too far" or "too high." In basketball, enough is never enough. At its best and worst, basketball is all about excess. Every day is Fat Tuesday on a basketball court.

"Did you see that? Did you see that?" screamed Double O as he lay on the floor and flailed his arms and legs. He laughed and hooted and cursed. Losing didn't embarrass him; he was proud of playing a game that could produce such a random, magical, and ridiculous highlight. There was no camera crew to record the event for *SportsCenter,* but it had happened nonetheless, and it would become a part of the basketball mythology at the University of Washington: *Do you remember the time that Old Indian scored on Double O? Do I remember? I was there. Old Chief scored seven straight buckets on Double O and won the game on a poster dunk right in O's ugly mug. O's feelings hurt so bad, he needed stitches. Hell, O never recovered from the pain. He's got that post-traumatic stress illness, and it's getting worse now that he plays ball in Cleveland. Playing hoops for the Cavaliers is like fighting in Vietnam.*

In that way, over the years, the story of Frank's game-winning bucket would change with each telling. Every teller would add his or her personal details; every biographer would turn the story into autobiography. But the original story, the aboriginal hook shot, belonged to Frank, and he danced in fast circles around the court, whooping and celebrating like a spastic idiot. I sound like some Boy Scout's idea of an Indian warrior, Frank thought, like I'm a parody, but a happy parody.

The other ballplayers laughed at Frank's display. He'd always been a quiet player, rarely speaking on or off the court, and now he was emoting like a game-show host.

"Somebody give Oh Shit a sedative!" shouted Double O from the floor. "The Old Indian has gone spastic!"

Still whooping with joy, Frank helped Double O to his feet. The old man and the young man hugged each other and laughed.

"I beat you," Frank said.

"Old man," said Double O, "you gave me a trip on your time machine."

IF SMELL IS the memory sense, as Frank once read, then he was most nostalgic about the spicy aroma of Kentucky Fried Chicken. Whenever Frank smelled Kentucky Fried Chicken, and not just any fried chicken but the very particular and chemical scent of the Colonel's secret recipe, he thought of his mother. Because he was a child who could not separate his memories of his mother and father and sometimes confused their details, Frank thought of his mother and father together. And when he thought about his mother and father and the smell of Kentucky Fried Chicken, Frank remembered one summer day when his parents took him to the neighborhood park to picnic with a twenty-piece bucket of mixed Kentucky Fried Chicken, and a ten-piece box of legs and wings only, along with a cooler filled with Diet Pepsi and store-bought potato salad and apples and bananas and potato chips and a chocolate cake. Harrison and Frank had fought over which particular basketball to bring, but they had at last agreed on an ABA red-white-and-blue rock.

"Can't you ever leave that ball at home?" Helen asked Harrison. She always asked him that question. After so many years of hard-worked marriage, that question had come to mean *I love you, but your obsessions irritate the hell out of me, but I love you, remember that, okay?*

On that day, Frank was eleven years old, young enough to sit on his mother's lap and be only slightly embarrassed by their shared affection, and old enough to need his father and be completely unable to tell him about that need.

"Let's play ball," Frank said to Harrison, though he meant to say, *Prove your love for me.*

"Eat first," Helen said.

"If I eat now, I'll throw up," Frank said. "I'll eat after we play."

"You'll eat now, and if you throw up, you'll just have to eat again, and then you'll play again, and then you'll throw up, so you'll have to eat again. It might go on for days that way. You'll be trapped in a vicious circle."

"You're weird, Mom."

"Yes, I am," she said. "And weirdness is hereditary."

"I'm weird, too," Harrison said. "So you got it coming from both sides. You don't have a chance."

"I can't believe you're my parents. Did you adopt me?"

"Honey, we certainly did not adopt you," Helen said. "We stole you from a pack of wolves, so eat your meat, you darling little carnivore."

Laughing, feeling like an adult because his parents treated him with respect and satire, Frank sat between his mother and father and almost cried with happiness. His chest tightened, and his mouth tasted bitter. He cried too easily, he knew, and sometimes had to fight-school-yard bullies who teased him about his quick tears. He usually won the fights and usually cried about his victory.

Sitting with his parents, Frank closed his eyes against his tears, blinked and blinked and thought of the utter hilarity of a dog farting in its sleep, and that made him laugh a little. Soon enough, he felt normal, like a kid made of steel and oak, and he could breathe easily, and he quickly ate his lunch of Kentucky Fried Chicken, but only wings and legs.

"Okay, I'm done," he said. "Let's play ball, Dad."

"I'm too tired," Harrison said. "I'm going to lie down in the grass and fall asleep in some dog poop."

His father was always trying to be funny. He was funny sometimes, maybe most of the time, but nobody could be funny all of the time. And being funny was sometimes a way of being dishonest.

A few years back, Harrison had told Frank's third-grade teacher that Indians didn't believe in using numbers that the science of mathematics was a colonial evil.

"Well," the mystified teacher had asked, "then how do Indians count?"

"We guess," Harrison had said with as much profundity as he could fake.

Okay, so maybe Harrison was funny because funny was valuable. Maybe being funny was usually a way of being honest.

"Come on, let's play ball," Frank pleaded with his father, who had flopped onto the grass with a chicken leg and a banana.

"I'm going to eat and sleep and fart," Harrison said.

"Dad, you said you'd show me something new."

"Did I promise you I would show you something new?"

"Well, no."

"Did I sign something that said I would show you something new?"

"No."

"That means we don't have an oral or written contract. We don't have an implied contract, either, because you don't even know how to spell 'implication.' So that means I'm going to eat chicken until I pass out from a grease overdose."

"Mom, he's talking like a lawyer again."

"Yeah," she said. "I hate it when he does that."

"And I can, too, spell 'implication,'" Frank said.

"Okay," Harrison said. "If you can spell 'implication,' your mother will play ball with you."

"I don't want to play ball with Mom, I want to play with somebody good."

"Hey, your mom is great. Why do you think I fell in love with her?"

"Mom, he's lying again."

"I'm not lying. Our dear Helen was a cannibal on the basketball court."

"Is that true, Mom?"

"I used to play," she said.

Frank looked at his mother. Sure, she was tall (five feet eight or so, the same height as Harrison), and she was strong (she grew up bucking hay bales), but Frank had never seen her touch a basketball except to toss it in a closet or down the stairs or into a room or out the door, or anywhere to get that dang thing out of her way.

"Mom, are you lying?"

"Have I ever lied to you?"

"You told me I was raised by wolves."

"Okay, have I ever lied to you twice in one day?"

"Mom, be serious."

"She is being serious," Harrison said. "She used to play those girls' rules. Three girls on defense, three on offense. Your mom was the shooter. Damn, I saw her score fifty-two points once. And then the coaches decided to play boys' rules. They didn't have to, but they wanted to see what your mom could do in a real game. And she scored seventy-three. I missed that one. If I'd seen that game, I would have proposed to her on the spot."

"I love you, too, sweetie," Helen said to her husband.

Frank couldn't believe it. He looked at his mother in her denim skirt and frilly blue top, with her lipstick and her beaded earrings and her scarf all matching perfectly, all of her life and spirit and world color-coordinated and alphabetically organized. How could his mother, who washed her hands twelve times a day, ever have played a game so fundamentally sweaty and messy?

"Mom, did you really play ball?"

"It was girls' basketball," she said, "so it doesn't really count."

She was being sarcastic, Frank knew, because she'd taught him how to be sarcastic.

"For the rest of your academic life," she'd told him on his first day of kindergarten, "whenever any teacher tells you that Columbus discovered America, I want you to run up to him or her, jump on his or her back, and scream, 'I discovered you!'"

He'd never been courageous enough to do it, but he always considered it. He always almost did it. He almost always ran home and told Helen how close he'd been to doing it, how he was sure he could do it the next time, and she hugged him and told him how smart and good and handsome he was. Helen was loving and crazy and unpredictable and gentle and voluble and bitter and funny and a thousand other good and bad and indefinable things, but she was certainly not a liar.

"Are you telling the truth?" Frank asked her. "Were you really a good basketball player?"

"People said I was good," she said and shrugged. "If enough people say you're good at something, then you're probably good at it."

"Okay, cool," Frank said. "Do you want to play ball with me?"

"Remember, you have to spell 'implication' first," Harrison.

"It's spelled 'D-A-D I-S A J-E-R-K,'" Frank said.

All three of them laughed. They were always laughing. That was what people said about the Snake Churches. People said the Snake Churches were good at laughing.

"Okay, okay," Helen said. "Let's play ball. But I'm not making any guarantees. It's been a long time."

So mother and son took to the court and played basketball. At first, she practiced shots while he rebounded her makes and misses and passed the ball back to her. She had a funny shot, a one-handed push, and she missed the first ten or twelve before her body remembered the game, and then she rarely missed. From ten feet away, then fifteen, then twenty, and twenty-five feet, she shot and made it and shot and made it and shot and made it and shot and missed it and then shot and made it and shot and made it and shot many times and made many more than she missed.

"Wow," Frank said to his mother as she shot. He kept saying it. It was all he could think to say. This was a new ceremony for them, for this mother and son. They'd created and shared other ceremonies. They baked cookies together; they told stories to each other at night; they made up love songs while she drove him to school; they gave silly nicknames to strangers in shopping malls; they made up stupid knock-knock jokes and laughed until milk sprayed out of their noses. But they'd never played a sport together, had never been this physical, this strong and competitive. Frank looked at his mother, and he saw a new woman, a different person, a mysterious stranger, and a romantic figure.

"Mom," Frank said. "You're a ballplayer."

Oh man, he loved her, and he felt like crying yet again. Oh, he was young and worshipful and sentimental, and he didn't know it, but his mother would always want her son to be young and worshipful and sentimental. She prayed that the world, filled with its cruel people and crueler philosophies, would not punish her son too harshly for being so kind and so receptive to kindness.

"Mom," Frank said. "Show me something new."

So Helen dribbled the ball toward the hoop, dribbled across the key, and shot a rolling left-handed hook that bounced around the rim and dropped in.

"Oh, sweetie! I love you!" Harrison shouted from the grass and sprayed chicken and banana into the air. "That was her favorite move, son, she never missed that one! And nobody ever stopped it. Hell, I never stopped it!"

"Do it again," Frank said.

So Helen shot the left-handed hook again. She shot it twenty times and made nineteen of them.

"She's beautiful!" Harrison shouted and ran to join his wife and son on the court. "Isn't she beautiful?"

Frank wondered if this was the best day of his whole life so far, if he would ever be this happy again. Those were extreme thoughts for an eleven-year-old, and Frank, though he was that eleven-year-old, understood he was being extreme, but it was the only way he knew how to be. It was the only way he'd been taught to be.

So mother, father, and son played basketball for hours, until it got dark enough for the streetlights to blink on, until it was too dark for even the streetlights to make any difference, until Frank could barely keep his eyes open, until Helen and Harrison took their exhausted son home and put him to bed and watched him sleep and breathe, and inhale and exhale and inhale and exhale.

ON THE FIRST anniversary of his father's death, Frank stepped outside to see what kind of day it was. He cursed the rain, stepped back inside to grab his Windbreaker, and walked to the covered courts over on Rainier Avenue. On a sunny day, fifty guys played at Rainier, but on that rainy day, Preacher was shooting hoops all by himself; he was always shooting hoops by himself. Two or three hundred set shots a day. One day a month, he closed his eyes and shot blindly and would never reveal why he performed such an eccentric ceremony.

"Honey, honey, honey," Preacher always said when asked. "Just let the mystery be."

On that day, Preacher's eyes were wide open when Frank joined him for a game of Horse.

"Hey, Frank Snake Church, what ever happened to you?" Preacher asked. He always asked variations of the same question when he saw Frank. "Tell me, tell me, tell me, what ever happened to Frank Snake Church, what the hell happened to Benjamin Franklin Snake Church?"

Preacher hit a thirty-foot bank shot, but Frank missed it. Preacher hit a left-handed hook shot from half-court, but Frank threw the ball over the basket.

"Look at me," said Preacher. "I'm a senior citizen and I've given Frank the 'H' and the 'O.' Ho, ho, ho, Merry Christmas. But wait, I must stop and ponder this existential dilemma. How could I, a retired blue-collar worker, a fixed-income pensioner, a tattered coat upon a stick, how could I be defeating the legendary Frank Snake Church? What the hell is wrong with this picture? What the hell ever happened to Frank Snake Church?"

"I am Frank Snake Church in the here and now and forever," Frank said and laughed. He loved to listen to Preacher rant and rave. A retired railroad engineer, Preacher was a gray-haired black man with a big belly. He stood at the top of the key, bounced the ball off the free-throw line, and off the board into the hoop.

"That was a garbage shot," Frank said. "You'd never take that shot in a real game. Never."

"Every game is real, every game is real, every game is real," Preacher chanted as Frank missed the trick shot.

"That's a screaming scarlet 'R' for you," said Preacher and called out his next shot. "This one is all net all day."

Preacher hit the fifteen-foot swish, and Frank also swished it.

"Oh, a pretty little shot by the Indian stranger," said Preacher.

"I ain't no stranger, I am Frank Snake Church."

"Naw, you ain't no Frank Snake Church," Preacher said. "I saw Frank Snake Church score seventy-seven against the Ballard Beavers in 1979. I saw Frank Snake Church shoot twenty-eight for thirty-six from the field and twenty-one for twenty-two from the line. I saw Frank Snake Church grab nineteen rebounds that same night and hand out eleven dimes. Yeah, I knew Frank Snake Church. Frank Snake Church was a friend of basketball, and believe me, you ain't no Frank Snake Church."

"My driver's license says I'm Frank Snake Church."

"Your social security card, library card, unemployment check, and the tattoo on your right butt cheek might say Frank Snake Church," Preacher said, "but you, sir, are an imposter; you are a doppelgänger; you are a body snatcher; you are a pod person; you are Frank Snake Church's evil and elderly twin is what you are."

Preacher closed his eyes and hit a blind shot from the corner. Frank closed his eyes and missed by five feet.

"That's an 'S' for you, as in Shut Up and Learn How to Play Another Game," said Preacher. "God could pluck out my eyes, and you could play with a microscope, and I'd still beat you. Man, you used to be somebody."

"I am now what I always was," Frank said.

"You now and you then are two entirely different people. You used to be Frank the Snake, Frank the Hot Dog, but now you're just a plain Oscar Mayer wiener, just a burned-up frankfurter without any damn mustard to make you taste better, make you easier to swallow. I watch you toss up one more of those ugly jumpers, and I'm going to need the Heimlich to squeeze your ugliness out of my throat."

"Nope, Frank now and Frank then are exactly the same. I am a tasty indigenous sausage."

"You were young and fresh, and now you're prehistoric, my man, you're only about two and a half hours younger than the Big Bang, that's how old you are. And I know you're old because I'm old. I smell the old on you like I smell the old on me. And it reeks, son, it reeks of stupid and desperate hope."

Preacher hit a Rick Barry two-handed scoop-shot free throw.

"I can't believe you took that white-boy shot," Frank said. "I'm going to turn you in to the NAACP for that sinful thing."

"Honey, I believe in the multicultural beauty of this diverse country."

"But that Anglo crap was just plain ugly."

"Did it go in?" Preacher asked.

"Well, it went in, but it didn't go in pretty."

"All right, pretty boy, let's see what you got."

Frank clanged the shot off the rim.

"My shot might've been ugly," Preacher said, "but your shot is missing chromosomes. You want me to prove it, or you want to lose this game all by yourself?"

"Here begins my comeback," said Frank as he took the shot and missed again.

"Spell it out, honey, that's 'H-O-R-S' and double 'E.' Game over."

"Man, I can't believe I lost on that old-fashioned antique."

"Sweetheart, I might be old-fashioned, but you're just plain old."

Frank felt hot and stupid. He tasted bitterness—that awful need to cry—and he was ashamed of his weakness, and then he was ashamed of being ashamed.

"Age don't mean anything," Frank said. "I walk onto any court on this city, and I'm the best baller. Other guys might be faster or stronger, maybe they jump higher, but I'm smarter. I've got skills and I've got wisdom."

Frank's heart raced. He wondered if he was going to fall again; he wondered if lightning was going to strike him again.

"You might be the wisest forty-year-old ballplayer in the whole city," Preacher said. "You might be the Plato, Aristotle, and Socrates of Seattle street hoops, but you're still forty years old. You should be collecting your basketball pension."

"You're twenty years older than me," Frank said. "Why are you giving me crap about my age?"

Frank could hear the desperation in his own voice, so he knew Preacher could also hear it. In another time, in other, less civilized places, desperate men killed those who made them feel desperation. Who was he kidding? Frank knew, and Preacher should have known, that desperate men are fragile and dangerous at all times and places. Frank wanted to punch Preacher in the face. Frank wanted to knock the old man to the ground and kick and kick and kick and kick him and break his ribs and drive bone splinters into the old man's heart and lungs.

"I know I'm old," Preacher said. "I know it like I know the feel of my own sagging ball sack. I know exactly how old I am in my brain, in my mind. And my basketball mind is the same age as my basketball body. Old, old, ancient, King Tut antique. But you, son, you're in denial. Your mind is stuck somewhere back in 1980, but your eggshell body is cracking here in the twenty-first century."

"I'm only forty years old," Frank said. He bounced the ball between his legs, around his back, thump, thump, between his legs, around his back, thump, thump, again and again, thump, thump, faster and faster, thump, thump, thump, thump, thump.

"Basketball years are like dog years," Preacher said. "You're truly about two hundred and ninety-nine years old."

Thump, thump, thump, thump, thump.

"I'm still a player," Frank said. "I'm still playing good and hard."

Thump, thump, thump, thump, thump.

"But why are you still playing so hard?" Preacher asked. "What are you trying to prove? You keep trying to get all those years back, right? You're trying to time-machine it, trying to alternate-universe it, but one of these days, you're going to come down wrong on one of your arthritic knees, and it will be over. What will you do then? You've bet your whole life on basketball, and playground basketball at that, and what do you have to show for it? Look at you. You're not some sixteen-year-old gangster trying to play your way out of the ghetto. You ain't even some reservation warrior boy trying to shoot your way off the reservation and into some white-collar job at Microsoft Ice Cream. You're just Frank the Pretty Good Shooter for an Old Fart. Nobody's looking to recruit you. Nobody's going to draft you. Ain't no university alumni lining up to financially corrupt your naive ass. Ain't no pretty little Caucasian cheerleaders looking to bed you down in room seven of the Delta Delta Delta house. Ain't no ESPN putting you in the Plays of the Day. You ain't as cool as the other side of the pillow. You're hot and sweaty, like an orthopedic support. You're one lonely Chuck Taylor high-top rotting in the ten-cent pile at Goodwill. Your game is old and ugly and misguided, like the Salem witch trials. You're committing injustice every time you step on the court. I think I'm going to organize a march against your ancient ass. I'm going to boycott you. I'm going to boycott your corporate sponsors. But wait, you ain't got any corporate sponsors, unless Nike has come out with a shoe called Tired Old Bastard. So why don't you just give up the full-court game and the half-court game and enjoy the fruitful retirement of shooting a few basketballs and drinking a few glasses of lemonade."

Frank stopped bouncing the ball and threw it hard at Preacher, who easily caught it and laughed.

"Man oh man," Preacher said. "I'm getting to you, ain't I? I'm hurting your ballplaying heart, ain't I?"

Preacher threw the ball back at Frank, who also caught it easily, and resumed the trick dribbling, the thump, thump, thump, and thump, thump.

"I play ball because I need to play," Frank said

Thump, thump.

"And I need yearly prostate exams," Preacher said, "so don't try to tell me nothing about needing nothing."

Thump, thump.

"I'm playing to remember my mom and dad," Frank said.

Preacher laughed so hard he sat on the court.

"What's so funny?" Frank asked. He dropped the ball and let it roll away.

"Well, I just took myself a poll," Preacher said. "And I asked one thousand mothers and fathers how they would feel about a forty-year-old son who quit his high-paying job to pursue a full-time career as a playground basketball player in Seattle, Washington, and all one thousand of them mothers and fathers cried in shame."

"Preacher," Frank said, "it's true. I'm not kidding. This is, like, a mission or something. My mom and dad are dead. I'm playing to honor them. It's an Indian thing."

Preacher laughed harder and longer. "That's crap," he said. "And it's racist crap at that. What makes you think your pain is so special, so different from anybody else's pain? You look up death in the medical dictionary, and it says everybody's going to catch it. So don't lecture me about death."

"Believe me, I'm playing to remember them."

"You're playing to remember yourself. You're playing because of some of that nostalgia. And nostalgia is a cancer. Nostalgia will fill your heart up with tumors. Yeah, yeah, yeah, that's what you are. You're just an old fart dying of terminal nostalgia."

Frank moaned—a strange, involuntary, and primal noise—and turned his back on Preacher. Frank wept and furiously wiped the tears from his face.

"Oh man, are you crying?" Preacher asked. He was alarmed and embarrassed for Frank.

"Leave me alone," Frank said.

"Oh, come on, man, I'm just talking."

"No, you're not just talking. You're talking about my whole failed life."

"You ain't no failure. I'm just trying to distract you. I'm just trying to win."

"Don't you condescend to me. Don't. Don't you look inside me and then pretend you didn't look inside me."

Preacher felt the heat of Frank's mania, of his burning.

"Listen, brother," Preacher said. "Why don't we go get some decaf and talk this out? I had no idea this meant so much to you. Why don't we go talk it out?"

Frank walked in fast circles around Preacher, who wondered if he could outrun the younger man.

"Listen," said Frank. "You can't take something away from me, steal from me, and then just leave me. You have to replace what you've broken. You have to fix it."

"All right, all right, tell me how to fix it."

"I don't know how to fix it. I didn't know it could be broken. I thought I knew what I was doing. I thought I was doing what I was supposed to do."

"Hey, brother, hey, man, this is too heavy for me and you, all right? Why don't we head over to the church and talk to Reverend Billy?"

"You're a preacher."

"That's just my name. They call me Preacher because I talk too much. I ain't spiritual. I just talk. I don't know anything."

"You're a preacher. Your name is Preacher."

"I know my name is Preacher, but that's like, that's just, it's, you know, it's nothing but false advertising."

Frank stepped quickly toward the old man, who raised his fists in defense. But Frank only hugged him hard and cried into the black man's shoulder. Preacher didn't know what to do. He was pressed skin-to-skin with a crazy man, maybe a dangerous man, and how the hell do you escape such an embrace?

"I'm sorry, brother," Preacher said. "I didn't know."

Frank laughed. He released Preacher. He turned in circles and walked away. And he laughed. He stood on the grass on the edge of the basketball court and spun in circles. And he laughed. Preacher couldn't believe what he was witnessing. He'd known quite a few crazy people in his life. A man doesn't grow up black in the USA without knowing a lot of crazy black folks, without being born to and giving birth to the breakable and broken. But Preacher had never seen this kind of crazy, and he'd certainly never seen the exact moment when a crazy man went completely crazy.

"Hey, Frank, man, I don't like what I'm seeing here. You're hurting really bad here. You maybe want me to call somebody for you?"

Frank laughed and ran. He ran away from Preacher and the basketball court. Frank ran until he fell on somebody's green, green lawn, and then Frank stood and ran again.

AFTER PREACHER'S DEVASTATING sermon, Frank didn't play basketball for two weeks. He didn't leave the house or answer the telephone or the door. He ate all of the food in the house and then drank only water and fruit juice. He was on his own personal hunger strike. Mr. Death, you are an obese bastard, Frank thought, and I'm going to starve you down until I can fit my hands around your throat and choke you. Frank lost fifteen pounds in fifteen days. He wondered how long he could live without food. Forty, fifty, sixty days? He wondered who would find his body.

Three weeks after Preacher's sermon, and after dozens of unanswered phone calls, Russell found Frank's address in his files, drove to the house, crawled through an unlocked window, and found Frank dead in bed. Well, he thought Frank was dead.

"You're breaking and entering," Frank said and opened his eyes.

"You scared me," Russell said. "I thought you were dead."

"Black man, you keep crawling through windows in this gentrified neighborhood, and you're going to get shot in your handsome African head."

"I was worried about you."

"Well, aren't you the full-service personal trainer? You should be charging me more." Frank sat up in bed. He was pale and clammy and far too thin.

"You look terrible, Frank. You're really sick."

"I know."

"I'm going to call for help, okay? We need to get you help, all right?"

"Okay."

Russell walked into the kitchen to use the telephone and hurried back.

"They'll be here soon," he said.

"What would you have done if you'd come too late?" Frank asked. "You know, part of me wishes you'd waited too long."

"I did wait too long. You're sick. And I helped you get sick. I'm sorry. I just wanted to believe in what you believed."

"You're not going to hug me now, are you?" Frank asked.

Both men laughed.

"No, I'm not going to hug you, I'm not going to kiss you, I'm not going to recite poetry to you," Russell said. "And I'm not going to crawl under these nasty sheets with you, either."

An ambulance siren wailed in the distance.

"Because, well," Frank said, "I know you're gay and all, and I care about you a bunch, but not in that way. If we were stuck on a deserted island or something, or if we were in prison, then maybe we could be Romeo and Juliet, but in the real world, you're going to have to admire me from afar."

MAUD PRESTON PALENSKE
MEMORIAL LIBRARY
500 Market St.
St. Joseph, MI 49085

"Yeah, let me tell you," Russell said, "I've always been very attracted to straight, suicidal, bipolar anorexics."

"And I've always been attracted to gay, black, narcissistic codependents."

Both men laughed again because they were good at laughing.

ONE YEAR AFTER Russell saved Frank's life, after four months of residential treatment and eight months of inpatient counseling, Frank walked into the admissions office at West Seattle Community College. He'd gained three extra pounds for every twelve of the steps he'd taken over the last year, so he was fat. Not unhappy and fat, not fat and happy, but fat and alive, and hungry, always hungry.

"Can I help you? Is there anything I can do?" the desk clerk asked. She was young, blond, and tentative. A work-study student or scholarship kid, Frank thought, smart and pretty and poor.

"Yeah," he said, feeling damn tentative as well. "I think, well, I want to go to school here."

"Oh, that's good. That's really great. I can help. I can help you with that."

She ducked beneath the counter, came back up with a thick stack of paper, and set it on the counter.

"Here you go, this is it," she said. "You have to fill these out. Fill them out, and sign them, and bring them back. These are admission papers. You fill them out and you can get admitted."

Frank stared at the thick pile of paper, as mysterious and frightening to him as Stonehenge. The young woman recognized the fear in his eyes. She came from a place where that fear was common.

"What's your name?" she asked.

"Frank," he said. "Frank Snake Church."

"Are you Native American?"

"Why do you ask?"

"Well, they have a Native American admissions officer here. Her name is Stephanie. She works with the Native Americans. She can help you with admissions. You're Native American, right?"

"Yes, I'm Indian."

"If you don't mind me asking, it's a personal question, but how old are you?"

"I'm forty-one."

"You know, they also have a program here for older students, you know, for the people who went to college when you were young—when you were younger—and come back."

"I never went to college before."

"Well, the program is for all older students, you know? They call it Second Wind."

"Second Wind? That sound like a bowel condition you have when you're old."

The young woman laughed. "That's funny. You're funny. It does sound sort of funny, doesn't it? But it's a really good program. And they can help you. The Second Wind program can help you."

She reached beneath the counter again, pulled out another stack of paper, and set it beside the other stack of paper. So much paper, so much work. He didn't know why he was here; he'd come here only because his therapist had suggested it. Frank felt stupid and inadequate. He'd made a huge mistake by quitting his Forest Service job, but he could probably go back. He didn't want to go to college; he wanted to walk the quiet forests and think about nothing as often as he could.

"Hey, listen," Frank said, "I've got another thing to go to. I'll come back later."

"No, listen," she said, because she was poor and smart and had been poorer and was now smarter than people assumed she was. "I know this is scary. I was scared to come here. I'll help you. I'll take you to Stephanie."

She came around the counter and took his hand. She was only eighteen, and she led him by the hand down the hallway toward the Native American Admissions Office.

"My name is Lynn," she said as they walked together, as she led him by the hand.

"I'm Frank."

"I know, you already told me that."

He was scared, and she knew it and didn't hate him for it. She wasn't afraid of his fear, and she wouldn't hurt him for it. She was so young and so smart, and she led him by the hand.

Lynn led him into the Native American Admissions Office, Room 21A at West Seattle Community College in Seattle, Washington, a city named after a Duwamish Indian chief who died alone and drunk and poor and forgotten, only to be remembered decades after his death for words of wisdom he'd supposedly said, but words that had been written by the mayor's white assistant. Mr. Death, Frank thought, if a lie is beautiful, then is it truly a lie?

Lynn led Frank into the simple office. Sitting at a metal desk, a chubby Indian woman with old-fashioned eyeglasses looked up at the odd pair.

"Dang, Lynn," the Indian woman said. "I didn't know you like them old and dark."

"Old and dark and bitter," Lynn said. "Like bus-station coffee."

The women laughed together. Frank thought they were smart and funny, too smart and funny for him to compete with, too smart and funny for him to understand. He knew he wasn't smart and funny enough to be in their presence.

"This is Mr. Frank Snake Church," Lynn said with overt formality, with respect. "He is very interested in attending our beloved institution, but he's never been to college before. He's a Native American and a Second Winder."

The young woman spoke with much more confidence and power than she had before. How many people must underestimate her, Frank thought, and get their heads torn off.

"Hello, Mr. Frank Snake Church," the Indian woman said, "I'm Stephanie. Why don't you have a seat and we'll set you up."

"I told you she was great," Lynn said. She led him by the hand to a wooden chair across the desk from Stephanie. Lynn sat him down and kissed him on the cheek. She came from a place, from a town and street, from a block and house, where all of the men had quit, had surrendered, had simply stopped and lay down in the street to die before they were fifteen years old. And here was an old man, a frightened man the same age as her father, and he was beautiful like Jesus, and scared like Jesus, and rising from the dead like Jesus. She kissed him because she wanted to pray with him and for him, but she didn't know if he would accept her prayers, if he even believed in prayers. She kissed him, and Frank wanted to cry because this young woman, this stranger, had been so kind and generous. He knew he would never have another conversation with Lynn apart from hurried greetings and smiles and quick hugs and exclamations. She would soon graduate and transfer to a four-year university, taking her private hopes and dreams to a private college. After that, he would never see her again but would always remember her, would always associate the smell of chalk and new books and floor polish and sea-salt air with her memory. She kissed him on the cheek, touched his shoulder, and hurried out the door, back to the work that was paying for school that was saving her life.

"So, Mr. Snake Church," Stephanie said. "What tribe are you?"

"I'm Spokane," he said, his voice cracking.

"Are you okay?" she asked.

"Yes," he said. But he wasn't. He covered his face and cried.

She came around the table and knelt beside him.

"Frank," she said. "It's okay, it's okay. I'm here, I'm here."

WITH STEPHANIE'S HELP, Frank enrolled in Math 99, English 99, History 99, Introduction to Computer Science, and Physical Education.

His first test was in math.

The first question was a story problem: "Bobby has forty dollars when he walks into the supermarket. If Bobby buys three loaves of bread for ten dollars each, and he buys a bottle of orange juice for three dollars, how much money will he have left?"

Frank didn't have to work the problem on paper. He did the math in his head. Bobby would have seven bucks left, but he'd paid too much for the bread and not enough for the juice. Easy cheese, Frank thought, confident he could do this.

With one question answered, Frank moved ahead to the others.

THREE WEEKS INTO his first quarter, Frank walked across campus to the athletic center and knocked on the basketball coach's door.

"Come in," the coach said.

Frank stepped inside and sat across the desk from the coach, a big white man with curly blond hair. He was maybe Frank's age or a little older.

"How can I help you?" the coach asked.

"I want to play on your basketball team."

The coach smiled and leaned toward Frank. "How old are you?" he asked.

"Forty-one," Frank said.

"Do you have any athletic eligibility left?"

"This is my first time in college. So that means I have all my eligibility, right?"

"That's right."

"I thought so. I looked it up."

"I bet you did. Not a whole lot of forty-one-year-old guys are curious about their athletic eligibility."

"How old are you?" Frank asked.

"Forty-three. But my eligibility is all used up."

"I know, you played college ball at the University of Washington. And high school ball at Roosevelt."

"Did you look that up, too?"

"No, I remember you. I played against you in high school. And I was supposed to play with you at UW."

The coach studied Frank's face for a while, and then he remembered. "Snake Church," he said.

"Yes," Frank said, feeling honored.

"You were good. No, you were great. What happened to you?"

"That doesn't matter. My history isn't important. I'm here now, and I want to play ball for you."

"You don't look much like a ballplayer anymore."

"I've gained a lot of weight in the last year. I've been in residential treatment for some mental problems."

"You don't have to tell me this."

"No, I need to be honest. I need to tell you these things. Before I got sick, I was in the best shape of my life. I can get there again."

The coach stood. "Come on," he said. "I want to show you something."

He led Frank out of the office and to the balcony overlooking the basketball court. The community-college team ran an informal scrimmage. Ten young and powerful black men ran the court with grace and poetry. It was beautiful. Frank wanted to be a part of it.

"Hey!" the coach yelled down to his players. "Run a dunk drill!"

Laughing and joking, the black men formed two lines and ran the drill. All of them could easily dunk two-handed, including the five-foot-five point guard.

"That's pretty good, right?" the coach asked.

"Yes," Frank said.

"All right!" the coach yelled down to his players. "Now run the real dunk drill!"

Serious now, all of the young men ripped off reverse dunks, 360-degree dunks, alley-oops, bounce-off-the-floor-and-off-the-backboard dunks, and one big guy dunked two balls at the same time.

"I've built myself a great program here," the coach said. "I've had forty players go Division One in the last ten years. All ten guys down there have Division One talent. It's the best team I've ever had."

"They look great," Frank said.

"Do you really think you can compete with them? Twenty years ago, maybe. But now? I'm happy you're here, Frank, I'm proud of you for coming back to college, but I think you're dreaming about basketball."

"Let me down there," Frank said. "And I'll show you something."

The coach thought it over. What did he have to lose? If basketball was truly a religion, as he believed, then he needed to practice charity in order to be a truly spiritual man.

"All right," the coach said. "Let's see how much gas you have left in the tank."

Frank and the coach walked down to the court and greeted the players.

"Okay, men," the coach said. "I've got a special guest today."

"Hey, Coach, is that your chiropractor?" the big guy asked.

They laughed.

"No, this is Frank Snake Church. He's going to run a little bit with you guys."

Wearing black jeans, a black T-shirt, and white basketball shoes, Frank looked like a coffee-shop waiter.

"Hey, Coach, is he going to run in his street clothes?"

"He can talk," Coach said. "Ask him."

"Yo, old-timer," said the point guard. "Is this one of those Make-A-Wish things? Are we your dying request?"

They laughed.

"Yes," Frank said.

They stopped laughing.

"Shit, man," the point guard said. "I'm sorry. I didn't mean no harm. What you got, the cancer?"

"No, I'm not dying. It's for my father and mother. They're dead, and I'm trying to remember them."

Uncomfortable, the players shuffled their feet and looked to their coach for guidance.

"Frank, are you okay?" asked the coach, wishing he hadn't let this nostalgic stunt go so far.

"I want to be honest with all of you," Frank said. "I'm a little crazy. Basketball has made me a little crazy. And that's probably a little scary to you guys. I know you all grew up with tons of crazy, and you're playing ball to get away from it. But I don't mean to harm anybody. I'm a good man, I think, and I want to be a better man. The thing is, I don't think I was a good son when my mother and father were alive, so I want to be a good son now that they're dead. I think I can do that by playing ball with you guys. By playing on this team."

"You think you're good enough to make the team?" the point guard asked. He tried to hide his smile.

Frank smiled and laughed. "Hey, I know I'm a fat old man, but that just means your feelings are going to be really hurt when a fat old man kicks your ass."

The players and Coach laughed.

"Old man," the point guard said. "I didn't know they trash-talked in your day. Man, what did they do it with? Cave paintings?"

"Just give me the ball and we'll run," Frank said.

The point guard tossed the ball to Frank.

"Check it in," Frank said and tossed it back.

"All right," said the point guard. "I'll take the bench, and you can have the other starters. Make it fair that way."

"One of you has to sit."

"I'll sit," the big guy said and stood with his coach.

"We got our teams," the point guard said and tossed the ball back to Frank. "Check."

Frank dribbled the ball to the top of the key, turned, and discovered the point guard five feet away from him.

"Are you going to guard me?" Frank asked.

"Do I need to guard you?" the point guard asked.

"I don't want no charity," Frank said.

"I'll guard you when you prove I need to guard you."

"All right, guard this," Frank said and shot a jumper that missed the rim and backboard by three feet.

"Man oh man, I don't need to guard you," the point guard said. "Gravity is going to take care of you."

The point guard took the inbound pass and dribbled downcourt. Frank tried to stay in front of the little guard, but he was too quick. He burned past Frank, tossed a lazy pass to a forward, and pointed at Frank when the forward dunked the ball.

"Were you guarding me?" he asked Frank. "I just want to be sure you know you're guarding me. I'm your man. Do you understand that? Do you understand the basic principles of defense?"

Frank didn't respond. Twice up and down the court, he was already breathing hard and needed to conserve his energy.

Frank set a back pick for his center, intending to free him for a shot, but Frank was knocked over instead and hit the ground hard. By the time Frank got to his feet, the point guard had stolen the ball and raced down the court for an easy layup.

"Hey, Coach," the point guard shouted as he ran by Frank. "It's only four on five out here. We need another player. Oh, wait! There is another player out here. I just didn't see him until right now."

"Shut up," Frank said.

"Oh, am I getting to you?" The point guard turned to jaw with his teammates, and Frank broke for the hoop. He caught a bounce pass, stepped past a forward, and hit a five-footer.

"Two for Snake Church," said Coach from the sidelines.

"That's the only hoop you're getting," the point guard said and hurried the ball down the court. He spun and went for the crossover dribble, but Frank reached in and knocked the ball away. One of Frank's teammates picked up the loose ball and tossed it back to Frank.

"Come on, come on, come on," the point guard shouted in Frank's ear as he ran alongside him.

Frank was slower than the young man, but he was stronger, so he dug an elbow into the kid's ribs, pushed him away, and rose up for a thirty-foot jumper, an impossible shot. And bang, he nailed it!

"Three points!" shouted Coach.

"You fouled me twice," the point guard said as he brought the ball back toward Frank.

"Call it, then."

"No, man, I don't need it," the point guard said and spun past Frank and drove down the middle of the key. Frank was fooled, but he dove after the point guard, hit the ball from behind, and sent it skidding toward one of his teammates, a big guard, who raced down the court for an easy layup.

"What's the score?" the point guard shouted out. He was angry now.

"Five to four, for Snake Church."

"What are we playing to?" Frank asked. He struggled for oxygen. Lactic acid burned holes in his thighs.

"Eleven," said the point guard.

Frank hoped he could make it that far.

"All right, all right, you can play ball for an old man," the point guard said. "But you ain't touching the rock again. It's all over for you."

He feinted left, feinted right, and Frank got his feet all twisted up and fell down again as the point guard raced by him and missed a ten-foot jumper. As his forward grabbed the rebound, Frank staggered to his feet and ran down the court on the slowest fast break in the history of basketball. He caught a pass just inside the half-court line and was too tired to dribble any farther, so he launched a thirty-five-foot set shot.

"Three!" shouted the coach, suddenly loving this sport more than he had ever loved it before. "That's eight to four, another three and Frank wins."

"I can't believe this," the point guard said. He'd been humiliated, and he sought revenge. He barreled into Frank, sending him staggering back, and pulled up for his own three-pointer. Good! Eight to seven!

"It's comeback time, baby," the point guard said as he shadowed Frank down the court. Frank could barely move. His arms and legs burned with pain. His back ached. He figured he'd torn a muscle near his spine. His lungs felt like two sacks of rocks. But he was happy! He was joyous! He caught a bounce pass from a teammate and faced the point guard.

"No, no, no, old man, you're not winning this game on me."

Smiling, Frank head-faked, dribbled right, planted for a jumper, and screamed in pain as his knee exploded. He'd never felt pain this terrible. He grabbed his leg and rolled on the floor.

Coach ran over and held him down. "Don't move, don't move," he said.

"It hurts, it hurts," Frank said.

"I know," Coach said. "Just let me look at it."

As the players circled around them, Coach examined Frank's knee.

"Is it bad?" Frank asked. He wanted to scream from the pain.

"Really bad," Coach said. "It's over. It's over for this."

Frank rolled onto his face and screamed. He pounded the floor like a drum and sang: *Mother, Father, way, ya, hi, yo, good-bye, good-bye. Mother, Father, way, ya, hi, yo, good-bye, good-bye. Mother, Father, way, ya, hi, yo, good-bye, good-bye. Mother, Father, way, ya, hi, yo, good-bye, good-bye. Mother, Father, way, ya, hi, yo, good-bye, good-bye.*

Coach and the players stared at Frank. What could they say?

"Hey, old man," the point guard said. "That was a good run."

Yes, it was, Frank thought, and he wondered what he was going to do next. He wondered if this pain would ever subside. He wondered if he'd ever step onto a basketball court again.

"I'm going to call an ambulance," Coach said. "Get him in the training room."

As Coach ran toward his office, the point guard and the big guy picked up Frank and carried him across the gym.

"You're going to be okay," the point guard said. "You hear me, old man? You're going to be fine."

"I know it," Frank said. "I know."

Red River Crossing

JOHNNY D. BOGGS

Born in 1962, Johnny D. Boggs grew up in South Carolina. After receiving a degree in journalism in 1984, Boggs worked at the Dallas Times Herald and the Fort Worth Star-Telegram before leaving to concentrate on his novels and freelance writing. He won the prestigious Spur Award from Western Writers of America in 2002 for his short story, "A Piano at Dead Man's Crossing."

He lives in Santa Fe, New Mexico, with his wife, son, and basset hound.

IF YOU'VE EVER met Abel Head Pierce, you know he's a hard man, and not always fair-minded. Honest, certainly, but I've never known him to own up to a mistake, and I have known him for forty-odd years. The closest he ever came to apologizing, or admitting that he was wrong, started with an incident that happened back in 1871 and then it wasn't until 1884 that Mr. Pierce hinted, in his own peculiar way, that he might have been a shade off being right during his dealings with Tom Griffin. I should know. I saw it all, at Red River Crossing, and later in Kansas, Texas, Arkansas, up the Texas Cattle Trail, and finally, thirteen years later, in Dodge City.

Folks call him Shanghai, and he strutted like a Shanghai rooster when I first met him in '55 during a trail drive to Louisiana. He sounded like one, too, the way he cussed in a high-pitched voice that pricked your skin worse than fingernails scraping a chalkboard. Mr. Pierce stood six-foot-four in his stocking feet, hailed from Rhode Island, but made his mark in Texas cattle.

In the years I had ridden for Mr. Pierce since that first drive to Louisiana, his wealth and power had grown. Down in Texas, and practically all over the West, Abel Head Pierce had a hard-rock reputation as an almighty shrewd businessman and a top-rate cattleman. By the spring of 1871, he was a thirty-seven-year-old rancher, ramrod and rapscallion, and he loved every minute of it when things were going his way. At Red River Crossing, things didn't go his way, and he blamed Tom Griffin.

Let me concede that he was absolutely right in doing so. At first, I mean. Tom Griffin accepted the blame for what happened. Tom Griffin, you see, could admit his own mistakes, but this one proved costly.

It came during the height of the long drives from South Texas to Kansas. The Red River was flooding—highest I've ever seen it—and I warrant there had to be sixty thousand cattle waiting to cross. Mr. Pierce realized the trouble, the danger, as we had three herds of two thousand each with too many neighbors. So we invited each trail boss to our camp for son-of-a-bitch stew and Sourdough Frankie's fine biscuits and strong coffee. After supper, Mr. Pierce gave his instructions.

"It's been a wet one, boys," he said, "and my steers have done so much swimming, they look more like sea lions that longhorns." Of course, Mr. Pierce added a handful of salty expressions to that statement, words that a Methodist would frown upon but a cowboy would surely enjoy. Then he turned serious.

"I'm not one who takes unnecessary risks when it comes to my cattle and my money. We need to separate these herds, so I'm asking you to back off ten or twelve miles each. Wait for the water to fall, then we can cross in good order. Problem with the way our herds are bunched together, if one stampedes, it'll play hell on all of us."

That coaxing might have worked, too, if not for Tom Griffin. A strong-willed Texan, Griffin had survived the War of the Rebellion and a string of lousy luck. That spring, he had his hands full fending off carpetbaggers with designs on taking his ranch from him.

"I supposed you'll be crossing first, Shanghai?" he said.

"Nope. Them Mexicans from Refugio County got here first."

"Well, I just don't see it, Shanghai," Griffin said. "There are so many cattle here if each of us backs up ten miles or so, hell, I'd be back where I started from, and I, for one, don't aim at missing the market in Abilene."

Move back, and they feared they'd lose their turn crossing the river, and every man jack of them wanted to get to the Kansas railhead first, when the buyers had plenty of money to throw around. "Hell," Griffin argued, "nothing is going to happen."

So they stayed put, and three or four days later, one of the herds spooked. A match, snapping twig, coyote, who knows what started it? But it happened. It didn't take much; and that stampede spread like a prairie fire. Another herd ran. And another. Every herd camped near the banks of the Red spooked. It proved to be one of biggest disasters and damnedest sights I ever saw. Mr. Pierce had been right, Tom Griffin wrong, and there would be hell to pay.

I COULD HEAR Mr. Pierce's curses from camp as I rode in that night with a couple of the boys and the body of Blue Ben draped in my sugans and tied behind the cantle of Clete Jarnigan's zebra dun. Reports were already coming in of dead cattle, busted-up wagons, and horses, but I knew the loss of Blue Ben would make things dangersome for everyone, but mostly Tom Griffin.

"Is that . . . ?" Mr. Pierce began.

"Yes, sir," I replied. "What's left of him anyway."

He cussed, kicked, and stormed around camp, screeching like one of those steam-powered organs aboard a steamboat, before stopping and staring at me.

"Whose herd stampeded first? You learned that?"

Well, I had, and though I hated to answer the question, I had to.

Mr. Pierce cursed Tom Griffin's name long and hard; then he ordered Clete and me to ride out and inform every trail boss, every wrangler, every belly-cheater and drover that there would be a funeral on the banks of the Red River shortly after dawn, and he would take it personal if they didn't show up.

"Jack," he called out as I swung into my saddle.

"Tell Tom Griffin if he comes to Blue Ben's funeral, I'll kill him. His men are welcome, but he isn't, not by a damned sight."

"Yes, sir."

IT WAS A mighty fine funeral. Mr. Pierce read from the Good Book, and though I heard some grumbling among the drovers and trail bosses, you can bet your boots no one bellyached within Mr. Pierce's earshot.

We threw up a cross over Blue Ben's grave, then moved out to try to separate the herds and get across the Red River again. That took a spell, ten days about if I recollect right. It took Tom Griffin even longer, only because Mr. Pierce ordered everyone not to assist the Rafter G, that he'd take it as an affront if anyone sided with that killer. For such a rawboned yankee, Abel Head Pierce threw a lot of weight, especially after what all had happened, and we were halfway to Kansas before Griffin ever got his beef across the Red.

Which could have ended things there, but that incident, Blue Ben's death, but mostly Tom Griffin's refusing to listen to reason, it festered something awful, stuck in Mr. Pierce's craw, and he wouldn't let it pass. Blue Ben was dead, but that wasn't half of it. We had lost better than two hundred head in the stampede—more than $7,000 at market price that year—and Mr. Pierce is a man who likes his money.

We sold our herds in Abilene, sent most of the boys back home, while Mr. Pierce and I waited at the Drover's Cottage for the Rafter G cattle to arrive. I remember sitting in the lobby, smoking a cigar, when a weary, ragged Tom Griffin walked inside and asked for a room.

"I'm sorry," the clerk told him. "We're full up."

That was a lie, and Tom Griffin knew it.

"Do you know who I am?" he asked.

"Yes, sir. But we're still full up."

"I've been bringing my beef to Abilene for four years. I've done business . . ." When he spotted Mr. Pierce, leaning against the balustrade, saw that laughter in Mr. Pierce's cold eyes, Tom Griffin left. He bunked that summer in his cow camp, and approached every cattle buyer in town, only to hear the same story. The summer crept by. September came and went, and the season ended, but Tom Griffin's longhorns remained camped outside town. Finally, he summoned enough courage, or swallowed down his pride, to brace Mr. Pierce at the Bull's Head Saloon.

"Listen, Shanghai," he said, "I was wrong at Red River Crossing, and I'm sorry about all that happened. I'm sorry about ol' Blue. Know he'd been with you for years, but . . . I ain't one to beg, sir, but I got a wife and two little girls, been on tick for so long . . . well, what do you want from me?"

"You want to sell your damned herd?" Mr. Pierce asked.

"You know I have to."

"Then I'll buy them from you, Tom. Ten dollars a head."

Tom Griffin looked as if he'd been gut-shot, and that bucket of blood turned quieter than a church on Monday morning.

"I could get better than that in Texas," Griffin said.

"But you aren't in Texas, Tom. And if you want to wait out the winter here . . ."

Everybody in Abilene knew that Tom Griffin had tried to wait out the winter the previous year, hoping for a better price, but that winter had been a hard one, and Tom Griffin's luck turned south. He had lost half his herd, sold out at a loss, forced to limp his way back to Matagorda County on tick and try again that spring. Griffin's face reddened, but he didn't lash out at Mr. Pierce, just stormed through the saloon doors.

WE DIDN'T SEE him again 'til November, when, hat in hand, he approached Mr. Pierce over breakfast.

"I'll take that offer," he said humbly. "At least I can pay off my crew, pay some of my bills, and get home to my family. Ten dollars a head, and I have fifteen hundred beeves, sir."

"Tom," Mr. Pierce said. "That was the price in October. The price today is eight dollars a head, if I like the way they look."

"I'd go broke selling out for that," Griffin snapped.

"You are broke, Tom. And you'll go broker waiting for a better offer in Abilene." Mr. Pierce's grin wasn't pleasant. "Word is the civic leaders don't want our business anymore. Abilene will be closed to the Texas trade come spring. Now, if you want to risk another winter, Tom, maybe you can push what's left of your beef to Ellsworth next year. If you can afford to pay any drovers or find anyone willing to work for you. Eight dollars, Tom. Cash money. Twelve thousand dollars. But if you wait 'til tomorrow, the price will be seven."

"You're one son of a bitch, Shanghai Pierce," Tom Griffin said through a tight jaw.

"Tell that to Blue Ben," he answered coolly.

WELL, TOM GRIFFIN sold his herd to Mr. Pierce that morning, who, in turn, found a buyer from a Kansas City packing plant willing to pay him $35.75 a head. By then, Griffin had ridden back to Texas, hoping he could make things right come next spring, but Mr. Pierce kept thinking ahead. Come roundup time, you couldn't find a vaquero or any man in South Texas fool enough to sign on with the Rafter G. We blackballed Tom Griffin, made him a man alone, and that's when I guess he started pulling the cork. I had never known Tom Griffin to take a drink, but after the spring of 1872 I seldom saw him sober.

Eventually, Mrs. Griffin took the two girls and moved back to her mother's in Sedalia, and Chemical National Bank took over the Rafter G. Shortly afterward I heard rumors that Mrs. Griffin had hired a rich Missouri lawyer, saying she'd rather live with the shame of divorce than be married to a worthless drunk. That's when Tom Griffin drifted to our camp one evening, asked if he could hire on for the drive, which had to make Griffin, in his cups or not, disgusted with himself. Mr. Pierce obviously enjoyed the opportunity to reply that he didn't hire walking whiskey vats to do a man's work. Tom Griffin rode back to the nearest saloon, and, by the time Mr. Pierce and I returned from Wichita that August, Tom Griffin had left the country.

THAT, ALSO, MIGHT have ended things, but the next year, just by chance, we ran into Tom Griffin in Hot Springs, Arkansas. His hair had turned white, his eyes rimmed red, but he looked quite happy when the two of us walked into the Avance Hotel.

"Well, Mister Pierce," he said pleasantly, "Mr. Street, do you have reservations with us?"

"You own this place, Griffin?" Pierce asked.

That brought a frown to the Texan's face, and he looked down at the ledger, mumbling something about reservations. Griffin, who once ran thousands of head over several sections of the best country a body could find in Matagorda County, wasn't anything more than a clerk.

"I damn sure want a room," Mr. Pierce said, "so hand over a key, boy."

Color returned to Griffin's face, and he looked up. "I'm sorry, gentlemen, but without a reservation, I can't help you. We're full up. Remember?"

Vengeance, I thought, recalling that time at the Drover's Cottage in Abilene, but Tom Griffin underestimated Abel Head Pierce, who stormed directly into the manager's office.

"Do you own this pigsty?" Mr. Pierce asked.

"Uh . . . I . . . well, only a half-interest, sir."

"How much to buy you out?"

"Sir?"

"You heard me. How much?"

"Mister Pierce, why, well, I couldn't take less than fifteen thousand dollars. This is—"

"Done."

I helped guide the stunned part-owner of the hotel to the bank—Mr. Pierce, naturally, rode—and there we recorded the transaction, and afterward returned to the Avance, where Mr. Pierce grabbed the key to a suite and another key to the adjoining room for me. When Griffin started to protest and threaten to alert the local constabulary, Mr. Pierce waved the duly noted deed in his face.

"I think I can take any room I want since I own this place, Tom."

Griffin's face turned ashen, and like a rooster, Mr. Pierce strutted up the stairs, stopping at the landing and calling down, "Tom?"

Meekly, the man looked up, steeling himself for the words he knew were coming.

"You're fired."

WELL, WE DIDN'T cross Tom Griffin's trail again for years. I had almost forgotten all about him until this saddle tramp showed up at our camp on the Brazos in the spring of 1884 when we were pushing a herd of two-year-olds to Dodge City by way of the cutoff.

"You looking for a job?" I asked. "Or just riding the grub line?"

Short-handed as we were after losing a couple boys to bad water, I felt so desperate I figured that bearded wreck of a man could at least ride drag for us.

Staring at me over his plate of beans, he wiped gravy with a frayed sleeve, and said, "Was . . .'til I recognized your road brand."

That's when I saw the man for who he was.

"Griffin?"

The dog started barking, and my stomach knotted as Mr. Pierce and Blue Ben II strode into camp, the pup just a nipping at Mr. Pierce's heels. Without a word, Tom Griffin, joints creaking, rose, dropped plate, fork, and coffee cup in the wreck pan, and headed toward his mount.

"Hold up there, cowboy!" Mr. Pierce called to the man's back, and to the dog. "Stay, Blue, stay."

Well, the dog didn't stay put at all, and when Tom Griffin turned around, Mr. Pierce recognized him immediately. Tom Griffin's hand dropped to his gun, but he was shaking so bad, I knew he wouldn't pull it.

"Griffin! By the saints, I thought you were dead." Mr. Pierce almost doubled over laughing, but he straightened and his face went cold when Tom Griffin spoke quietly.

"I am dead, Shanghai. You killed me years ago. And because of what?" He pointed at the pup, the spitting image of ol' Blue Ben who had been killed at Red River Crossing back in '71. "Because I got that damned dog of yours killed in a stampede? I didn't start the stampede, Shanghai. It was an accident. Still, I took responsibility for it, but you couldn't let that lie, could you? I lost my wife. My girls. My ranch. My damned dignity. Because of a dog?"

Still shaking, Tom Griffin spun, making a beeline for the remuda.

Blue Ben II began barking, and, to our surprise, took off chasing that old cowhand.

"He's right, Mister Pierce," I said to my boss's back.

"Like hell."

"You never cared one whit about that dog," I reminded him, "until he got killed."

"Maybe, but that son of a bitch over yonder cost me seven thousand dollars, Jack. I haven't forgotten that, even after thirteen years."

"No, sir, but I figure Tom Griffin's paid that debt. With interest."

Mr. Pierce looked at me for what seemed the longest time, and his face softened a bit before he strode away, calling out again, "I said hold up there, cowboy!"

Well, much to my surprise, Mr. Pierce offered Tom Griffin a job, riding drag maybe, but a job, at thirty a month and a bonus at Dodge City. Even more shocking, Griffin took the offer. He said something to me, a few weeks later, that all he had ever known really was cattle, all he ever wanted to do was ranch and cowboy, and now, after thirteen years, he had that chance again. He promised he wouldn't let Shanghai Pierce down.

Yes, he was a broken man by then. Mr. Pierce had broken him, yet, I thought, Mr. Pierce was coming around, mellowing a bit. Besides, Blue Ben II took a shine to Tom Griffin. Every morning we'd find that bluetick pup curled up in Griffin's sugans, and Ol' Griff would feed that obnoxious little dog breakfast and supper. They became something of a fixture on that drive.

We pushed the herd up to Red River Crossing, and that's when it happened again. Another stampede, only there weren't dozens of herds and sixty thousand cattle around, just our own. A lightning strike sent the herd thundering right through camp, wrecked the hoodlum wagon, turned over the chuckwagon, maimed fifteen horses, and killed twenty-one head of cattle before we got them turned and milling.

I'm still not sure how it happened, how he did it, or even why, but we found Tom Griffin's crushed body back in camp, near the blackjacks and smoldering cookfire. The best we could figure it is that Tom, who had been night-herding, had dived off his horse, or maybe it had stumbled, but he had picked up that quivering little puppy, frightened half to death, and tossed it clear of the stampeding cattle. Tom Griffin had saved Blue Ben II's life, even if it had cost him his own.

He wasn't dead when we found him, but I knew he wouldn't last long, not with death's rattle in his throat, not as busted up as his innards had to be. He asked to see Mr. Pierce, his voice stronger than it rightfully should have, and while Sourdough Frankie searched desperately for a bottle of rye in the ruined chuckwagon, Mr. Pierce knelt beside the dying cowhand, cradling the dog in his hands.

"Shanghai," Tom Griffin said, "you want to tell me something?"

"I sure do, Tom," Mr. Pierce said, but Tom Griffin died before Abel Head Pierce could say anything else. He sat there for the longest time, the puppy whimpering in his arms, the only sound around. Finally, seeing the boys worried, restless, and confused, and Mr. Pierce apparently badly shaken, I announced that we'd bury Tom Griffin at Red River Crossing and Sourdough Frankie would carve his name on a piece of board from the destroyed hoodlum wagon.

"No." Mr. Pierce placed the dog on Tom Griffin's chest. Stiffly, he rose and looked every mother's son of us in the eye. "We're taking him to Dodge. Tom Griffin will finish the drive, by thunder, and we'll give him a funeral to remember him by."

WELL, MR. PIERCE is a man of his word, so once we had outfitted ourselves, we salted down Tom Griffin's broken body in a coffin Mr. Pierce bought in Spanish Fort, loaded him in the hoodlum wagon, and hauled him to Dodge. Our drovers didn't care much for that at all—coffins and dead bodies giving even the strongest cowboy a bad feeling—but they knew better than complain or quit on Shanghai Pierce. No one talked about our odd cargo, and we covered the rest of the trail without incident.

Once in Dodge City, after selling the herd and paying off the crew, Mr. Pierce gave us instructions that we would all attend Tom Griffin's funeral and whoever didn't show up would rue the day. The service would

begin at nine o'clock sharp at the Union Church, and by 8:55 that morning every drover we had stood in his Sunday best, which they had
bought for the funeral, and hat in hand. A few had brought along their
whores, just to increase the turnout.

"This is not worth a tinker's damn," Mr. Pierce told the parson. "Tom
Griffin's funeral will draw more than a dozen thirty-a-month drovers,
by God, and three chirpies."

The parson nodded, and the funeral was put on hold. To hell with the
town ordinance prohibiting the packing of firearms, Mr. Pierce told us,
so we outfitted ourselves, mounted up, and rode through Dodge, round-
ing up every person who dared open a door or walk the streets. Mr.
Pierce even persuaded the city and Ford County peace officers to help
bring crowds out to see Tom Griffin off to Glory.

Better than a thousand people packed the Union Church and
crowded several blocks around to hear the sky pilot say a few words and
the choir sing a couple nice hymns. Then—I served as a pallbearer—we
walked Tom Griffin, the old coffin we had bought in Spanish Fort replaced by a beautiful one that the undertaker swore would last a century, to Prairie Grove Cemetery, and I'll be damned if the mourners
didn't follow us there.

Trailing the pallbearers and coffin, Mr. Pierce led a riderless black
horse, one boot placed backward in the stirrup, and a whore, dressed in
white except for a black armband, carried that yipping little puppy dog,
Blue Ben II, in her arms.

With ropes, we lowered Tom Griffin's oak casket into the grave,
tossed some wildflowers on it, and stepped back to hear Abel Head
Pierce address the crowd and, after thirteen years, make his peace with
Tom Griffin.

Or so I thought.

Well, like I said, if you've ever met Abel Head Pierce, you know he's a
hard man, and not always fair-minded. Honest, certainly, but in forty-
odd years I've never known him to own up to a mistake. The closest he
ever came to admitting he was wrong happened at Prairie Grove Cemetery in Dodge City, Kansas, in July of 1884, but instead of apologizing,
instead of praising Tom Griffin, he kept his eulogy short.

"Ladies and gentlemen," he said in that abrasive voice, "we're here to
bury Tom Griffin, a drover my segundo, Jack Street, hired for some
damned reason. Because, Christ a'mighty, this dumb son of a bitch that

we're burying didn't have brains enough to stay in his damned saddle. Instead of trying to save my cattle, hell, he figured to spare the life of this stupid mongrel. It cost him his life, and me fifteen horses, twenty-one head of prime beef, a hoodlum wagon, chuckwagon, and four extra days at Red River Crossing. One thousand, three hundred, twenty-two damned dollars, and seventeen cents, Lord a'mighty. Tom Griffin, you ignorant bastard, rot in Hell. Now let's all head over to the Long Branch for a morning bracer. Amen."

SAY WHAT YOU will about Mr. Pierce—likely, I have heard it already—and while he is contrary, abrasive, and ruthless, I think there was more to that eulogy than slander and sacrilege. The Dodge City newspapers all ran front-page articles about Tom Griffin's funeral—proclaiming it bigger even than Marshal Ed Masterson's back in '78—although none printed any of Mr. Pierce's salty language, and that story spread all across Kansas, even on to Missouri and down in Texas. What's more, fourteen years have passed, but you'll still find folks from Dodge to San Antonio who remember Tom Griffin, not as a run-down drunk, but as a cowboy who died under the hoofs. Maybe they don't know what happened in 1871, a lot of them laugh about Mr. Pierce's graveside tirade, but mostly they recall that Tom Griffin gave his life for a dog, which sets pretty high among most folks. His marble tombstone still stands at Prairie Grove Cemetery, and the epitaph "Here Lies A Cowhand"—on Mr. Pierce's dime, though he'll never say so—hasn't faded, which is more than you can say about most drovers' graves. Old trail hands still tell big windies about Tom Griffin, and that's something you can attribute to Abel Head Pierce.

He didn't apologize, not exactly, but that's as close as you'll ever hear one whispered from Mr. Pierce's lips.

Come Back

RICHARD CASS

Richard Cass was born in Boston, Massachusetts, and graduated from Boston Latin School, Colby College, and the MFA program at the University of New Hampshire. He lived in New England until 1993, when he moved to Oregon.

His short fiction has been published in magazines such as Potomac Review *and* Gray's Sporting Journal *and has won prizes from Redbook, Playboy, and the Pacific Northwest Writers' Conference. He's grateful for all his teachers, including Thomas Williams, Jr., Ernest Hebert, Ursula K. Le Guin, and Molly Gloss.*

JOHN SANG SCHUBERT lieder to the dead salmon that passed on the slime line, but the cannery management in Juneau didn't favor self-expression. They didn't actually fire him—he was a good worker—until he muscled a fat chinook right off the moving rubber belt and tried to kiss it good-bye.

He wandered south after that, painting houses in the summer, drinking beer and carving birds in the winter, until he fetched up in West Beach. Linda, his on-again off-again wife, laughed when he decided to fish commercially.

"Better me than some hard-hearted Harry," he said. "At least they know I'll treat them right."

And fishing turned out to be what he was born to do. He trolled for salmon whenever and wherever it was legal, from southern Oregon up into British Columbia, and did well enough to pay off his boat. He built a cedar-shingled cabin far up the Nehalem River, almost high enough that the tides didn't draw.

After two years, Linda got tired of being alone so much and moved to Portland to live with a guy who cooked in a Cuban restaurant.

✵

ONE MORNING IN May, John trolled the turn of the tide, right outside Tillamook Bay. He looked east into the sun at precisely the moment a charter boat coming out over the bar met a big wave at the wrong angle and capsized.

He pulled in his gear and steered the *Bogart* toward the entrance to the bay. An explosion spewed clouds of black and orange into the air. Faint sorrowful songs started playing in his head.

By the time he arrived, eight or ten small boats were circling the site, mainly getting in each other's way. He stood off, upwind, where he could see the smoke and burning diesel, but couldn't smell it. He picked up the microphone.

"Albert? You there? Come back."

Across the oil slick, a lean and shirtless man stood up in a flat-bottomed skiff, holding it steady in the outgoing tide. Albert should have been inside the bar, crabbing and watching the tourists in his rentals. The two of them had fished together until Albert's second heart attack. John missed his slow spare voice over the radio on those night-sweeps offshore.

Albert raised his hand to his mouth, and his voice boomed out of John's radio speaker.

"One survivor. Lady deckhand." Albert spent his own words like money.

"Coast Guard?" The *Bogart*'s engine raced.

"On their way."

His oil pressure gauge was climbing, from idling so long, and John didn't want to add to the confusion by breaking down in the middle of all this. He backed the *Bogart* out of idle and rumbled away.

"Going to fuck the fishing, too," Albert said.

Under the stinking oil sheen, shards of fiberglass fluttered in the whirl and bubble of the disturbed ocean.

As if to prove him wrong, a ball of smelt flashed under the ocean's surface a few yards off.

Big king salmon slammed into the mass of bait, then cruised back through to gulp the dead and injured.

When his oil pressure dropped into the safe zone, he turned for home.

☼

ALBERT WAS RIGHT—the fishing was fucked for a while, though whether because the *Two-Step* had sunk, John couldn't say. He'd seen it happen before, not the sinking, but that inexplicable shift in the bite: it was on, it was off. There was nothing you could do about it, and no one to blame.

He sailed the *Bogart* up into the Queen Charlotte Islands for a while to keep busy, and his luck began to run. He landed 4,500 pounds of salmon in a little over a month, and returned to West Beach on the third of July, for a rest.

The Fourth of July was the beach town's signature holiday. It drew thousands from all over the Northwest, like flies to meat. The seven miles of sand beach seethed day and night with crowds and bonfires, barking dogs, greasy kerosene torches, drunks, and howling children. Being in it was painful—even being nearby was annoying. John usually took the *Bogart* out beyond the breakers in the afternoon and stayed to watch the fireworks.

The morning of the fourth, he tied up to the end of a finger pier at Love Marina. Sitting on the *Bogart*'s fantail in a plastic-mesh lawn chair, he felt the sun try to burn through the offshore clouds. A rap on the hull brought him out of a daydream.

"Captain Stevens?"

His mouth tasted like he'd been sleeping. He could just see the top of her head. "John's fine."

"Permission?"

"Sure."

She was thin as wire rope, her tanned arms stringy with muscle. She wore a tight navy T-shirt. A band of red webbing belted her jeans, and her deck shoes were black with grease, the right sole bound to the upper with duct tape. She climbed over the railing as if she'd done it all her life.

"I'm not selling any fish," he said. Sometimes tourists came down to the dock, expecting a bargain.

"Not buying any."

She looked around, and he saw her disapproval. He wasn't the neatest fisherman in the world, but everything was where he needed it.

"Kinda messy, init? I'm Gina."

"Mmm." His chair creaked.

"You fishing this week?"

"Not today," he said. "You know what you're doing?"

Every day he heard the commercial captains bitching because nobody wanted to work. If she was experienced, he knew three of them who'd take her on the spot.

"No one will hire me."

Then he knew who she was. "That's a great technique, insulting the guy you're asking for a job."

A flush rose up her neck, but she didn't look away. "Sorry."

"What happened?" He gestured south.

She crossed her arms and prepared to deliver the story.

He shook his head.

"Not the canned version. What you learned."

"Always wear a life jacket. Don't trust anyone but yourself. Everyone thinks I'm bad luck now—I wasn't running the boat."

He'd never needed a mate before.

"Trial run," he said. "Be here at four."

"You like doughnuts?"

GINA STEPPED ONTO the deck at five minutes of four, carrying a brand-new orange backpack and a flat waxed box. Her teeth were luminous in the dock lights.

"Krispy Kremes. Got them on the way to day care."

The nearest store was Beaverton, thirty miles away. Had she driven that far for doughnuts?

"There's a head down below," he said.

She tossed her backpack down the hatch and nodded.

"I want to try right outside the bar, first thing." He needed to know if she was going to be queasy. Most fishermen, the lucky ones anyway, survived more than one wreck in their working lives.

"You trust my luck?"

"I'm not superstitious that way."

They trolled within a quarter-mile of where the *Two-Step* had gone down, and she didn't react, except for one long stare into the depths.

When they tied up at the end of the day, Gina came aft and stood in front of him, fists on her hips. In the light mist, her oilskins showed creases from the package.

"That didn't go too well," she said.

He felt useless—if he could comfort a fish, he thought he ought to know how to reassure a human. She was a calm sailor, her movements precise and economical—her presence in the boat had lighted his day in a way he was afraid to look at too closely. He counted out some bills and handed them to her.

She shook her head. "We didn't catch shit."

"You worked. We said it was a trial run."

She started to protest, but he cut her short.

"Tomorrow," he said. "Same time. No doughnuts."

THEY FISHED EVERY day for a week before he conceded to himself that it really didn't work. She was perfectly competent, but too worried about pleasing him. They didn't catch anywhere near what he would have caught by himself. As much as he liked having her around, he had to let her go.

Friday afternoon, he paid her off, then offered her a lawn chair and a beer. He expected her to refuse, as she had all week, but she must have known that he wanted to tell her something. She sat down, stretched out her legs, and popped the can.

"It's not working," she said. "We're like two different-sized gears."

"The work's getting done." He wasn't sure why he wanted to argue.

"Except we're not catching fish. I appreciate the chance, John. I do."

"But?"

"I'm better at the social fishing. Helping the sports bait up and reel 'em in. I like being needed."

"We are who we are."

She bent the empty can in half and worked it back and forth. "I ap preciate your taking a chance. It made a difference—I got a spot on Larry Karpen's boat."

John stared at his can. Larry Karpen was a slob; he didn't take care of his boats.

"You've met him?" he asked. "You've seen the boat?"

"Got to climb back on somehow, John. I'm not going to hairdresser school at this point in my life."

"I think about getting off the water all the time," he said.

Her face softened. She picked up the backpack.

"You're full of crap," she said. "You'd mold up on land, green as a tree."

She kissed him full on the mouth, tasting like salt and soap and iron. But she pulled back quickly.

"I'll be fine," she said. "The Coast Guard's on everyone now. Karpen won't get away with anything."

"Tight nets, then," he said.

"Lines, John. We're fishing different methods now. Tight lines."

BY OCTOBER, JOHN was over missing her.

Then, one Saturday, while he was sitting at the same pier where Gina first came aboard the *Bogart,* Albert climbed on board, holding a cigar box full of currency. "One of Karpen's albacore boats went down. Yesterday morning."

"Everyone?"

Albert nodded. No one in West Beach had missed John's hiring Gina.

"Insurance on the deckhands—we're collecting for her baby," Albert said. "Little girl, one and a half."

John opened his wallet, dumped all the bills in the box, and started to unknot his lines.

GOING OUT OVER the bar, it was nearly dead calm. On the far side, he throttled back and drifted.

He latched the wheel on course, due west. The sun was dropping into the cold blue water. A faint song, bright as stars and silver-skinned, drifted out from behind the shoulder of Neahkhanie Mountain— someone up there was having a party. He couldn't hear the tune clearly enough to identify, but it sounded like old rock'n'roll.

He climbed up onto the *Bogart*'s rail, a can of beer in one hand, and peed into the kelp as it slipped under the keel. He thought for an instant about stepping off the rail, into the forty fathoms of sea, where Gina lived now.

His VHS radio coughed to life.

"John? John Stevens," Albert said. "You out there? Come back."

Once a Cowboy

MAX EVANS

Max Evans was raised on two different ranches, his father's and one owned by his widowed aunt, which he helped run. At age eleven he went to work on Ed Young's Rafter EY on Glorieta Mesa south of Santa Fe. By the time he was fourteen he was drawing regular cowboy wages and in all he spent seven years on the Rafter EY or being loaned by Young to many neighboring ranches as everyone did during the Depression. In a story too long to tell here, Max got his own ranch over in the northeast corner of New Mexico in what he calls the Hi-Lo Country. He ran that operation for eight years and also did day labor for big ranches all around him. Then he became a successful professional painter and metamorphosed into a writer. He has written twenty-eight books, including The Rounders *and* The Hi-Lo Country*, both of which were made into major movies, and* Bluefeather Fellini*, which he considers his masterpiece. He now lives in Albuquerque, New Mexico.*

YOU NEVER QUITE get to know anyone—anyone at all. Most especially how they'll end up. Even if you've been through decades of bar, car, and horse wrecks, like I had with ol' Rusty Carver.

I see him now as I ride this damn forest line fence that's been kicked down in places by newcomers. They drive their gas-greedy SUVs up as far as possible, then walk the fence line on the U.S. Forest side, kicking weak posts loose so the boss's cows can get out and cause weeks of hard riding to gather. Some we never find.

My mind's image of ol' Rusty was clear as spring water. He was mounting a green horse. He could just barely reach the stirrup. But he cheeked the bridle and swung his body in the saddle, smooth and easy, riding out circling the round pole corral, getting the feel of how the horse moved, how he reined, ready for him to buck if he thought he had to.

As I dream-watched ol' Rusty, I thought of how different we looked. He was about five-eight and had so much hard, round muscle that he didn't seem to have—or need—any bones in his body. Well, except for his hands. The bones sure showed big there.

Everyone in our country dreaded shaking hands with him. He didn't know it, but he was a hand-crusher.

His nose was broken from tree limbs that horses had run him into—and other things, such as rocks, fists, and a skillet his longtime girlfriend Shirley Mae had swatted him with.

He had a round scar on one side of his belly and one on his back where a Nazi sniper had shot him during World War II. I reckon he'd healed up fine because he never said a word about it in all the years I knew him. Not one damned word.

Now me, Roy Barrett, I was six-foot-two of bones tied together with beef jerky. My nose had never been broken, but it did bend over about a half-inch to the south from the cartilage being torn loose. I can't recall how it happened, except I was having fun getting drunk.

It wasn't hard to remember most things we'd shared, but some I couldn't call up any closer than a coyote howling in the next county.

I sure remember, and my spine still feels the time I roped the seven-year-old outlawed steer around the neck and he jumped off in an arroyo, jerking me and my horse over the side, where we all fell in a pile. The horse got up before I did, and the steer as well. They both tried to run in different directions. Ordinarily, that would have been natural, except I was in between them with the rope wound around my middle. I felt like I was one of those poor people that magicians put in a box and then drop the blade down, cutting them smack dab in half. Luckily, I was still in one piece, except my waist was pulled down to about thirteen inches.

Now, I reached out and grabbed the rope on each side of me. No matter how hard I pulled, I couldn't get any slack in the rope with a thousand-pound horse tied hard and fast to one end and a thousand-pound steer on the other.

That makes an even ton.

Ol' Rusty had been following on a good bay cow horse, his rope down to heel up the steer if I was unlucky enough to catch the wild shit-splattering son of a bitch.

Well, my eyeballs were being pushed out of my head by all my insides that had been shoved upward from the rope around my middle. I saw things in a blur, but here's how it went when I double-checked it later.

Ol' Rusty's double eagle eyes—and brains faster than a war room computer—saw my entire problem in a glance. He spurred right along the bank of the arroyo and threw his loop over the steer's head, jerking him down hard. He bailed off the bay and flew through the air like a red-tailed hawk, landing rolling in the bottom of the arroyo not unlike a big round rock, and got up pulling his pocket knife out, opening the blade, and cutting the ropes in two, right where they were tightened against the addled steer's neck as he stumbled up to his feet.

Rusty yelled, "Hold the rope that holds your horse," being an efficient cowboy and rescue squad all at once.

I had been doing this with one hand all along, but now I could use two. The well-trained cow horse turned, looking down from the rope where it was tied to the horn like he was supposed to do.

The world was flat full of blurs. One went by me going south.

The steer had charged my savior with his head down some. Our luck just kept on running, and so did the big steer. One horn had gone on one side of Rusty and one on the other. He was trying to shove my best friend toward—and possibly through—the far side of the arroyo bank, but Rusty was knocked down, and all the steer did was step on him with two of his four feet, ripping the back of his shirt for about a foot and removing only a six-inch strip of hide—Rusty's hide, not the steer's.

I want everything clear here.

I also found out later—as we so often do in this puzzling life—that I had a wide belt all the way around my waist that was also missing hide—my hide, not the steer's.

It's a good thing we'd been working in a sandy part of the arroyo or we might have gotten hurt.

When old Rusty got up and looked things over, he said with a good deal of seriousness, "We're gonna have to ride back to headquarters and get some more ropes."

He was twenty years older than me and had been a mentor for longer than that, so I just nodded my head yes, thinking the fifteen-mile ride back over rocky hills, one rocky mountain and four rocky canyons would be good exercise for both men and beasts. It surely was.

RUSTY CARVER HAD saved my life and other little particles so many times I pretty near cried as I looked back on the long years with him. I would have wept a keg-full all right, except the smiling and the giggling got in the way. As a fair example, the long weekend trip we made to the wonderful little hamlet of Hillsboro, New Mexico, and then on over to El Paso would do.

Now, Hillsboro is in the eastern foothills of the Black Range, where the great Apache warriors Victorio, Nana, and Lozen fought to a standstill two thousand U.S. cavalrymen and infantry as well as about six hundred civilian militia. Me and ol' Rusty have worked cattle over every damn battlefield in their wild history. There was big gold and silver booms there and all sorts of other history, too wonderful for me to remember right now.

A feller just naturally favors a place where he has a good time. I would have liked it if I'd spent half my time in jail. You see . . . Hillsboro is a one-bar, two-church town. My favorite kind. You can get in a lot of sinning and saving all in one little place. These little wonderful havens were the foundation, the cement, and glue of the entire West at one time. Now the *New West* has made them scarce as picnics in a dust storm.

Hillsboro's one great bar, the S-Bar-X, is named after a cow brand. They hardly ever ran out of whiskey, even though I can honestly say that a couple of times the miners, cowboys, artists, and other wastrels have had them down to less than three bottles. I actually witnessed the time they ran plumb out of beer. Some people got real cranky and had little nervous fits.

Hillsboro has two good restaurants most of the time, one gas station, one motel and a museum or two, art galleries, and antique stores. It was a good place to drink and dance, you see. Ol' Hoss Hogan had a little band that played weekends at the S-Bar-X. He tried to dress like a cowboy, but you could still tell he was a fix-it-upper repairman on the side. However, by nine o'clock at night, he sounded like Guy Lombardo, Patsy Cline, and Hank Thompson all at once.

Shirley Mae taught first grade over at the county seat—Hot Springs. And she was there waiting for us. She was built a little like Rusty, except for her milk glands. They were a half-gallon apiece. But she had a kind and pretty face framed in thick brown, curly hair that made her big brown eyes seem to shine like little headlights.

My girl, Cindi, tended bar right here where the fun-havin' people were gathering. She was kinda tall and skinny like me, except for her butt. It was wider than her shoulders. Before I ever dated her, a local miner showed his appreciation for beauty by saying a sort of dumb thing: "When Cindi walks, her butt looks like two corn-fed pigs in a gunny sack." Even so, it was enough of a compliment to make me take notice. Careful notice.

Well, we got us a table and got down to drinking. I hope some of the young will also remember how valuable it is to have a girlfriend for a bartender. The drinks seem to heavy up a bit. The band was playing, most everybody was dancing and things got louder and louder. Friday night in the high desert makes more than the coyotes howl. It smelled real good—full of spilled drinks, lung-killing smoke, sweaty citizens, and other noisy-scented things.

Now Rusty dances slow with his shoulders all bunched up as if he was afraid his head was gonna fall off, and he looked down at his and Shirley Mae's feet like he was afraid they were gonna cripple one another. Suddenly he stopped, raised his head up, and howled, trying to really get the sound through the ceiling to the moon outside.

It must have worked because every one in the S-Bar-X caught the howling disease. Hoss Hogan and his Good Boys—that's the name of the band—played louder to be sure they were heard, and the place turned into a yelling, drinking, dancing heaven. There wasn't but one fight that night, and it was outside. People were having so much fun, they didn't even bother to go watch. Now, that's having fun in anybody's town.

Cindi started trying to get everybody out by closing time, which is two o'clock in the morning in New Mexico. By three, there wasn't anybody left but the four of us.

Since it was too near sunup to go to sleep, I said, "Cindi, you got tomorrow off. Hellsfire, let's head down to El Paso."

Rusty jumped in, his little tiny eyes opening wide enough so you could see they were dishwater blue: "That's the best thing I've heard since cattle was a dollar a pound." I couldn't recall when that was, but the girls seemed willing. Cindi had a purse full of tips and got us a bottle of bourbon to keep us awake till we got to the great Del Norte Hotel in El Paso, Texas.

Shirley Mae drove her Ford until we rolled into Las Cruces, where she got sleepy. Rusty took a drink out of the bottle—big one—and decided he'd drive so we'd all be safe for the upcoming adventures in the great Del Norte.

We were on the outskirts of El Paso at daylight when a siren caused me to take both my hands off Cindi and quiver like I'd been shot in the butt with a flaming arrow. Rusty pulled over after the cop drove alongside for about a mile, making mad pull-over signs. He got out seeming somewhat irritated and asked Rusty for his driver's license.

He didn't have one that he could find. He said, "Shirley's got one. Let me have it, hon."

The cop said, "That won't quite work, sir."

"Oh," said Rusty.

"What is your name, sir?"

"All I can remember right now is Rusty."

"OK, uh-huh, OK. Mister Rusty, did you know you were speeding?"

"Speedin'?"

"Yes, sir, ninety miles an hour in a fifty-five-mile zone."

Rusty grinned real appealing-like and bragged: "Sure, I knew it. I was trying to get home before I got drunk."

The cop didn't know what to say for a minute. I didn't know what to say for a minute, but Shirley Mae evidently did. She got out of the car, moved around the back, smiling so sweet you'd think she'd just swallowed a chocolate bar, and motioned the red-faced cop to her. They talked, and they talked some more.

The cop got back in his patrol car. Shirley Mae got back in her car on the driver's side. As ol' Rusty scooted over, he asked, "What did you tell him?"

"Just what I told you the first night we met."

Rusty damn near wrinkled all the hide off his forehead trying to remember what it was she'd said.

Sure enough, we made it through the city of El Paso to the great Del Norte Hotel right at full service, sunup. I emptied Cindi's bottle so it wouldn't evaporate in the upcoming heat of the Mexican border.

WE SLEPT UNTIL midafternoon and had a good breakfast of *huevos rancheros* in the coffee shop along with a couple of nice bloody Marys with our coffee.

By eight that night, the great round bar was full of visitors mostly enjoying themselves. There were local businessmen, gold and mercury smugglers, ranchers, oil lease men from farther east in West Texas, and even a few plain old working cowboys like me and Rusty.

The tables and booths in the large lounge were mostly full, and a mariachi band was tuning up. So were we four. The air was full of fun and action. Nobody noticed the deadly cigarette smoke in those days. Just goes to show you how easy even the brightest of people are to brainwash. Course, in our own bunch, we only had one genius, and that was Shirley Mae.

I know it's hard to believe, but things got better. The mariachis were strolling and playing. Some people left the famous circular bar, so big that you had to have a hunter's eye to see all around it, but others filled their empty places as fast as popcorn farts. The table next to the bar emptied, and that sharp-eyed Shirley Mae moved and claimed it for us. Now we were set comfortable with a good view of the whole wonderful place.

We had no more than got our second wonderful drink than that crazy Rusty Carver said to me, "Hey, Roy, let's go over to Juarez, where things are really wide open." The rest of us were silent, staring at him like he was a rabid skunk. That ain't a pretty sight to stare at.

Then Shirley Mae broke the crushing silence, sweetly: "Now, Rusty, dear, Juarez is certainly a freewheeling place, a place to let loose, especially for men. However, I don't feel we should crowd our luck driving any more while drinking."

Rusty meekly said: "It ain't but a half a mile. We could walk."

Since Rusty realized there wasn't a single certainty in what he'd just said, he got up and danced with Shirley Mae. I did the same with Cindi. We were snuggling while we moved, and I couldn't see a single hard rock anywhere on the dance floor. Everything was sure keen. We just got mellow as cherry Jell-O, and everything we said broke us up laughing. Everybody at our table was a goddamned comic and had an audience sitting there who knew how to appreciate those flint-edged quips and showed it. Fun. Fun. I tell the cockeyed world.

I said something like, "You know, if we got up in the morning and there wasn't a single chicken left in the world, there would be panic in the streets."

Of course, I was simply observing, seriously, how everybody was going crazy over the fried chicken joints just beginning to sprout up all over the country. Well, not all over. Hillsboro doesn't have one. Anyway, this just rocked everybody back. Cindi was laughing so dang hard she had to put her head down on the table. Shirley Mae was so full of mirth, she was holding her stomach with both hands and had her eyes closed so tight they were squirting out tears. Ol' Rusty was leaning over, slapping at his knees, about to fall out of the saddle. These two big ol' college football players came over to get our girls to dance. That was fine, but the girls didn't want to. And the young men were so impolite as to insist before the girls could stop laughing. After the third "no thank you," one of them pulled Cindi half up, spouting off, "Ah, come on, Slim. It'll do you good."

I don't know what it was that caused me to stand up. Maybe it was him calling Cindi "Slim" before he'd had a chance to see that wonderful big butt. Maybe it was the crude, macho way he butted in. I don't know. Hell, I just stood up in resentment and was knocked down before I could say more than, "Didn't you hear the . . ."

I was a little dizzy, but I rolled away fast to escape the kicks I expected to follow, and even that was too slow.

Ol' Rusty took a shortcut right across the table, spilling a few drinks and breaking a few glasses. That wasn't nothing compared to what he did to the invaders. Rusty was very limited as a bar fighter. He just had two punches. That great big bony hand-crushing left to the belly or ribs and then a sort of overhand right to the cheekbone.

Down the big kid went, flat as a penny on the pavement, and still as a mummy's ass.

There was no way his companion wanted to enter this sudden competition. But being good at competition was how he was getting through Texas Western University. Besides, what was worse, people were watching to see what he would do.

Whup. Whap. And he joined his friend on the ballroom floor. However, he moved a little bit, and Rusty went down and whapped him on the side of the jaw. Rusty was always a true gentleman, and this last proved it. He could have kicked him instead.

There were evidently folks present who didn't understand loyalty and protecting the hearth and all that.

The El Paso jail for drunks and derelicts was underground in those days. That's where we all spent the night—safe from atomic bomb attacks. Since I had only received and not delivered a punch, this detention was puzzling. Also, when the law arrived we were all trying to explain that we were the pickees, not the pickers. If Cindi and I had shut up and let Shirley Mae do her trick talking, all the trouble to follow could have been avoided. There's no use saying more about the jail. Hell, most everyone who experiences it once decides not to let it happen again. Ever.

The courtroom was full of hangovers. There were other kinds of criminals, of course, but we were with the majority for one of the few times in our lives.

Our turn came. Cindi, Shirley Mae, and me, ol' Roy Barrett, were fined for resisting arrest, drunkenness in a public place and three hundred dollars in broken glass. We paid up. Even so, I was puzzled by how four whiskey glasses and a cheap little ash tray could mount up to three hundred dollars. Maybe they were imported crystal and I'd been having too much fun to notice.

Then there stood Rusty before the judge, his hat held in front of his chest with his head down like he was praying. I knew better. He was being tried for assault. He was straining his brain matter trying to keep straight all the things Shirley Mae had told him, such as: "Now, dear, don't be afraid. I know this judge. My uncle helped him get appointed, and he's an art lover."

Rusty's little pig eyes opened up so you could tell he heard. "An art lover?" he said.

"That's right, he collects from Tom Lea, José Cisneros, and all kinds of fine artists. He even thinks he's an artist himself. Half the basements and closets in El Paso hide at least one of his paintings." She went on to close the deal out: "Now, you have no doubt noticed how he asked every defendant what their occupation was. Well, when he does that, you tell him you're an artist and he'll be easier on you."

Rusty stared and stared. This was asking a bit much for a hard-rock cowboy and efficient bar-room brawler to actually admit in public that he was an artist.

It was finally Rusty's turn to be questioned.

"And Mister Rusty Carver, what is your occupation?"

Rusty choked. He turned his hat in his hands. I thought the tough old son of a bitch was gonna fall dead as year-old dung right there.

"Well?" Judge Chavez asked.

"Your honor, sir, I'm an artist."

The judge relaxed back in his chair, his hands locked together across his chest, and beamed kindly down on our dear desperate friend.

"I'm a portrait artist, your honor, sir."

"Oh, a portrait artist, huh. Are you good?"

"Well, I s'pose I am."

"Modesty in an artist is very rare, my son. I'd bet you are very good."

"I sure hope you win your bet, your honor, sir."

Cindi and I were hopeful. Shirley Mae was just swelling with pride.

Judge Chavez paused, his nostrils flaring. "Do you think you'd have time to paint me?"

Political machinery was running through the judge's head. I could see it. The thought of a free portrait was perhaps turning the wheels of justice.

"Well, your honor, sir, I'm out of art supplies right now."

The judge leaned forward with serious intent, his pen poised above a blank paper and said, "Well, son, give me a list and we'll see what we can do about that."

My God. We all breathed. It looked like it had worked. Then, *then*, my dearest friend and Shirley Mae's closest loving friend said, "Well, let's see, your honor, sir. If I had a broom and a bucket of fresh shit I believe I could get an exact likeness."

The entire courtroom gasped and stared up and down and even sideways as the judge turned that shade of purple you see in mountain crevices as the sun sets in the peaceful West. There was no doubt in my mind that my very best friend was going to be sentenced to hang until he was that same shade of purple.

Shirley Mae became a heroine of the first order as she charged past the guard and the judge's all-around man and pulled the judge's head next to her whispering mouth.

He shook his head at first, still dangerously purple. Then he lessened to red and then to his natural, nice olive. Now he was healthy again and occasionally shook his head in agreement to whatever in the hell Shirley Mae was saying. Then she smilingly glared at us with kind assurance and I for one felt safe and warm.

The judge, amidst slight confusion, calmly dismissed Rusty's case for lack of evidence. There were a few protestations, but simply lifting his manicured hand, palm out, was enough to bring a welcome silence.

We finally followed Rusty's wishes and went to Juarez, and Rusty asked Shirley Mae to marry him. Like the feller said, "In those days you could do anything in Juarez you were big enough to do and still pay for." Nowadays, of course, you've got the dope smugglers instead of the gold smugglers. But there's a big difference here. It takes many mean and greedy bastards to get the dope for the dopers. It takes good miners to get the gold for the smugglers. Yeah, I miss the miners. Miners ain't nothing but cowboys who can't ride.

We had one hell of a fun time in Juarez, Mexico, before heading back to the Hillsboro country. As I think back on ol' Rusty now, he wasn't near as dumb as some people might think. The first thing he did when he escaped hanging was marry Shirley Mae. That's what I call plumb wise and wonderful.

It was about impossible to figure how a man that smart could suffer such a terrible blow later. You can't build any final forts against the future no matter what the experts tell you.

SHIRLEY MAE AND Rusty pitched in their savings, mostly hers, and made a good down payment on a little white-painted, five-room frame house in Hillsboro. He went on working with me on the Ladder Ranch and she continued teaching first grade in Hot Springs. They soon had one cute little daughter, Mary Anne, and another in the chute. A family had been cemented. On weekends in the spring and summer he helped her patch up the place real good and make a good garden of tomatoes, corn, green beans, and most important of all, chile. And every winter he killed a deer to round out the bounty.

The best I'd done was finally get engaged to the new bartender at the S-Bar-X. Cindi had run off to Tucson, Arizona, with a used car dealer. She'd been fun.

However, my new—and I hoped forever—love had been raised on a ranch until her father lost the place when she was eighteen years old. She was still pissed about that, blaming the U.S. Forest Service, the Bureau of Land Management, and above all the "Do-Gooders." She just said it once so as not to be a whiner. "Five generations of us fighting droughts, blizzards, cow disease, low prices and now, where bear, cows, and antelope roamed there's a bunch of trashy trailer houses and the water's turned sour as cat shit."

I never did know all of it. What I did know was Susie Lou was a strange but good looker. She had auburn hair worn in a ponytail and oddly enough, considering the red showing in her hair, eyes as black as Geronimo's. She walked back and forth around that S-Bar-X bar like she owned it. She had everything that makes up a young woman a man would want to spend his old age with, moving smooth as water in an irrigation ditch. The mother ditch.

She laughed at all the silly things us humans do and at the same time she could get tough and mean as a badger if you got out of line smart-assing. She also got along great with Rusty and Shirley Mae. That just about cinched it.

I didn't have anywhere to put her on the Ladder, and I hadn't got up the guts to mention it. So when I heard about those forty-eight horses a feller wanted to get rid of over near Hatch, I got ol' Rusty to go with me and take a look.

The man had a combination farm and cow ranch most commonly called a stock farm. The man who owned the horses was over northeast, a ways from Mountainair, and said his name was Tom Nothing, but most everyone called him Nothing Tom. Well, we walked around the corral and looked over Nothing's forty-eight horses. They were every color from bays to paints and every shape and condition from bony to fat.

"What do you want for 'em?" I asked.

"Hell," he said, "I don't know. A couple of 'em ate a little loco weed. The effects ain't shown up yet, but who knows? Huh."

I couldn't give him an answer.

"Some of them is a little green and some of them has been rode hard with a lot of living with dried sweat," he added.

"What do you want for 'em?"

"Some of them has been kid ponies and one or two has been bucked out in rodeos."

I was beginning to show signs of irritation. Even Rusty had taken his five-inch-brim greasy old Stetson off and was scratching his thick-haired gray head.

"For the last time, how much do you want?"

"What you got to trade?"

"Well, let's see, we got ten bred heifers between us that the Ladder lets us run for free."

I looked at Rusty and he looked at me. Then we both looked way off across the desert mesa only a half mile to the west waiting the fatal answer.

"They in good shape?" Tom Nothing asked.

"Yeah," I said.

"Yeah. It's a trade if you deliver them right here," he said.

It was done.

Then we did what all cowboys have to do on their own at least once in their lives. We quit the Ladder, where we had hard but good jobs, and went in business for ourselves.

We owned one good cowhorse apiece and the rigging that goes with 'em. Rusty's cousin over at Hot Springs had two pack mules we borrowed. We used most of the little savings we had and with the hesitant blessings of Shirley Mae and Suzie Lou, headed out across country. We were now cowboy entrepreneurs and aimed to come home in a few weeks with lots of money and other goods to make our women happy and secure. I aimed dead on to ask Suzie Lou for her hand and everything else tied to it.

We headed north along the Rio Grande at first, then angled off northeast later. We had decided to ride a different horse each day and that way we could be testing while we were trading. It didn't take long to realize these horses had spent more time on loco weed than it first appeared. If a tree limb touched them on the head, some of the horses would just fall down and wrap around the tree. We couldn't get them up. So we'd have to tie a rope on their feet and drag them away and then tail them up like a dying cow. It was turning into the damnedest mess a feller ever saw.

I was riding a good-looking sorrel, plumb shiny, and every time he'd see a shadow from a fence post or a tree, it didn't matter, he'd drop his head down and examine it carefully, then jump just as high and far as he could. That sure slowed things down. It wasn't quite so bad if you weren't riding them. Some of them would suddenly see a cow trail and just jump straight up and fall down on it. Sometimes more than once. But the ones that got my total attention were the ones that would lift their heads to a sudden breeze that had blown across a waterhole way off somewhere. They'd run around in circles, their heads down, until they found a sink place or a bare patch and just stop and drink. That invisible water must have tasted pretty good cause they'd switch their tails and walk away acting satisfied with all that dusty air they'd swallowed. One really did smell water at a farmer's water trough and just fell into it. He must have got water in his lungs. He died. One mare went up to an arroyo bluff and just walked off it, hitting her head and breaking her neck. She didn't hardly kick before she was still forever.

We lost four head before we sort of got the know-how to sort of handle them.

We made our first trade on the fifth day out. A small rancher needed a gentle horse for his kids. Rusty really surprised me. He was a genuinely good liar.

"That little sorrel mare there was ridden by my brothers' kids over at Las Cruces all the time," he said. "Hell, his three-year-old rode her in a Fourth of July parade."

"Well, I'm gonna take your word for it, but this little bay here is a mite too spooky for my kids."

We made the trade and the man had told the truth, mostly. Spooky was not the right word, however. That sucker bucked so hard, Rusty had to run into him three different times with his own good horse to keep me from being thrown hard.

When the new horse finally stopped, I told Rusty: "We made a hell of a good trade there. We'll swap this bastard to a rodeo stock contractor. This is the kind of buckin' stock they're prayin' to find."

"Yeah," the great liar said.

The very next ranchhouse we came upon was about five miles westerly. The feller took a liking to another sorrel mare we had.

"How old is she?"

Rusty ran up right quick, pushed her lip back, and said: "She shows to be a coming five." Rusty had always been good at teething a horse's age, but now he was also fast, and all those natural muscles stopped folks from doubting his word.

Rusty went on and said: "Why, three of my little nieces and nephews rode this horse to school at the same time down at Nutt." Now, Nutt, New Mexico, is famous for being nothing but a bar between Hatch and Deming. There sure as hell ain't no school there.

We traded that fourteen-year-old sorrel mare for a bull with one nut. That was fine with me. We might have to eat the half-loaded critter to keep going on our trail of riches.

After a trade was done and the handshake made, we'd hear bragging through their laughter such as, "That ol' horse is spavined."

"That ol' horse has been foundered and has a bad ankle to boot."

We heard our victims spout such things as: "That milk cow ain't had a calf in three years. You couldn't get a drop of milk out of her with an oilfield suction pump. Ha ha ha."

We got to having a lot of fun out of this. It's always a good thing because the joke was just as much on us as them. Oh, it went on and on for weeks. 'Course, what these gloating local traders didn't know was this: as soon as we were out of hearing, we nearly fell off our own crazy horses laughing about the shadow-jumping, air-drinking trick horse they now owned.

We weren't gaining much yet, but we knew now we didn't have much to lose, if anything. In the fun department, we were many rocky miles ahead. All this fun puzzles and pains even more when you know what happened to old Rusty later on.

We tried to camp out one night and count up. We had a hundred and seven-dollar gain in the cash department. Some few cattle, bulls, cows and heifers of various colors and conditions. Sixteen new horses—some lame one way or another and four or five that were working real good. We had about half our loco'ed stock left to trade. 'Course, they were the craziest of the forty-eight.

When we were trading after three o'clock in the afternoon, we stalled by teething, checking out every joint on the horse, cow, or whatever was on the docket. Rusty and I held endless sidebar conferences and then about sundown we'd make the trade. We'd shake hands in the old-fashioned way that used to hold water better than the tightest contracts you can get now.

Invariably, the traders would ask us to stay for supper and the night. The feed was always better than the crackers and sardines we'd gotten down to.

We had trouble every night, though, when people were so generous. You see, we had so many trading tales to discuss that it was impolite to just bust a gut laughing at midnight or after. Not only that, it would wake up and scare hell out of our host and hostess thinking they had a couple of real nuts in their place. Well?

We spent a lot of evenings planning what we were going to get our women with our profits. Rusty wanted to buy the lot next door so Shirley Mae could have room to raise the flowers she loved so much as well as the vegetable garden they both cultivated. I was heavy on getting

a little house like Rusty's and a diamond ring for that special finger on
Suzie Lou's hand.

"Hellsfire," I told Rusty. "I may just buy the S-Bar-X for her."

"Well, by damn," he said. "That's what I call a wedding present."

Over by Mountainair in the rolling hill and mesa country, we acci-
dentally ran onto a bootlegger. He was friendly from the start, knowing
that if we were any form of the law, we would not have the sad mixture
of stock we had.

He was holding a really good thirty-thirty Winchester. I could tell
Rusty really wanted it for a deer rifle. His old .30-.40 Krag was about
done in.

So we settled for a little tradin' talk over some of the best corn-made
white lightning I ever tasted. Damn, we sure had fun. We stayed three
days. Old Jake finally got drunk enough on his own concoction that we
traded him a beautiful pinto mare that didn't go crazy but every other
day—this was her day off—for the Winchester and three crock jugs of
homemade whiskey.

Then we got the hell out of there.

Old Jake would have a hangover next day—the day that paint mare
was scheduled to go crazy and kick at shadows, sunlight, cedar trees,
barn doors, or humans.

When we got to Mountainair we traded another kid horse for a good-
looking cow and calf to a feller just west of town. Damned if it wasn't a
good old pony. He had six kids, and they all took turns riding him,
happy as a fried chicken dinner with biscuits and gravy.

And that's exactly what we had for lunch. Mister Hawkins insisted on
us dining so luxuriously on his wife's cooking. We tried to appear reluctant but damn near knocked one another down getting to the table. We
did give him a couple of drinks from ol' Jake's jugs. And we all ate. With
the kids and his wife and a visiting sister and her two kids, there were
too many to count.

After three cups of coffee and some killer tobacco, Mister Hawkins
said, "I can tell you fellers been tradin' loco'ed horses and I counted 'em
perty close in your"—he hesitated before he said it—"remuda. I was a
horse trader for thirty years. That's how I traded for this fine place here.
There's a twenty-acre pasture right out there. I suggest you put all the lo-
cos in there, and we'll turn the rest of your stuff"—yeah, he called our

walking goods "stuff"—"and I'll pass the word around and we'll see what happens. If you get rid of them, you can just give me whatever you like. Loco'ed horses sometimes get over it in a few years, sometimes minutes. But there's a little shortage of *using* horses right now."

Rusty pitched right in at this: "They've all been rode several times. We did it ourselves."

"Well, well, well," he said, increasing the volume each time. "That means they'll show better than I thought."

Mister Hawkins's trading blood was beginning to fire. It took about two weeks, and that was fine with us. Mrs. Hawkins seemed to have an unlimited amount of chickens to fry, and she could cook biscuits and gravy that would make a heroin addict quit cold for just one serving. And that ain't much of an exaggeration.

The horses behaved and reined out pretty good most of the time. There was one day when a skinny ol' gray stud tried to mount the hood of a man's new pickup, and another time a little chestnut mare we'd traded for lit out in a dead run. She did a full circle in the pasture, slid to a stop and turned around and retraced the whole thing, her ears laid back and her beautiful chocolate mane and tail streaming out in the sunlight.

Now this would have been a beautiful sight to a circus horse trainer, but to a bunch of ranchers, cowboys and part-time farmers, this was a puzzle. It didn't puzzle me. We'd traded one loco'ed horse for another. However, when she slid to a stop and looked around, spotting the little gathering, she stood right in front of Rusty.

He smiled as if he knew everything in the world, reached out and patted her on the forehead, saying softly, sickeningly, "My little darling, just like I trained you. Thank you for the fine show." He eased a loop over her head, and a bean farmer bought her for his wife for an astounding forty dollars.

It was time to go home. We were traded out. We had to settle up with Hawkins. He was smarter half asleep than both of us at our best, so we had to cheat a little to even the odds. We took the last gallon of ol' Jake's whiskey and just kept toasting such things as "to the hospitality of the Hawkins family . . . to the beautiful Hawkins children . . . to the best fried chicken in the world . . . to new friends and old memories." If we hadn't had to put Hawkins to bed, we'd have gone on all day and far into the night. As it was, we watched while Mrs. Hawkins threw a cover over him. Rusty asked her if she had an envelope. She did. He stuffed some bills in it, licked and sealed it and placed it on the fireplace mantle. Mrs. Hawkins smiled knowingly. We saddled our own horses—the two we'd left home with—and got the pack mules ready. We gathered our new horses, cows, bulls, and heifers up and headed out across country as far off any trail as we could. We were aiming in the general direction of Hillsboro, way off southwesterly.

A FEW DAYS later, tired, hungry, and with the sardine diarrhea, we stopped, looking down from a hill above our town. We were on the far eastern edge of the Sterling Roberts ranch, I think. We counted up our money. We had six hundred twelve dollars and seventeen cents to split up.

There were twenty-six horses, none of them loco'ed where you could tell by looking, but a lot of them limping. There were nine milk cows, from Holsteins to Jerseys and a couple of brindles. Some of them had even given milk at one time. We had four cold bulls, one hot one and another with one nut, three burros, two mules, and a Rolf collie dog who was about to have pups. Of course, Rusty had his Winchester.

The only thing we could figure out was the split on the money and we had figured hard. Before even facing our beautiful women, we gathered the little courage and energy we had left and pushed this bunch of livestock up the road north past Jimmy Bason's F-Cross Ranch and way on up into the U.S. Forest land of the Black Range, opened a gate and drove them scattered out in the vast Gila Wilderness. We'd lied so long on the trading trail that we now lied to ourselves about how all our livestock would heal and fatten up and then we'd gather them and hold a big sale. What few the lions, bears, and coyotes would miss couldn't be penned in that huge and wild country with a dozen top cowboys and that was about all there was left in the whole of Sierra County. The Rolf collie bitch would turn into a fair cowdog. Shirley Mae fell in love with her, though, and we never got to use her much.

We mounted up, leading the two pack mules. After having spent two days near Hillsboro, we finally headed straight for the S-Bar-X bar. It was all downhill right to the front porch. Then two steps up and four more to the door. We'd made it.

IT WAS A Thursday. Shirley Mae would be home from Hot Springs for the weekend on Friday night. So we had time to sip a few drinks and talk over our next move. Suzie Lou evidently had a day off, so we sat at a table and relaxed.

No matter how we figured, that three hundred odd dollars we each had pocketed wasn't going to last long, and it sure as hell wasn't going to put us in business for ourselves. Before we could admit we were going to have to go back to cowboying, Ginger, the relief bartender came over and handed me an envelope. She turned around and whipped up to get away from our table before I could ask her about it. I unfolded the letter. It was from Suzie Lou. My eyes blurred over as I read it. The gist of it was that she loved me but didn't see any future for her in Hillsboro, and she didn't see any for me anywhere else.

I wanted to yell out about the lonely beauty of the whole damn surrounding country and the fun a fella could have if he worked it right, but all I did was say to my best friend, "Suzie Lou left the country."

Rusty just said, "Awww, shit. What did she do that for?" with disappointment showing on his old broad, busted face.

I don't care what people say, when this happens you get shook up. There was a rock in my throat I couldn't have washed away with a barrel of beer.

Ol' Rusty and ol' Roy were sure surprised when Art Evans, the foreman of the Ladder, told us the boss knew we'd be back and had just hired a couple of gunzels (phony cowboys) to help out until we returned.

Art was a hell of a good cowboy and a fine feller, but he had to issue the orders the big owner gave. Our first punishment was building a mile and a half of fence in solid rock. We got blisters bigger than silver dollars digging those post holes with regular hand diggers and a heavy steel bar. We finally had to use dynamite on most of the post holes.

Then we were exiled to Farber Camp, a powerful forty miles from nowhere. There were a hell of a lot of cows in the Farber pasture to be checked out and a count made.

We pulled six good horses over with the Ford pickup and a six-horse trailer the boss had bought from a broke racetrack runner.

Farber Camp held a pretty fair three-room shack that had actually been painted twenty years back, and it had recently been left vacant by a cowboy and his wife who took off for Montana. Art Evans told us that they had left some grub there, as was customary. He said there was enough for a month.

There was plenty of pinto beans and sowbelly and a starter of sourdough bread. There was also a rare luxury—three boxes of Post Toasties.

The next morning for breakfast I poured us out a big bowl each of the corn flakes. Rusty had our thick bacon ready, but I was still scrounging around looking for some canned milk to eat them with. I looked everywhere but the outhouse. There was no cockeyed canned milk. Rusty seemed a little disappointed, but I was half mad.

"Rusty," I said with much conviction. "We are surrounded by big pastures. These pastures are grazing over seven hundred head of mother cows. All those mamas who have calves have milk."

"Let's saddle our horses," he wisely added.

We rode a long way. It was a nice feeling, though. All we wanted was one cow to give us enough milk for the breakfast of delicious Post Toasties. We'd eaten the sowbelly before we left. A good thing.

The Ladder had over two hundred thousand acres of mostly rough rocky land, but good grass for the cows and brush of all kinds to feed the numberless deer, elk, bear, mountain lions, coyotes, foxes, wild turkeys, and even quail in the lower flatlands. As we rode along side by side, our heads down looking for cow sign, as cowboys do their entire lives, we saw the tracks of most of these wild critters. Then I pulled up and stared a minute across mesas, breast-shaped foothills, and smaller rolling hills where you could find great meadows. I looked all the way across the Black Range, dark bluing the lighter blue of the sky, and into the mighty Gila Wilderness. No, I didn't feel small in this vastness. I *knew* that. I just felt at home. Just like old Nana and his little tiny surviving tribe had felt and fought so damn well to save what I so easily viewed.

We saw a lot of cows, but in widely scattered bunches. Most of them had been sucked dry by their calves. Finally we found the cow we were looking for. She and about ten more head of mothers were returning from a drink at a spring down below. She was the only one that had a full bag. The other cows were flabby-bagged, and the reason why was their calves were with them. It was obvious this big old cow had a late calf, and she'd hid it while she went for water.

We were taking down our ropes, angling off so she wouldn't booger, waiting till they hit the open meadow just up ahead.

Now, me and ol' Rusty had made a lot of little punkin' roller rodeos around the country, trying out bull-doggin',' bronc riding, and calf roping, but about the only thing we'd ever won much at was wild cow milking. Whichever one of us got position first roped the horns. If you caught the neck, it choked them and made a cow mad and harder to mug. Rusty usually mugged because he was a lot stronger than me.

I had brought along an oversize Coke bottle to get our breakfast milk in.

We pulled our hats down over our eyes.

The little bunch of cows hit the opening. We spurred after them. Damned if that old sorrel horse didn't put me just right to fit a loop around her neck just as she hit the brush. Rusty bailed off his horse and was fighting tree limbs and brushy entanglements to get to her head and mug her, so I could squeeze a teat or two and get us a Coke bottle full of milk.

Now several things had already gone to hell and back twice. Not only had I caught her around the neck instead of the horns, but deep next to her chest. Now she could get mad without hardly choking. She did that. She was bellering and bawling in bass. And she ran through the thickest skin-plowing bushes she could find. There were millions of them bushes. Old Rusty was hanging onto her horns with a hand on each, but she was flinging him up and then down. She was dragging him a spell, then turning back and stepping all over his legs with hard, sharp, fast-moving hoofs. Skin ripped off, but Rusty held. I was running after them through that same hide-loving brush. Every now and then I'd stick my head in her flank, grab a teat with one hand and try to squeeze milk in the small opening of the big Coke bottle.

I mostly missed it because of the thrashing about. My cowhorse was trying his best to hold the rope tight, but she twisted and turned so many different ways it was impossible. I must have had about an inch of cloudy milk in the bottle when she got loose bowels. Of course, she was swinging her tail all the time, hitting me all over, but especially in the face. So now, with the added weight on her tail she whopped me across both eyes and I damn near went blind. I was forced to wipe the brown-green stuff out of my eyes, and it made the bottle slick and harder to hold, and some of it was getting into the milk. Course, I was too busy at the time to know it. Then, too, there was a little blood from my scratched face mixed with the cow shit and then into our breakfast milk.

The second time she whapped me across the face with that dirty old tail, I not only went blind; I got mad.

I was calling her names I usually reserved for child molesters, wife beaters, crooked politicians, and road ragers. I used all these expert names and more when I fell down under her and she kicked me in the side of the head. I was thinking maybe she'd kicked my left ear off, but I knew damn well she'd ripped at least half my hat brim loose because it was flopping in my face.

After several years passed in about fifteen minutes, I had the bottle three-quarters full of dark-colored milk.

I yelled, "We got the milk, we got the milk! Rusty, hang on till I get my horse."

He yelled back, "There ain't nothing left to hang on with but my arms. The rest of me is in pieces in the bushes."

I sympathized as I got on my horse with my thumb over the bottle top to save every drop of the precious liquid. It was difficult to believe, but it happened: We hit a little opening, Rusty plowed his worn-out heels in the ground and stopped the old cow. She was getting kind of worn out, herself. I spurred my horse up, loosening the rope. Rusty jerked the loop wide and off over the cow's head. By God, we'd done it!

The cow took off bellering in the direction of her calf. Rusty was standing in the way. One horn grazed a trail on the outside of his rib cage and several hundred pounds of cow knocked him rolling.

He lay still. The cow tore more brush apart vanishing in broad daylight. I got down carefully, so as not to spill our milk, and went over to see if Rusty was dead. My knees buckled and I sat right down by him. With my free hand I tried to roll him over faceup. It worked. He sat straight up.

"You got milk?" he said.

I proudly held the bottle out where he could see.

"That there looks like chocolate milk," he said.

"Now ain't that something," I said. "A cow that gives chocolate milk."

He stared at me so hard I got scared.

"Something is wrong with your hat," he said.

Before I could move, he reached out and jerked my hat brim. It all came off. I was wearing a little cap with no bill. What a feeling of inadequacy for a working cowboy. Terrible. By gollies, I got home with the funny-colored milk. The sun had been coming mostly straight down on my face. I didn't know it until about sundown, but I was burned red as a woodpecker's head. My cap that had once been a hat didn't do the job.

And I'm ashamed to admit that my best friend Rusty refused to let me pour the milk on his Post Toasties. I had strained it several times through a dish towel into a little pitcher, but he kept saying there was cow shit in it and always would be. He poured water and a spoon of sugar on his cornflakes and ate them with no expression of appreciation on his face at all.

Of course, one has to make allowances in special situations. Rusty's face looked like it had been pounded for an hour with a steak softener and had barb-wire dragged across it until the barbs wore off. His shirt and even his Levis were ripped and skinned from the cow's front feet and the strangling brush. There was just no way you could foresee the tough old bastard's futile future.

Anyway, I had strained that milk over and over through clean dish-towels until the chocolate had turned plain gray. That was the best I was ever going to do for my Post Toasties milk. And by doggies, I want the world to know that I poured half that little pitcher of semi-chocolate milk on my cereal and ate every damn flake and spooned what was left out of the bowl, making the most gluttonous sounds. As everyone says, a man has got to do what has to be done, and I'm still here to tell about it.

The second day of actually working cattle for the benefit of the Ladder outfit, we were riding along with our heads down looking for fresh cow sign. Without even looking up, Rusty said, "You look just like a rabbi on horseback with that little skull cap."

I didn't hesitate. I reined my horse around, rode to camp, and drove all the way to Hot Springs to buy me a new hat. I couldn't go to headquarters for the spare hat I had there. I'd have to explain to the other cowboys forever. My face was red as a monkey's ass in every way.

THE OWNER FINALLY let us go back working under Art Evans, and the Hillsboro world moved on and on with cattle prices going up and way down like always. A few miners grubbed enough gold from the hard hills to keep their bodies and dreams barely alive. Some of the artists who had drifted here stayed, but most, like the world around, moved on to other little colonies, then still others. But there was an amalgamated core community here that was both solid and bizarre.

A big movie star bought a half-serious, half-play ranch over across

the state border in southeastern Arizona and Rusty got the job as foreman with Art Evans's recommendation. It seemed far away, but actually
it was only a half-day's drive. So Rusty got back to Hillsboro to be with
Shirley Mae about twice a month. This raise in pay, combined with his
mate's teaching wages, allowed them to raise their two daughters perty
good. The girls were just one year apart and were both running straight
A's in high school. That meant college scholarships would come if the
grades held up, and they did.

I kept looking for another Suzie Lou, wondering how many chances
at such a woman a cowboy's God would grant. I hated to quit the Ladder
outfit, but I had the itch to hunt for something I hadn't found, whatever
the hell that was.

I worked up near Hi Lo in the northeastern part of the state for a few
years. Here I was catty-cornered completely at the other end of the state
from where I'd come. It's really good cattle country, but old Jim Ed Love,
who owned the J L outfit, was so cockeyed unpredictable I finally had to
pull out of there to keep from throwing a rock or something at him.
One minute he was sweet-talking you into doing twice the amount of
justified work and the next second he was sweet-talking you and meant
it. Course, that was his way of keeping us dumb-ass cowboys confused
and doing what he wanted.

I worked up there for several years—on three different outfits—and
still had the same saddle and maybe a hundred fifty dollars more money
than I'd had the day I left the Hillsboro country. I told ol' Wrangler Lewis
and Dusty Jones who had worked for Jim Ed most of their lives, "This
cowboyin' has got me stiffened up all over, but the one place that
counts."

Dusty said, "Me, too."

Then he looked way off at the sky for bird migrations and sadly went
on, "However, I sometimes wish my dinger was as stiff as my neck."

That was too much truth for me to handle. A week later I quit the Hi
Lo Country and started working dude ranches in Wyoming and Colorado. The dudes were only there in the summertime, and these dude
outfits kept their play cattle in the barns in the winter. I didn't have to go
out in sixty-mile-an-hour blizzards and feed freezing cattle with a freezing cowboy riding a freezing hay wagon. Why in hell hadn't I figured
this out before my temples turned gray?

It was easier work for sure. There was more women available, as well as more whiskey. Some of these women, even rich women, seemed to like me, but even if I could have put up with holding my hand out behind me with my palm up, I never seemed to be able to hook up with one that suited. I sure fought my head to do it, though, but the money didn't make them anywhere near Suzie Lou.

Cowboys, unfortunately, aren't much on writing letters. Me and ol' Rusty mailed about one a year for awhile, then none. Shirley Mae wrote me three or four times a year, no matter what. The girls were going to graduate from New Mexico State University on the same day this year. Time flies faster than falcons. Before Art Evans and his wife retired, he got ol' Rusty a sort of easy horse wrangling job on the Ladder. I went back and thought I'd finish up with Rusty there. Twenty years' age difference isn't so much when one of you is twenty-five and the other is forty-five, but now it was like a thousand years.

The first thing I noticed was certain crazy things we'd done in our youth had gone missing in Rusty's head. He covered up real quick by answering, "Well, yeah, whatever" and such like.

Shirley Mae had been retired for five years and with Rusty's faltering help had their little place in town pretty shiny. She was sure wanting Rusty to retire with her, but for plain working cowboys, there was no such thing as retirement pay. Finally, Ralph Moon, the new foreman, had to let him go. Shirley was sure happy to have him home, even if he was getting a little forgetful a mite more than most. Rusty had gone to wrangle the horses every now and then without his pants on. And once he'd even gone out barefooted and no shirt. 'Course, he never forgot his hat.

A famous TV mogul and his movie star wife—at the time—bought the Ladder and were turning the whole damn thing into a buffalo ranch. That is right. Over two hundred thousand acres of buffalo. I don't have anything against buffalo. I just wasn't raised to work them. I was goin' crazier than I was natural born. That is crazy. I had to go.

Then, luck finally hit me right between the horns. A Texas oil man had bought a play-pretty ranch a few miles southerly from town and to everyone's surprise, his wife, Dottie Eastman, took to it and went and started raising and breeding Arabian horses like she'd been born to it. She wouldn't hardly ever go back to his Midland, Texas, headquarters with him.

One day, he had a hunting party of longtime, rich friends driving and climbing around after elk. Carl Eastman fired on a big five-by-six and just as the elk fell, so did he, both deader than a bleached cow skull.

I went over one week later. I sat in that big fancy kitchen and had coffee with that big fancy woman, stayed all day and stayed all night, and had me a top-paying job helping raise and train them Arab horses on this big fancy ranch before the sun came up that next morning.

A week after I'd been employed on the Dottie outfit, she took some meat out of the freezer and cooked us up the best damn elk steak I ever tasted. I was sure enjoying life like never before. I silently thanked old Carl Eastman for being such a good shot.

'Course, my tires was flattened a little every time I visited Rusty and Shirley Mae. He was always so happy to see me that he'd forget and crush my hand. He might be old and getting soft everywhere else, but those damn hands could still turn a chunk of steel into baking powder. But it was getting damn near impossible to talk about the old days and great times we'd shared. He would remember a snatch or so, then his eyes would go to a place unknown. Finally, it hurt my heart so bad, I told Dottie this would be the last time I could take watching him disappear like that. To her credit, she said, pushing at her dyed red hair, with those wonderful fifty-year-old blue eyes wide as a baby's, "No, darling. You have to see it through. He would, for you."

She was right, of course, and at that moment, I realized I had finally moved up from Suzie Lou.

When I got to their house and parked the pickup, I knew something was wrong. There wasn't anybody in the house and their dog was gone. Ol' Rusty had just wandered off out of town, walking across the foothills west toward the F-Cross Ranch and the Ladder on beyond. With the help of their little mongrel dog, Buckshot, Shirley Mae and several more citizens found him. I met them walking back into the edge of the one and only main drag of Hillsboro. Shirley Mae was holding his hand, leading him slowly along with the little black and white dog by their side. The rest of the town folks walked respectfully behind.

When she saw me, she smiled a tiny bit and said, "Buckshot trailed him . . . or I might never . . ."

I took his other hand and tried to visit on the way back to the house.

"That old bay horse is hiding in the outhouse," I told him. That's all. He didn't even know I was there or anywhere else as far as that goes.

It got worse almost daily now. One of their daughters lived in Portland with her husband and two grade-school kids. The other one was divorced in San Diego, working at a computer firm trying to support three stair-step boys alone.

They managed at great hardship to come for a couple of days, each a month apart. About all they could do was clean everything up and cook several meals ahead and put them in the freezer. Then they had to get to El Paso and take flights back home and hold their worlds together there. That's just the way of it.

I brought up to Shirley Mae about putting him in a good permanent care home in Las Cruces. I'd checked it out myself. Shirley Mae finally said "no" for the last time. "Not while I can move." A month later, she fell dead, just wore out. The girls came. The cowboys from all around came. Most of the town of Hillsboro came. We buried her up on the windy hill where all cow-mining towns have their graveyards. The wind blew like hell.

The daughters dressed Rusty up in a suit he'd only worn twice in twenty years. One held his hand on one side, her sister did the same on the other. He smiled and said something unintelligible every now and then.

Some black yearling steers with white faces lined up along the fence, all in a row, staring at the people at the cemetery. A red-tailed hawk shot down out of the huge sky, screamed once and whirred off out of sight over the hills.

We all went down to the S-Bar-X and got a little drunk telling great stories on and about Rusty's wonderful wife. The girls stayed home with their dad, and the next day, Dottie and I went with them to Las Cruces and got all the papers done to keep him there. I told them, "Don't let the nature of things ruin your families. Just come when it's really possible—not impossible. I'll go see him every week. All we need to know is how he's treated. He doesn't recognize any of us anymore."

They took off to the El Paso airport, and I drove me and Dottie back to the ranch.

Dottie and I went to visit him once a week. I could sit there and tell stories about all the cowboy wrecks, all the drinking, all the rodeoing, and more, for a while. Then his not hearing, not knowing, began to wear on me. I told Dottie not to come with me anymore. It was doing more harm than good. They kept him clean, but his pajamas were hanging on his bones where all those muscles used to be. He looked backward into his head, seeing nothing in front. I don't think he weighed a hundred pounds.

Then I started falling behind on my visits. I only went twice a month now, and feeling guilty about it. I hadn't been to see my best friend in a month. But somehow this day I felt better. I didn't dread it so much. Maybe looking at the varied landscape around the ghost town of Lake Valley caused this. It sure was beautiful with all the odd shaped little canyons and valleys that you come upon like a surprise present. The golden fall grass was up a foot high. It looked like patches of ripe wheat on the rolling hills, and what cattle I spotted were fat.

Just before I got to the three or four buildings on the left of the road, I could see a great grouping of those breast-shaped hills that were scattered all over this country. To the left, near the road, was the opening to the old Bridal Veil Mine that once had silver ore so rich you couldn't even blast it properly. They had run a rail line into the mine and backed the cars in, cutting the silver loose with double handsaws, dropping it directly into the ore cars.

On around past the three or four buildings, all on the left side of the road, if you looked carefully up on the right-hand hill, you could see another windy graveyard. A little distance on from there was Skeleton Canyon, where Victorio, Nana, and the great female warrior and medicine woman, Lozen, had lured a bunch of drunken miners and soldiers into a destructive ambush.

I wondered why I'd never really looked at all the detailed beauty and history here before. I decided right there that folks go all the way through their little lives and miss seeing the things that matter most.

LATELY, I'D GONE into Las Cruces on Saturday to miss the Sunday obligatory rush to these places of the old and the stricken. I was stopped at a red light near the university when I saw something that would make an old-timer pray for total darkness. The last few years, I'd noticed cell phones grafted on most folks' ears. A man stood there holding one in each hand, talking first into one, then the other, so fast it appeared he was watching tennis. By God, I couldn't wait to report this sighting to Rusty.

I'd usually arrive just before lunchtime and push Rusty in a wheelchair to the dining room to eat. Well, he had to be fed by the nurses, by hand, so I did that, too, when I was there. The only thing in his room was pictures of Shirley Mae and his daughters hanging just above the table by his bed. About a year earlier, I'd fixed a place to hang his best hat below the pictures. I was a little early for lunch, so I started off talking about the fun we'd had on our wonderful loco horse-trading trip. There in the wheelchair, he never even moved. He was gone way off in another world that didn't belong to me, yet.

Just the same, I went on about him tradin' a good-looking loco'ed horse for an even better-looking outlaw. I reminded ol' Rusty about what he'd said: "All right, it's a deal if you'll throw in a paid-up doctor bill with the horse."

It was time. I got hold of the wheelchair to take him to lunch. Suddenly he started whining and trying to turn his head. It wasn't a complaining whine—just a desperate one, a solid little cry from long ago. I thought he might hurt his neck straining back. And one fist—the bones still big, the only thing left on him that wasn't shriveled to mostly nothing—reached out for the wall. I was puzzled. But then without a thought I took his big old Stetson hat from the wall, placing it on his head as near as possible to the way he'd worn it all his life. Rusty's whining stopped instantly. He put both his hands back in his lap, leaning forward some as if he wanted his horse to move out.

I pushed him through the halls of smells you never forget. The old. The dying. The urine. We rolled on into the dining room. A couple of the service ladies who recognized me waved. There were others at his table. Some were awkwardly feeding themselves. Others were spoon-fed by impatient employees.

I pulled an empty chair over by Rusty, intending to place his hat on it. To my astonishment, he beat me to it. He set the hat upside down so as not to tilt the brim out of its natural line. Then Rusty settled down in the wheelchair, not moving anything but his mouth as I scooped the soft food into what seemed to me an untasting, unfeeling body. Afterward, I wiped his mouth and chin carefully and replaced the hat properly on his head at the exact right angle, and I pushed him back to his room.

I sat on the bed where the side bars had been dropped. Then I took his long bony hands in mine. I looked as hard as I could straight into his eyes. I strained. Nothing. Absolutely nothing.

Just as I was standing up, I thought I felt the tiniest squeeze from each of his once-powerful hands. But I got nothing else from any part of him. He had gone to the place beyond the planets. I got up and left. I knew I'd never see him again.

BACK OUT IN Lake Valley, I drove leisurely along enjoying the wonderful land all over again. Then I remembered that a large fifth-generation rancher had been unable to hold it together with all the bureaucratic conditions put on his lovely land. Impossibilities had descended from many sources. He either had to sell it or lose it, thereby becoming an old worn-out pauper.

Suddenly I saw the first development house going up on the fresh-torn earth. How had I missed it on the drive down this morning? How? Then I knew. I'd just on this very day learned to see without looking down at the ground for animal tracks.

A lost sadness covered me, and penetrated inside, seizing every particle of my being. Then I was no longer here. I was worse off than Rusty. Then from somewhere I realized he would never know about the residences and residents to come. He would never have to bear seeing this special landscape smothered with dwellings or know that the deer, the cattle, the coyotes, and the mountain lions would soon be gone to that other place he now inhabited.

My eyes blurred with wetness so thick I could hardly see the road. I wiped them with my shirt sleeve as clean as I could. At just that second I looked back visualizing both sides so gleefully thinking we'd skunked one another when actually we'd broken even, unknowingly trading one loco'ed horse for another. Then I smiled just before I laughed out loud so hard I damn near ran off the road and had another wreck.

Snow Cave

PETE FROMM

Pete Fromm is the unprecedented four-time winner of the prestigious Pacific Northwest Booksellers Association Award for Book of the Year. His work includes How All This Started, Dry Rain, Indian Creek Chronicles, *and, most recently,* As Cool As I Am.

Pete Fromm lives with his family in Great Falls, Montana.

HIS SON'S TEETH had stopped chattering, and Carl said, "I bet hunter safety never touched on this. Not even close. You and me, bud, we're sailing uncharted waters."

Colton remained silent.

Carl waited in the darkness, but then couldn't help himself. He flicked on the flashlight, pointing it at the ceiling, careful not to light his face from underneath, the old Halloween spook. This was scary enough as it was.

They were lying on their sides, the silvery sheet of the space blanket only inches below the slick, icy, hard roof of the snow cave. Only a casket, Carl thought, could be gloomier. Or colder. "Snug as a couple of bugs, aren't we?" Carl said.

"Dad. You should save the batteries. In case we need them later."

"Good thinking," Carl said. "Good thinking. And I know that." He made a show of sweeping the light around. "Just checking, doing a little housekeeping before we turn in." He sneaked a glance at Colton's face, gray with fear he hoped, not hypothermia. "How you doing, buddy?" he asked. "Really?"

Colton made himself smile. "Okay. Don't think I'll be getting that much sleep though."

Carl laughed like it was a great joke. The slimy, cramped cave held the sound close, leaving it so quiet afterward that their breathing sounded huge. "We're like grizzlies," Carl said. "Denning up."

"Just for a night though, Dad. Not the whole winter."

"Nope. Cozy as this is, I'm with you on that one." Then he asked, "You got the time?" Somehow he'd left his watch at home, part of the clutter on his dresser.

Colton wrestled with his coat sleeve, his mitten. "Seven fifteen," he said.

Exactly twelve hours since they'd left the car. Half that since it started snowing. Snowing like Carl had hardly seen in his thirty-four years. And definitely a first for Colton's twelve. Nice start to his hunting career. Just a day out, no need to check the weather.

"Dad," Colton said.

"What, bud?"

"The light."

"Oh, right." He twisted the head of the mini-Mag, plunging them back into the blackness Carl dreaded. Blackness thicker than any he'd ever imagined. Blackness you could float in. "Darker than the inside of a cow in here," he whispered.

Colton didn't answer.

"Dark as a pocket. Darker than a banker's heart." He was wracked by a bout of shivering. "Let me know, Col', if you start getting too cold."

"I'm too cold," Colton answered, then said, "Just kidding. I'm okay. I mean, I think we're going to be cold all night."

"You might be right," Carl admitted, letting the silence stretch before saying, "Colder than the balls of a brass monkey. Colder than a well digger's ass. Than a—"

"Dad," Colton interrupted. "'You don't have to do that. Cheer me up.'"

"Okay," Carl said.

Deepening his voice, Colton said, "'You know, if you guys would quit talking, you might even fall asleep tonight.'"

Carl tried to chuckle. "Got me there," he said. God, how many times had he said that? Standing at the boys' door, Colton and his younger brother, Jaydon, unable to shut it down for the night, the two of them thick as thieves, always plotting some new scheme or adventure.

Carl's throat tightened until he had to fight simply to remember how to breathe. He wanted to turn on the flashlight more than he'd wanted most things in his life. But Colton would warn him again about the batteries. Colton warning him. The twelve-year-old the dad.

He pictured Marie and Jaydon at home, what they must be going through. Well, not quite yet. Marie'd be watching the clock now, going through the motions with Jaydon, letting him watch a movie, microwaving him some popcorn, leaving her to concentrate on her worry. But there'd be no calls until ten or so, midnight maybe. Carl had stayed out too long often enough before to assure that. Now Marie would be more steamed than worried, ready to set into him for keeping Colton out so long. Especially in this weather.

Picturing them, the light of their home, the warmth, the plain ordinariness of another night there, the TV on, Marie folding laundry in front of it, the boys fighting against finishing their homework, Carl felt sure he'd suffocate.

He snapped on the flashlight. He gasped in a huge breath, as if it were light he breathed, not air.

He felt his son's hand touch his arm, stared down at it there, the heavy deer-hide mitten groping toward his hand. "Why don't you let me hold it, Dad?" Colton said. "Really, I'm all right. I'll use it less than you."

"I, I just wanted to make sure you had your hat on," Carl said.

"I do, Dad. 'You lose seventy-five percent of your heat through your head, you know.'"

Carl said, "Well, you do."

Colton found his father's hand, and worked his mitten into it, slipping around the mini-Mag's thin barrel. He reached forward with his other hand and wrestled the shoelace off of Carl's wrist and around his own.

"Strap the cord around your wrist. If we drop it, we could spend the rest of the night looking for it. Hell, it could freeze to the floor."

"Got it," Colton said, and watching him, Carl wanted to hug him like he hadn't since he was a toddler. But every movement brought more cold, more wet touches, and the cave was tight enough to make anything like a hug seem more like a stranglehold.

Colton twisted the light off, and Carl sucked in an involuntary gulp of air, as if he were submerging again, diving deeper than ever.

For a long time after, neither of them spoke. They sat huddled, listening to their own breathing, each other's.

"Be light in another twelve hours," Carl said, when he couldn't stand another second of the black quiet.

"We should try to sleep. 'You know, if you just fall asleep, we'll be there faster, we'll be there before you know it.'" Carl's strategy during any long car trip.

"You think you can sleep?" Carl asked.

"Can try."

"Okay. You take the first shift. I'll stand guard."

"Stand?"

"Lie, then. Lay. Whichever it is."

"Lie."

"Okay, smart boy."

They were quiet a long time, Carl feeling his son's every shiver. "You know, Dad, that always cracked us up. What you said about sleeping making the trip go faster. Like it was this secret time travel technique you'd discovered."

"Well, I—"

"We knew what you meant. It was just the way it sounded, you know? Sleeping making something faster."

Carl listened to Colton shift, the crackling of the branches beneath them. An elbow, or something, bumped him under the chin.

"You know what?" Colton went on. "Jaydon and I, we still call going to sleep dropping into warp drive. Like it will skip us over a bunch of hours. Get us straight to morning. Not waste a second. At warp speed, you know, like in *Star Trek*."

Carl shook his head, struggling to hold it together. "I get no respect," he said, but he was there in their bedroom with them, just two boys making fun of their dad, making up their own language, the darkness far from complete, the glow-in-the-dark stars on the ceiling, the gurgling hum of the fish tank, the old Superman poster dimly visible, the chains that had held him bursting apart, flying away from his chest.

"Okay," he said, speaking slowly, trying to maintain. "You drop into warp speed, buddy. I'll be right here."

"Warp drive, Dad."

"'Night, Colton."

"Don't let the bedbugs bite."

"The bedbugs' asses are frozen solid tonight."

"Mine, too."

And with that, like he'd always been able to do, except in the damn car on those long trips, Colton fell asleep. It seemed only seconds before

Carl heard his breathing slow, ease deeper. It'd be a cold day in hell, Carl thought, before he could sleep in this tomb. Then he half smiled. It was a cold day in hell already.

He promised himself he would not try to look at Colton's watch. He guessed it was maybe an hour before he inched his hand out, found Colton's mitten, slipped his own around it, barely moving, barely touching, not daring to do anything that might wake him. But touching him gave him strength, and he didn't try to inch back his sleeve to get at the watch. He didn't even think of the flashlight until he felt it. He just held his hand.

He thought back to the fire-building attempt before the snowcave, after smothering his panic, admitting they were completely turned around, a phrase Colton had corrected with one word. "Lost."

He carried matches in his pack, the ones he'd told Colton about when they'd packed, telling him he didn't have to take his own, even though he'd said, "Dad, in hunter safety they said everyone should always have their own gear. In case you get separated."

"It's your first hunt, Colton. I wouldn't miss a second of it for anything. We won't get separated."

"But—"

"Colton, I've been doing this since I was your age. I've got everything in my pack. It's always there."

He'd browbeaten him. Made him leave his stuff at home. Now, Carl couldn't remember what he'd been thinking. If.

The matches that he always carried were there, and they acted exactly as if they'd been there since he was twelve. The sulfur crumbled off when he tried to strike them. If anything, they fizzled for a second, nothing more than a quick glow, a wisp of smoke, only smelling like a real match. Colton hadn't said a word. Carl patted his pockets for a lighter, a book of paper matches. But he didn't smoke. There wasn't a chance of anything like that being there.

He'd ransacked his pack then, dropping his candle into the snow. Colton pawed after it, but Carl snapped, "Forget it. We'd have to *light* it."

He'd stopped then, his hand inside his pack. He pulled out the flashlight. The night was falling fast, hastened by the ungodly fall of snow, flakes as big as moths, hardly any air between them. He twisted the top, and a weak, yellow light seeped out. "Goddamn it," he whispered. He'd never once had to use any of this stuff.

Colton dug in his pocket, pulled out his own mini-Mag, brand-new, brand-new batteries. It shone like a searchlight.

"Good boy," Carl managed. "You don't have any matches in there, do you?"

Colton shook his head, still sparing him.

Carl pulled the small, silver crinkle of factory folded space blanket out of his pack. "I've got this," he said. "And two Power Bars. Probably eight or nine years old."

"The chewing will warm us up."

"Good boy," Carl said again. Without him, he knew he'd still be wrapped in panic, charging headlong through the snow until a tree brought him up short. "I don't have a shovel, or anything, but we should probably start thinking shelter before it gets any darker. I've got the bone saw. We could build a lean-to."

It was Colton who suggested a snow cave. It was something they'd talked about in hunter safety. With their arms and legs, their boots, they shoved snow together into as big a pile as they could, clumsily scraping down to something like bare ground, leaving an igloo-sized hump in the center of their clearing. They fell against it, packing it down, throwing on more. Then Colton dropped down and started burrowing into the side of the mound, scooping out their lair. "This is just like when Jaydon and I built that one on our deck," he said.

Carl took the snow he scraped out and built a tunnel entrance, thinking Colton simply didn't know enough yet to be afraid. The night inside that cave gaped before Carl like a black hole. Colton and his brother hadn't even thought to ask about sleeping in the snow cave they'd built on the porch.

By the time Colton said he thought the hole was big enough, they were both exhausted and the nightfall was complete. At least the cold was deep enough to mostly keep them from getting wet. By the last light of Carl's flashlight they cut boughs with the saw, for the floor. Colton crawled in with his flashlight on, calling to Carl when he had the branches spread. Carl wedged himself in after his son.

If anyone was going to be the hero of this, it would be Colton.

The space blanket was only really big enough for one. They pulled it over themselves, keeping off the touch of the roof, holding in some heat, maybe. Carl guessed you'd have to be wrapped inside it for it to do any real good.

❂

CARL WOKE TO Colton whispering, "Dad?" It was pitch-black, and for an instant Carl thought Colton was sick, had crossed the hallway to his and Marie's bed. "Dad," he said again, "It's really cold. Way colder."

Carl tried to sit up, the space blanket an icy sheet against his face. He bumped his head on the ceiling. "Dad," Colton said. "Wake up."

He was supposed to be, Carl remembered, standing guard. But Colton was right about the cold, he could feel that already. "What time is it?" he asked, wrapping his arms around himself as best he could, rubbing them up and down.

The flashlight came on like lightning, both of them ducking away, closing their eyes. Colton struggled with his coat sleeve and mitten, baring his wrist. "Three thirty, Dad. Three thirty in the morning."

Their breaths fogged the stale air, the space blanket's silver foil dulled heavy with frost.

"You don't have a thermometer on that thing, do you?"

Colton re-covered his wrist. He turned off the light. "I don't need one. I'm freezing."

"Me, too," Carl said.

They stayed still for a minute, freezing. Then Carl said, "You think we can move around enough until we're spooned? Without knocking this whole igloo down?"

"Spooned?"

Carl shivered. "Me wrapped around you. My front to your back. It's what me and your mom call it."

"Yeah. Okay. I think we can try. I think we need to."

They discussed the move, and then, turning the light back on, Colton swung his legs over Carl, Carl tugging at his coat, twisting him around. They knocked the space blanket completely off, wedging it into the base of the wall.

As they maneuvered, Carl worked his back to the door, keeping Colton as far from the outside air as possible. When he wrapped his body around Colton's he was shocked to find him trembling all over, shivering violently. "God, Col', why didn't you wake me up?"

"I did."

His face pressed against Colton's head, Carl could feel his son's teeth chattering. He bit his lips, ashamed that hours ago he'd thought things were as scary as they'd get. He struggled behind his back, searching for the space blanket, finally having to pull off a mitten and pull it up over them again, doing his best to spread it out without being able to lift his head to see what he was really doing. "Is that any better?" he asked. "You doing okay?" The sharp crinkling of the blanket drowned any answer Colton could have given.

Satisfied with the blanket, or giving up on getting it any better, Carl repeated his question.

"Yeah," Colton said. "It's a little better. How'd it get so cold?"

"I was sleeping on guard," Carl admitted.

"That didn't make it cold."

"No. I know. I fell asleep. It must have, I don't know. There wasn't anything like this on the weather."

"The weather was *wrong*?"

Carl wrapped his arm over Colton, hugging him. How could he possibly still be joking? How much did he not know about this kid, the depths his strength went to?

"You all set?" Colton asked.

"Set?" Carl said.

"For morning. The blanket I mean. Do we need the light anymore?"

"I, no, no, we don't need it. Go ahead."

The light went out. Carl continued to hug his boy. "I think I hate the dark more than the cold," he whispered, his mouth inches from Colton's ear.

"The dark isn't going to kill us," Colton said.

"Nothing's going to kill us, Col'. Don't worry about that. We're already ten hours through the dark. Another four hours, that's all. Then it'll be light enough to see and we'll figure out where we are and beat feet for the truck."

"How do we figure out where we are?"

"We'll see the dawn, the east, get our bearings that way. I know this place well enough. Mom'll have people out looking, too."

"What if it's still snowing like yesterday?"

"When was the last time you saw it snow like that for more than a day?"

"I've never seen it snow like that at all."

"Right. We'll be good. Even if it's still snowing, we'll be able to see enough to see which side of the sky gets light first."

"Okay," Colton said, more, it sounded to Carl, to stop talking than out of any kind of conviction.

Colton dozed a couple of times before seven, but not Carl. The cold was painful, his back tightening, his shoulders hunched until his muscles hurt enough to make him cry. But there was no moving possible, and even if there were, he wouldn't risk disturbing what rest Colton could get.

Between dozes, Colton checked his watch until finally he said, "Almost quarter to seven."

"Okay, buddy. I'm going to go out. I'm going to watch the sky, make sure we don't miss the dawn."

Colton said, "Okay."

"I'm going to wrap you up in the space blanket, all the way around you. I think that's the only way it really works."

"I got to pee, Dad. I got to go out, too."

"Okay." He forced himself to gasp out some sort of laugh. "I wish you hadn't said pee. Now I don't know if I'll make it in time."

Colton didn't try to laugh back.

Wriggling out of the tunnel, pushing out the almost solid plug of fresh powder, a stunning rush of crystalline air flooding around him, Carl started to crouch up too soon, breaking apart most of the tunnel against his back. He swore.

Colton, crawling up his rear, said only, "Just go."

Carl reached his feet, turned, and helped Colton straighten up, pulling on his coat and arms. Mittens in their teeth, they struggled through their clothes, fingers fighting buttons, zippers.

Finally, just in time, they peed into the darkness, only a foot or two from what was left of the cave entrance. Already Carl's fingers were useless. His nostrils stuck together with his first breath, and he panted through his mouth. Forty, he was guessing. Forty below. Without the wind. But no stars. How could it get that cold without clearing?

"Fuck," Colton stuttered, Carl able to hear the clatter of his teeth. "I peed all over myself."

"It's okay. No problem."

"For a second it felt good. Warm, you know."

Carl ached all over, but the cold wouldn't let him relax, even let his shoulders sag. "This cold, wind's got to be out of the north." The shivers made his voice shake. "I know the truck's east. The road. That way. It can't be more than a few miles. Four maybe, at the most."

"We can't walk in the dark."

With the light they could. Maybe. Keep the wind on their left. The goddamn wind. Carl couldn't tell if it was still snowing, or if the wind was stinging his cheek on its own. "You have the light?" he asked.

Its cone of light shot out, tiny outside the cave. "No snow," Carl said, the first bit of luck they'd had since leaving the truck.

Sweeping the beam around, Colton said, "Must've snowed another foot after we went in." Without a word, he sat down in the broken tunnel.

No tracks for any search party. They both knew that.

"Colton?"

"God, this wind," he said.

"Go back in," Carl said. "Wrap yourself in the space blanket like a burrito."

Without moving, Colton asked, "Can you feel your feet?"

"What?" Carl wriggled his toes. "Enough to know they're freezing."

"I can't feel mine. Not since we woke up that time. Got spoony."

"Mean they're numb? Tingly?"

"I mean they're not there."

"Half an hour, Col', we'll have daybreak. We'll get out of here."

Colton was already on his belly, slithering into the cave, disappearing. Carl sat in the tunnelway, as much a door as he could be. He listened to the harsh crackle of the blanket. "Wrap it tight as you can."

Colton didn't answer. It just went silent.

Half an hour later Carl saw the east lighten. He looked away, then back, the change subtle enough he thought it could be little more than hope. He turned that way, the wind, sure enough, scraping against his left cheek. "Got it," he shouted. He kicked a big arrow in the snow. "Colton, we're gone. I've got east."

Colton didn't answer and Carl fell to his knees, then his belly. It was dark enough yet that he had to feel for the entrance, only inches away. "Some light, Colton. Some light would help."

But then he found the tunnel and slithered in. Maybe it was the wind block, but it did feel warmer inside the cave. Carl felt around for Colton, the blanket snapping under his mittens. "Come on, Colton, wake up. Time to go."

Colton mumbled something and a few seconds later Carl found his hands, twisted the mini-Mag on, the room flashing brilliant. Colton had gotten himself mostly burritoed, though his feet stuck out of the bottom of the wrap.

"Colton, buddy, I found east. It's time to go. Let me give you a hand." He'd always been hard to get to bed, and just as hard to get out. Carl took off one of his own mittens and rubbed Colton's bare cheek with his bare hand. Neither felt warm.

"Colton," he said. "Colton?"

"I'm cold, Dad," he said.

"I know, buddy, me, too. But we're out of here now. It's time to go."

"I'm too tired."

"No, no. We'll get you moving. You'll warm up that way." Lying flat in the snow, Carl could barely raise up to his elbows. He pawed inside his coat for the last Power Bar. "Here," he said, tearing the foil with his teeth, biting off a corner of the rock-hard bar. "Eat this. Put it in your mouth. Suck on it like before. Until it gets soft."

"I'll eat later."

Carl shone the light straight into Colton's face. He barely flinched. The skin was past gray, a pasty white, drawn up tight over his cheeks, slack around the mouth. "We've got to get you moving, buddy," he said, trying to lift him by the shoulders.

But Colton was dead weight. Exhausted, Carl dropped his forehead down over his boy's chest. Through the space blanket, the wool and polypropylene, he heard the steady thump of his heart. For years he had carried Colton with him everywhere, on his shoulders in the grocery store, slung on a hip, or across his arm before that. He'd ride on his shoulders until his legs would fall asleep, the tinglies.

Without quite admitting that his boy was too big now for Carl to even dream of carrying, let alone stagger with through four miles of thigh-deep snow, Carl wriggled down to his son's legs and tucked his feet inside the space blanket, folding them in tight, his decision made for him.

Back at his head, Carl stroked Colton's cheek, waking him again. "Colton? Colton, buddy. I'm going to go for help. I have to go now. It shouldn't take more than a couple of hours. It's getting light outside. You won't be in the dark."

Colton nodded. "Okay, Daddy. I'll be okay."

Colton hadn't called him daddy in years. Carl leaned in and kissed his son's cheek. He pressed the Power Bar into his hand. "Keep eating. Eat it all. I'll leave the rifles. Fire a shot now and then, for the searchers to hear. I'll flag my way out. We'll be back home before you know it."

"Okay," Colton said. He was shivering again, which Carl hoped was a good sign. "Thanks, Dad."

"I'll run the whole way," he promised.

"Be careful," he said.

Carl kissed him once more, something he used to do every day. "You go ahead and leave that light on. You won't need it much longer. You don't need to save the batteries."

"I'll be okay."

"Okay. Don't worry. I'll be right back." He gave him what hug he could, and inched backward out of the tunnel.

Outside, Carl poked the rifle butts down the tunnel entrance, saying, "There you go," though Colton didn't answer. He wedged both their day-packs into the broken tunnel, making a door, but leaving enough room for a little air to make it in.

He stood, the wind cutting him instantly. "I'll be back," he shouted, so Colton could hear him through the snow. "Fast as I can."

And then, though his own feet were hardly more than wooden blocks, Carl began to run, toward the light, the wind at his left. He caught his breath every hundred yards or so, tying a piece of orange flagging to whatever branch looked obvious.

The snow was at least knee-deep, thigh-deep in places, and drifting now under the wind. Carl fell again and again, though it felt less like a fall than a simple tipping over. Each time he struggled up, tied another piece of flagging, checked the wind direction, pushed on. At one point he thought he heard a shot behind him, but he wasn't sure. He smiled anyway, picturing Colton back there, keeping his head, doing what had to be done.

By the time Carl reached the road he'd lost all sense of time. He felt like he'd been walking, stumbling, for hours. And now the logging road stretched blank and trackless before him, despite the searchers Marie must have sent out at daybreak. He stood on it, looking up, and then down. He tied the last of his flagging, a ten-foot streamer, to a brittle chokecherry branch overhanging the road. Everything was buried deep, blazingly white, all exactly the same. Up or down?

Biting his lip, nearly crying for the first time yet, Carl chose down. He pushed through the snow for what he guessed was two miles, before giving up, turning around, trying up. More than an hour later, maybe two, he passed his flagging. Snow began to ease down, nothing like yesterday, no worry about burying his trail.

WHEN THE SEARCHERS found him, Carl stopped, straining to hear what he could no longer hope were engines, even as the pair of huge trucks, chained up on all fours, plowing snow with their bumpers, their grills, chugged around the bend behind him.

Teetering, he let them roll up to him, their windows coming down. "You Carl Delman?"

Carl said, "What time is it?"

The man leaning out the passenger window said, "Almost four."

Carl staggered, said, "We made a snow cave. My boy's in there. Have you got him already?"

Radios crackled. The driver spoke into the mike, turning away from Carl. Men came from the other truck. Someone poured a cup of something hot from a thermos. Carl drank, couldn't tell if it was cocoa or coffee. "We found your flagging. Your trail," the man said.

Carl straightened. They were trying to get him into the truck, next to the heater. They hadn't answered him. "Have you got Colton yet?" He knew that if he started to get warm, even if he sat down, he might not be able to get moving again.

The men looked at each other, down at the snow. "We followed your trail. We saw *your* trail."

"Then we have to go. Right now. He's waiting."

The driver, the only one still in the truck, kept talking into his radio. The others kept working on Carl, trying to get him into the truck. They gave him a little Halloween-bag Snickers bar. "They're on their way there now," the driver said, leaning out the window. "The other half of the team. How far off the road?"

"Miles. Hours. We got to go, too. I do. He was getting awful cold."

Getting a promise of a ride to his last streamer of flagging, Carl let himself be talked into the pickup. He sat by the door, the heater burning his cheeks. They told him he'd only been about three hundred yards from his truck when he'd given up and turned back up the road. The driver muscled the truck around, a three-cornered turn with about seventeen corners.

The heater hadn't touched his feet before they lumbered back down to his trail. The men in both trucks insisted he wait, that he warm up, that he let the others bring his son out for him. Carl pushed his shoulder against the door, stumbled off up his own track, widened now and flattened by the team of searchers ahead of him. The other's had no choice but to fall into step behind him.

The trail now was like a highway, the other searchers half an hour ahead. Soon Carl was in the middle of the pack. The searchers turned on their headlamps. Not long now.

The radio on the driver's hip crackled, cleaving the steady swish of their legs in the snow, the deeper huffs of their breathing. The world beyond their headlamps was full black, the cold even more daunting in the darkness.

Without breaking stride, the driver keyed the mike strapped to the shoulder of this jacket. Carl couldn't make out the voice on the other end. Only the driver's voice, his quick, "The father's here with us."

There was something else from the other end, and the driver stopped. Drawn up against the cold, each wrapped in their own thoughts of home and warmth, the rest of the crew nearly piled into him. Carl looked up, saw one of his scraps of flagging caught and fluttering in the driver's headlamp.

"Sir," the driver said. Every eye on him, his face deer-bright in the glare of headlamps, the driver glanced to the ground, held his hand up like a shield. "Sir, they've reached your snow cave. They found your son."

Carl sagged, the relief stealing the last scraps of his strength. But before his thank God reached his lips, what the driver hadn't said made it through, and Carl straightened back up. He put one foot in front of the other. And then again. When he stepped to go around the driver, the driver held out his hand, put it on Carl's shoulder, held him back. Leaning in close, almost as close as Carl had been to Colton just before he'd left him, the driver whispered, "Sir, I'm sorry."

Carl pushed past the driver, stepping into the darkness. Wordlessly, the others fell into step around him, giving him the light he needed to go on.

By the time they reached the snow cave, the first team had Colton's body out, wrapped tight in the space blanket, head to foot in his silvery shroud. The cave itself lay in ruins, the searchers still hurrying then to get to Colton, not yet paying the respect due a gravesite. Their headlamps, as they looked at the ground, glinted off the bright brass casings poking out of the snow, Colton firing into the cold, signaling his rescuers, until both rifles were empty.

On his knees, knowing that the searchers would have to carry them both out, that he had no will left to take one more step forward, Carl carefully unwrapped Colton's head, his shoulders. His face was the same, asleep, frost still thick on his hat and collar, the last of his breaths frozen there.

His arms were drawn up tight to his chest, his knees as well, and in his fist Carl saw his mini-Mag, still pointing out, ready to light his way. Carl twisted the end of the light and it flashed on immediately, still bright, and Carl knew he wouldn't be able to stand again, that the searchers would have to drag him out like their second body, while he lay in the snow, picturing his boy dying in the dark, saving his batteries for when he'd need them later, using his head.

The Last Running

JOHN GRAVES

John Graves was born in Texas and educated at Rice and Columbia univer-
sities. He has published a number of books, chiefly concerned with his
home region.

He currently lives with his wife on some four hundred acres of rough
Texas hill country, which he described in his book Hard Scrabble.

THEY CALLED HIM Pajarito, in literal trader-Spanish interpretation of his surname, or more often Tom Tejano, since he had
been there in those early fighting days before the Texans had flooded up
onto the plains in such numbers that it became no longer practical to
hate them with specificity.

After the first interview, when he had climbed down from the bed
where an aching liver held him and had gone out onto the porch to
salute them, only to curse in outrage and clump back into the house
when he heard what they wanted, the nine of them sat like grackles
about the broad gray-painted steps and talked, in Comanche, about
Tom Texan the Little Bird and the antique times before wire fences had
partitioned the prairies. At least, old Juan the cook said that was what
they were talking about.

Mostly it was the old men who talked, three of them, one so decrepit
that he had had to make the trip from Oklahoma in a lopsided carryall
drawn by a piebald mare, with an odd long bundle sticking out the back,
the rest riding alongside on ponies. Of the other six, two were middle-
aged and four were young.

Their clothes ran a disastrous gamut from buckskin to faded calico
and blue serge, but under dirty Stetsons they wore their hair long and
braided, plains style. Waiting, sucking Durham cigarettes and speaking
Comanche, they sat about the steps and under the cottonwoods in the
yard and ignored those of us who drifted near to watch them, except the
one or two whom they considered to have a right to their attention.

Twice a day for two days they built fires and broiled unsymmetrical chunks of the fat calf which, from his bed, furiously, Tom Bird had ordered killed for them. At night—it was early autumn—they rolled up in blankets about the old carryall and slept on the ground.

"They show any signs of leaving?" Tom Bird asked me when I went into his room toward evening of the second day.

I said, "No, sir. They told Juan they thought you could spare one easily enough, since all of them and the land too used to be theirs."

"They didn't used to be nobody's!" he shouted.

"They've eaten half that animal since they got here," I said. "I never saw anybody that could eat meat like that, and nothing but meat."

"No, nor ever saw anything else worth seeing," he said, his somber gray eyes brooding. He was one of the real ones, and none of them are left now. That was in the twenties, he was my great-uncle, and at sixteen he had run away from his father's farm in Mississippi to work his way to the brawling acquisitive Texas frontier. At the age of eighty-five he possessed—more or less by accident, since cattle rather than land had always meant wealth to him—a medium-large ranch in the canyon country where the Cap Rock falls away to rolling prairies, south of the Texas Panhandle. He had buried two wives and had had no children and lived there surrounded by people who worked for him. When I had showed up there, three years before the Comanches' visit, he had merely grunted at me on the porch, staring sharply at my frail physique, and had gone right on arguing with his manager about rock salt in the pastures. But a month later, maybe when he decided I was going to pick up weight and live, we had abruptly become friends. He was given to quick gruff judgments and to painful retractions.

He said in his room that afternoon, "God damn it. I'll see them in hell before they get one, deeper than you can drop an anvil."

"You want me to tell them that?"

"Hell, yes," he said. "No. Listen, have you talked any with that old one? Starlight, they call him."

I said that neither Starlight nor the others had even glanced at any of us. Tom Bird said, "You tell him you're kin to me. He knows a lot, that one."

"What do you want me to say about the buffalo?"

"Nothing," he said and narrowed his eyes as a jab of pain shot through him from that rebellious organ which was speaking loudly

now of long-gone years of drinking at plains mudholes and Kansas saloons. He grunted. "Not a damn thing," he said. "I already told them."

Starlight paid no attention at all when I first spoke to him. I had
picked up a poor grade of Spanish from old Juan in three years but was
timid about using it, and to my English he showed a weathered and not
even disdainful profile.

I stated my kinship to Tom Bird and said that Tom Bird had told me to
speak to him.

Starlight stared at the fourteen pampered bison grazing in their
double-fenced pasture near the house, where my great-uncle could
watch them from his chair in the evenings. He had bred them from seed
stock given him in the nineties by Charles Goodnight, and the only time
one of them had ever been killed and eaten was when the governor of
the state and a historical society had driven out to give the old man
some sort of citation. When the Comanches under Starlight had arrived,
they had walked down to the pasture fence and had looked at the buffalo
for perhaps two hours, hardly speaking, studying the cows and the one
calf and the emasculated males and the two bulls—old Shakespeare,
who had killed a horse once and had put innumerable men up mesquite
trees and over fences, and his lecherous though rarely productive son,
John Milton.

Then they had said, matter-of-factly, that they wanted one of the animals.

Starlight's old-man smell was mixed with something wild, perhaps
wood smoke. His braids were a soiled white. One of the young men
glanced at me after I had spoken and said something to him in Comanche. Turning then, the old Indian looked at me down his swollen
nose. His face was hexagonal and broad, but sunken where teeth were
gone. He spoke.

The young man said in English with an exact accent, "He wants to
know what's wrong with old Tom Bird, not to talk to friends."

All of them were watching me, the young ones with more affability
than the others. I said Tom Bird was sick in the liver, and patted my own.

Starlight said in Spanish, "Is he dying?"

I answered in Spanish that I didn't think so but that it was painful.

He snorted much like Tom Bird himself and turned to look again at
the buffalo in the pasture. The conversation appeared to have ended, but

not knowing how to leave I sat there on the top step beside the old Comanche, the rest of them ranged below us and eyeing me with what I felt to be humor. I took out cigarettes and offered them to the young man, who accepted the package and passed it along, and when it got back to me it was nearly empty. I got the impression that this gave them amusement, too, though no one had smiled. We all sat blowing smoke into the crisp evening air.

Then, it seemed, some ritual biding time had passed. Old Starlight began to talk again. He gazed at the buffalo in the pasture under the fading light and spoke steadily in bad Spanish with occasional phrases of worse English. The young Indian who had translated for me in the beginning lit a small stick fire below the steps. From time to time one of the other old men would obtrude a question or a correction, and they would drop into the angry Comanche gutturals, and the young man, whose name was John Oak Tree, would tell me what they were saying.

The story went on for an hour or so; when Starlight stopped talking they trooped down to the carryall and got their blankets and rolled up in them on the ground. In the morning I let my work in the ranch office wait and sat down again with the Comanches on the steps, and Starlight talked again. The talk was for me, since I was Tom Bird's kinsman. Starlight did not tell the story as I tell it here. Parts I had to fill in later in conversation with Tom Bird, or even from books. But this was the story.

WITHOUT KNOWING HIS exact age, he knew that he was younger than Tom Bird, about the age of dead Quanah Parker, under whom he had more than once fought. He had come to warrior's age during the big fight the white men had had among themselves over the black men. Born a Penateka or Honey Eater while the subtribal divisions still had meaning, he remembered the surly exodus from the Brazos reservation to Oklahoma in 1859, the expulsion by law of the Comanches from all of Texas.

But white laws had not meant much for another ten years or so. It was a time of blood and confusion, a good time to be a Comanche and fight the most lost of all causes. The whites at the Oklahoma agencies were Northern and not only tolerated but sometimes egged on and armed the parties striking down across the Red, with the full moon, at the line of settlements established by the abominated and tenacious

Texans. In those days, Starlight said, Comanches held Texans to be another breed of white men, and even after they were told that peace had smiled again among whites, they did not consider this to apply to that race which had swarmed over the best of their grass and timber.

In the beginning, the raids had ritual formality and purpose; an individual party would go south either to make war, or to steal horses, or to drive off cattle for trading to the New Mexican *comancheros* at plains rendezvous, or maybe just reminiscently to run deer and buffalo over the old grounds. But the distinctions dimmed. In conservative old age Starlight believed that the Comanches' ultimate destruction was rooted in the loss of the old disciplines. That and smallpox and syphilis and whiskey. And Mackenzie's soldiers. All those things ran in an apocalyptic pack, like wolves in winter.

They had gone horse raiding down into the Brazos country, a dozen of them, all young and all good riders and fighters. They captured thirty horses here and there in the perfect stealth that pride demanded, without clashes, and were headed back north up the Keechi Valley near Palo Pinto when a Texan with a yellow beard caught them in his corral at dawn and killed two of them with a shotgun. They shot the Texan with arrows; Starlight himself peeled off the yellow scalp. Then, with a casualness bred of long cruelty on both sides, they killed his wife and two children in the log house. She did not scream as white women were said to do, but until a hatchet cleaved her skull kept shouting, "Git out! Git, git, git."

And collecting five more horses there, they continued the trek toward the Territory, driving at night and resting at known secret spots during the days.

The leader was a son of old Iron Shirt, Pohebits Quasho, bullet-dead on the Canadian despite his Spanish coat of mail handed down from the old haughty days. Iron Shirt's son said that it was bad to have killed the woman and the children, but Starlight, who with others laughed at him, believed even afterward that it would have been the same if they had let the woman live.

What was certain was that the Texans followed, a big party with men among them who could cut trail as cleanly as Indians. They followed quietly, riding hard and resting little, and on the third evening, when the Comanches were gathering their herd and readying themselves to leave a broad enclosed creek valley where they had spent the day, their sentry on a hill yelled and was dead, and the lean horsemen with the wide hats were pouring down the hillside shouting the long shout that belonged to them.

When it happened, Starlight was riding near the upper end of the valley with the leader. The only weapons with them were their knives and Starlight's lance, with whose butt he had been poking the rumps of the restive stolen horses as they hazed them toward camp below. As they watched, the twenty or more Texans overrode the camp, and in the shooting and confusion the two Comanches heard the end of their five companions who had been there afoot.

"I knew this," the leader said.

"You knew it," Starlight answered him bitterly. "You should have been the sentry, Know-much."

Of the other two horse gatherers, who had been working the lower valley, they could see nothing, but a group of the Texans rode away from the camp in that direction, yelling and firing. Then others broke toward Starlight and the leader a half mile above.

"We can run around them to the plain below," the son of Iron Shirt said. "Up this creek is bad."

Starlight did not know the country up the creek, but he knew what he felt, and feeling for a Comanche was conviction. He turned his pony upstream and spurred it.

"Ragh!" he called to the leader in farewell. "You're dirty luck!" And he was right, for he never saw the son of Iron Shirt again. Or the other two horse gatherers either.

But the son of Iron Shirt had been right, too, because ten minutes later Starlight was forcing his pony among big fallen boulders in a root tangle of small steep canyon, each of which carried a trickle to the stream below. There was no way even to lead a horse up their walls; he had the feeling that any one of them would bring him to a blind place.

Behind him shod hoofs rang; he whipped the pony on, but a big Texan on a bay horse swept fast around a turn in the canyon, jumping the boulders, and with a long lucky shot from a pistol broke Starlight's pony's leg. The Comanche fell with the pony but lit cat-bouncing and turned, and as the Texan came down waited crouched with the lance. The Texan had one of the pistols that shot six times, rare then in that country. Bearing down, he fired three times, missing each shot, and then when it was the moment Starlight feinted forward and watched the Texan lurch aside from the long bright blade, and while he was off balance, Starlight drove it into the Texan's belly until it came out the back. The blade snapped as the big man's weight came onto it, falling.

Starlight sought the pistol for a moment but not finding it ran to the canyon wall and began climbing. He was halfway up the fifty feet of its crumbling face when the other Texan rode around the turn and stopped, and from his unquiet horse, too hastily, fired a rifle shot that blew Starlight's left eye full of powdered sandstone.

He was among swallows' nests. Their molded mud crunched under his hands; the birds flew in long loops, chittering about his head. Climbing, he felt the Texan's absorbed reloading behind and below him as the horse moved closer, and when he knew with certainty that it was time, looked around to see the long caplock rifle rising again. . . . Watched still climbing, and guessing at the instant, wrenched himself hard to the right, seizing the roots of a cedar that grew almost at the top of the cliff.

The bullet smashed through his upper left arm, and he hung only by his right, but with the long wiry strength of trick horsemanship he swung himself up and onto the overhanging turf of the cliff's top. A round rock the size of a buffalo's head lay there. Almost without pausing he tugged it loose from the earth and rolled it back over the cliff. It came close. The Texan grabbed the saddle as his horse reared, and dropped his rifle. They looked at each other. Clutching a blood-greasy, hanging arm, the Comanche stared down at a big nose and a pair of angry gray eyes, and the young Texan stared back.

Wheeling, Starlight set off trotting across the hills. That night before hiding himself he climbed a low tree and quavered for hours like a screech owl, but no one answered. A month later, an infected skeleton, he walked into the Penateka encampment at Fort Sill, the only one of twelve to return.

That had been his first meeting with Tom Bird.

WHEN TELLING OF the fights, Starlight stood up and gestured in proud physical representation of what he and others had done. He did not give it as a story with a point; it was the recountal of his acquaintance with a man. In the bug-flecked light of a bulb above the house's screen door the old Indian should have looked absurd—hipshot, ugly, in a greasy black hat and a greasy dark suit with a gold chain across its vest, the dirty braids flying as he creaked through the motions of long-unmeaningful violence.

But I did not feel like smiling. I looked at the younger Indians expecting perhaps to find amusement among them, or boredom, or cynicism. It was not there. They were listening, most of them probably not even understanding the Spanish but knowing the stories, to an ancient man who belonged to a time when their race had been literally terrible.

In the morning Starlight told of the second time. It had been after the end of the white men's war; he was a war chief with bull horns on his head. Thirty well-armed warriors rode behind him when he stopped a trail herd in the Territory for tribute. Although the cowmen were only eight, their leader, a man with a black mustache, said that four whoa-haws were too many. He would give maybe two.

"Four," Starlight said. "Texan."

It was an arraignment, and the white man heard it as such. Looking at the thirty Comanches, he said that he and his people were not Texans but Kansas men returning home with bought cattle.

"Four whoa-haws," Starlight said.

The white man made a sullen sign with his hand and spoke to his men, who went to cut out the steers. Starlight watched jealously to make certain they were not culls, and when three of his young men had them and were driving them away, he rode up face to face with the white leader, unfooled even though the mustache was new.

"Tejano," he said. "Stink sonabitch." And reached over and twisted Tom Bird's big nose, hard, enjoying the rage barely held in the gray eyes. He patted his scarred left biceps and saw that the white man knew him, too, and reached over to twist the nose again, Tom Bird too prudent to stop him and too proud to duck his head aside.

"Tobacco, Texan," Starlight said.

Close to snarling, Tom Bird took out a plug. After sampling and examining it and picking a bit of lint from its surface, Starlight tucked it into his waistband. Then he turned his horse and, followed by his thirty warriors, rode away.

In those days revenge had still existed.

He had been, too, with Quanah Parker when the half-white chief had made a separate peace with Tom Bird—Tom Tejano the Pajarito now, looming big on the high plains— as with a government, on the old Bird range up along the Canadian. There had been nearly two hundred with Quanah on a hunt in prohibited territory, and they found few buffalo and many cattle. After the peace with Tom Bird they had not eaten any more wing-branded beef, except later when the Oklahoma agency bought Bird steers to distribute among them.

They had clasped hands there in Quanah's presence, knowing each other well, and in the cowman's tolerant grin and the pressure of his hard fingers Starlight had read more clearly the rout of his people than he had read it anywhere else before.

"Yah, Big-nose," he said, returning the grip and the smile. Tom Bird rode along with them hunting for ten days and led them to a wide valley twenty miles long that the hide hunters had not yet found, and they showed him there how their fathers had run the buffalo in the long good years before the white men. November it had been, with frosted mornings and yellow bright days; their women had followed them to dress the skins and dry the meat. It was the last of the rich hunting years.

After that whenever Tom Bird passed through Oklahoma he would seek out the Indian who had once pulled his nose and would sometimes bring presents.

But Starlight had killed nine white men while the fighting had lasted.

DRESSED, TOM BIRD came out onto the porch at eleven o'clock, and I knew from the smooth curve of his cheek that the liver had quit hurting. He was affable and shook all their hands again.

"We'll have a big dinner at noon," he told Starlight in the same flowing pidgin Spanish the old Comanche himself used. "Juan's making it especially for my Comanche friends, to send them on their trip full and happy."

Still unfooled, Starlight exhumed the main topic.

"No!" Tom Bird said.

"You have little courtesy," Starlight said. "You had more once."

Tom Bird said, "There were more of you then. Armed."

Starlight's eyes squinted in mirth which his mouth did not let itself reflect. Absently Tom Bird dug out his Days O' Work and bit a chew, then waved the plug apologetically and offered it to the Comanche. Starlight took it and with three remaining front teeth haggled off a chunk, and pretended to put it into his vest pocket.

They both started laughing, phlegmy, hard-earned, old men's laughter, and for the first time—never having seen Tom Bird out-argued before—I knew that it was going to work out.

Tom Bird said, "Son of a coyote, you . . . I've got four fat *castrados*, and you can have your pick. They're good meat, and I'll eat some of it with you."

Starlight waggled his head mulishly. "Those, no," he said. "The big bull."

Tom Bird stared, started to speak, closed his mouth, threw the returned plug of tobacco down on the porch, and clumped back into the house. The Indians all sat down again. One of the other older men reached over and picked up the plug, had a chew, and stuck it into his denim jacket. Immobility settled.

"Liberty," Starlight said out of nowhere, in Spanish. "They speak much of liberty. Not one of you has ever seen liberty, or smelled it. Liberty was grass, and wind, and a horse, and meat to hunt, and no wire."

From beyond the dark screen door Tom Bird said, "The little bull."

Starlight without looking around shook his head. Tom Bird opened the door so hard that it battered back against the house wall, loosening flakes of paint. He stopped above the old Indian and stood there on bowed legs, looking down. "You rusty old bastard!" he shouted in English. "I ain't got but the two, and the big one's the only good one. And he wouldn't eat worth a damn."

Starlight turned his head and eyed him.

"All right," Tom Bird said, slumping. "All right."

"Thank you, Pajarito," Starlight said.

"Jimmy," the old man said to me in a washed-out voice, "go tell the boys to shoot Shakespeare and hang him up down by the washhouse."

"No," John Oak Tree said.

"What the hell you mean, no?" Tom Bird said, turning to him with enraged pleasure. "That's the one he wants. What you think he's been hollering about for two whole days?"

"Not dead," John Oak Tree said. "My grandfather wants him alive."

"Now ain't that sweet?" the old man said. "Ain't that just beautiful? And I can go around paying for busted fences from here to Oklahoma and maybe to the God damn Arctic Circle, all so a crazy old murdering Comanche can have him a pet bull buffalo."

Starlight spoke in Spanish, having understood most of the English. "Tom Tejano, listen," he said.

"What?"

"Listen," Starlight said. "We're going to kill him, Tom Tejano. We."

"My butt!" said Tom Bird, and sat down.

IN THE AFTERNOON, after the fried chicken and the rice and mashed beans and the tamales and the blistering chili, after the courteous belching and the smoking on the porch, everyone on the ranch who could leave his work was standing in the yard under the cottonwoods as the nine Comanches brought their horses up from the lot, where they had been eating oats for two days, and tied them outside the picket fence, saddled.

After hitching Starlight's mare to the carryall, without paying any attention to their audience they began to strip down, methodically rolling their shed clothes into bundles with hats on top and putting them on the back of the carryall. Starlight reeled painfully among them, pointing a dried-up forefinger and giving orders. When they had finished, all of them but he wore only trousers and shoes or moccasins, with here and there scraps of the old bone and claw and hide and feather paraphernalia. John Oak Tree had slipped off the high-heeled boots he wore and replaced them with tennis sneakers.

A hundred yards away, gargling a bellow from time to time, old Shakespeare stood jammed into a chute where the hands had choused him. Between bellows, his small hating eye peered toward us from beneath a grayed board; there was not much doubt about how *he* felt.

The Indians took the long, blanketed bundle from the carryall and unrolled it.

"For God's sake!" a cowboy said beside me, a man named Abe Reynolds who had worked a good bit with the little buffalo herd. "For God's sake, this is nineteen damn twenty-three?"

I chuckled. Old Tom Bird turned his gray eyes on us and glared, and we shut up. The bundle held short bows, and quivers of arrows, and long, feather-hung, newly reshafted buffalo lances daubed with red and black. Some took bows and others lances, and among the bowmen were the two old men younger than Starlight, who under dry skins still had ridged segmented muscles.

"Those?" I said in protest, forgetting Tom Bird. "Those two couldn't . . ."

"Because they never killed one," he said without looking around. "Because old as they are, they ain't old enough to have hunted the animal that for two whole centuries was the main thing their people ate, and wore, and made tents and ropes and saddles and every other damn thing they had out of. You close your mouth, boy, and watch."

Starlight made John Oak Tree put on a ribboned medal of some kind. Then they sat the restless ponies in a shifting line, motley still but somehow, now, with the feel of that old terribleness coming off of them like a smell, and Starlight walked down the line of them and found them good and turned to raise his hand at Tom Bird.

Tom Bird yelled.

The man at the chute pulled the bars and jumped for the fence, and eight mounted Indians lashed their ponies into a hard run toward the lumpy blackness that had emerged and was standing there swaying its head, bawling-furious.

Starlight screeched. But they were out of his control now and swept in too eagerly, not giving Shakespeare time to decide to run. When the Indian on the fastest pony, one of the middle-aged men, came down on him shooting what looked like a steady jet of arrows from beside the pony's neck, the bull squared at him. The Indian reined aside, but not enough. The big head came up under the pony's belly, and for a moment horse and rider paused reared against the horns and went pinwheeling backward into the middle of the onrushing others.

"Them idiots!" Abe Reynolds said. "Them plumb idiots!"

One swarming pile then, one mass with sharp projecting heads and limbs and weapons, all of them yelling and pounding and hacking and stabbing, and when old Shakespeare shot out from under the pile, shrugging them helter-skelter aside, he made a run for the house. Behind him they came yipping, leaving a gut-ripped dead horse on the ground beside the chute and another running riderless toward the northeast. One of the downed hunters sat on the ground against the chute as though indifferently. The other—one of the two oldsters—was hopping about on his left leg with an arrow through the calf of his right.

But I was scrambling for the high porch with the spectators, those who weren't grabbing for limbs, though Tom Bird stood his ground

cursing as Shakespeare smashed through the white picket fence like dry
sunflower stalks and whirled to make another stand under the cottonwoods. Some of the Indians jumped the fence and others poured
through the hole he had made, all howling until it seemed there could be
no breath left in them. For a moment, planted, Shakespeare stood with
arrows bristling brightly from his hump and his loins and took someone's lance in his shoulder. Then he gave up that stand, too, and whisked
out another eight feet of fence as he leveled into a long run down the dirt
road past the corrals.

They rode him close, poking and shooting.

And finally, when it was all far enough down the road to have the perspective of a picture, John Oak Tree swung out leftward and running
parallel to the others pulled ahead and abruptly slanted in with the long
bubbling shriek, loud and cutting above all the other noise, that you can
call rebel yell or cowboy holler or whatever you want, but which deadly
exultant men on horseback have likely shrieked since the Assyrians and
long, long before. Shakespeare ran desperately free from the sharp-
pointed furor behind him, and John Oak Tree took his dun pony in a line
converging sharply with the bull's course, and was there, and jammed
the lance's blade certainly just behind the ribs and pointing forward, and
the bull skidded to his knees, coughed, and rolled onto his side.

"You call that fair?" Abe Reynolds said sourly.

Nobody had. It was not fair. Fair did not seem to have much to do
with what it was.

Starlight's carryall was headed for the clump of horsemen down the
road, but the rest of us were held to the yard by the erect stability of Tom
Bird's back as he stood in one of the gaps in his picket fence. Beside the
chute, Starlight picked up the two thrown Indians and the saddle from
the dead horse, the old hunter disarrowed and bleeding now, and drove
on to where the rest sat on their ponies around Shakespeare's carcass.

Getting down, he spoke to John Oak Tree. The young Indian dis-
mounted and handed his lance to Starlight, who hopped around for a
time with one foot in the stirrup and got up onto the dun pony and
brought it back toward the house at a run, the lance held high. Against
his greasy vest the big gold watch chain bounced, and his coattails flew,
but his old legs were locked snugly around the pony's barrel. He ran it
straight at Tom Bird where he stood in the fence gap, and pulled it
cruelly onto its hocks three yards away, and held out the lance butt first.

"I carried it when I pulled your nose," he said. "The iron, anyhow."

Tom Bird took it.

"We were there, Tom Tejano," Starlight said.

"Yes," my great-uncle said. "Yes, we were there."

The old Comanche turned the pony and ran it back to the little group of his people and gave it to John Oak Tree, who helped him get back into the carryall. Someone had caught the loose pony. For a few moments all of them sat, frozen, looking down at the arrow-quilled black bulk that had been Shakespeare.

Then, leaving it there, they rode off down the road toward Oklahoma, past the fences of barbed steel that would flank them all the way.

A cowhand, surveying the deadly debris along the route of their run, said dryly, "A neat bunch of scutters, be damn if they ain't."

I was standing beside old Tom Bird, and he was crying. He felt my eyes and turned, the bloody lance upright in his hand, paying no heed to the tears running down the sides of his big nose and into his mustache.

"Damn you, boy," he said. "Damn you for not ever getting to know anything worth knowing. Damn me, too. We had a world, once."

The Teachings of Bronc Buster Billy Brown

DRUM HADLEY

Drum Hadley was a poet among poets in the 1960s, hanging out with the major voices of his generation—Allen Ginsberg, Lawrence Ferlinghetti, Charles Olson, Gary Snyder. Then he moved to a ranch on the Mexican border.

His latest collection of work is Voice of the Borderlands.

Hadley's poetry and his life are devoted to sustaining a way of life. He started the Animas Foundation, and with others, the Malpai Borderlands Group. Both organizations help support ranching in harmony with the environment.

CROP FAILURE

The Man Called Billy Brown

The wildest, horse-ridin'est, whiskey-drinkin'est,
Woman-chasin'est cowboy
Who's rode all of this desert country
From Texas along the Rio Grande a-sowin' his wild oats
And a-prayin' for crop failure.
"I'm a lover and a fighter and a wild horse rider
And I'm a pretty fair windmill man too," old Billy would say.
"Do you savvy? Are you listenin'?"

Tall, skinny Texan in black high-heeled boots,
A dancer who moves on his toes into the stirrups.
Legend of horse breaking gone to Mexico to escape the Law.
Near sixty years old, hair beginning to grey,
Four-inch-brim sombrero pulled way down
Over his eyes to keep the desert sun from burning.
His wages go to fine gear, rawhide, horsehair hackamores,
Bits, a pair of silver spurs with the letters "BILLY,"
A tooled saddle, soft batwing chaps.

A pretty tough hombre, some people say,
If another man doesn't return his Southern-drawled politeness.

THE NATURE OF A COWBOY

I. The Hiring of Billy Brown

"There just ain't many old-time cowpunchers around,
Who know as much about horses as he does.
You sure oughta get him to ride them colts,
And you'd learn a lot from him too," Bud says.
"Well," says Drum, "we've got five colts he could ride.
They're all started but one.
I don't think they'd buck or hurt him,
But my wife'd sure throw a terrible fit
If I brought another drinker to the ranch.
We've already got Roberto and Walter and Juan.
And Carlos and Berto would go along with 'em,
And old Billy would sure set 'em off,
If they got the chance."
"Well, would your wife get over it?" says Bud.
"I guess she'd cool off, Bud, in maybe three or four weeks."
Bud throws his saddle onto his horse, laughs, and rides away.
"Well, the quicker you do it, the quicker she'll get over it."

—*Voice of* BUD ROBBINS

ON THE SQUARE OF THE RED-LIGHT HOUSES IN AGUA PRIETA

Billy Brown worked for Chapo Varela at the Rancho Nuevo in the Cajón Bonito. Chapo paid Billy Brown to ride colts, but he paid him with mares instead of money.

II. Hunting for Billy Brown

The lights blinking red and orange and blue and green,
Old lime paint flaking off the adobe walls,

The horns, the music of the mariachis playing,
Soft light, yellow and warm inside.
"I'm a lover and a fighter and a wild horse rider
And just a pretty fair windmill man. Do you savvy, are you listenin'?
Goddamn, I think I been off with a darn *puto*.
I took her back to one of them rooms.
I took her clothes off and she didn't have no chichis!"
"*Dame un* piece, price," one says.
"*Se levanta pura madre,*" says another.
A coyote calling off in the desert country to the South,
Yip yip yip oooooooooooooourh.
"My goddamn false teeth are loose," Billy says.
"I don't know whether I could bite one of 'em on the tittie or not,
But I'm a-gonna try."
He goes and gets another one,
Comes back after a while.
"She was old enough not to lie to me.
You know the young ones, they'll all lie.
We talked about horses.
I don't know how much a horse does think,
But they're like a woman. They understand quite a bit,
But in a hundred years from now—
Why, I've seen people a-killin' themselves,
Runnin' around tryin' to get things done—
In a hundred years from now, it won't make any difference,
Rich or poor, so you better smell the goddamn flowers.
Smell 'em while you ride on by.
You know," says Billy Brown, "I think I'll get me a pack outfit,
A Springerville tree, take these old mares,
If I can't legally get 'em across the borderline,
And ride on South to Sahuaripa.
That's where they got them big chi-chis."

A pretty green-eyed girl comes to sit
On the lip of the bar stool beside him.
"Green, green, how I like green," says Billy Brown.
"You know, I never could figure out which I liked best,

Green eyes or green grass.
I think I used to like green eyes best,
But now, I think I like green grass."

—*Voice of* BRONC BUSTER BILLY BROWN

THE STUDY OF ANCIENT LITERATURE

III. By the Old Cantina Oak Wood Bar Billy Brown Considers the Bible Genesis, Chapter 19, Verse 26: Lot Fleeing from the Wrath of the Lord

"You know, that Bible's not a bad book," Billy Brown says.
"It's a little slow in parts, but they fight,
They drink the booze, they sleep with other men's wives.
Why, it's got almost everything in it.
One time, I bet a feller a case of Jim Beam whiskey
The Bible even told about a man a-sleepin with one of his daughters.
That was the story about that old feller Lot who was on the dodge,
And runnin' from the Law, and him and his daughters slipped off.
They went to live in a cave for a while.
Well, after they'd been there in that cave for about three years,
These young fillies was a-comin' along in their teens,
And they was a-feelin' kinda hot and twisty like.
Do you savvy, are you listenin'?
Now their old daddy, he liked to drink the booze.
Well, one night these girls ups and gets their old daddy drunk,
And when they had him pretty good and lickered up,
After he'd gone to bed, one of these fillies,
Feelin' kinda hot and twisty like,
Why, she climbs into the bed with him.
Well, her old daddy gives her the business, he does.
And because he had those drinks a couple of thousand years ago,
I won that case of Jim Beam whiskey!
Do you savvy, are you listenin'?"

—*Voice of* BRONC BUSTER BILLY BROWN

A BOTTLE OF JIM BEAM WHISKEY

IV. Bringing Billy Brown to the Ranch to Ride Colts

Slip him up to the camp by the spring, quick,
So none of the other cowboys will see him,
Catch that wild look, quit their work,
And run off on a rampage to town.
"Billy, I can't take you out there," I tell him.
"Not if you've got any more
Bottles of Jim Beam whiskey.
It's too much to do to Diana.
We've done enough to her already.
You don't have any more, do you?"
"No! No!" Billy says.
But when he gets up to the spring somewhere,
He finds one down in the curls of his bedroll.
Goddamn, that's three more days of wild drunkenness
I'll have to go through.
But when he gets good and drunk, I do get the secret
From him, about where he'd hid some more.
I may have had to unscrew those back hinges
Off his locked truck, but I got that damn bottle.
"Billy do you have any more whiskey?"
I ask him the next day.
"NO, NO," he says.
"Can I have any I find then, Billy?"
"Well, I guess so," he says.
Goddamn, I got Billy Brown that time.
Got his bottle of Jim Beam whiskey.
Got it now and it's hidden away, too.

—*Voice of* BRONC BUSTER BILLY BROWN

BY THE SANDY PICKET CORRAL

V. To Hackamore the Colt

"Where is Billy? I'll bet he's studyin' his witchcraft." Roberto
    laughs.
Roberto and Drum are waiting for him by the sandy picket corral.
Moved him last week from his camp by the spring.
"Where is old Billy?"
"Hell, he's fallen asleep again in the bunkhouse.
We've got our ropes ready.
We need him to come help us,
To give us some of his magic, to slip a hackamore easy
Onto this jumping, kicking, little Bayleaf colt."
Two weeks later, finally, he comes walking, bowlegged, down
By the sandy picket corral to hackamore the colt.
Listen to the sound of the rope.
His thrown rope swishes through the air.
Ropes him quick with a hoolihan loop.
Hollers to us to come help pull.
"Pull, pull hard on the rope!
Watch that colt. He's rarin'!
Don't let him go over backward.
If he hits on his top knot, it'll kill him.
Get a hitch over your hip on that rope.
Get his ear! Get his tail!
Get his ear! Lift his tail!
There, we got him stopped."

—*Voices of* BRONC BUSTER BILLY BROWN *and* ROBERTO ESPINOSA

A PAT ON THE ASS

VI. In These Flying Seconds

The stillness goin' by too fast.
"Quick, before he quits restin' and starts fightin' again,
Tie up that colt's back foot. Hobble him in front,
Hobble him behind,

Sideline him!
Sack him out with a light saddle blanket,
While he stands there, quiverin' with his eyes all wide."
Billy ropes him time and again,
Holding him close by the hackamore lead,
Takes off the foot ropes, drops a loop over his rump,
Twitches it to scare him, to teach him to lead.
In less than an hour from when he first felt the rope
Settle around the soft mane hair on his neck,
The colt's got a saddle on, following Billy around the corral.
"Billy, that sure was a pretty job," says Drum.
"Well you know," Billy says, breathing a little hard,
"Just about the time you get old enough
To know what you're doin',
You're so old and sored up,
You can't do it anymore.
Instead of takin' a pretty girl off to bed her down somewhere,
You just want to sit here,
And drink a cold beer or give her a pat on her ass.
Where is she?
I'm not that old yet.
Come on. Let's get a drink of water.
We'll ride the rest of these colts before the sun goes down.
We'll ride 'em all down the canyon a ways."

—*Voice of* BRONC BUSTER BILLY BROWN

TO BE TIED HARD AND FAST

When Billy Brown was dying in the veterans' hospital,
In Tucson, Arizona, he kept trying to escape,
Like the mule Mike, back to his *querencia*
the big, wild, open country of the Sierra Madre.

The nurses had put handcuffs on him.
They were made of plastic,
but in his weakened condition,

They might as well have been made of steel.
He said, "Drum, cut me loose . . . cut me loose."
This poem is called "Cutting Loose in the Springtime."

CUTTING LOOSE IN THE SPRINGTIME

I.

Billy Brown, being an old Texas cowboy,
Was a hard and fast tie man.
That means he tied his rope solid,
Or fast, to the saddle horn, as against dallying.
Dallying means to take turns of the rope around the saddle horn,
To hold an animal you've got roped,
So if something happens and you start to get into a wreck,
You can let your rope slide around the saddle horn,
Or take those dallies off the horn.
Billy only dallied roping little calves in a corral,
'Cause, he said, you had to learn it when you were young,
Or you couldn't do it well enough to keep from losing
A finger, or a hand, or a thumb.
Billy carried a knife strapped to his chaps right above his thigh
    bone,
So if he had a cow brute, or some critter roped,
And he was tied hard and fast,
And was maybe riding a spinning, pitching colt,
With the coils of that rope winding around him,
He could pull his knife free, and start cutting loose.

II.

Sometimes, Spring comes whirling up these desert canyons
From the South so strong, I'd cut loose and go a-prancing . . .
With one of these light seeds that flies up towards the canyon rim.
Sometimes, those sweet scents of the Springtime
Come whirling up these draws from Mexico so strong,
When the blood-weed starts greening up,
And the mourning doves start calling long,
Long into the beginning of the morning.

III.

When the Spring winds come blowing down the ridge lines,
And you feel them blowing along the creased lines of your skin,
Who would tell Springtime to be still,
Or to go away from the rims of these dry canyons and hills,
Till all the honey and all the humming bees,
And those light blue eyes are gone?
Who would tell the Springtime to be still?

GETTING THE JOB DONE

Another Rancher's Tale

Another rancher at Ben's table begins telling
About the Bureau of Land Management.
"A young man comes to the door of our house in town.
Him and his agency manage the Bureau of Land Management
On our ranch.
My cowboy's driven him forty miles to town for help.
'I'm from that group of eight vehicles that didn't quite make it.
Up Guadalupe Canyon,' he says.
'We stayed a couple of days.
We placed some mistnets to catch bats.
I think they must of washed away 'cause I can't find 'em.
Mine was the last vehicle to leave.
I stayed lookin' at plants and birds.
It was a real nice day, and I just drove right into
That creek without lookin'.
That truck had four-wheel drive,
But the tires must of hit a soft spot.
There was so little water, I didn't imagine
I might be in trouble. I guess I should of known.
The truck stalled in the middle of that creek.
I set for two or three minutes tryin' to start the engine.
Where I was, it hadn't hardly rained, but I think
There must of been rain somewhere up the canyon.
When I looked out of the window of that truck,
The water was gradually risin' up the side of the door.

I stayed, tryin' to start that truck till the whole truck body
Started rockin' and then floatin'.
Then the water started comin' in through the window.
I rolled down the downstream window
And climbed out onto the hood.
The truck was rockin' like all get-out.
I jumped for shore but didn't quite make it.
I thought maybe I'd better walk back to my camp,
To try and pull myself together.
When I got back to camp I saw that a great big limb
From a sycamore tree'd fallen right on top of my tent,
And smashed it like a pretzel.
I hate to think what would of happened
If I'd been in that tent.
I went to bed and woke this morning and hoped
It all had been a bad dream . . .
But no such luck.
I hate to think what would of happened if I'd of been in that tent.
I dunno, I think maybe somebody's tryin' to tell me something.
I lay there in my sleeping bag,
Thinkin' of the birds and the beautiful canyon,
'Cause I hated to think of that government truck,
With the creek flowin' over the hood.
I got up and walked to the truck to get the canteen,
Where it was hangin' on the pickup bed,
'Cause I thought I might need some drinkin' water.
I guess I really went back to see if that truck was still there.
I was surprised to see it.
I waded to the truck and crawled into a window
To try the starter.
The engine barely turned. I thought it was best
To leave it while the battery still had some juice.
I'd been readin' a copy of Ernest Hemingway's
Islands in the Stream.
Left it on the dashboard. The last I saw,
It was floatin' down the creek. I had a refrigerator-freezer
That plugged into the cigarette lighter.
It hadn't floated out of the window yet.

The frame's restin' on the sand in the creek bed.
All the wheels're covered with sand.
You can just see a little bit of one front wheel,
And the creek water flowed over the engine all night.
What do we do?' the BLM guy asked me.
'Well,' I said, 'I reckon I could bring my bulldozer
Three miles up the canyon and pull you out.'
'I dunno about that,' he says.
'I'll have to call Government Services Agency who leased
The trucks to the BLM,
To see what their correct procedure is in a case like this.
We don't want to get it out in a way
That they won't authorize.'
So he made the call.
The office said to tow that truck two hundred and fifty miles
To Las Cruces, but he didn't have no money to rent a tow bar.
I took him to the tow bar rental garage,
And offered to loan him the sixty-seven dollars for that tow bar.
He called the Bureau of Land Management in Las Cruces,
To see if they'd pay back the loan.
'They probably will,' a nice girl said,
'But it may take an awful long time for the paperwork to be pro-
      cessed.'
After a day or two, he left the ranch and Douglas,
Being towed behind another government truck that'd been sent to
      save him.
He thanked me for my help, and for my cowboy bringin' him
      into town,
And for the meals my wife gave him, and the use of my bulldozer,
And the telephone, and the loan of sixty-seven dollars.
I thanked him for his help in managin' my ranch."
"Yep," says Bill Bryan, "with a little help
The government sure gets the job done."

To Go Up a Little Waterfall

Walter and Drum were in upper Guadalupe Canyon,
The country was very rough, almost too rough,
Even for cattle raised in Guadalupe, to make a living.

They were having trouble driving forty head of replacement
    heifers
Up a little waterfall towards the source of Guadalupe.
Walter was about sixty-five. Drum was thirty-two.
Walter had been raised in the canyons of the Guadalupe watershed.
They were at that place where four little canyons
Came together to spill into Guadalupe.
The lion-hunting Glenns called this area "Lion Canyon."
The homesteading Johnson family called it "Guadalupe above the
    Box."
The Mexicans and Drum called it *"De los Pilares por Arriba."*
Roberto called it "Salsipuedes Canyon," which meant "get out, if
    you can."
In that place there was an opening that could hold
About as many heifers as Walter and Drum were driving.
But the heifers would have to take the first step to go up a little
    waterfall,
And then higher into the basin of Lion Canyon,
From there, to the North, would be an easy drive.
Walter and Drum were sitting on their horses, at that joining place,
Waiting for one of the heifers to take the first step to go up the
    waterfall,
That first heifer in front of the waterfall didn't want to go,
They couldn't get close to push her, because the other heifers were
    in the way.
From Drum's young point of view, he felt that he and Walter had
    already
Waited quite awhile for the cattle to move.
So, after Drum couldn't stand to wait any longer,
He rode his horse up a ways, maybe thirty steps,
Over to where Walter was sitting on his horse, Red.
Drum asked if Walter thought, maybe, the heifers would go on up
    the waterfall.
"Well," said Walter, "I guess maybe they might go up the country
    now."
Then, he took down the coils of his saddle rope, and ran all the slack
Back through the honda, so the loop would not catch one of the
    heifers

Then, as though the weight of the coils of his rope were a rock, he
    threw it,
Still holding to the last coil, so that he could recoil
and throw the rope again if he had to.
The coils hit her in the buttock. The heifer jumped.
She led the others up the waterfall, and higher up into Lion
    Canyon.
They sat on their horses for another little while,
To make sure that the heifers could see
The easier country ahead, and also the good grass feed.
That little drive done, Walter and Drum turned their horses
To head down Guadalupe towards home.
That night at dinner, as was the custom with cowboys, they talked
    about the day.
Since Walter was so much older and more experienced,
With cattle and horses and rough country,
Drum asked, "How much longer would you have waited
To push all those heifers up the waterfall if I had not ridden over?"
"Well," said Walter, "When you're a-drivin' cattle through a rocky
    country,
And there's a real bad place that you're in, and you don't know
    what to do,
I've found, if you'll just wait longer than you could ever think,
That's the quickest way to go through."

GATHERING THE REMNANT

Summer Morning

When the morning sunlight hits these blue mountaintops,
When the mockingbirds begin to call,
And the breeze blows cool down the canyon,
We'll stop here a moment to watch, on old Tico horse.
Maybe we'll hear a calf bawl,
Maybe a cow will step out from behind a bush
While these long shadows flow away into the West,
Along the mountains where the ridgelines go . . .
Till that burning round ball of the sun

Lifts over the ridgeline, and it's morning.
Drum slaps the coils of his saddle rope
Against the right leg of his chaps.
"C'mon, Tico horse," he says,
"Let's go gather what's left of the remnant."

Continuity

ELMER KELTON

Author of over forty novels, Elmer Kelton has been writing for more than fifty years. Four of Elmer Kelton's books have won the Western Heritage Award from the National Cowboy Hall of Fame, and seven have won the Spur Award from Western Writers of America.

He is the recipient of numerous other awards, among them the first Lone Star Award for lifetime achievement from the Larry McMurtry Center for Arts and Humanities at Midwestern State University. He was given a lifetime achievement award by the National Cowboy Symposium. The Texas Legislature proclaimed Elmer Kelton Day in April 1997.

A native of Crane, Texas, Kelton served in the U.S. Army, including combat infantry service in Europe. He and his wife, Ann, have been married over fifty years. They have two grown sons, a daughter, four grandchildren, and five great-grandchildren.

ED WHITLEY WOULD always remember where he was and what he was doing when the old man had his heart attack: in the dusty corrals behind the barn, preg-checking a set of Bar W black baldy heifers.

It was not a dignified job for a cowboy who would much rather be on horseback, doing something else—anything else. It was not the pastoral western scene depicted on calendars or Christmas cards, and certainly not the stuff of song and story. It was messy work and smelled a little, but it had become an economic necessity of life for a rancher in a time of tight or negative profit margins. A dollar saved was better than a dollar earned, for it was not subject to income tax.

To Ed's knowledge, his father had had no previous indications that a coronary was imminent. If there had been, the old man had remained tight-lipped about them. Tom Whitley had always regarded aches and pains as a personal affront, to be borne in silence. To complain was to give them importance.

Ed's probing fingers had just confirmed the presence of a developing calf when he saw Tom fall against the steel squeeze chute, one hand grasping for a rail, the other clutching at his chest. The old man's eyes were wide in surprise and pain and confusion, his mouth open for a cry that choked off before it started. Ed jerked his arm free and ripped off the shoulder-length plastic glove that had covered his hand and sleeve. He caught Tom and eased him to a sitting position on the ground.

Ed's grown son Clay vaulted over the crowding-pen fence and came running, along with ranch hand Miguel Cervantes.

The old man wheezed, "I'm all right. It's just that sausage I had for breakfast."

Ed knew better. He had seen that look before, when his neighbor Alex Hawkins had collapsed and died at the bankruptcy auction that sold out his cattle and rolling stock two years ago.

"Help me get him to the pickup," he shouted.

HE HAD NEVER understood how doctors could have such a dispassionate attitude in the face of suffering and human mortality. With no more emotion than if he was reading the cafeteria menu, the emergency-room doctor confirmed Ed's opinion that his father had suffered a heart attack.

"We will not know the extent of muscle damage or blockage until we have done an angiogram. We must assume, though, that it has been severe. I do not wish to sound alarmist, but you had better prepare yourself and your family for the worst."

"Dad's got a constitution like a horse. He hasn't had a sick day in his life, hardly."

"With an eighty-year-old heart, it may take only one."

Tom was eighty-two, if one wished to be technical about it, but he acted as if he were twenty or thirty years younger. He rode more miles a-horseback than Ed and far more than Clay, who lived in town and held down an eight-hours-a-day job at the feed mill. Clay helped at the ranch on weekends.

Tom persisted in wrestling fifty-pound feed sacks two at a time when Ed was not looking. Somewhere in his sixties he seemed to have made up his mind not to get any older, but not to die, either. He had gotten away with it, except for a little arthritis in his joints that occasionally forced him into minor retreat but never into surrender. He had also come into increasing reliance on reading glasses. But he still ate beef for dinner and supper every day, using his own teeth.

In the back of his mind Ed had known his father could not live forever, but he had never allowed himself to dwell upon that. He could not visualize the ranch without Tom Whitley. From Ed's earliest memories, Tom and the home place had been one and the same, inseparable. Tom's father, Ed's grandfather, had acquired the nucleus of the ranch around the turn of the century, homesteading four sections under Texas law. Tom had been born there and over the years had more than doubled the size of the place. With Ed's help he had cleared the land debt so that the ranch now was free and clear.

"Ready to pass on, without no encumbrance," Tom had said when they paid the final note. But Tom had shown no inclination to pass it on. Now Ed had to face the shattering probability that the time had come. Nothing would ever again be as it had been. He could see no continuity between the past and the future. Losing Tom would be like cutting a tree off from its roots.

They moved Tom into the intensive care unit. The hospital had rules about visitation, but it was lax on enforcement in regard to family members. Ed never asked permission to stay in the room with his father, and nobody contested him. For a long time Tom seemed to be asleep. He was hooked to a monitor, its green screen showing heartbeats as a series of bobbles up and down from a straight line. Ed would watch the screen awhile, then stare at Tom, forcing up old memories as if he had to retrieve them now or lose them as he was losing his father. Most were pleasant, or at least benign.

He could not remember a great deal about his grandfather. The face that came to his mind's eye owed more to old photographs than to life. He knew that Morgan Whitley had come of age in the waning years of the great trail drives and the open range. The ranch's outside fence still retained segments of the original wire and posts that Morgan had installed some ninety years ago, though the toll of time had caused most to be rebuilt in recent years. Even when replacing it, Tom and Ed had coiled and saved some of the rusty old wire and hung it on the barn wall as a keepsake, for Morgan's strong hands had once gripped it. A lively imagination could fantasize that his fingerprints were still fixed upon the steel strands.

Many ranches had unbroken family ownership into the third, fourth, and fifth generations. It conveyed, in a peculiar way, a sort of immortality to those who had gone on. This continuity fostered a reverence for the land as if it were a living member of the family. It engendered in the later generations a strong urge to protect and improve rather than to mine the land for immediate gain at the expense of the future.

But Ed feared for that continuity when Tom was gone. Tom's boots made big tracks, as his father's had before him. Ed felt inadequate to fill them. His life had been relatively easy compared to Tom's and to Morgan's. Most of the building had been completed before he had come of age. He had inherited the fruit without having to dig through the rock and plant the tree.

This was Saturday, so Clay was not on duty at the mill. He had remained at the corrals to finish the day's job. It was an unwritten tenet of ranch life that not even an emergency should interrupt work in progress if any alternative was available. Ed arose from the hard chair as Clay and Ed's wife Frances came into the room. Neither asked aloud, for they could not be certain that Tom would not hear. Ed answered just as silently with a shrug of his shoulders, followed by a solemn shaking of his head. Frances slipped her arm around his waist, offering him emotional support. Clay said his young wife Susan was downstairs with their five-year-old son. The hospital did not allow children into ICU.

Clay moved close to his grandfather's bedside and stared down gravely into the lined face that had been a part of his daily life as far back as memory went. Tears welled into his eyes.

When Ed had been a boy, Tom had been demanding of him—often unreasonably demanding, in Ed's view. He remembered a time when Tom had taken a dislike to Ed's way of mounting a horse and had made him practice getting on and off until Ed had thought his legs would collapse. Tom had drilled him mercilessly in the art of roping, making him do it over and over, day after day, until he rarely missed a loop. Not until years later did Tom confide that his own father had done the same thing to him. It was not enough to pass on property. It was necessary to pass on knowledge and skills if the property was to have meaning and continuity.

Tom had mellowed by the time his grandson had come along. He had shown infinitely more patience in teaching Clay the cowboy trade. At those rare times when discipline was called for, Tom had walked away and left that painful duty to Ed.

Odd, Ed thought, how sometimes the further apart people were in age, the closer they seemed in their relationships with one another.

The boy had learned diligently, polishing the horseback skills passed down from his great-grandfather Morgan through Tom, then through Ed and finally to Clay.

Frontier realities had limited Morgan Whitley's formal schooling to a couple of years, though he had acquired a liberal education in the school of practical experience, with graduate honors in hard knocks. Better times had allowed Tom to finish high school before turning to a full-time career as a working cowpuncher and eventual partnership with his father.

Ed, the third generation, had gone on to earn a degree in animal husbandry at Texas A&M. It was an accomplishment Tom had always regarded with a conflicting mixture of pride and distrust. "Most of what I know about a cow," he had often declared, "you ain't goin' to find in no Aggie textbook."

Tom's eyelids fluttered awhile before he opened his eyes, blinking as his vision adjusted itself to the fluorescent lights of the hospital room. He focused first on Tom and Frances, then let his gaze drift to Clay. At first he seemed confused about his surroundings. Ed grasped his father's hand to keep him from tearing loose the tube that fed him glucose.

Anyone else might have asked how he had come to be where he was or what kind of shape he was in, but not Tom. He had always been one to take care of business first. "You-all finish with them heifers?"

Clay said, "We did, Granddad—Miguel and me. They were all settled but three."

"Hell of a note, stoppin' work to rush me in here like this when there wasn't nothin' wrong except that sausage. I could tell the minute I ate it . . ."

Ed said, "It's a lot more than the sausage. Doctor says it's your heart." He stopped there. He thought it best not to tell his father how serious his condition really was unless it became necessary to prevent him from climbing out of bed. It would be like Tom to get in the pickup and head for the ranch in his hospital gown if they wouldn't give him his shirt and Levi's.

Tom grumbled, "Probably just overdone myself workin' that squeeze chute. Never did see that we need to preg-test those heifers. You can tell soon enough which ones come up heavy with calf and which ones don't."

Ed could have told him, as he had before, that checking the heifers early for pregnancy allowed for culling of the slow breeders before they had time to run up an unnecessary feed bill. Moreover, high fertility was a heritable characteristic. The early breeders were the kind a rancher wanted to keep in his herd, for they passed that trait on to their offspring. The slow ones were a drag on the bottom line.

But to Tom, that had always been an Aggie textbook notion. He distrusted selection judgments based on records or mechanical measurements. He preferred to rely upon his eyes.

He had not thought much of artificial insemination either, when Ed had first brought it to the ranch.

Tom had not always been so reluctant to try new ideas. Neither, for that matter, had Ed's grandfather Morgan, up to a point. Though Morgan had been a product of the open range, he had built a barbed-wire fence around the perimeter of his holdings as soon as he had been financially able to buy cedar posts and wire. That had allowed him to keep his own cattle in and his neighbors' out. He had gradually upgraded the quality of his herd through use of better sires without his cows being subject to the amorous attentions of inferior stray bulls.

But as the years went by, Morgan had become increasingly conservative, content with things as they were and quick to reject the innovations of a younger generation. He had looked askance upon the advent of the automobile and truck as tools of the ranching trade. He argued that anything he needed could be carried by a good wagon and team. As for cattle and horses, they could walk anywhere it was needful for them to go; they didn't have to be hauled.

He and his son had almost come to a fistfight over Tom's purchase of a light truck. In time he became accepting enough to ride in a truck or car, but to the end he stubbornly refused to place his hands on the wheel of one.

Tom often told about building his first horse trailer. He had long wished for a way to eliminate the waste of time involved in riding horseback to a far corner of the ranch to do a job, then returning home the same slow way. It took longer to get there and back than to do the work. He acquired the chassis of a wrecked Model T and stripped it down to the wheels and frame. Atop this he built a three-sided wooden box with a gate in the rear. Crude though it was, it could haul two horses, pulled by the truck.

Morgan had ridiculed the idea. "First thing you know, you'll never see a cowboy ridin' anymore, or a horse walkin'."

Gradually, however, the horse trailer became a regular and accepted fact of survival in the ranching business. It allowed more work to be done in less time and with less labor.

Through thrift and careful borrowing, Tom had managed to add on to the ranch, each addition and each mortgage coming over Morgan's strong objections and predictions of imminent ruin. He had brought a telephone to the ranch, and a gasoline-driven generator to furnish limited 32-volt power so the two houses and the barn could have electric lights. He had even bought Morgan a radio in hopes it would keep his widowed father from feeling so lonely when he sat alone at night in the original old ranch house. At least, he argued, Morgan could keep up with the world news.

"You're wastin' your money," Morgan had declared. "I won't ever listen to the thing. I won't even turn it on."

Tom had often delighted in telling about the time a few weeks later when conversation somehow turned to country music, and old Morgan exclaimed, "Say, that Uncle Dave Macon can sure play the banjo, can't he?"

The aging open-range cowboy had died just before the outbreak of World War II, leaving Tom to run the ranch after his own lights. Tom had sometimes wondered aloud how his father would have reacted to the technological innovations that war and its aftermath had wrought upon the ranching industry.

Tom had cross-fenced the ranch for better control of grazing. He had replaced the generator with REA electricity. But in time he had settled into the same brand of conservatism as his father when it came to modern innovations. He treated with skepticism many of the ideas Ed brought home from A&M.

"Aggie textbook notions," he would snort. Some he accepted after a time. Others he never did.

DESPITE HEAVY MEDICATION, Tom awoke in the early morning hours, as he was accustomed to doing at home. Ed's back ached from sitting up all night in the straight hard-backed chair. He suspected that hospitals purposely installed uncomfortable furniture to discourage visitors from staying too long. Tom stared at his son with concern in his eyes.

"You ever get anything to eat last night?"

"I slipped away for a bite with Frances while Clay was here."

"You better go and get you some breakfast, else you'll be the one sick in here instead of me."

"Later. I don't want to miss seein' the doctor."

"Ain't no doctor goin' to show up this early unless he's still here this late."

"I'll be all right."

Tom stared at him awhile. "Sure, you'll be all right. Ever since you were old enough to straddle a horse, I've been tryin' to get you ready for this. Now it's come time, ready or not."

Ed realized his father was not just thinking about Ed's immediate need for nourishment. "Don't you be talkin' thataway. You'll be out of here in a few days if you'll do what they tell you."

"I'm goin' out of here in that long black wagon. We both know that. I could feel old St. Peter breathin' on my neck half the night. But you'll be all right. What you goin' to do about Clay?"

"What's there to do about him?"

"You'll have to talk him into leavin' that piddlin' job at the mill. You'll need his help full-time when I'm gone."

Ed's throat tightened painfully. He did not want to talk about this, but Tom was persistent. He seemed to sense that he did not have a lot of time to get the talking done.

Tom said, "He's a good boy, even if he *has* got some newfangled ideas. Some of them'll work, and some won't. You'll have to get a feel for how tight to hold the reins, and how loose, same as I did with you and my daddy did with me."

Ed did not know how to reply. It hurt too much to acknowledge what Tom was saying. "You'll come through this all right," he said, though the words were hollow. He knew differently, and so did Tom.

Tom said, "That's the way of the world. It's up to the young ones to keep movin' forward, and up to the older ones to keep the young from runnin' the train off of the track. And it's why the old have to pass out of the picture, so the train won't come to a stop altogether and maybe even slide back down the hill."

"Things wouldn't ever be the same out there without you."

"They ain't meant to be. If my daddy had had his way, we'd still be drivin' cattle afoot to the railroad. If *his* daddy had had his way, there wouldn't even be no railroad. We don't none of us—old or young—ever have it just the way we'd want it, and that's probably a good thing."

THOUGH SOME RANCHERS saw Sunday as just another day for work—it seemed there never were enough days to do it all—Tom Whitley had always accepted Sunday as a day of rest. It was fitting, Ed thought later, that on a Sunday he slipped away into his final rest. Helplessly Ed watched the monitor screen as the line jumped violently up and down, then flattened. The most strenuous efforts of doctor and nurses could not alter the inexorable course of nature.

Frances was with Ed at the end, and so was Clay. It helped, not having to face this dark moment alone.

Ed said quietly, "I don't know how we'll survive without him, son."

"What did he do when *his* dad died?"

"He picked himself up and went his own way."

Clay gently laid a hand on his father's shoulder. "Then that's what we'll do."

The return to the ranch after the funeral was one of the most trying ordeals of Ed's life. He tried to find comfort in the fact that nothing physical had changed. The entrance gate, the headquarters layout, all looked the same as he drove in. Four horses stood near the barn, waiting for someone to fork hay into the steel rack. Either Tom or Ed customarily did so in the late afternoon. A Jersey milk cow stood outside the milk-pen gate, patiently awaiting the bucket of ground feed that would be poured for her as she took her place in the stanchion. All these things were the same as they had been for years and years. In these, at least, there was constancy.

But Tom's red dog, tail wagging, came out to meet the car. It watched Ed and Frances get out, then looked expectantly for its master. It turned away, its tail drooping in disappointment. It retreated toward the house where Tom had lived since Ed's mother had died, and Tom had turned the larger, newer house over to Ed and Frances. Ed watched the dog and felt anew the pain of loss.

"We'll have to get Red used to comin' to our house for his supper," he said.

Frances nodded. "It'll take him a while to quit missin' Tom."

Ed winced. "I doubt I ever will."

✦

THE DOG NEVER did become accustomed to staying around the bigger house. It did not have to. Clay resigned his job at the feed mill, and he and Susan moved into Tom's house. Though it was old and still bore much of Morgan Whitley's imprint, as well as Tom's, it had most of the modern conveniences that a town girl like Susan was used to.

Clay's being around all the time helped Ed's adjustment to the change. Before, Ed had tried to see to it that he and Miguel did the heavier and more menial work, leaving the lighter chores for Tom. Now Clay and Miguel took on most of the heavier lifting, and Ed found himself doing more of the things that Tom had regarded as his own province. Ed resented it a little at first, though he kept his feelings to himself. It seemed they now considered him an old man who had to be sheltered. He was not old, not by a damn sight. But after a time he began to appreciate their deference. His back did not hurt as much as it used to, and he found himself able to spend more time on horseback, riding over the country the way he liked to do.

It warmed Ed's soul, too, to look toward the older house and see Clay's boy Billy riding a stick horse in the front yard. It was high time, Ed thought, to find a pony so the boy could start learning to ride. Billy's cowboy education had been neglected in town. Ed would get him a rope, too, and a plastic steer head to attach to a bale of hay so he could learn to throw a loop around the horns.

Ed sensed that something had begun to nag at Clay. His son became subject to long periods of thoughtful silence, as if he had something on his mind that he was reluctant to voice.

Whatever the problem was, Ed decided the time had come to bring it into the open air. One possibility had occurred to him early. "Is it Susan and that house? I know it's old, and I guess it's got Dad's brand all over it. My granddad's, too. But she's welcome to redo it any way she wants to. It's her house now."

Clay seemed surprised at the thought. "The house is fine. She loves it. We like the idea that we're the fourth generation of Whitleys that's lived in it, and Billy's the fifth. It's like they're all still with us, that nobody's gone."

Ed wished he could see it that way. Tom *was* gone. The root had been severed. The feeling of continuum was lost.

"Well, if it's not the house, what's the trouble?"

Clay frowned, and he took a while in bringing himself to answer. "I've been workin' on an idea. I've been kind of shy about bringin' it up because I don't know how you'll take it."

"Spill it, and we'll find out."

"You've heard them talk about cell grazin' plans, where they take a pasture and fence it up into twelve or fifteen small paddocks. They throw all their cattle onto one at a time and move them every two or three days. That way most of the ranch is restin', and the grass has a chance to grow. It makes for a healthier range."

Ed could only stare at him.

Clay took a sheet of paper from his shirt pocket and unfolded it. Ed recognized a pencil-drawn map of the ranch. Clay placed a finger on the spot that marked the headquarters. "I've figured how we can divide up all our pastures with cheap electric fence and have ourselves four grazin' cells. It's worked on lots of other ranches."

"But this isn't some other ranch." Ed's impatience bubbled to the top. He could imagine Morgan's or Tom's reaction to such a farfetched idea. "Where did you ever come up with such a radical notion—some Aggie textbook?"

Aggie textbook! Ed wondered for a moment how that expression had popped into his head. Then he remembered. He had heard it from Tom—more times than he wanted to recall.

Looking deflated, Clay studied the paper. "I've had the idea for a long while. I knew better than to try it on Granddad, but I thought you might give it a chance."

"He would've said what I did."

"In the same voice, and the same words, more than likely." Clay managed a wry smile through his disappointment. "You even look like him at a little distance. Funny, you were worried that things could never be the same with Granddad gone. But you've fitted right into his boots."

Ed pondered on what Tom had said about it being the responsibility of the young to originate fresh ideas while the old held the reins, loosening or tightening them as the need came.

Ed compromised, as Tom often had. "Tell you what: we'll try your idea, but we'll go at it slow. We'll take the northeast pasture first and see how it works out. In two or three years, if we like it, we'll talk about doin' the rest of the place. This is a drastic change you're throwin' at me."

"As drastic as Granddad buyin' the first truck, or buildin' the first trailer? Or you startin' artificial insemination and preg-checkin'?"

Ed stared toward the old house. Billy was in the front yard, playing with the red dog. Red had taken right up with the boy, tagging along with him as he had tagged after Tom. Ed thought about Tom, and about Morgan Whitley. The word came to him from somewhere. "Continuity."

Clay puzzled. "What do you mean, continuity?"

"Just thinkin' about somethin' your granddad said. I'll tell you some-day, when it's time for *you* to think about it."

Looking Glass

WILLIAM KITTREDGE

William Kittredge has written a memoir, Hole in the Sky, *collections of essays, short stories, and novels, including a series of Western novels.*

He grew up on a ranch in southeastern Oregon, farmed until he was in his thirties, studied at the Writers' Workshop at the University of Iowa, and became the Regents Professor of English and Creative Writing at the University of Montana until his retirement. He has received numerous prestigious awards, including a Stegner Fellowship at Stanford, two Writing Fellowships from the National Endowment for the Arts, two Pacific Northwest Bookseller's Awards for Excellence, and the PEN Award. He was coproducer of the movie A River Runs Through It.

He also, with Annick Smith, edited The Last Best Place: A Montana Anthology. *He lives in Missoula, Montana.*

SIMON FANTARA STANDS on a sandy bar at the edge of the Clearwater River, which was known as Kookooskia. He is thinking of Looking Glass, the warrior chieftain for the Nez Perce, people who said Canada was Grandmother's Land in those days when they believed Queen Victoria owned it and was grandmother to the world.

The U.S. Cavalry was winning the battles, and there was nothing left but escape, Joseph aimed the people north on their way to the Bear Paw Mountains of Montana where Looking Glass died and Joseph gave up because the children wailed in the cold. There could be no fires and no light and all they had suffered for was lost. The wind was filled with snow as Looking Glass died on the cut bank above Snake Creek. Simon Fantara tries to become Looking Glass, imagining losses and lies.

Mists lift away into the forests beyond the green twists of water and black boulders. Some people thought it was no sin to tell a lie the first time, and that there was no sin in telling it a second time. But three times? Tell that many lies and you become someone else. Simon Fantara imagines dying in the Bear Paw Mountains.

"So leave," Corrie said, and her eyes were golden and solemn behind her amber-colored glasses.

Simon Fantara had his nights of driving the freeway up to Santa Barbara or out to some honky-tonk tavern on the edge of the Mojave, anywhere so long as it took the night. The great rows of sprinklers sighed and whirled over the desert alfalfa fields in the early morning as he drove and Corrie slept beside him.

Their first morning together, on the sloping lawn above the swimming pool, they played badminton after coming out of the sauna. She gave him the uphill side.

"Don't want to pick on a cripple," she said, and he wondered if she thought of him as an old man because his right leg had been broken so many times and so badly he had to wear a chrome-plated brace buckled to his thigh and curved under the sole of his boot. It was the kind of thing she kept on saying, which didn't bother him because anybody knew it took a certain amount of smart-ass to survive.

Simon was barefoot that morning and his leg hadn't hurt enough to bother, the sunlight was discolored by haze from fire in the mountains north of Ojai, and Corrie was a pleasure to watch as she beat him, until she fielded his serve and stopped. "That's enough," she said. "I'm sorry."

"I'm always beating people," she said, looking up at him with her head turned so the morning was red in her hair. She said she had never been able to cure herself.

"Makes my kidneys ache," he said, as if that meant anything. That evening on the hillside above Malibu the world seemed green beside the imitation Moorish house her father bought her the first time she was married, vines climbing to the iron-work balconies, and they went back in the sauna and that second night got drunk on mescal again and slept wrapped in blankets on the lawn. At daybreak the edge of sunlight came sparkling toward them from the ocean toward Catalina, and four days later she had him downtown trying out for a Chrysler commercial. He was, after all, a Champion of the World.

CORRIE HAD BEEN gone three days without saying she was going anywhere when Burton Davis called, saying he had this deal in Montana, where Simon would play Indian, and Simon hitched his four-horse aluminum trailer to rattle along empty behind his yellow Continental, and crossed from Malibu in San Fernando and then over to Bakersfield and north, not thinking in the hot wind of the valley with the windows open and the air-conditioning off until he checked into a motel on the outskirts of Lodi, a line of wood-frame shacks painted orange, only blocks from the Holiday Inn where he could have stayed.

Back to it now, he thought, and he knew this was foolishness, his old life in motels being the last thing he was after. He cut the plastic around the cap of a pint of Johnny Walker Red and when it was gone he wasn't sleepy.

With morning just beginning to show he crossed Donner summit over the Sierras and curved down into Reno and a three hundred and fifty-eight dollar hour at a crap table on the second floor of Harold's Club. Walking out he won two hundred back on a dime slot as four stars spun into a row.

Simon slept in the Lincoln just south of Pyramid Lake, stopped in the twilight outside Winnemucca to puke while traffic thundered on toward night in the east, his head aching after five shots of Johnny Walker in a glaring Lovelock barroom, nothing to puke but the whiskey and three pickled sausages from a half-empty plastic jar. Simon wiped his mouth and had a sense of having gotten away. The desert was quiet and empty under the smoky light, and he thought of turning north to find a ranch in the unknown country around the Black Rock Desert and taking up a cowhand life.

North of Wells he was off the freeway and onto narrow pitted asphalt rising and falling through scrub-brush sand hills, a dark line in the beginning of morning. The highlands were soft and undulating. Like the palms of the first buckskin gloves he'd ever owned, that was what he thought. Those gloves had been bought with wages earned starting colts the summer he was fourteen.

Those gloves had been chewed and stitched by the women in their camp alongside the Bitterroot River, a willow ramada and three tin-roofed, rotting houses built of cottonwood logs that had been bulldozed into a heap and burned on a fall day in the late fifties, after that one-eyed and crazy old man named Daddy Clock-Stocking was carted off to die with relatives on the reservation near Browning.

Corrie said he had too much imagination. She said that was why they liked him. "You're willing to be anybody," she said. "So they love you. Why wouldn't they?"

And she was right, it was easy enough. Simon slept through the day in Twin Falls, Idaho, while the air conditioner hummed and the television picture revolved.

THE BLOND GIRL from Salmon shook her bracelets and talked about the man she loved, who had gone north to roughneck in the oilfields around Calgary, and stayed. She said she was going to find that man. Simon told her about the old days in Calgary, parties every night and the wild cow milking with Oscar Dodson the year they started out, and driving to the snowy mountains off west with the girls from Shelby, and going back to the mountains with Jackie Belle Deer the summer Simon had won bareback and the bull riding and the all-round money at Calgary. He told the blond girl from Salmon about the dust hanging above the willow corral at Boulder Cabin before sunrise as he stood by the juniper centerpost with seventy head of geldings circling counterclockwise around him and then reversing when he flipped his seagrass riata underhanded and dropped the loop over the head of a long-legged bay with scabbed withers, somebody's traveling horse: Catching the horses one by one for the men behind him trailing bridles and hackamores and then those men going down the taut rope toward the trembling animal to touch the flaring muzzle and slipping the cold steel snaffle bit into the mouth of whatever horse it was they wanted for that day.

The blue '61 Ford pickup and the camper and Jackie Belle Deer and the flush days of going from one show to another with Jackie Belle, and Jackie Belle taking off with better than twenty-five grand and that calf roper named Verlon Perkins and who could blame her after the summer his leg was smashed against a bucking chute in Jacksonville, Oregon.

"You'll never marry me," Jackie Bell said. "I got to take care of myself." Who could blame her for that? Only a fool would go at life imagining that his talent for staying on horseback would get him through, even if you owned a buckle, heavy silver, and gold, the size of a man's hand, engraved with your name: Simon Fantera, Champion of the World.

OUT ON THE northern plains just short of Canada, Simon parked under trees by the Tree House Motel in Havre. He stood up at the bar and one of the old men turned to him and said, "Hell, been a long time."

"We got old," the man said.

An hour or so later Simon was drunk and a black-haired girl named Mary Ann was watching him drink and Simon was watching the Miller

High Life clock, yellow-edged and plastic, a rotating sphere with the time on one side and an imitation glass of beer on the other. He'd told the girl named Mary Ann that the color of whiskey and water was a color for remembering. "Makes me think of fishing," he said. "That's pretty," she said, and she drifted away.

The summer he was thirty, completely down, crutches under his arms after Jackie Belle left, Simon hocked the buckle in Reno and bought some food and then called Benny Jackson in Elk River, Idaho. "You might as well come on up," Benny said, "if you're crippled."

Benny had wired money for bus fare but Simon got the buckle out of the hock shop instead, and hitchhiked, waving his crutches until a car stopped, and wore away the summer scuffing around to serve tap beer in Benny's bar in Elk River, shacking up with Benny's wife while Benny was off team roping in California.

Things to do in Elk River, Benny's hometown. Screw Benny's pride-and-joy behind his back and feel sorry for Benny because he'd married such a woman to get his hands on her father's bar.

THE LEAD SLUG that would strike him center in the forehead, take after take, until it was right, suitable to print. Simon imagined the blow being soft as a hummingbird strike before death. The dry brown stain painted across his chest was another skin ending at the whiteness of his neck. Makeup people out at Bear Paw would do his face. It had to be right as the bullet struck, and Looking Glass died.

"What it is, see," the director said, "is simple. You stare off like you were watching the military coming, and then you're shot. You fall forward. It's against the rules of physics, but who gives a shit?"

Swallows nested in the bluff above Snake Creek, and off west there was dust curving up behind a yellow Buick convertible. Simon stood with his face painted and did not fall, and Looking Glass lived until the dust fell away. The sixth take was perfect, the camera eye widening in jump cuts. Behind Looking Glass there was eastern sky, that falling man becoming faint and grainy against it as the jagged alpine Bitterroot Mountains under first snow were imposed over the dark old forests of the Selway, the Clearwater, Kookooskia, where Looking Glass was the war chief.

The Hard Way

ELMORE LEONARD

Elmore Leonard's first published story, "Trail of the Apache," was in Ar-
gosy magazine in 1951. Between then and 1961 he published thirty short
stories and five novels in the Western genre. His novel Hombre was chosen
one of the best Westerns of all time by the Western Writers of America. As
the market for Westerns disappeared, he began to write crime novels and
has earned extraordinary critical success as well as bestsellerdom. He is the
recipient of the Grand Master Award of the Mystery Writers of America.
Many of his novels have become successful movies.

He lives with his wife, Christine, in a suburb of Detroit, Michigan.

TIO ROBLES STRETCHED stiffly on the straw mattress,
holding the empty mescal bottle upright on his chest. His sleepy eyes
studied Jimmy Robles going through his ritual. Tio was half smiling,
watching with amusement.

Jimmy Robles buttoned his shirt carefully, even the top button, and
pushed the shirttail tightly into his pants, smooth and tight with no
blousing about the waist. It made him move stiffly the few minutes he
was conscious of keeping the clean shirt smooth and unwrinkled. He
lifted the gun belt from a wall peg and buckled it around his waist, inhaling slowly, watching the faded cotton stretch tight across his stomach. And when he wiped his high black boots it was with the same
deliberate care.

Tio's sleepy smile broadened. "Jaime," he spoke softly, "you look very
pretty. Are you to be married today?" He waited. "Perhaps this is a feast
day that has slipped my mind." He waited longer. "No? Or perhaps the
mayor has invited you to dine with him."

Jimmy Robles picked up the sweat-dampened shirt he had taken off
and unpinned the silver badge from the pocket. Before looking at his
uncle he breathed on the metal and rubbed its smooth surface over the

tight cloth of his chest. He pinned it to the clean shirt, studying the inscription cut into the metal that John Benedict had told him read *Deputy Sheriff.*

Sternly, he said, "You drink too much," but could not help smiling at this picture of indolence sprawled on the narrow bed with a foot hooked on the window ledge above, not caring particularly if the world ended at that moment.

"Why don't you stop for a few days, just to see what it's like?"

Tio closed his eyes. "The shock would kill me."

"You're killing yourself anyway."

Tio mumbled, "But what a fine way to die."

Jimmy left the adobe hut and crossed a backyard before passing through the narrow dimness of two adobes that squeezed close together, and when he reached the street he tilted his hat closer to his eyes against the afternoon glare and walked up the street toward Arivaca's business section. This was a part of Saturday afternoon. This leaving the Mexican section that was still quiet, almost deserted, and walking up the almost indiscernible slope that led to the more prosperous business section.

Squat gray adobe grew with the slope from Spanishtown into painted, two-story false fronts with signs hanging from the ramadas. Soon, cowmen from the nearer ranges and townspeople who had quit early because it was Saturday would be standing around under the ramadas, slapping each other on the shoulder thinking about Saturday night. Those who hadn't started already. And Jimmy Robles would smile at everybody and be friendly because he liked this day better than any other. People were easier to get along with. Even the Americans.

Being deputy sheriff of Arivaca wasn't a hard job, but Jimmy Robles was new. And his newness made him unsure. Not confident of his ability to uphold the law and see that the goods and rights of these people were protected while they got drunk on Saturday night.

The sheriff, John Benedict, had appointed him a month before because he thought it would be good for the Mexican population. One of their own boys. John Benedict said you performed your duty "in the name of the law." That was the thing to remember. And it made him feel uneasy because the law was such a big thing. And justice. He wished he could picture something other than that woman with the blindfold over her eyes. John Benedict spoke long of these things. He was a great man.

Not only had he made him deputy, but John Benedict had given him a pair of American boots and a pistol, free, which had belonged to a man who had been hanged the month before. Tio Robles had told him to destroy the hanged man's goods, for it was a bad sign; but that's all Tio knew about it. He was too much *Mexicano*. He would go on sweating at the wagonyard, grumbling, and drinking more mescal than he could hold. It was good he lived with Tio and was able to keep him out of trouble. Not all, some.

His head was down against the glare and he watched his booted feet move over the street dust, lost in thought. But the gunfire from upstreet brought him to instantly. He broke into a slow trot, seeing a lone man in the street a block ahead. As he approached him, he angled toward the boardwalk lining the buildings.

SID ROMAN STOOD square in the middle of the street with his feet planted wide. There was a stubble of beard over the angular lines of his lower face and his eyes blinked sleepily. He jabbed another cartridge at the open cylinder of the Colt, and fumbled trying to insert it into one of the small openings. The nose of the bullet missed the groove and slipped from his fingers. Sid Roman was drunk, which wasn't unusual, though it wasn't evident from his face. The glazed expression was natural.

Behind him, two men with their hats tilted loosely over their eyes sat on the steps of the Samas Café, their boots stretched out into the street. A half-full bottle was between them on the ramada step. A third man lounged on his elbows against the hitch rack, leaning heavily like a dead weight. Jimmy Robles moved off the boardwalk and stood next to the man on the hitch rack.

Sid Roman loaded the pistol and waved it carelessly over his head. He tried to look around at the men behind him without moving his feet and stumbled off balance, almost going down.

"Come on . . . who's got the money!" His eyes, heavy lidded, went to the two men on the steps. "Hey, Walt, dammit! Put up your dollar!"

The one called Walt said, "I got it. Go ahead and shoot," and hauled the bottle up to his mouth.

Sid Roman yelled to the man on the hitch rack, "You in, Red?" The man looked up, startled, and stared around as if he didn't know where he was.

Roman waved his pistol toward the high front of the saloon across the street. SUPREME, in foot-high red letters, ran across the board hanging from the top of the ramada. "A dollar I put five straight in the top loop of the *P.*" He slurred his words impatiently.

Jimmy Robles heard the man next to him mumble, "Sure, Sid." He looked at the sign, squinting hard, but could not make out any bullet scars near the *P.* Maybe there was one just off to the left of the *S.* He waited until the cowman turned and started to raise the Colt.

"Hey, Sid." Jimmy Robles smiled at him like a friend. "I got some good targets out back of the jail."

Aiming, Sid Roman turned irritably, hot in the face. Then the expression was blank and glassy again.

"How'd you know my name?"

Jimmy Robles smiled, embarrassed. "I just heard this man call you that."

Roman looked at him a long time. "Well you heard wrong," he finally said. "It's Mr. Roman."

A knot tightened the deputy's mouth, but he kept the smile on his lips even though its meaning was gone. "All right, mester. It's all the same to me." John Benedict said you had to be courteous.

The man was staring at him hard, weaving slightly. He had heard of Sid Roman, old man Remillard's top hand, but this was the first time he had seen him close. He stared back at the beard-grubby face and felt uneasy because the face was so expressionless—looking him over like he was a dead tree stump. Why couldn't he get laughing drunk like the Mexican boys, then he could be laughing, too, when he took his gun away from him.

"Why don't you just keep your mouth shut," Roman said, as if that was the end of it. But then he added, "Go on and sweep out your jailhouse," grinning and looking over at the men on the steps.

The one called Walt laughed out and jabbed at the other man with his elbow.

Jimmy Robles held on to the smile, gripping it with only his will now. He said, "I'm just thinking of the people. If a stray shot went inside, somebody might get hurt."

"You saying I can't shoot, or're you just chicken scared!"

"I'm just saying there are many people on the street and inside there."

"You're talking awful damn big for a dumb Mex kid. You must be awful dumb." He looked toward the steps, handling the pistol idly. "He must be awful dumb, huh, Walt?"

Jimmy Robles heard the one called Walt mumble, "He sure must," but he kept his eyes on Roman, who walked up to him slowly, still looking at him like he was a stump or something that couldn't talk back or hear. Now, only a few feet away, he saw a glimmer in the sleepy eyes as if a new thought was punching its way through his head.

"Maybe we ought to learn him something, Walt. Seeing he's so dumb." Grinning now, he looked straight into the Mexican boy's eyes. "Maybe I ought to shoot his ears off and give 'em to him for a present. What you think of that, Walt?"

Jimmy Robles's smile had almost disappeared. "I think I had better ask you for your gun, mester." His voice coldly polite.

Roman's stubble jaw hung open. It clamped shut and his face colored, through the weathered tan it colored as if it would burst open from ripeness. He mumbled through his teeth, "You two-bit kid!" and tried to bring the Colt up.

Robles swung his left hand wide as hard as he could and felt the numbing pain up to his elbow the same time Sid Roman's head snapped back. He tried to think of courtesy, his pistol, the law, the other three men, but it wasn't any of these that drew his hand back again and threw the fist hard against the face that was falling slowly toward him. The head snapped back and the body followed it this time, heels dragging in the dust off balance until Roman was spread-eagled in the street, not moving. He swung on the three men, pulling his pistol.

They just looked at him. The one called Walt shrugged his shoulders and lifted the bottle that was almost empty.

WHEN JOHN BENEDICT closed the office door behind him, his deputy was coming up the hall that connected the cells in the rear of the jail. He sat down at the rolltop desk, hearing the footsteps in the bare hallway, and swiveled his chair, swinging his back to the desk.

"I was over to the barbershop. I saw you bring somebody in," he said to Jimmy Robles entering the office. "I was all lathered up and couldn't get out. Saw you pass across the street, but couldn't make out who you had."

Jimmy Robles smiled. "Mester Roman. Didn't you hear the shooting?"

"Sid Roman?" Benedict kept most of the surprise out of his voice. "What's the charge?"

"He was drinking out in the street and betting on shooting at the sign over the Supreme. There were a lot of people around—" He wanted to add, "John," because they were good friends, but Benedict was old enough to be his father and that made a difference.

"So then he called you something and you got mad and hauled him in."

"I tried to smile, but he was pointing his gun all around. It was hard."

John Benedict smiled at the boy's serious face. "Sid call you chicken scared?"

Jimmy Robles stared at this amazing man he worked for.

"He calls everybody that when he's drunk." Benedict smiled. "He's a lot of mouth, with nothing coming out. Most times he's harmless, but someday he'll probably shoot somebody." His eyes wandered out the window. Old man Remillard was crossing the street toward the jail. "And then we'll get the blame for not keeping him here when he's full of whiskey."

Jimmy Robles went over the words, his smooth features frowning in question. "What do you mean we'll get blamed?"

Benedict started to answer him, but changed his mind when the door opened. Instead, he said, "Afternoon," nodding his head to the thick, big-boned man in the doorway. Benedict followed the rancher's gaze to Jimmy Robles. "Mr. Remillard, Deputy Sheriff Robles."

Remillard's face was serious. "Quit kidding," he said. He moved toward the sheriff. "I'm just fixing up a mistake you made. Your memory must be backing up on you, John." He was unexcited, but his voice was heavy with authority. Remillard hadn't been told no in twenty years, not by anyone, and his air of command was as natural to him as breathing. He handed Benedict a folded sheet he had pulled from his inside coat pocket, nodding his head toward Jimmy Robles.

"You better tell your boy what end's up."

He waited until Benedict looked up from the sheet of paper, then said, "I was having my dinner with Judge Essery at the Samas when my foreman was arrested. Essery's waived trial and suspended sentence. It's right there, black and white. And kind of lucky for you, John, the judge's in a good mood today." Remillard walked to the door, then turned back. "It isn't in the note, but you better have my boy out in ten minutes." That was all.

John Benedict read the note over again. He remembered the first time one like it was handed to him, five years before. He had read it over five times and had almost torn it up, before his sense returned. He wondered if he was using the right word, *sense*.

"Let him out and give him his gun back."

Jimmy Robles smiled, because he thought the sheriff was kidding. He said, "Sure," and the "John" almost slipped out with it. He propped his hip against the edge of his table-desk.

"What are you waiting for?"

Jimmy Robles came off the table now, and his face hung in surprise. "Are you serious?"

Benedict held out the note. "Read this five times and then let him go."

"But I don't understand," with disbelief all over his face. "This man was endangering lives. You said we were to protect and . . ." His voice trailed off, trying to think of all the things John Benedict had told him.

Sitting in his swivel chair, John Benedict thought, Explain that one if you can. He remembered the words better than the boy did. Now he wondered how he had kept a straight face when he had told him about rights, and the law, and seeing how the one safeguarded the other. That was John Benedict the realist. The cynic. He told himself to shut up. He did believe in ideals. What he had been telling himself for years, though having to close his eyes occasionally because he liked his job.

Now he said to the boy, "Do you like your job?" And Jimmy Robles looked at him as if he did not understand.

He started to tell him how a man elected to a job naturally had a few obligations. And in a town like Arivaca, whose business depended on spreads like Remillard's and a few others, maybe the obligations were a little heavier. It was a cowtown, so the cowman ought to be able to have what he wanted. But it was too long a story to go through. If Jimmy Robles couldn't see the handwriting, let him find out the hard way. He was old enough to figure it out for himself. Suddenly, the boy's open, wondering face made him mad.

"Well, what the hell are you waiting for!"

JIMMY ROBLES PUSHED Tio's empty mescal bottle to the foot of the bed and sat down heavily. He eased back until he was resting on his spine with his head and shoulders against the adobe wall and sat like this for a long time while the thoughts went through his head. He wished Tio were here. Tio would offer no assistance, no explanation other than his biased own, but he would laugh and that would be better than nothing. Tio would say, "What did you expect would happen, you fool?" And add, "Let us have a drink to forget the mysterious ways of the

American." Then he would laugh. Jimmy Robles sat and smoked cigarettes and he thought.

Later on, he opened his eyes and felt the ache in his neck and back. It seemed like only a few moments before he had been awake, clouded with his worrying, but the room was filled with a dull gloom. He rose, rubbing the back of his neck, and, through the open doorway that faced west, saw the red streak in the gloom over the line of trees in the distance.

He felt hungry, and the incident of the afternoon was something that might have happened a hundred years ago. He had worn himself out thinking and that was enough of it. He passed between the buildings to the street and crossed it to the adobe with the sign EMILIANO's. He felt like enchiladas and tacos and perhaps some beer if it was cold.

He ate alone at the counter, away from the crowded tables that squeezed close to each other in the hot, low-ceilinged café, taking his time and listening to the noise of the people eating and drinking. Emiliano served him, and after his meal set another beer—that was very cold—before him on the counter. And when he was again outside, the air seemed cooler and the dusk more restful.

He lighted a cigarette, inhaling deeply, and saw someone emerge from the alley that led to his adobe. The figure looked up and down the street, then ran directly toward him, shouting his name.

Now he recognized Agostino Reyes, who worked at the wagonyard with his uncle.

The old man was breathless. "I have hunted you everywhere," he wheezed, his eyes wide with excitement. "Your uncle has taken the shotgun that they keep at the company office and has gone to shoot a man!"

Robles held him hard by the shoulders. "Speak clearly! Where did he go!"

Agostino gasped out, "Earlier, a man by the Supreme insulted him and caused him to be degraded in front of others. Now Tio has gone to kill him."

Jimmy ran with his heart pounding against his chest, praying to God and His Mother to let him get there before anything happened. A block away from the Supreme he saw the people milling about the street, with all attention toward the front of the saloon. He heard the deep discharge of a shotgun and the people scattered as if the shot were a signal. In the space of a few seconds the street was deserted.

He slowed the motion of his legs and approached the rest of the way at a walk. Nothing moved in front of the Supreme, but across the street he saw figures in the shadowy doorways of the Samas Café and the hotel next door. A man stepped out to the street and he saw it was John Benedict.

"Your uncle just shot Sid Roman. Raked his legs with a Greener. He's up there in the doorway laying half dead."

He made out the shape of a man lying beneath the swing doors of the Supreme. In the dusk the street was quiet, more quiet than he had ever known it, as if he and John Benedict were alone. And then the scream pierced the stillness. "God Almighty somebody help me!" It hung there, a cold wail in the gloom, then died.

"That's Sid," Benedict whispered. "Tio's inside with his pistol. If anybody gets near that door, he'll let go and most likely finish off Sid. He's got Remillard and Judge Essery and I don't know who else inside. They didn't get out in time. God knows what he'll do to them if he gets jumpy."

"Why did Tio shoot him?"

"They say about an hour ago Sid come staggering out drunk and bumped into your uncle and started telling him where to go. But your uncle was just as drunk and he wouldn't take any of it. They started swinging and Sid got Tio down and rubbed his face in the dust, then had one of his boys get a bottle, and he sat there drinking like he was on the front porch. Sitting on Tio. Then the old man come back about an hour later and let go at him with the Greener." John Benedict added, "I can't say I blame him."

Jimmy Robles said, "What were you doing while Sid was on the front porch?" and started toward the Supreme, not waiting for an answer.

John Benedict followed him. "Wait a minute," he called, but stopped when he got to the middle of the street.

On the saloon steps he could see Sid Roman plainly in the square of light under the doors, lying on his back with his eyes closed. A moan came from his lips, but it was almost inaudible. No sound came from within the saloon.

He mounted the first step and stood there. "Tio!"

No answer came. He went all the way up on the porch and looked down at Roman. "Tio! I'm taking this man away!"

Without hesitating he grabbed the wounded man beneath the arms and pulled him out of the doorway to the darkened end of the ramada past the windows. Roman screamed as his legs dragged across the boards. Jimmy Robles moved back to the door and the quietness settled again.

He pushed the door in, hard, and let it swing back, catching it as it reached him. Tio was leaning against the bar with bottles and glasses strung out its smooth length behind him. From the porch he could see no one else. Tio looked like a frightened animal cowering in a dead-end ravine, more pathetic in his ragged and dirty cotton clothes. His rope-soled shoes edged a step toward the doorway, with his body moving in a crouch. The pistol was in front of him, his left hand under the other wrist supporting the weight of the heavy Colt and, the deputy noticed now, trying to keep it steady.

Tio waved the barrel at him. "Come in and join your friends, Jaime." His voice quivered to make the bravado meaningless.

Robles moved inside the door of the long barroom and saw Remillard and Judge Essery standing by the table nearest the bar. Two other men stood at the next table. One of them was the bartender, wiping his hands back and forth over his apron.

Robles spoke calmly. "You've done enough, Tio. Hand me the gun."

"Enough?" Tio swung the pistol back to the first table. "I have just started."

"Don't talk crazy. Hand me the gun."

"Do you think I am crazy?"

"Just hand me the gun."

Tio smiled, and by it seemed to calm. "My foolish nephew. Use your head for one minute. What do you suppose would happen to me if I handed you this gun?"

"The law would take its course," Jimmy Robles said. The words sounded meaningless even to him.

"It would take its course to the nearest cottonwood," Tio said. "There are enough fools in the family with you, Jaime." He smiled still, though his voice continued to shake.

"Perhaps this is my mission, Jaime. The reason I was born."

"You make it hard to decide just which one is the fool."

"No. Hear me. God made Tio Robles to his image and likeness that he might someday blow out the brains of Señores Rema-yard and Essery." Tio's laugh echoed in the long room.

Jimmy Robles looked at the two men. Judge Essery was holding on to the table and his thin face was white with fear, glistening with fear. And for all old man Remillard's authority, he couldn't do a thing. An old Mexican, like a thousand he could buy or sell, could stand there and do whatever he desired because he had slipped past the cowman's zone of influence, past fearing for the future.

Tio raised the pistol to the level of his eyes. It was already cocked. "Watch my mission, Jaime. Watch me send two devils to hell!"

He watched fascinated. Two men were going to die. Two men he hardly knew, but he could feel only hate for them. Not like he might hate a man, but with the anger he felt for a principle that went against his reason. Something big, like injustice. It went through his mind that if these two men died, all injustice would vanish. He heard the word in his mind. His own voice saying it. Injustice. Repeating it, until then he heard only a part of the word.

His gun came out and he pulled the trigger in the motion. Nothing was repeating in his mind, now. He looked down at Tio Robles on the floor and knew he was dead before he knelt over him.

He picked up Tio in his arms like a small child and walked out of the Supreme into the evening dusk. John Benedict approached him and he saw people crowding out into the street. He walked past the sheriff and behind him heard Remillard's booming voice. "That was a close one!" and a scattering of laughter. Fainter then, he heard Remillard again. "Your boy learns fast."

He walked toward Spanishtown, not seeing the faces that lined the street, hardly feeling the limp weight in his arms.

The people, the storefronts, the street—all was hazy—as if his thoughts covered his eyes like a blindfold. And as he went on in the darkness he thought he understood now what John Benedict meant by justice.

Among the Living Amidst the Trees

BRUCE MACHART

Bruce Machart's short fiction has appeared in Zoetrope, Five Points, Story, *and* Glimmer Train, *among other publications. His work has been cited by the Texas Institute of Letters, and he is the recipient of numerous awards and fellowships. He teaches at North Harris College in Houston, Texas.*

For Lee K. Abbott

HALF PAST QUITTING time on Friday, a day we began by liquefying a family of possums in the debarker, and Garrett and me are driving the drive we drive five times a week. Route 96, from the paper mill in Silsbee, where we turn logs into loose-leaf, to Jasper, where we head home to shake the bark dust from our jeans and blow it from our noses and wash it from our hair before we take our women out for dancing and beer. Friday evening in the full steamy blaze of East Texas summer, and someone's gone and let those little lovebugs out from wherever it is they keep them holed up the rest of the year. Garrett's drinking a tallboy, working a toothpick around in his mouth and cursing the black mash of bug guts on his Silverado's windshield. He's scratching his wiry red sideburns like they're overrun with mites, glazing and smearing the front glass over again and again with the wiper/washers. "These sumbitches is freaks of nature," he says. "Fucking and flying what all at the same time."

"And dying," I say. Straight forward through the windshield I can't see a thing, not a bit of the road, but on either side the forest is wet and green and rustling with breeze. Garrett's leaning his head out the window now and then to get a better look at the road, cursing when he catches a bug in his teeth. I'm staring straight ahead into the aftermath of a bug orgy gone bad, and the whole time there's green streaking by in the corner of my eye—the trees, the undergrowth, a whole forest full of little live things waking up for the nightlife.

"Yessir," Garrett says, "Dying in mid-lay. Sounds good until you figure they probably don't even get their rocks off. They're probably just thinking those hold-on thoughts, you know, imagining about nuns or unpaid bills or a car crash, and then—Smack! Windshield. The great hereafter and beyond. All that shit."

"You think bugs even got rocks to get off?" I say.

Garrett takes his foot off the gas and shoots me a look like maybe I've slid over next to him on the bench seat and asked could I hold him awhile, then something outside catches his eye. "Well, whatever in blazing hell is wrong with the critters around here today?" he says, kicking hard on the brakes and sliding the truck to a stop on the gravel shoulder. "Possums all ground up like chili first thing in the morning. Fuck bugs. And now lookit," he says, tossing his empty back into the truck bed. "Lookit here at these dogs doing it human style."

And there they are, sure enough having canine relations right down in the ditch next to a rusty corrugated culvert, the one on top some sort of hound mix—part beagle, part blue tick, maybe—and so in need of a meal that from up on the highway he looks to be all rump and rib cage. His little bitch, she's missing an ear, and he's got her pinned down tight, her back against the far bank of the weed-choked ditch. The old boy, he's going at it in that churning-butter, dog-lay way. Even so, I can't help thinking there's a twinkle of something tender about these two, the way her front paws are wrapped up around the scruff of his collarless neck, the way he's intent on licking where her ear used to be all the while he has his way with her. And his way is a strange way, after all, for a dog. "They're doing it missionary," I say, and it seems silly to admit, but the whole thing slicks my guts with a kind of greasy, nervous guilt, the likes of which I haven't felt since my wife caught me playing my own fiddle in the shower one time last year. "Let's go," I say. "Give the old boy some privacy."

"Privacy?" Garrett says, fishing what's left of the six-pack from off the floorboards. "When you want privacy with Glenda, tell me something, you generally haul her out here to the side of the highway?"

Garrett's the kind of man who does more talking than thinking. Just this week, when one of these shirt-and-tie reporters who've come nos ing around since the murder asked Garrett if he thought Jasper was a racist town, old Garrett looked into the camera and spit between his teeth. "Hell no," he said. "We done elected blue-gums both as mayor and sheriff. Now what's that tell you?" Even so, Garrett every now and again makes good plain sense, so as crossways as it seems to be sitting on the side of the highway watching these dogs ravage one another, I've got to give the man his due. I crumple my empty and crack open a new can.

"At-a-boy," says Garrett. "We ain't going nowhere. This is something you don't get to see but once, if ever, and we're gonna just sit right here and drink a cold beer and see it."

AFTERWARD, ON THE way home, we decide we'd rather be drunk early than clean. We're halfway there as it is, and Conway Twitty's on the radio singing about whiskey and women and hasn't once yet mentioned a shower or soap, so there's maybe one of those subliminal messages working on account of that. Besides, the way all these reporters have been jammed into Slyder's Saloon since those sick bastards dragged Mr. Byrd down a rutted road until there wasn't anything left to drag, we figure we'd best get there early if we want a table level enough to set a longneck on. Instead of showering, once we clear the cloud of lovebugs we crank down the windows to let the wind blast the dust from our hair. Outside, the sun is just beginning to hunker its way west, setting the treetops ablaze in such a way that the whole sky goes over to a kind of deep and waxy pink lipstick color. Garrett guns the engine and we speed toward home, breathing deep through our noses and shaking our befuddled heads at what we've just seen. It's a yeast farmer's wet dream out, too. The kind of hot and juicy you ought to be able to bottle and sell in drugstores. With the windows down, the forest smells akin to what you might get if you boiled Pine-Sol on the stovetop while roasting a sack of rain-soaked soil in the oven.

When we cross Route 190, Garrett veers left onto Main and spits out the window. Traffic's as heavy as it gets in a small town. High school kids with nowhere to be but on the streets, big sweating men trying to get home from work, all of it made worse by the news crews mulling around double-parked vans with their satellite antennas reaching up high as old pines, all of them just waiting for air time so they can send word to the world of what a backward and bloodthirsty bunch of hicks we all are.

"If I was that dog," Garrett says, "I'd a never let my lady know there was an alternative to the dogstyle. She's liable to get it in her head the old way's degrading or something, least if she's like Sandy she would. Hell, sometimes I get so tired of the same old thing I'd damn near do it on the side of the road just to spice things up, you know? Ten years of walking on that-time-of-the-month eggshells and what do I get? But you wouldn't know nothing about that, now would you, Mr. Newlywed. Your Glenda's a grinder, is she not?"

Now, maybe if someday we find ourselves making conversation somewhere in a locked-tight and soundproof and windowless room, and Garrett's tongue is tore clean out of his mouth and he's got both arms ground down to stumps so he can't write or do that sign language the deaf folks use, maybe then I'll tell him straight away that yes, he's absolutely right. A grinder, I'll say. No two ways about it. I'll tell him how matter-a-fact she *does* like to do it on the highway, preferably while I'm driving, and in the living room, with the lights on and the curtains thrown wide. In the ladies' room stall at Slyder's one Saturday night. I'll tell him about the rooftop, so help me God, when a new moon gave the night fully over to darkness and I arched myself beneath her, crawfishing my way backward, scooting up the shingled slope from eave to peak, all the while pressed between the hot sliding softness of my wife and the roof rash rising on my elbows and ass. I'll tell him about the shingle grit I'd picked grain by painful grain for a week from my skin.

Hell, put us in a room with no ears and I'll even embellish some things, but not now. Not here. In this little neck of the Big Thicket, words bounce around from tree to tree, house to house, and mouth to blathering mouth, so I don't say a thing. A year back, the night before Glenda and I got married, her daddy, Tricky, threw us a party at Slyder's, rented the whole place out. This was in the days before he found out about his cancer, before his black hair turned loose of its gray scalp, and when he pulled me a new Lone Star from the ice and twisted her open he put his big, thick-skinned hand on the back of my neck and told me to be careful where I let my mind wander, especially when Glenda wasn't around to keep it penned up. Glenda's mom, he told me, had run out on him because he one time *thought* about cheating. He said news—true or otherwise—travels that damn fast or faster here in Jasper. Said all he was doing was having a dirty daydream about the new drive-thru girl at the Cream Burger, and when he got home the old lady had cleared out. "And all I done," Tricky said, holding his beer bottle like a microphone, "was lean in a little when this gal handed me my lunch so I could see what she had working under her shirt."

That's just the way it is around here, so I don't tell Garrett a thing. I don't mention how in the early days, after I'd run into Glenda at the Easy Clean Laundromat she inherited from her grandma and we'd been out a time or two, she took to taunting me. About how one night, while we walked along Coon Creek out back of my place, she'd crouched behind a sweet gum tree and stepped out of her dress before wading through the tangle of shoreline shadows and into the water. "Come on," she said, working water with cupped hands over her moonlit skin. "Get in here. You aim to be a man tonight or not?"

Instead, I let Garrett drive and I drink what's left of my beer and I try not to think too much about Glenda, about how her skin shines even in the darkness, even beneath the water; about how Garrett's wife, Sandy, spends her lunch break away from the police-station filing room where she works and eats instead at the laundromat, where she fills my wife's head with the latest horror stories about the way James Byrd was killed, about the root-riddled road that ripped his body apart as he thrashed and slid, chained behind his murderers' truck; about how Mr. Byrd used to smile and whistle while washing his work clothes on Sunday nights; about how Glenda's started talking lately about going out to Huff Creek Road so she can see where it happened, so she can smother her imagination in the reality of it, no matter how gruesome; about how tore up she gets nights on account of her daddy and his cancer; about how some nights she lets loose to crying even while we're making love, and how it hollows me out so that I think nothing will ever fill me up again.

Some nights I'll sleep in restless fits, the muscles of my lower back burning with spasms so that I dream I'm an animal with a boot on my neck and a red iron searing another man's initials into my hide. Every night this week, after I think she's cried herself to sleep, I've jerked awake to a bed half full and the sound of her voice in the hall. Even over the telephone, Tricky will have her in stitches, and through the cool hum of the air conditioner her quiet laughter will push its way into the room. I'll prop myself up in bed and feel the kinks in my back turn loose. And I'll listen, trying to imagine what he's saying, how he's managing to make her laugh.

"I can't push it out of my mind," Glenda will tell him. "I'm serious,

Daddy, I keep seeing it. Over and over. His body tearing apart on that road, and it's not like I knew him that well, but I keep expecting him to walk into the store and set his laundry bag on one of the machines and nod and smile at me while he feeds dollars into the change machine. I keep hearing his whistling. He had such a pretty way of whistling, so high and sweet for a man his size, and he wasn't showy about it either. You could tell he wasn't doing it for anyone but himself."

And then she'll stop talking and start listening, her bare feet sliding across the hardwoods while she paces, her breathing loud enough to hear, and then she'll let loose the slightest of half-swallowed laughs. "It's just that I don't know what I'm ever going to do without you," she'll say, and I'll wonder how a man gets to be man enough to hear that and go on telling jokes. Man enough to give of himself exactly what's needed.

You aim to be a man tonight or not? It stings more than a little to think about it, but as Garrett pulls into the back lot behind Slyder's and tilts the rearview down so he can watch himself run a comb through his tangle of red curls, all I can think is that more and more, when I'm alone with my wife, it's not the wild sex I'm after. I don't want all the gymnastics or the risk of being seen or the shingle grit stuck in my skin. Instead I want her to laugh, to wink at me while stepping out of her skirt, to turn off the lights and shut the bedroom door and pull me with her beneath three or four quilts so that I can have her all to myself, so I can duck my head beneath the covers before we make love and see her skin glowing there in the darkness, calling to me in some shiny new language only I can understand, lighting my way while I reach out and hold her and keep her from crying and answer her in the voice of the man I've somehow managed to become.

INSIDE, STANDING BACK of the bar, Stu Slyder is damn near salivating at all the business coming his way on account of this murder. If you'd lived here all your life like I have, and you happened upon Slyder's tonight, aiming to have a long sit-down with the boys over a few cold ones, you'd no doubt stop at the door and marvel awhile, wondering if you'd taken a wrong turn somewhere, maybe stumbled across some secret white-collar society in your yellow-dog town. There are guys in neckties everywhere. Back at the pool table. Bellied up to the bar. And instead of the familiar stink—sawdust and sweat and spilled tap beer—the place is ripe with the smell of aftershave. Stu is smiling his gap-toothed smile, trying to keep his shirt tucked in despite the downward slump of his belly. He's sliding bottles across the bar, slicking the stray hairs of his comb-over back with the palm of his hand. It don't take much of a man, I'm thinking, to get rich off his hometown's troubles.

Garrett makes his way back from the bar and hands me a longneck. "Lookit that leech," he says. "Teeth on him, he could eat corn on the cob through a picket fence, and *would* too if he thought he could make a buck doing it. Promise him ten dollars for the pleasure and he'd kiss your ass on the steps of city hall and give you an hour to draw a crowd."

"He counts all his money after tonight," I say, "the price is liable to go up."

"Sounds about right," he says. "He's a counter, sure enough. Always did like that math. Sucked up to Mrs. Earlich so bad in algebra class you'd have thought her big tits reached out all the way to his desk."

Looks of Stu's new brick house up on the highway, I'm thinking, maybe we all should have sucked a little of that tit. He's a tight-ass, all right, but he ain't stupid. Besides, this is the only bar in town with a dance floor. And they still got Bob Wills on the jukebox. And then there's Glenda's daddy, Tricky, huddled as per usual around the big corner table with his fellow pipefitters playing forty-two, every one of their heads sheared clean as summertime sheep. They're slapping dominoes on the tabletop and scratching the backs of their necks and no doubt comparing notes on the Harleys they've got ready to roll out back. Six months back, after Tricky's first couple chemo sessions, all the boys of the pipefitters' local shaved their heads. It was a hard man's brand of brotherhood, and the night they did it Tricky walked into the bar, and when he saw them his eyes filled with a liquid look of something like love. These are rough-hewn and heavy men, men with calluses thick as rawhide, men who aren't afraid to keep something tender beneath their rib cages, and to expose it to the elements when occasion calls for it, no matter how it hurts. Tonight, it's these men and their laughter and the cold bite of beer on my teeth that set me at ease, despite the fact that Stu Slyder is talking quiet-like to one of these hair-gelled reporters, leaning in close enough to kiss the guy. He reaches across the bar and takes a sharply creased greenback from the man, some high denomination, I'm guessing, and I catch Garrett's eye and nod in that direction.

"A value-added whore," Garrett says. "I shit you not. Put a quarter in his ear and his teeth fold back."

"Save us some seats over by Tricky," I say. "I'll call the girls."

Garrett nods and I make my way to the pay phone in the back near the ladies' room. As soon as Glenda picks up the phone she says, "Where are you and why aren't you here?"

"Got sidetracked," I say. "We hit some gravel on the way home, started sliding and slid clean over to Slyder's. Go get Sandy and meet us here, would you?"

"Figured as much," she says. "Already got the quilt in the truck, so don't get too drunk on me. I got plans for you yet tonight."

"Looks of this place," I tell her, "the whole world's got plans tonight, and they mostly include Slyder's. You wouldn't believe the out-of-towners."

"Well hang in there, old timer. I'm on my way. Is Daddy there?"

"Him and the whole crew."

"Well then it can't be *that* bad. They'd just as soon drink water as mingle with strangers."

"Then keep your headlights on bright when you pass over Coon Creek and you oughtta see them all bending down for a drink. I'm serious, sugar. I ain't ever seen the likes of this. I keep thinking of what my cousin Ty said after that school bus went into the ravine last year out his way and all those kids drowned. He likened living in Harlingen that week to being in the freaking zoo, and on the wrong side of the bars, too. Strangers gawking at you, getting on the TV and twisting things all around."

"Now hold on, baby doll," Glenda says. "I'm coming. If something's going to get twisted tonight, it better be me around you."

BACK AT THE table, Garrett's holding forth with Tricky and the boys, throwing his hands around like he's on a Sunday morning church show and something holy's taken hold of him. I grab a couple new beers from the bar, and when I sit down he winks at me, popping a toothpick into his mouth. Next to Tricky are the Hooper twins, DJ and Teke, and their cousin Nelson, three massive men with shining scalps. You put this foursome in the bed of a pickup, the bumper would throw sparks going down the road. Now Garrett works his toothpick around in his molars awhile, then he plucks it from his mouth and points it at me. "So then the foreman, old Henderson, he tells us to fire up the debarking drum, and it ain't but seven-thirty and already it's hot as the devil's dick out, and let me tell you something about your son-in-law here, Tricky. He reckons he'll stand right in front of the debarker's vents while I run the first load of logs, figures he'll get a blast of fresh sappy air in his hair when I hit the pneumatics. So I crank that big bastard up and load it with pine and tumble them logs barkless and clean, real quick work, but when I release the valves and the vents spring open, all I hear is this poor boy cussing and carrying on. I mean, he's howling, so I shut the machine down and haul ass around to him thinking something's gone wrong, maybe he's hurt, and there he is, bloody as a blind butcher. Shit's in his eyes. He's spitting it out his mouth. And then it hits me. It's them possums again. We've caught them nesting time to time in the debarker drum when the heat gets bad. And I shit you not, we must've tore a half dozen or more of them little sumbitches to shreds."

Garrett stops now for effect while the boys start chuckling, looking at me sidelong, then he tilts his beer back and slams it empty on the table. Even I can't help but smile. "Yessir," he says. "Tricky, your boy here was wearing possum insides *all over* his outsides."

IT'S WHEN THE women show up that things begin to get ugly, but not on account of them. Sandy, she's decked out with that black hair pulled back tight as the skirt that's riding up on those wide, hand-hold hips. Garrett talks a lot of lonesome-man trash, but his woman's got on her the kind of grade-school-teacher good looks that can drive a man to mischief when he's alone in the shower. As for Glenda, her hair's done up in pigtails. Her skin, it's got the sheen of something well buttered to it, something so shining and bright you could kill the main to Slyder's breaker box out back and so long as she was there you'd still have enough light to drink by. They're lovely, the both of them, and they don't mind hearing it.

"There's my girl," Tricky says, pushing himself back from the table and slapping a palm against his knee. "Ain't she a peach?"

Glenda smiles, puts a hand on her hip and bats her eyes, then plops into his lap. "I'll bet you say that to all the girls who get your laundry done free for you."

"Sure do," he says, playing a domino from his hand. "Thing is, unless something's changed around here, and things rarely do, every girl who fits that bill has got her ass right this minute in my lap."

"How you feeling, Daddy? You know you're not supposed to be drinking a bunch of beer."

"Well it ain't going to kill me, now is it?" he says.

DJ and Teke raise eyebrows at each other and reach for their cigarettes. Nelson smooths a hand over his shaved scalp, says, "You're too
damn stubborn to die, you old fart, so quit talking your sympathy talk
and shake the dominoes. These women came to dance, no doubt, not to
hear your bellyaching."

DJ and Teke nod and blow smoke from their noses. Garrett and me,
we take the hint and haul our ladies to the dance floor, or what's left of it,
given the crowd. Somebody's gone and paid a half dollar to hear Willie
Nelson sing about blue eyes and rain showers and heartbreak, and when
Glenda leans her head back into the crook of my elbow I can smell the
honeysuckle lotion she smooths into her skin after showering. She tick-
les her fingers on the back of my neck while we turn and slide around
the floor. On her face, wet-eyed worry.

"That Willie Nelson knows a thing or two," she says, closing her eyes.

"So do you," I whisper.

Six months back, when Tricky came straight from the doctor's on a
Saturday afternoon to give us the bad news, Glenda and I were making
love in the shower, and while we dance and Willie sings and Glenda
leans forward, pressing her face to my chest, I'm in two places at once.
My feet are sliding in time to the music, but my mind is under that spray
of water with her, both of us lathered with soap, Glenda with a foot up
on each side of the tub so she could bend her knees and lower herself
down onto me while I blinked water from my eyes and held her hips,
watching them fall and rise. "Every time we come here it's raining," she'd
said, working herself against me. It's an old joke between us, one that deserved its silly little answer. "Every time it rains here we're coming," I
told her. Then the door rattled and the muscles in Glenda's hips
twitched and Tricky's voice was hot and thick as the bathroom steam.
"You rabbits get on out of there," he said. "I've got something needs
telling."

And now, as Willie winds it down and Garrett and Sandy dance over
close to bump hips with us and laugh, Glenda lifts her face back from my
chest and I see her dark eyes are drowning, and still she manages a smile.
"I was thinking about your daddy catching us in the shower," I tell her.

She takes my hand and we stand there awhile, waiting for the next
record to play. "I was thinking about Mr. Byrd," she says. "Sandy says
they had to hunt with dogs for the missing pieces. Spent half a day draw-

ing spray-paint circles on the ground where they found his dentures or keys, a hand with a ring still on its finger—like that. Can you imagine?"

"I can't," I say, sliding her into the first three steps of a waltz. I mean to say something else, but instead a hard little fist of muscles starts clinching down low in my back, and I'm listening to the whisk of our boots on the dance floor and holding my wife a little too tight for good dancing, and all I can think about is those dogs on the side of the highway, about how the one on top took the trouble to lick clean his little woman's wound, about how even animals find ways to be kind.

I loosen my grip on Glenda's hand and lead her into a spin. Her pigtails whip the air and the hem of her dress parachutes out and she lets loose of a little squeal. I reel her back in, stepping long on the hard note of the waltz as I pull her in tight. She slips her fingers into the back pocket of my jeans, and I'm about to tell her about the dogs, about how Garrett called their position human style, but that's when the music stops, and so do we.

We stop and turn and Stu Slyder is standing by the jukebox with the electrical cord in his hands. He's turning up the television set over the bar with the remote control. Up there on the screen is the slick-haired man I saw earlier pressing creased money into Stu's hand, and he's standing now in front of Slyder's, his lips curled up in such a way that folks in living rooms all over God's creation will know that it pains him just to be here, to be standing amidst our kind. This whole town stinks something fierce, he might as well be saying.

"Turn that mess off," Garrett hollers, but Stu's not having any of it.

"Fixing to be Candid Camera," he says, "so ya'll be on your best behavior."

On the television, the reporter is gesturing wildly, talking about the town and the men who'd spent many of their adult years in prison. "For all we know, the murder could have been planned in this very bar," he tells us. "This is where the suspects were arrested. Just out back of where I stand right now, in the parking lot, police tell us that the blood-spattered chain they allegedly used to drag the victim to his death was recovered from the bed of the suspects' truck."

Glenda steps close behind me, reaching her arms around my waist. Stu Slyder is taking baby steps toward the television set, beaming at this windfall of publicity. The bar, loud and alive with talk and music a minute ago, is now taken with the kind of quiet you mostly hear in churches or hospitals.

"Channel 3 News has since learned that the blood found on the chain and on one of the suspect's shoes matches the type of the victim, James Byrd Jr., and we have reports that other members of the upstart Aryan group have been known to frequent this establishment."

"What a bunch of horse shit," Garrett says.

Then the reporter opens the door and we begin to see ourselves on the television screen. I stand there stunned, my toes gone numb in my boots while the camera pans around the room and there I am, wide eyes rimmed in red, my work shirt faded and frayed near the embroidered name tag. Glenda's visible only as arms wrapped around my waist, and then we're gone, off screen, just like that, and I see what the reporter wants the world see, a table full of hulking, hard-looking men with shaved heads and lit cigarettes, dominoes standing in rows before them. Tricky and Nelson and the Hooper twins, they sit there fixed in the lights of the camera while this reporter talks about the Aryan Nation and the KKK and skinheads, and when Glenda pushes me out of her way and stomps over to the camera, for a moment I watch her, the real her, and then I turn back to the television and see her there, her pigtails bobbing behind her as she spits at the reporter and swings around to point a finger at the camera man, and at me—at all of us glued to the screen.

"They ain't skinheads, you asshole!" she screams. I'm right there, not ten feet from her, but what I feel instead of pride or love or some impulse to protect her is an acid-hot drip in my guts, a kind of embarrassment you feel for people you don't know when they come unglued on afternoon talk shows. "That's my daddy," Glenda says, and then she's flailing away at the camera and Tricky is up in a hurry, wrapping her in his big sunburned arms, and I just stand there, the only one left watching the screen, marveling at the television version of my life.

It's not until Stu Slyder steps in that I snap out of it. He's up there onscreen, his fat blue tongue visible through the gap in his teeth as he moves between the camera crew and Glenda, as he stutters and sputters and rants about the First Amendment and then—never mind that Tricky's got her in his arms, never mind that it's all under control—then the fat bastard leans in with two rigid fingers and thumps Glenda up high on the chest, just below the tender skin of her neck, and that's all it takes.

I haven't hit anyone since high school, haven't been hit since my father one time backhanded me in the jaw for getting smart with him about something I can't even remember anymore. But tonight it comes so natural I would swear it's something you're born with, the backward snap of the elbow, the instinctive grip of the other man's collar. The spill of adrenaline into your veins when you make blood spray from another man's nose. My knuckles crack with the impact, and the sound of it is sharp as the fireside pop of hickory kindling, only louder. His head, it snaps back and I jump him, slamming him to the floor. He's on his back, pinned down with that ridiculous flap of comb-over hair dangling around his ear, and I keep throwing punches, knocking his big head against the hardwoods with each blow until his eyes glaze over with a bloodshot brand of fear I've never seen before.

Then he kicks his legs hard and throws all his weight to one side and I'm caught for a moment off balance, reaching down to catch myself when he throws himself forward, slamming his forehead into my mouth, and I don't know if the cameras are still rolling or not, don't know if Glenda is burrowing her face into Tricky's chest or staring down at me with the same kind of unease I'd felt for her not a minute before. All I know is that my eyes are awash with hot white light, and that I've got blood in my mouth for the second time in a single day, and that mine tastes sharply of iron, and that Garrett is leaning down and hoisting me up by my belt saying, *Holy shit, Hoss, that was a serious big can of whup-ass,* and that when my vision comes back the first thing I see is the reporter with his microphone at his side and his eyes on the floor, probably praying I'm done swinging for the night.

Then we're making a break for it, shuffling past the pay phone for the back door, getting the hell out of there. In the parking lot, the moon is throwing light off the chrome of the pipefitters' Harleys as they kick them to life. Garrett's laughing hard, howling into the night, asking, *When did you get to be such a shit kicker?* as he loads Sandy into his truck and cranks it up. Glenda shoots me a long and blinking and altogether confused look, a look you might give your husband if, say, you caught him jerking off in the shower, then she climbs up into the driver's seat of my truck and slams the door. I circle around to the passenger side, breathing in the exhaust of all these loud engines, and before I get in I spit a fat wad of blood into the parking-lot gravel, and there, at my feet, half a tooth floats yellow and broken in a thick pool of red.

✿

IN THE TRUCK, I don't know what to expect. A stern talking-to, maybe. A ride home and a night spent alone in bed while Glenda walks the halls talking quietly into the telephone. Instead, there's an unexpectedly cool swirl of air pouring in through the windows and, outside, a drift of clouds running up on the moon. There's the hum of tires on concrete and the rumble of the engine through residential back roads to the outskirts of town, where Glenda steers over an old logging bridge and puts the headlights on bright and slows to a crawl, centering the truck on the dirt road while we bounce in and out of ruts and over roots and the chassis squeaks and shimmies. "Not afraid of ghosts," Glenda says, "are you, sugar?"

I inhale and the night air saws away at the exposed nerves of my tooth. Tree branches lean in to brush the truck's front quarter panels. Glenda, she keeps on driving.

"Don't know," I say. "Never met one."

A mile or so up, the road is roped off with yellow police tape. Glenda kills the engine and grabs the flashlight from beneath the seat. "Night like tonight," she says, "can't get any weirder, I'm thinking."

I climb down from the truck and duck under the tape, following my wife as she pans the flashlight beam from one side of the road to the other. All around us there's the clatter of falling branches and the hissing of the breeze and the frogs speaking up from the trees. The road falls off on each side into ditches littered with weeds and debris, and I begin to wonder just how the hell you can drive a man into these woods and drag him from your truck, how you can cave his head in with the heel of your boot and then hold him down, your knee on the back of his neck, while your buddies hitch chains to his ankles. I'm wondering how you can stand over him—no matter what damn color he is, no matter what you believe—smoking a cigarette until he comes to and you see the fear widening in his eyes. I'm trying to imagine how it might have played out, how it all might have looked, but what I see instead are Stu Slyder's bloodshot eyes, and now I'm wondering just what the hell I'd been thinking back at the bar.

Up ahead, Glenda stops and squats over a red ring painted onto the hard-cooked dirt. "Dear God," she says, shining the light up the road. "Look at them all."

And there, by God, they are: dozens of them, some big enough to outline a trash can lid, others so small you could cover them with a coffee cup, and no pattern or order to them whatsoever. We walk up the road and Glenda bounces the light around from red circle to red circle, and the moon stays back behind the clouds, and the forest seems rightfully alive and loud. And they just go on forever. I'm thinking you could pull me apart however you pleased and no matter how you tried you'd never end up with enough pieces to fill these rings. I'm thinking there's a lesson in that, a lesson I might could stand to learn, something about how there's always more to you than what you might think, but then Glenda bends down and traces a finger around one of the red circles and it's all I can do to stand there and watch her.

"He could whistle like you wouldn't believe," she says, "a not-a-care-in-the-world kind of whistle, the same way Daddy used to." She looks back at me with an arm outstretched, and when I go to her there's nothing left but to get down on my knees there beside her in the dirt and watch while she flattens out her hand and rubs this circle of paint into the earth. "Just whistling like that," she says, wiping her hand on my jeans, "ought to be enough to keep you alive."

On the walk back, Glenda turns the flashlight off. I freeze and look around long enough to see that I can't see a thing, so I bring her in tight, and I hold her there in the darkness, and when she leans her head back from me I get ready to walk. But then her lips are on me, and they're open, and my mouth is all of a sudden so full of her that it's like I'm being kissed all at once by everyone in my life who ever loved me in the least.

BACK AT THE truck, Glenda throws a quilt down in the bed and we undress each other there in the dark before climbing in. It's habit, something I'm so accustomed to that I don't question it until we're wrapped up together with the quilt over our heads, until she pulls one of my legs up between her own and I can feel her there, the soft and swollen wetness of her. Her breath pushes hot against my chest and my tooth is screaming, a sharp pain that burrows down through the meat of my gums and into my jaw, and I want like hell here to tell Glenda that we don't have to do this, that we can just lie here awhile and go to the house, that I understand what just happened out on this road. Truth is, though, that I can't put it into words, not just yet, and all I know is that her skin is so soft it pains me to even think about letting her go, and her breathing is steady and slow, the breath of the deeply dreaming, and I'm thinking she might sleep through the night for the first time all week. Still I can sense that she's waiting, waiting for me to say something, so I tell her the first thing that comes to my muddied mind. "Garrett and me," I tell her. "We saw a couple dogs today. Up on Route 96. Doing it missionary."

She rolls back, pulling me up onto her. She presses her mouth against my cheek and I can feel her smiling there in the dark. She whispers, "You did not," and slips me inside.

I close my eyes, swallowing hard as I push myself into her. "Did too," I say, and then we're wrapped up in warmth, wrapped up in each other and in the sounds of the forest around us, the wind and the trees and the insects almost mechanically loud, like they've been working all night to find the right riff, and with a little work I hear them not as a whole but as single instruments, the same way you can when you focus in to find the bass line as you step onto the dance floor, so your feet know whether to polka or two-step or waltz, except something's not right. Here I am, a man making slow love to his wife in the back of a pickup truck not half a mile from where another man was just this week murdered, and the forest has something too deep to its melody, something too low-down and rumbling. Despite the quilt over our heads, it's all of a sudden a slightly brighter night, and I'm sure, right up until the voice bounces around in the trees, that the moon's found its way out of the clouds.

But then it comes, my name called out like it's a question all in itself, and for the second time tonight I'm thinking about how Tricky caught us in the shower, only this time I'm not remembering it so fondly. This time I'm feeling again the hot flush of my ears and the nervous twitching in Glenda's hips, the way time stops for just a sliver of a second when two grown people who love each other freeze in the middle of their most private moment and hope like hell they're both hearing things. It's settling into me the way grit can settle into a man's skin that headlights don't feel the same as moonlight, and then I hear it again.

"Hey, bud," Garrett says. "You in there?"

I duck out from the covers, throwing the quilt over Glenda, and when she pokes her head out her pigtails are frazzled with static. She looks like a schoolgirl who's been caught by her daddy doing backseat, midnight things, and I feel something warm and altogether newly formed ballooning wide in my chest. "Nice timing," I say, and Garrett comes over, his truck's headlights throwing his long shadow over us as he walks our way, scratching a toothpick around in his sideburns.

"Hell, you two," he says, "ain't enough *ever* enough?"

Glenda smiles without showing teeth, and I can tell she's not embarrassed. I can tell she's flattered, flattered to be young and wild and lovely enough yet to make even the likes of Garrett shake his head with envy.

Now the moon really does come skulking out from the clouds, and when my tooth throbs I realize I'm smiling. Glenda's toes are curling around in my leg hairs, telling a little joke of their own, and when I look over her lips are pressed into a girlish grin and it's clear that she's more than happy to let me do the talking.

When I look back at Garrett he's shuffling his boots in the dirt. His eyes shift quick from Glenda to the ground.

"Out looking for more dogs to gawk at?" I ask.

"I wish," he says.

"What, then? They looking for me back in town?"

"They are," he says, and then he turns to Glenda. "They already came by our place. Sandy said you had some wild idea about coming out here and having a look."

"She's got lots of wild ideas," I tell him, but Garrett just rolls his eyes and keeps talking. Old Stu's hot, he's saying, wanting to press charges, wanting some payback. "I dropped Sandy at the police station on the way. She thinks maybe she can talk Sheriff Duecker into cutting you some slack, but all the same I wanted to warn you. You'd be in a fast river of shit if they found you out here."

"They bothered Tricky and them yet?"

"I doubt it. They tore off toward the highway when we ditched the bar. They're probably bellied up to another game of forty-two down in Kirbyville by now."

"Well, hell," I tell him, standing up in the bed of the truck. "I better get on into town then and turn myself in before they get back. Last thing Tricky needs is to come home to cops at his door and people talking all over town about his son-in-law the fugitive."

Glenda leans back against the cab and shakes her head. Her eyes water and sparkle in such a way that I know she's trying hard not to laugh. "I don't guess they'll need to frisk you," she says, and I look down at myself, a man with flecks of sawdust in his chest hair, a man wearing nothing but moonlight and pale skin and not-so-white socks. A man I don't yet fully recognize.

"I hate to do it, Glenda," Garrett says, "but I'm going to turn my back now so you can get dressed." And then he does; he turns and walks away and waits with his back turned, leaning on the door of his truck while Glenda fishes around in the quilts and hands me my jeans. I stand there awhile before putting them on, and I wink at my wife, and I look out into the forest where the crickets and frogs are still carrying on.

"You gonna bail me out?" I ask, and Glenda grins as I step into my pants. She stands, letting the quilt fall away from her. "I believe I will," she says, and I nod and smile and buckle my belt, and her skin is shining so bright and warm it's a wonder I don't melt.

Vital Signs

VALERIE MINER

Valerie Miner is the award-winning author of thirteen books, including novels and collections of short fiction. Her work has appeared in journals such as The Georgia Review, Salmagundi, New Letters, Ploughshares, The Village Voice, Prairie Schooner, The Gettysburg Review, Ms., The Times Literary Supplement, The Women's Review of Books, The Nation, *and others. Her stories and essays are published in more than fifty anthologies. She has won fellowships and awards from the Rockefeller Foundation and the National Endowment for the Arts, among others.*

Valerie Miner is a professor and artist in residence at Stanford University. She and her partner live in San Francisco and Mendocino County, California.

THEY ARRIVED IN the full heat of a late August morning, high-spirited children released from an overlong car journey. Matsuda navigated the turquoise Camaro swiftly along the dirt road, and they alighted in a cloud of golden dust. Felipe first—Felipe always first—bouncing toward me, grinning in his campy, flirty, I-know-you'll-always-love-me way.

He was right about that love, but I practiced dignified affront. "Fourteen hours late?" I called archly. After all, it was my fiftieth birthday, and this celebratory weekend with best friends had been shortened half a day because—well, I could just guess—because Felipe was late for a deadline. Or he forgot to pick up his special birthday shirt from the cleaners.

He won, of course—right arm around my waist, the other switching sun hats with me—cooing, "I get to try on the crown, don't I? Since my birthday is in a couple of weeks. I have to see if I like being fifty!"

"And if you don't?" I laughed between his kisses.

"Hey, hey," called Eleanor, extricating her long legs from the backseat with Hepburnesque grace. "You can't start the party without us." She looked especially trim in her white T-shirt and little red shorts. In my next life, I resolved, I would be lanky.

"That's right," Greg grumbled, combing sweaty black curls behind his ears. "We may have traveled economy, but we count too." How had they persuaded Greg, who always got carsick, to sit in the back?

Matsuda, Felipe's new boyfriend, stood by the purring Camaro, watching us curiously. A red baseball cap shaded his eyes, a long dark ponytail looped over the back strap.

I hadn't seen my friends for six months. Now that we lived in different parts of the country, at each reunion I found myself looking cautiously for evidence of aging. Yes, I was a little obsessive; fifty was still young these days. Young middle age. These people—"The Symposium," Felipe mockingly named us years ago—meant more to me than anyone in my life. The Symposium and my partner, Victoria.

We had met in our late twenties, seasoned citizens of a troubled world we were determined to change by teaching in the Oakland high schools. All of us were active in our union, but we each wanted more than that—a place where we could talk about issues personally, worry out ethical questions with rigorous, good-humored friends. And so, once a month we met for a potluck dinner and serious discussion about literacy outreach to parents, the value of compensatory education for gifted kids, the socially weighted definition of "gifted." The five of us were in our prime—professional, political, sexual.

Over the years, some of us came out; some got married, unmarried, remarried. Andrew and Greg became parents. Everyone went into therapy. I could never find the language to describe our relationship. Years before, we had abandoned the identity of discussion group. Although we still loved to argue megapolitics, these days we also talked job security, health difficulties, hairstyles, and mortgage payments. If the word weren't so overused, I'd say we had become a voluntary "family."

This morning, my first reaction on seeing them was relief. I had begun to worry when they didn't arrive for last night's dinner. It was a three-hour drive north from the Bay Area on sometimes twisting, difficult roads. (Then, early today, there was that fiery sunrise, an overbright red blur slashing across the new sky . . . Sailor's warning? Did it apply to highway driving?) Silly to fret, I could see that now, as they stretched their legs, admired the view from our ridge, and ambled around the new deck.

Strangely, it had been ten years since we had all spent a weekend at this particular place, a small parcel of Mendocino hill country Victoria and I used as a summer retreat. I'll never forget that July weekend when they helped build the cabin: everyone had a good time; some were more skillful carpenters than others. Greg was a natural at roof shingling. Felipe, who suffered vertigo, spent his time hammering down the kitchen floor. (He did such a dreadful job that we had to yank out most of those nails the following Monday, after the gang drove back to the Bay Area.) Today, Felipe's first destination was the kitchen, where he enthusiastically admired his fine craftsmanship.

After bagels and fresh ground coffee—their offering for being so late—we walked around the land and I showed them sleeping quarters. I always feel more comfortable as a visitor once I've met my bed. Eleanor was happy to camp on our couch. At the bunkhouse, Felipe and Matsuda would stay in the big room; Greg took the loft with a view of Cow Mountain.

Andrew and his family would stay down the hill. Most of the other members of our land cooperative, except for Rosemarie, were away this week. So we could put up Andrew, Kimiko, and the boys at the big cabin by the pond when they arrived—*if* they arrived—tonight.

"Of course they'll arrive, Maryann." Felipe laughed at me. "Where does a small, skinny person find the energy for all this silly worry? After twenty-odd years, you're still waiting for us to be on time, *amiga*."

This was meant to be the perfect weekend, a triumvirate celebration of fifty. Oddly, we were all born within a month: Andrew first, me ten days later, then Felipe—late of course—in mid-September. He joked that we were triplets, separated after a very arduous labor in which the mother of us all birthed Andrew in Boston, me in San Francisco, and then had the good sense to retire to Merida, where she raised Felipe, the most well-adjusted sibling. We had planned the party for years.

"Fourteen hours late." I widened my eyes, hurt as well as pissed off.

"Ah, but weren't we worth waiting for, butterfly?"

WE WOULD EAT lunch under the oak in the dappled sunshine. I unfurled the canary yellow tablecloth—a fifteenth-anniversary gift from Victoria—which glowed even more golden in this bright afternoon against the rolling Mendocino hills. Yellow jackets hovered around a decoy plate, interrupting us only occasionally with a low buzz—café conversation from a distant table. I inhaled well-being, friendship, and glorious late-August heat.

Lunch, catered by Felipe and Matsuda, wasn't what I had pictured. As they unpacked salami and cheese and iceberg lettuce and sliced white bread, Victoria gave me one of those "Relax, it ain't in your control" winks, and I returned to my nascent practice of tranquility. The sandwich was a fine guy meal; I sneezed at the familiar taste of Dad's favorite horseradish mustard.

The geographical "where" of the Symposium had become trickier to identify over the years. Only Felipe was still teaching high school, still evangelizing physics to Oakland teenagers. Eleanor now traveled the country as an education writer. Diplomatic Greg worked at the school board. Andrew became a super-canny consultant in online educational materials. Much to my surprise, I had turned into a professor of education in Seattle, where I had been lucky enough to meet Victoria. Felipe joked that while the rest of us launched into larger worlds, he had no imagination, no ambition. In truth, I believed that Felipe kept teaching because he was the best one. (What did that mean? How could you say someone was the most generous? The most compassionate? All virtues were circumstantial, temporal. Maybe I was simply saying I loved him the most.)

Above us, Spanish moss drooped down from the knotted branches of the live oak. Eleanor and Greg were arguing about Jerry Brown—a debate they might have finished years ago if the man didn't continually reincarnate. Felipe was asking Victoria about her Saturday choral group. She had a beautiful voice—a big woman's voice—but long ago traded in concert dreams for a job as a school counselor and Saturdays singing with her friends. The table became cluttered with bottles of Pepsi, Corona, Calistoga water, Handley chardonnay; a vat of mayo; a bowl of fragrant, sweaty blackberries. Matsuda seemed distracted, twiddling his ponytail, looking off toward the western hills; did he know the weather blew in from that direction? I should have tried to bring Felipe's new lover into the conversation, but I wanted to sit back and watch my old friends. Our charmed weekend had begun; we ate too much and caught up on gossip and laughed at Felipe's ridiculous jokes. Eleanor passed out photos of our Thanksgiving gathering. Greg showed pictures of his son's high school graduation. Young Jonathan was starting Berkeley this week, in a physics honors program recommended by Uncle Felipe.

AS WE CLEARED the table, Felipe suggested casually, "Hey, Maryann, let's go for a walk after lunch."

Sure, I nodded, taken aback because usually, after a midday engorgement like this, we'd all go hiking together.

To shake a vague uneasiness, I thought back to their Christmas visit long ago, when I was finishing grad school in Minneapolis. We all walked *across* frozen Lake Calhoun, Felipe playing a queenie Jesus, sashaying on the solid water. Thought back to the August we stayed at Eleanor's family cottage on the Jersey shore, taking long rambles every afternoon. But there would be no invigorating communal hike this afternoon; everyone was finking out. Matsuda wanted a nap. Greg needed to finish the *Times* crossword, and Eleanor had some last minute galleys to review. Each slipped off, promising to do dishes later.

The dishes, that's what clued me in. Every family had rituals, and doing dishes together was ours. We had all survived enough childhood kitchen fights to have a firm regimen. One scraped, one washed, two dried, and one put away. Everyone had a task. No coffee, no walk, no future until the dishes were done.

ALONE NOW, FELIPE and I sat across from one another, listening to the lonely wind riffling through golden grasses. Even the bees had left. Felipe fiddled with his thread bracelet; I now recalled a matching one on Matsuda's tanned wrist.

"All right," I said, picking up a blackberry. "Tell me what's going on." Had he been fired for rabble-rousing at school? Was he finally making progress with the Merida project?

Anxiety rarely visited Felipe's sturdy face. I noticed his hair thinning on top. Lights of silver winked from the beard under his full, mauve lips. I searched his brown eyes and saw my friend of twenty years ago: Felipe suing the school board for tracking black students into industrial arts. Felipe confiscating half a dozen guns from Asian gang kids in his neighborhood and then absentmindedly leaving the arsenal in his trunk for six months. Wonderfully fierce Felipe battling homophobic Proposition Six and, winning that round, initiating a Gay Pride Week at school. This was familiar, smart, whimsical, maddening Felipe.

Felipe facing a terrible change.

Ragged breath reached my lungs.

"I have some bad news." His voice got louder. "Maybe not bad"—the words faded in and out—"just a little hard."

No longer could I see his face. I struggled to keep myself warm and steady, hands gripping the sides of the picnic bench. A bleating noise threatened, louder and louder in gaudy colors.

"No, no," I heard myself ranting. Of all my friends, Felipe would remain safe from HIV. Since two negative tests (the second just to check the first) ten years ago, I had relinquished fear. We were dealing with a community pioneer, who chaired the mayor's AIDS Education Board.

He reached for my fist, which was slowly pounding a blackberry into the gold tablecloth.

"It's all right," he said gently.

"No it's not," I spat back. "It isn't true. Not now. There's a mistake."

"I've had three tests," he shrugged.

"Well"— I gulped hot, dry air—"you'll be fine, of course." I raced ahead—simultaneously by myself, away from Felipe, and ushering him with me to safety. "With the protease inhibitors. It's just a chronic illness now."

He shook his head—sympathy, fatalism in sad, dark eyes.

Jays barked from a tree near the ridge.

Ashamed of how I ripped the story from his telling. I allowed my fingers to relax in his and we held hands as the purple juice seeped along random threads of the linen cloth.

"Matsuda's T-cells," he explained with relief, "are much better, responding to the cocktail. Last test, there was no HIV detectable in his system."

Wind shifted, and I noticed early fog rolling in, imagined how it had started at the coast an hour ago. He was telling me that his new boyfriend of six months had got bored with safe sex. Turning the pale green ring around his finger, Felipe said they were theoretically monogamous, but that it was tough on Matsuda to be the twentyish lover of a middle-aged man, especially of someone so preoccupied with work and politics and . . .

He registered my incredulity, stopped.

Goosebumps on his solid, muscular arms. Was it going to rain? No, I wasn't cold. He shivered.

"Shouldn't you get a sweater or something?"

He smiled—fondly, wisely, older than I had ever seen him. "A nap," he answered. "I'll just lie down for a while."

"Yes, yes," I encouraged. "Rest, it's the fastest route to recovery."

Before I could feel foolish, he said, "I love you."

"I love you too, Felipe."

❉

BACK IN THE cabin, I stared out the window at the ghostly moss—tawdry Christmas tinsel rusting in the late-summer fog.

Suddenly, a knock at the door. Greg and Eleanor peered through the back window.

I opened the door and we hugged. Then, in sighs and silence, we washed the sticky lunch plates. The aroma of horseradish mustard and lemon Joy pervaded the close air of our small cabin.

Eleanor stepped back from the sink, snapping her dishtowel. "I think we're being too WASP about this."

Greg sniffed in agreement.

I waited, drying spots off the glass pitcher.

Eleanor was waving those long, graceful arms. "We're all just taking the news politely. He wants to tell us individually, discreetly, and that's the end of that. On with the party!" Her voice rose. I always admired the quick swell of Eleanor's anger. "He wants us to move along with the weekend . . . argue about the fall elections . . . plan the dinner menu."

"So what can we do?" Greg's face was drawn. The quietest and the most observant of us, he was also the most practical. Here, however, he looked lost.

I had almost forgiven his lie about the crossword.

Eleanor paced back and forth to the window. "This isn't just Felipe's news. It belongs to all of us."

"It's Felipe's life," I said, "Felipe's—"

"Now don't even start thinking that," she commanded. "My father treats lots of HIV, and he swears by these new drugs."

I wondered if the whole weekend would be like this—all of us arguing the same stale, desperate reassurances.

"Well"—Greg swallowed his familiar impatience with Eleanor—"it's mostly *his* news. His and Matsuda's."

"Matsuda!" Eleanor declared. "It's so creepy to have him here this weekend. I mean after what he did to Felipe."

"Felipe would say they 'did it' together," I objected. (Why did we call him Matsuda? I wondered. Because Felipe did. Roy, Ray; once I knew his first name.)

"Don't give me that 'luck of the draw' shit. Matsuda lied. He was screwing around and promising Felipe he was monogamous. I feel like shooting the little teenybopper."

Was he a teenybopper? No, he was twenty-three or twenty-four, almost the age we had all been when we first met.

"No weapons!" Greg raised his hand. "Felipe threw out the guns he confiscated from the kids six or seven years ago."

Eleanor and I laughed half-heartedly.

We agreed to tell Felipe we were worried, that we loved him—not only individually, but as a group. None of us was maudlin enough to say "family" out loud.

"At dinner," Greg suggested. "After the second glass of wine, we'll bring it up then. We'll be brief, but clear." I watched Greg returning to his comfortable, competent skin.

Hard to say much more. We were all so shaken by the news. Each of them left for a solo walk.

A FEW MOMENTS later, the phone beeped. Andrew ringing from Corning. He, Kimiko, and the boys *were* making progress on their way south from Mount Shasta. Originally, they had planned to come for lunch, but I felt no irritation. (Safety, that's all I cared about. *When* didn't matter. Just four safe people.)

"We'll arrive by 6 P.M., easily," he said. "Meanwhile, do you want any olives?"

"Olives?"

"We're sampling at the Olive Pit," he rasped loudly over the background noise. "And we thought we'd bring an hors d'oeuvres tray. Nuts, artichoke hearts, and—what do you want—kalamatas? niçoise? Moroccan?"

"T-cells," I spit into the phone, careening suddenly from rage to grief. "We could use some T-cells."

"He's told you?" Andrew's familiar voice softened.

I sobbed. Finally.

"That's it," he said. "Cry. You never let go." Behind him, I heard a dinging cash register, voices murmuring through brine and oil.

I couldn't stop.

He waited.

"This is a ridiculous phone call," I inhaled, pulling myself together.

"I love you," Andrew said.

I broke down.

DESPITE THE DARKENING chill, everyone remained determined to have a proper country Saturday afternoon. (Autumn already? I wondered. Sometimes fall came early in Mendocino, but I prayed for the weather to cheer up.) Eleanor, training for a marathon, declared she would go running in nearby Hendy Woods. Felipe was resolutely refreshed from his nap and decided to accompany her.

As they drove toward the gate, Greg, Victoria, Matsuda, and I walked downhill to the pond. Too cold for swimming, but we could bird-watch, read, talk.

One toe in the pond, Matsuda deemed the temperature perfect.

This strong, muscular young man cut through the water like a dancer, gracefully sidestroking to the distant cattails. Back and forth: crawl, breaststroke, dog paddle. We watched, mumbling plans about dinner, when to light the charcoal. Greg closed his eyes, seemed to nap. Victoria took my hand, and I stared at the crimson of her whimsical manicure, teasing her about turning into a lipstick dyke. Lovely hands, one of the first things I noticed—her firm gentleness. I used to believe self-sufficiency was the noblest virtue, but now I wondered what I would do without Victoria's wackiness and practical intelligence.

Matsuda lifted himself from the water, nimble as a silkie, dried off, and stretched out on his towel, eyes closed. Like all silkies, a creature of mysterious powers.

Since I had been reading, it took me a while to register the noise. Victoria was already waving to Rosemarie, who ambled down the hill, almost keeping pace with her wonderfully silly dog, Kipper. Tensing, I glanced at the innocent sleepers. Years before, when we first bought the acreage with three other friends, Rosemarie argued for preserving it as women-only land. Eventually, she compromised, allowing men on weekends and special occasions. This was both a weekend and a birthday, so what was I anxious about?

Victoria squeezed my shoulder reassuringly, then called, "Rosemarie! Terrific! Come meet our friends, Greg and Matsuda."

Of course Victoria realized we had all mellowed over the years. Even Rosemarie had invited her uncle last summer. She probably wouldn't even notice Victoria's femme fingernails.

Kipper, the West's most elegant cocker spaniel, bounced toward us in a jingle of tags.

I grinned at this flurry of brownish blond curls. Such a welcome contrast to dour, practical Rosemarie.

Greg and Matsuda nodded hello.

I scooted over, remembering how she enjoyed afternoons reading by the pond.

Book in one hand, towel in the other, she stood peering into the green water. "Do you mind if I swim?"

Greg and Matsuda shrugged at the unnecessary question, and it took me a couple of beats to realize Rosemarie hadn't brought a suit. Ordinarily we skinny-dipped in the pond. Maybe Rosemarie had forgotten this was a guest weekend. Maybe she didn't care. The guys wouldn't know that Rosemarie was not only suitless, she was also breastless, having made a courageous recovery from a double mastectomy two years before.

I twisted through embarrassment for the boys, anger at Rosemarie, admiration for Rosemarie, a pang for Felipe. Patched grey and white and darker grey, the sky closed in on us.

Kipper sniffed intently around the base of the old willow. Greg asked Matsuda computer advice, and I wondered how he could converse so civilly with Felipe's potential murderer. The afternoon was spinning fast and slow.

A maverick wave of sun cast Rosemarie's long shadow across the yellow grass. She was a tall, fit woman, big-boned, and I was touched by the puckering flesh in her thighs and a faint purple varicose streak in her right calf. I almost missed the moment she pulled off her T-shirt and deliberately poised herself to dive into the murky water. Greg glanced away, but Matsuda's face was observant. Her chest was flat, slightly concave against the sturdy ribs, and the scars were, as always, smaller than I expected—the right one virtually invisible, the left one red against pale Danish skin. Matsuda studied Rosemarie's long, balletic arch into the pond and followed the passage of a spectral green mermaid until she surfaced at the cattails. Another shape-shifter.

"Nice dive," Matsuda nodded.

Victoria smiled. "Yes, she captained her college swim team."

At the sight of Rosemarie floating, the dog barked, jumping jerkily at the deck's slippery edge.

Rosemarie yelled inaudibly from the cattails.

Greg reached over to calm Kipper.

Rosemarie shouted louder. "Don't let her too close to the edge; she can't swim."

This was the tension breaker we needed, and the four of us howled at the notion of a cocker spaniel, this natural-born water dog, unable to swim. Maybe Rosemarie was developing her own weird sense of humor after all these years.

Kipper quivered with excitement at her friend's voice and our fits of laughter. Suddenly, propelled by her own giddiness, she skidded and flew into the pond.

Rosemarie screamed. "Save her! Save her, someone; she can't swim!" Stroking frantically toward the dock, she screamed, "Somebody, help!"

Kipper's sweet face wrenched with panic. She practiced some primal paddling instinct, clearly losing.

The next sound: Matsuda crashing into the water. He dove precisely, yanking a terrified dog by the scruff of her neck.

Rosemarie had made it halfway across the pond. This must have been happening very fast, but I felt frozen in slow motion, imagined us back in wintry Minneapolis, Lake Calhoun cracking, all of us falling in, slipping down, down.

Matsuda's long black hair sprayed across his face as he struggled to stay afloat with wiggling Kipper. Pressing toward the dock, he treaded water, finally managing to hand the sad, wet dog up to me. A minute later, Rosemarie reached the ladder.

She leapt on the dock. "Thank you, thank you," she shouted down to the grinning St. Christopher. "You saved her!" Rosemarie lifted the dog from my embrace.

I was grinning, too—then saw spots of blood along my forearm where I had held Kipper, noticed a rusty screw protruding slightly from one of the dock boards. My blood? The dog's? Matsuda's?

"Naughty, naughty dog," Rosemarie lectured Kipper, who had run off to the safe grasses, nervously shaking dry. Pulling on her shirt and shorts, Rosemarie hurried after the dog, then turned back. "Thank you, thank you!" she called to Matsuda.

He smiled.

I could see Felipe loving the sweetness in those shy eyes.

Her voice scratched through the warming afternoon, high and fast.

"Ridiculous, really—a water dog who can't swim. Maybe it's why I love her."

I rubbed my arm. The blood was gone now.

Matsuda nodded gently and waved to Rosemarie.

FOURTEEN YEARS BEFORE maybe fourteen and a half, because it was a winter night—we were sitting in a secondhand hot tub under the bay tree in Eleanor's backyard. There we were, pretending to be unselfconscious about our naked bodies, all of us looking up to identify constellations, making up names for unknown ones, whispering about our futures. Felipe spun fantasies about his Yucatan summer program for East Oakland kids. Greg toyed with running for State Assembly on a radical schools platform. Eleanor was going to found a magazine for activist teachers. I was newly in love with Victoria, and together we planned to work a year in Chile. Another year in Tanzania. The night sky grew more brilliant as we argued means versus ends, long- and short-term commitments. Everything was possible; all we had to do was choose.

FELIPE APPEARED AS I rooted beneath the deck for briquettes.

Flushed, a little winded, he declared, "Great run! Three miles. Some serious hills. Frankly, I was kind of surprised I could keep up with Eleanor."

I grinned at the bloom in his cheeks. He and Matsuda ran off to buy wine for dinner.

Eleanor looked refreshed by her shower. "Let's start the artichokes." She took my hand, winking and waving to Felipe. "Washing, peeling, cooking artichokes takes forever."

Working at the sink, I listened to the water groaning from the outside faucet where Greg was taking a quick wash. Normally, our makeshift shower was one of summer's joys—standing there on a hundred-degree afternoon letting water clean and calm your body—but ablution was more penance than pleasure in this dreary weather.

When Eleanor's wet, sandy hair was slicked back, she always reminded me of a baby rabbit my brother raised. Soft, moist, vulnerable, and throbbing with quixotic growth. Any minute, the marathon runner and famous author would emerge.

It wasn't until long after the Symposium began that we realized three of us had suicide in our families—Greg's mother, Eleanor's sister, my little brother. Curiously perhaps, given all our other intimacies, we never really spoke about these deaths. People who haven't known suicide always wonder "how." Those of us who have suffered it are paralyzed by "why." We asked neither question, just nodded to that familiar expression of loss we recognized in one another. All that we shared was unspoken—sadness, guilt, cautiousness, a kind of elastic tolerance. Someday, I imagined, we would talk about suicide. Someday I'd forgive myself, my parents, for the disappearance of my beautiful teenage brother.

Eleanor scrubbed the artichokes vigorously. We always let her take charge of the vegetables; otherwise she would persecute us with detailed pesticide reports. I filled a big pot with water for the artichokes, squeezed in the juice of three tender Meyer lemons, and added a few garlic cloves.

"God, I'm glad we survived that run," she sighed. "I was terrified he was going to keel over. Those pills affect his balance. I just decided to quit once I was convinced we had put on a good-enough show."

I thought about Felipe's triumphant smile.

"What a relief to get him back in the car in one piece. Did he say anything about the run? Did he look all right to you?"

No, not all right. Jubilant. Exultant. "You put on a good-enough show," I said.

Her blond eyebrows lifted faintly over doleful eyes.

Artichokes prepared, she set upon the potatoes. I failed to persuade her you can't remove every nick of soil.

Into the salad bowl, I tossed fresh basil and arugula from Greg's garden, and veg we bought at the Mendocino Farmers' Market: shallots, green-red-orange peppers, seedless cucumbers, those little yellow lightbulb tomatoes.

"Hey, look what I found." Greg toweled his black curls with one hand and held out a brightly wrapped package with the other. "On the picnic table outside."

I could smell it from across the room: Rosemarie's famous dill wheat baguette. Still warm as Greg handed it to me. The card said, "For Matsuda and his friends, from Kipper and her friend."

"That was sweet of her," Eleanor said.

"You don't know," Victoria shook her head. "It's a bloody miracle."

"Matsuda, the miracle worker!" I sniffed.

"Let's just enjoy the bread," Greg cajoled. "And the evening."

I swiveled toward the counter to hide my tears, remembering Rosemarie's stalwart response to the diagnosis; her determined recuperation from surgery—all those exercises; then her passionate grasping at what life offered—taking kayak lessons, baking classes. The dill wheat was my favorite of her breads.

Victoria had almost finished preparing the green beans and cremini mushrooms, marinated in her garlic vinaigrette. Garlic—there was always *mucho* garlic in a Symposium feast—the key to our good humor, Greg insisted.

Almost dry now, Greg sat at the table, playfully lining up the six bottles of vino Felipe and Matsuda had brought home.

I COULD HEAR the wine mavens in our outside shower, whooping and giggling over the spray of hot water.

"Look," called Victoria, pointing out the bay window. "Look, sun!"

When I raised my head, the room had lightened in color and weight and spirit. We were floating.

"Right," I grumbled to settle myself, in no mood for a good mood. "Perfect timing: sunrise at 5 P.M."

"No, see!" she shouted through my petulance.

"Yes," declared Eleanor. "A rainbow—over the hills."

I walked to the back deck. "Hey, you guys," I shouted. "Hey, Felipe, Matsuda—a rainbow!"

Immediately, I felt foolish, interrupting their shower, childishly needing them to enjoy this—a goddamned rainbow—as if we'd all been astral-projected to Disneyland.

In seconds, they appeared on the grass, barefoot, towels around their waists, holding hands. Together, we watched the rainbow shimmering in the sky, reflected in the water. Buttery yellow, lime green, robin's-egg blue, lipstick pink, lavender. We named the colors. I peered through a translucent red at the stand of Douglas fir. We counted the bands—Greg saw seven, Felipe nine. Eleanor insisted there were really only three. The arch grew longer, stronger, stretching from the vineyard ridge to the far side of the valley. Carefully, I followed the silken trail. If I held my gaze, could I reach the end before any colors evaporated? I wanted my friends to come with me; surely, together we would make it.

Instead, I stood back, savoring their bickering laughter.

❂

ELEVEN YEARS AGO, they all flew up to Seattle for Thanksgiving. "All" had a different meaning then. Andrew hadn't met Kimiko yet; Eleanor was married to Cecil. Often, in those early days, Greg's son Jonathan joined Symposium celebrations; but on this holiday, he was staying with his mother, as agreed in Greg's and Nola's tense but generally amicable custody arrangement. I was sorry to miss the boy, although perhaps at seven Jonny—or Jonathan, as he preferred now—was too old to be the Symposium mascot. That November weekend passed happily with our ritual rambles, vociferous arguments, high and low cultural forays, and elaborate homemade dinners. Especially during the pre-fat-and-fiber days, each meal was an extravagant cooking competition. Somewhere in the Pike Place Market, Felipe found a long blond wig. During our last night together, we lounged around the fireplace with chocolate cookies and brandy and coffee, taking turns fashioning the wig into coiffures for karaoke roles—Cher, Elvis, Bob Marley, Judy Garland, Aretha—brunettes all of them.

Late in the evening, my phone interrupted. It must have been ringing a long time because the nurse shouted at me when I finally answered . . . They didn't know much about the head-on collision: Nola was dead, and Jonathan remained in critical condition. We drove Greg to the airport and waited with him for a flight—any flight, any price—to San Francisco. Three hours later, they left, Felipe ushering Greg onto the plane. We would send their clothes with Eleanor on Monday.

Early the next morning, Felipe called to report Jonathan was pulling through, although his left leg was pretty shattered.

Greg had collapsed with exhaustion in Felipe's guest room.

ALMOST 8 P.M. and no sign of Andrew, Kimiko, and the kids. (Dear, distracted Andrew. Sometimes we called him Lucky Andrew, because, despite his career roulette, he always evaded disaster. Felipe thought luck came with his charming green eyes. When Kimiko first got pregnant, Andrew had no job. Then, just before Joey was born, he was headhunted for a hot position in computer consulting.) No telling when Andrew would finally pull up. We were all hungry and tired after a long day, so we lit the charcoal.

Of course, just as Greg lifted the perfectly cooked salmon from the grill, Andrew's forest green SUV crunched down the hill in the hazy evening afterlight.

Kisses. Hugs. The melt-in-your-mouth salmon was shoved into the oven to stay warm while we unloaded the car. Two little boys raced around the cabin, noisy as a gang of ten. Kimiko washed out a handkerchief spotted by Luke's bloody nose. From dark red dots on the cabin floor, I could tell the poor kid was still descending that mountain. The reel fast-forwarded: Carrying bags upstairs. Unveiling the olive tray. Pouring champagne. And finally—9 P.M. maybe—we sat down to the birthday feast.

Andrew and Kimiko entertained us with harrowing tales of backpacking with toddlers on Mount Shasta. Then we recited our stories: the long lunch, jogging, swimming, St. Christopher's rescue. Andrew raised a glass to Matsuda, the hero.

I told myself to relax—Felipe was right, we all survived on oxygen and chance. I concentrated on loving my friends, but couldn't stifle the vengeful wish that Matsuda choke on a fishbone.

Wine flowed. Felipe had good taste; god knew how much he had spent on this plonk. Of course, the food was divine—Eleanor's well-scrubbed, tender artichokes; Victoria's dream beans; Greg's masterful salmon, which was just a little dried out from its exile to the oven during welcoming ceremonies. Kimiko and Andrew had selected five types of specialty olives. The contest winner was a green olive stuffed with sun-dried tomatoes. Our moods lifted. It was possible to forget, for minutes at a time. And then, like coughing breaking the spell of a scherzo, Felipe's diagnosis erased my sense of well-being.

"Felipe," I heard myself saying. If I didn't do this now, I never would. Eleanor nodded encouragement.

Felipe cast me a warning glance, refilled his glass with dark cabernet, and began to tell a joke.

"Felipe," Greg interrupted, gently holding his arm.

Good, I thought; Greg, the diplomat among us, would be the best messenger. He had been especially close to Felipe since Jonathan's accident.

Silence.

As I waited for Greg's speech, I imagined Felipe raising his glass, consecrating the wine.

Actually, our friend looked cornered, angry—but grudgingly returned Greg's smile.

"Felipe"—Greg massaged his old friend's shoulder—"Maryann has something to say."

My courage almost evaporated, I made it brief and simple.

"Felipe," I sighed, "we have something to tell you as a group. I mean we're friends together—as well as individually." God, I was screwing this up, sounding like a TV therapist.

Victoria watched me closely.

"I'll make this short," I reminded myself. "We just need to say, we love you."

Felipe reached for Matsuda's hand.

The room was thick with wordlessness, not even a note from the children. I began to perceive Matsuda's bravery in facing this weekend, and to understand that Felipe might not have been able to come without him.

"Each of us. And all of us are here to do anything you need. And we won't do anything you don't want."

Felipe nodded. Enough. I could hear his unspoken protests of self-sufficiency. But he could no more talk than cut our ties.

"And," I continued, "we want to say we're sorry about the diagnosis. Diagnoses. Concerned for you and Matsuda."

Victoria wiped her eyes. Greg filled my glass.

Joey pierced the solemn quiet. "Cake, Mommy, didn't you say there would be birthday cake?"

We all followed Kimiko's firm instructions to eat another helping of vegetables before we even thought about dessert.

Felipe disappeared outside for his usual post-dinner smoke.

As they started clearing the table, I too slipped out.

He leaned against the redwood deck railing, staring into a landscape of fog. From our ridge, the valley looked like a foamy river. The bases of first-growth sequoias were so thickly veiled in mist, they might be a cluster of young trees caught in a night flood.

When he turned, I could see most of his face through the cigar smoke—the serious expression was hard to read.

"Are you mad at me?" I asked feebly. Not—How are you? May I join you?

His body was still; his eyes narrowed.

"Yes," he finally whispered.

I hung my head, warned myself not to dare cry.

He lifted my chin.

"And also, no," he said.

Felipe's arm on my shoulder, mine around his waist, we turned back to watch those treetops reaching through the fog. I breathed in the cool night, not bothering to look for stars in the overcast sky. We stood that way for a long time, listening to the frogs and crickets, inhaling musky smoke, letting the mist rise around us.

A VOICE SQUEAKED from the doorway. "Greg says to tell you we're all hungry for cake." Joey peered up at us with shy defiance.

"Oh, are we?" Felipe laughed and lifted the boy ceremoniously, a sacrifice to camouflaged stars. Joey giggled.

Felipe set him down and said, seriously, "Yes, some of us have come a long way for cake."

Laughing, we followed our buoyant messenger into the warm room, which seemed to have grown higher and wider in our absence.

"Finally!" Eleanor exclaimed. "You know, you can't put off turning fifty this way."

I shrugged, grinning.

Greg passed a cup of coffee and squeezed my hand.

Eleanor must have worked on the cake's design for a week. The 12 × 12 sheet was divided into three isosceles triangles. Andrew's section showed a family dancing around a computer. In mine perched a little country house. Felipe was portrayed as a teacher at the blackboard, singing. In the middle of all our lives stood three fat, garish pink candles, "5–0," flames screaming.

A round of "Happy Birthday." Clapping. Silent supplications from the honorees before we blew out the candles. Then, unabashed wishes from the others.

"I wish Luke's nose will stop bleeding by bedtime," Kimiko sighed.

"I hope the sun comes out early tomorrow," said Eleanor.

"I want some cake," said our little friend.

"About time!" Felipe stood and cut the first piece for Joey.

As Greg passed out the other slices of Eleanor's gorgeous cake, Victoria sang a sixteenth-century Italian birthday song her grandmother had taught her. I felt happier than I had all day.

"What's this?" A wail from the far end of the table.

Before anyone could answer, Joey was pointing accusingly to his father.

"Cake," Andrew answered, innocent, exhausted from the endless drive through bounteous California landscape with his two precious children. "Chocolate cake," he managed. "You love chocolate cake."

"This isn't chocolate!" Joey shouted. "I can't eat this."

"He's right," Eleanor struggled. "It's carob. I mean you guys have got so health conscious, I thought you'd prefer it."

Joey was bawling.

Greg tried gently, "It's delicious, Joey, really. And it's good for you."

"Ugh," he screamed.

Kimiko reached forward, stroking his hair, taking over from a depleted Andrew.

The child didn't want consolation; he wanted chocolate.

"I don't like things that are good for me!"

Felipe laughed the loudest. "I know what you mean, Joey."

ELEANOR GOT HER wish; the next morning was brilliantly sunny, hot enough for swimming by 10:30 A.M. She, of course, went for a run. The kids loved playing with their parents in our battered, patched inner tubes. Matsuda swam laps. Greg sat with his feet in the water, finishing a mystery novel. Felipe stretched out on a purple flowered towel, working on his tan.

Felipe raised his head every once in a while, squinting at the kids and growling like a sea monster. They squealed with excitement, spattered him with water. All so normal, as if three of us hadn't turned fifty this year, as if . . .

SINCE GREG HAD a meeting in the city, we packed up and headed to the house for an early lunch. Matsuda, Greg, and Felipe took the lead, carrying the cooler and deck chairs and foam pads. Andrew hoisted Luke on his shoulders and held big Joey's hand.

Kimiko and I stayed behind, stacking inner tubes and beach balls. As she bent down to collect one of Luke's plastic frogmen, I noticed a trickle of red streaking along her right thigh. Another on her left leg.

I whispered, "Kimiko." Then, trying for Victoria's light matter-of-factness in the face of real life. "You're bleeding down your legs."

"Oh, Christ," Kimiko said, more irritated than embarrassed. "Since having the boys, my periods arrive without any warning." She cupped pond water and rinsed off her legs.

"We've got Tampax and pads in the privy," I offered.

"Thanks." She shook her head. "I guess I should be grateful—it's how/why we have Joey and Luke. It's a sign of life."

THE GRIZZLED SEA monster had turned into a bucking bronco, chasing Joey and Luke around the table as Victoria finished lunch preparations. Then Felipe sank down on the couch, resolutely regaling us with a string of puns from his dreadful joke repertoire. The kids sat at his feet, swapping riddles with him. We finished the birthday cake for dessert—all of us except Joey, who had sworn to boycott carob for the rest of his long life. Greg started the dishes. Eleanor pulled out her electronic calendar and subdued the unruly mob into making definite Thanksgiving plans—her house in Berkeley this year. And was pumpkin pie acceptable to Master Joseph?

"Guys," Greg said with almost Monday-morning sobriety, "I have that meeting at seven tonight . . ."

Felipe roared loudly, prancing around Greg, wiggling his ragged tail and batting the air with menacing hoofs. Luke and Joey followed the bronco's lead, corralling Greg in a circle of neighs and whinnies and giggles.

MATSUDA HONKED THE horn. Felipe and the kids snorted fiercely. Greg, Andrew, and Eleanor carried bags out to the car.

Twenty minutes later we were still hugging, pressing last-minute messages on one another. Greg ran back to the house for a missing thermos, Eleanor for her lost reading glasses. Matsuda straightened his backward red baseball cap. Felipe closed his eyes momentarily.

Suddenly everyone was waving, a cluster of large and small organic pinwheels spinning. As they pulled away, Felipe jauntily tilted my sun hat over his brow. We were all shouting and blowing kisses. They disappeared into dust, the engine sound fading as they looped down far hills toward the gate.

"OH, NO," LUKE moaned into the vacant afternoon. "I'm going to miss Felipe."

The adults looked from one to another helplessly.

"Don't worry," reassured his big brother, "he's not a very old horse. He'll be back soon, galloping the hills."

We laughed.

"Hey, Dad, how old is Felipe?" Joey asked. "The same age as you, right?"

"Yes," Andrew grinned. "Felipe is fifty this summer."

"*Fif*-ty!" Joey's face grew doubtful.

The road dust in my contacts was making me tear. I closed my eyes and saw Felipe's big smile. Oxygen and chance, I remembered.

"That's *oooold*," said Joey.

"Not old enough," I called, doing my best to assume the spirit of a bucking bronco.

Aground and Aloft

STEVEN PATTERSON

Steven Patterson grew up on the California coast and lived for many years in the high desert of Idaho. He graduated from the Iowa Writers' Workshop, where he was a teaching-writing fellow, and has since returned there as a visiting professor. He has also been a fellow at the Sun Valley Writers' Conference.

Currently he lives with his wife in Iowa, where the mountains are just memories.

I FLY IN deep river canyons and come to rest where flat land is scarce. My day is a hopscotch route, up and down, up and down. For the dwellers of remote outposts I am a taxi service, mail carrier and delivery van. On occasion I am called on to be an ambulance driver, an emergency outlet arcing over the granite peaks. Once I have been a hearse of last resort, bearing out the body of a drowned river runner as cargo in the tail, cinched up tight in his sleeping bag. But these are details that don't change my waking day. I attend to the variables around me: the steep slopes, the jutting trees, updrafts and crosswinds and density altitude. My importance doesn't lie in what I carry or where I go. I am responsible for my skill with the yoke, a knowledge of flaps and throttle, an eye for the condition of the air. It is my task to settle the machine to the earth in impossible places, like alighting at the bottom of a soup bowl.

I make runs out of Cascade, where I work for Chimp Atherton. His name is on the hangar and the planes. My husband, Ron, and I hired on eighteen years ago, when it was just the three of us. Today there are four pilots, Chimp not included, as well as two mechanics and three women who run the office and take radio calls. Now, in the summer, is our busiest season. Every pilot and every plane will work steady through until the aspen groves turn yellow and quaky. Then we will bolt skis to a couple of the Cessnas and deliver groceries and mail to some of the ranches that get snowed-in. But the work is slower in winter. Two of the summer pilots head down to Arizona and run a flight school, and then appear again when the rivers here are high with snowmelt.

I prefer the taxi and supply flights, ferrying cargo around, traveling routes I can see in my sleep. Chimp likes some of the fancy flying, chartering for the Forest Service Aerial Fire Attack when the ridges start to burn. Powell, a moustache with a man attached, likes to get up there and tool around for hours, so he volunteers for the Fish and Wildlife trips to monitor gray wolves they have marked with radio collars. I'm not much for adventure these days, though. When I go up I want to know exactly when I'm coming down again. I want to picture the landing before I ever take off.

It has been a little more than eight months since my husband's plane went down in a distant valley. No one was there to watch it happen. Civilians have some fancy notion about airplanes always going off the radar, a scenario of instant alarm and emergency protocols. But wilderness flying does without such gadgetry, which is expensive and often useless for the terrain. We rely instead on a system of self-reporting, and trouble is usually confirmed by absence. After Ron was two hours overdue and no one could raise him on the radio, the rest of us took off in a little buzzing squadron and traveled his planned route back to his departure point. There was no evidence of him or the plane that day, nothing so halting as a smoke plume. It would have been better to have known before the sun dropped, before we all had to come in for unwanted landings and I paced the hangar all night, throwing wrenches against the metal siding when things got too quiet. That would have been a cleaner cut, I think, something easier to gather and repair. But it was late the next afternoon when a Forest Service helicopter spotted the wreckage, and the day after that when I could finally view it for myself.

I have not been in the air since. Four weeks afterwards I drove myself to Mexico with the dogs on the mattress in the back of the VW. It was an annual trip Ron and I made for more than a decade, a couple of months we sought away from the snow and the engine whine. We hadn't managed to get there in a couple of years, but suddenly it was where I needed to be. We had seasonal friends on the beaches, ones outside the fraternity of flight, who knew me as a good kayaker and a half-decent watercolor artist. I parked the van in various campgrounds for more than half the year, watching as the whales migrated south offshore and then north again before I had gone. I resisted for a while, but then I took their lead.

The early morning is bright and cool. Chimp is doing his pre-flight on the little Piper, running his hand along the struts. There are no big fires yet in early July, so he's flying a single, rich fisherman into the deep wilderness for the day. It's an expensive charter, and his passenger is in the parking lot wearing about a thousand dollars worth of Orvis gear and practice-casting with a beautiful cane rod. When Chimp sees me on the tarmac he comes over.

"It's going to be nice air this morning, Wayva," he says. "But this afternoon could get squirrelly."

"Well, Chimp. You just summed up most of the summer season. Any other wicked insights you feel like sharing?"

"Wayva." He frowns. He puts one hand on my shoulder and dips his head to indicate that he's getting personal. "I feel like it's right to have these chats as you ease back in."

"You know it's nothing but babytalking me, Chimp. If you trust me, you'll let me scout my own air."

He removes his hand. "If I didn't trust you, you wouldn't be flying my plane."

"Fair enough," I say.

He points me to the red Cessna. "You'll take out the 206 today. You've got some passengers for Moose Creek, and also some gear for that river outfitter on the Middle Fork."

I nod. "You're worrying for no reason," I tell him. "I feel ready. Ready steady."

MY BREATH DRAWS short today as I fly. I haven't been up in months and the sight from this altitude is as much strange as familiar. I remember the details of the setting but for some reason not the shock of its dimensions. Out the cockpit window the landscape is a series of ranges that recede into the haze. Some high spots are bare scars of rock above a slope of tumbling scree; others bristle with firs like the tight teeth of a comb. High, white fields of snow adhere to many northern slopes, and below them the countless little lakes that cup the runoff, too many to be named. The slanting morning sun lights up the ridges but leaves the canyon bottoms dark in shadow. It makes the repetition even more obvious: a low spot for every high one, a fall for every rise.

I am probably the only woman pilot in the air at this moment well beyond each visible horizon. That's because mountain air is ruled by men. Fathers pass the particular knowledge to sons. The only female evidence tends to be the voices on the radio, beaming a signal out of the home fields in Salmon or Stanley or Hamilton. I learned from Ron, sitting beside him for years like a trucker's wife, one short haul after another into the wilderness. I had my license when we met, but I wasn't fit for the backcountry, only for the long, paved, civilized strips. He taught me the physics, and most especially he gave me the experience. It's the experience that is crucial, for practice counts most when returning to the earth in the mountains. Each landing demands a singular approach, often blind, and so a pilot relies on the faith of precise, visual recall.

I remember once bringing the plane down on a particularly difficult strip for the first time. I had timed the drop perfectly and worked the throttle like a pro, so the wheels hit the ground like I had just rolled off a ramp. I turned and grinned at Ron, who stared straight ahead and nodded at the passing ground. It was a display of approval—no lapse in technique he could criticize. I turned back and watched a little rise approach. I knew that at the top of it the strip doglegged, so I waited and then turned the wheel right. The runway went left. We bounced through rock and sagebrush, and then I turned back to correct too hard and tilted the plane so that the wingtip scraped before we bounced back hard on all wheels. He was responsible for the plane and its damage, and his disappointment was deep. The full measure of it was demonstrated when he did not allow me to fly back out. I wouldn't have wanted to, but a less angry pilot would have insisted it upon me as a penance and a timely lesson of terra firma. He let me out of it, something I preferred at the time but which I learned to view as a blunt delivery of mistrust. I worked hard to never earn that penalty again, although I failed in the end.

A sun low in the eastern sky is calming to a pilot, because morning air is the best for flying in the backcountry. It is cool and relatively still, just the kind of dense and stable platform a plane needs for proper lift. After about 10 A.M. the heat of the day starts to tear the air apart. Pilots learn the science that is involved: solar and orographic influence, diurnal reactions. We know that everything starts to move invisibly according to the topography: in updrafts, downdrafts, flowing through river canyons or whipping across them. Canyons that meet may cause a convergence effect. Canyons that narrow are likely to produce a Venturi effect. Warm, dry air lifting up the steep slopes meets cool, moist air at higher altitudes, and thunderstorms bloom. This is all precise, studied data. But for canyon flying it is meant to be cautionary and superfluous. A wilderness pilot knows to avoid flights from late morning to late afternoon, when all the facts describe air that is essentially unknowable. Luck starts to count for something during those hours, and relying on luck at all is a sure sign that the pilot has erred.

The three passengers in the back are Forest Service, kids nearly. They won't see a road for weeks where they're going, and they have obviously spent their last night in town getting ready for the absence, toasting their fortune with cheap beer. All of them are sleeping it off after having to make this early flight. It's a common ceremony, something I see every summer. They want one last, long taste before the mountains devour them. Now they'll join up with a trail crew in the Wilderness Area for a long stint without luxury. Wilderness designation prohibits anything mechanized or motorized, so while some of their softer counterparts elsewhere clear timber with chainsaws, they go at it with axes and crosscuts. They will ache in their tents every night from the strain. But I know it's something these boys choose. They're alike—they believe in the superiority of labor.

They remind me of my son, Henry. He used to have the same kind of stubble under his lower lip as one of these boys, the same languid comfort of his muscles. From childhood, Henry always preferred a path going uphill. He built radios from kits instead of buying them made. He chose summer trail work instead of a job back in town and nights at the drive-in. Ron and I wanted to shake him of this idea at first, to make his life an easier one. But we got to realize the earnestness it came from. Henry wanted to struggle so he could rest in comfort, so he could know his idleness was deserved. I'm not sure where he got this strength. It's not something I see in myself.

I see the first stop of the day and start to circle so I can survey for air traffic and animals on the ground, obstacles of any kind. Indian Creek, is a USFS air strip on the Middle Fork of the Salmon, which is busy with commercial float trips in the summer. There are tie-downs at one end of the strip but little else in the way of services or facilities. The runway is bi-directional, something not common in the backcountry. An upstream landing is indicated in the morning when a typical down-canyon flow of cool air provides a headwind. I breathe hard before I let us start to fall.

✺

THE PASSENGERS HELP me unload two large, heavy coolers sealed with tape. The boat I am supposed to meet has not arrived, so we haul everything to the edge of the meadow the strip is carved in, above the river and a small beach. The air is still chilly and everything is wet with dew. We sit on the coolers and wait.

"This is my last year on the trails," one of the boys says to me.

"Starting to drag ass?" I ask.

He snorts like I've insulted him. "I'm going to train with the fire crew out of McCall. Next year I'll be smokejumping."

Another boy laughs. "We call him 'Smoker' in camp, but that's on account of how powerful his farts are."

"Don't start with that shit." The first boy shakes his head. "When I'm gone, you'll remember sucking my fumes as the closest to greatness you ever got."

The third boy looks at me. "Don't mind him. He's high on his own gas."

This really gets the first one going. "Come again? I'm sorry; I forgot you can't even come once. You need to stretch and shellac it to keep it up."

"At least I got prospects, man. You couldn't get lucky if your sister took food stamps," says the third one.

"The only action either of you ever saw was a wet sock you balled up in your hand," says the second.

The three of them laugh softly, shaking their shoulders. Then suddenly in my presence they are quiet and embarrassed, looking at the trees or up the river. I know they think they've crossed a line with me, gotten too rough. I don't tell them, but I enjoy the chest out bluffing of men. It reminds me of Ron and Henry giving each other soft thumps like this, father and son jabbing and dodging. For a moment it makes me feel warm.

After about fifteen minutes the raft comes into view. We watch it float toward us. The guide strains at the oars to bring it into the beach, hops out and tugs it with a tow line, then anchors the rope with a heavy rock. He comes up the beach smiling.

"Waiting long?" he asks.

"I shouldn't be waiting at all," I say. "I need to keep moving while I've got the weather."

"Sorry. You could have left the stuff and gone," he says, trying to apologize.

"I only get paid if I make sure you get it. Now you got it."

He pulls off the tape and checks the supplies. The coolers are filled with tubs of ice cream, packages of hot dogs and buns, containers of potato salad. Stashed on the side are several packages of sparklers, and I realize for the first time that today is the Fourth of July, and these are the celebration provisions. I'm not sure how I forgot.

"We want to do it right for the guests," the guide says. "It'll be a fine surprise at camp tonight."

"Nice touch," I say.

The boys help him load the coolers on the raft while I untie the plane. I think of the boaters still around the fire upstream, sipping their coffee before the thrill of the day's rapids, maybe unaware that one of their guides has slipped out early on this secret mission, certainly unaware of me and my cargo. I know I can take off downstream and they will never know I was here. But safety suggests that I do not depart with a tailwind. So I will end up buzzing over their heads at relatively low altitude, and they will tip back their heads and stare. The cleverer among them may notice the missing boatman and figure out the surprise before they even make camp. This is something I cannot help.

IF YOU SPEND enough time in a cockpit, the noise of a single piston engine seems at times to disappear. These are the moments when every setting is correct for the circumstance. You get a feeling like you're soaring on your own power, aloft and alone. Some pilots get great pleasure out of these spells of reflex and bliss. I've always been taught they are among the most dangerous occasions. If you get out of your head that means the plane is flying you. But a pilot must always fly the plane, every second. An aircraft will obey the air and its own physics. A pilot is there to control these same things, modify and shape them. Flying is all intention and guile, steering the elements. It is not a surrender to the wind. That's what kites do, and kites will crash as often as they ascend.

Ron always liked to tell me this. We honeymooned in a little C180, and he whispered to me about stall speed and turbulence. I would nuzzle him at night, camped under the outstretched wing, and he would name the forces that could pluck me from the sky. He always identified inattention as the foremost, the gravest sin. He wanted badly for me to respect the machines and the skies, to cherish the beauty of the labor of flight, and fear nothing but my own lack. If I strayed, I would not escape the eventual consequence: I would meet the ground and augur in. "Propellers scoop rotten post holes," he said. "But they dig a pretty good grave." The way he squeezed my hand made it more tender than our vows.

Last summer Ron started to lapse. He began talking of flying as having transcendence, making it a mystical act. When he went up, he said, he could feel himself slip from his earthbound weight. A man doesn't change his beliefs like that without a reason, and I knew the reason was me. He knew that such talk would terrify me, having taught me the fear himself. We argued every morning before we took off in different directions, and each night he would touch back down with a fierce smile. Sometimes I was there to see it aimed at me, a jab for my transgressions. And sometimes I was still out, in a cabin in a steep river canyon, sitting on the edge of another man's bed, and I could feel that smile burn like hot iron in my chest.

He knew about the affair but we didn't talk about it, allowing it instead to follow us around like a stray dog. It glided through canyons and over ridge tops with us, breathing on our necks with a stale heat. When I caught a transmission of his on the radio I could hear the strain of its company in his voice. He never addressed me directly anymore, only referred to me as a bothersome idea that wouldn't focus entirely or disappear either.

"Canyon traffic," he would say, "be advised. Squalls in a ten-mile line eastbound above Elk City. Pilots, wives and swindlers, beware. Over."

I enter the Selway River Canyon from the west a few miles above Selway Falls. This is the approach for Moose Creek, a big Forest Service strip with a ranger station and enough room to accommodate the big DC-38 for fire control. I take care not to drag the plane in on a slow, mushing approach, because this is where the winds of two converging canyons meet, making them unpredictable. I don't want to be surprised this close to the trees.

THE RANGER STATION at Moose Creek has been around since the twenties. The current ranger, Dino, has been stationed for six years, and I've known him since the beginning. He is a gruff but decent man in his forties, making him still younger than me, even though he's got the crust of an old-timer.

I walk from the plane to the station, leaving the boys with a quick farewell to grab their own gear and hustle on to find their crew. Dino is already walking out to meet me, presumably since he recognized Chimp's plane.

"Come out to pester the Feds, have you?" he asks.

"You're spending my taxes out here, Dino. I wanted to check if you were mowing the grass."

"You look good, Wayva." He takes my hand for a gentle shake, but we do not embrace. It's a disrespect he would not show any pilot.

"And you look like you combed your hair with a rock," I tell him.

"Are you on schedule?" he asks. "Can you have a cup of coffee?"

We head for the oldest building, the one called the "Honeymoon Cabin," which serves as a cookhouse during fire season. A few from the fire and trail crews are still eating breakfast, so we carry our cups outside to a picnic table.

"You're taking it easy this year," he says. "We usually see you by April."

I nod at the coffee. "I spent a lot of the winter down on the beach in Baja in the van. I've been back only about six weeks, looking things over at the house."

"I guess we haven't talked since the memorial service."

"That sounds right," I say.

He takes a long breath. "I hope you won't mind me telling you again how sorry I am."

"I'm pretty used to it," I say. "It's about the only thing I hear these days."

He stops breathing like I've hooked him in the gut. "I can't know how it is for you, Wayva. All I know is Ron was a good friend to a lot of people. And Henry was a fine, strong boy."

I let him off the hook like I am accustomed now. "I appreciate that, Dino. It means something coming from you."

"It's true." He grins with relief. "Hard to take losing the good ones."

"Everyone's good to someone, don't you think?"

"I don't know," he says. "The fire guy they got out here this summer, the crew chief, he's a pretty useless specimen. Hard and mean. He could just as well get caught in a big burn and end up as nothing but a little smoking grease. I'm pretty certain no one around here would miss a step."

"That's the way it is with those firefighting bastards, isn't it? They breathe so much smoke some of them start spitting it."

"Yeah," he says. We've drifted off the centerline of the conversation and he doesn't know how to angle back. I don't feel like helping him right now.

I toss what's left of the coffee. "I'd better get up and out of here before I get stuck."

"Sure, I understand." He takes my cup and we head for the plane. "I'm glad to see you again. I'm glad you're in the air. It would make Ron and Henry proud, I think."

"You know," I say, "people keep telling me that, too. Truth is, being back up makes me feel defiant. I don't know why, but it seems like their air I'm trespassing in."

He stops and looks at me as I open the cockpit door, his mouth downturned just a bit. "Don't believe that."

"I can't help it." I climb into the seat and latch the door behind me. Dino's still there holding out the two coffee cups. I grin and slide open the window. "You want to know what funny feels like? It's being scolded by dead men for rising."

HENRY NEVER SHOWED any zeal for serious flying. He had his license and about 100 hours of flight time in open country, but he didn't desire the demanding training for the wilderness. This may seem like a heartbreak for two formidable prop-head parents, but the boy was so sweet about it that it was impossible to be upset. He would ride copilot with Ron or me once or twice nearly every week of his life. When he turned eighteen and spent summers on the trail crews he would travel in and out with one of us every time. For years we had him wear the cockpit headphones and we would narrate the entire trip as we went—every throttle adjustment, every landscape feature that might suggest airflow— spelling out the ether, trying to train him to be an expert before he ever took the yoke. Not once did that boy ever roll his eyes sideways at me or his father, not that I saw. He held his head up in a serious fashion and scanned the terrain, nodded at our comments, smiled at our bad jokes. He must have known for years before we did that ours was a family trade he would not follow, but he never complained to us or took up an angry defense of his liberty, claiming his father and I were encroaching. He decided to go along, to give us that comfort which parents are so often denied. And I never expressed to him how full that made my heart, that gift of tolerance for his hardheaded folks. I think about that all the time, and sometimes I can convince myself that a sensitive boy like Henry would have known without my saying.

In the last couple of months before the crash I lost that boy to Ron. I deserved it. Everyone knew about my affair. The unavoidable thing about the wilderness is that for all the vast acreage the human community is tiny. There are only a few dozen inhabited lodges and ranches, a handful of Forest Service posts. Communication is by a couple of radio frequencies, party-line fashion. The same small batch of pilots provisions everyone. So while distances are great, in some ways the isolation is an illusion. Secrets are hard to keep in the mountains.

Ron moved out of the house and rented another in Cascade, and Henry went with him. I had not felt much love for Ron in many years, and he knew it, even though it pained him. So my infidelity was not so much a shock as it was a confirmation of failure for him. It was dreadful, but it was not unexpected. For Henry, though, I believe that revelation tainted me. I think of the change as something biological. I know how babies respond to the scent of their mother—it is pacifying and alluring, something I imagine as sweet like cream. You know how it works when you cradle an infant, or a bawling six-year-old burrows his face into your neck and you rock him to comfort. The very fragrance of your skin is a bond. I don't think this ever really leaves us, even though we grow to claim reason over instinct. I believe that afterwards, when everybody in town knew my secret and Henry had to face me, attentive to my sin, that scent spoiled. From the way his eyes watered I think I had turned tinny and bitter. At the time of the crash he hadn't spoken to me in three weeks.

A few miles behind me is the spot their plane went down. I need to circle back in the wide part of the canyon now if I am to align a safe approach. What I remember—the thing I try and focus on—is that turn radius and airspeed are proportional, and understanding this relationship is crucial for a backcountry pilot. I wonder—would it help me now to remember my son's easy laugh instead? It could fill my head if I let it. Or should I try and soothe myself with the calculation that an airspeed of 130 knots in a 30-degree bank would present a turn radius of 2599 feet? Maybe the latter, since the canyon here is less than a mile wide. At 70 knots I could lower my turn radius to 753 feet, keeping the canyon walls away from me but also dropping the engine RPMs to roughly the pitch that comprised Ron's one-note singing voice, the entirely unapologetic drone he massacred radio tunes with. To avoid that I think I'll keep some of my speed and turn more sharply to compensate, even knowing that exceeding a medium bank can be disorienting without a visual horizon, and the impulse to "bank and yank" is generally a hazardous one. I am well aware that passengers tend not to appreciate steep turns, particularly in constricted terrain, and a good pilot always considers the comfort of travelers in any calculations. But what is inescapable is that I am the only traveler here, and I cannot make myself comfortable.

The strip comes into view. Now it is important to block out stray thoughts and concentrate. I remember, for example, that terrain and runway gradient usually dictate landing upstream, but also that this instance is an exception. Shearer USFS is an unmanned airport on the Selway. At an elevation of 2634 feet . . . maybe it's 2364 . . . the strip lies deep in a narrow river canyon. An upstream landing, designated runway 36, is not advised—this heading is best suited for departures. Inexperienced pilots are urged to use this strip for emergencies only, at which time a downstream landing is recommended. I can't seem to remember that number designation, but that's not crucial. Pilots should note that a high ridge presents a formidable obstacle as the aircraft descends. After clearing the ridge, pilots are advised that a 4:1 descent slope is required to make the field with adequate braking distance. Depending on climatic conditions and the aircraft weight, once a pilot is committed to this landing there is often no go-around option. Planning and preparation for such a landing is essential.

I AM ALONE on the ground. Shearer is the kind of strip that sees one or two aircraft a day in the summer. There are two cabins off in the trees, but they are almost always empty since the Forest Service lost the bulk of its budget. A private lodge lies a couple of miles downstream, but no one is likely to show up for a visit. The caretakers there are busy holding back the wilderness, and the guests have paid a wad of cash to fall off the map. In any case, I'm heading upstream, toward the ridge I had to clear on approach. Last October, Ron, with Henry beside him, wrecked at full speed into that rocky slope. The last time I flew into the mountains was to circle that spot, peering down two days later at that impossibly small jumble of metal debris. There was hardly a scar or a scorch in evidence. It was almost as if the crash had happened silently and without violence, my husband and son just absorbed into the hill. I could not put my plane down. I just looped and looped until finally my gauges told me I needed to return home.

It's late morning now and the chill has been wrung from the air. I stuff my jacket in the plane. The trail is easy to find in the short grass of the runway, so I get on it. There is no worry of being on the wrong path—along this part of the river there is only one. It goes upstream and down, close to the banks. At some points there is rockfall that narrows the canyon, so the river rushes only a few feet away.

I get to a wide, sandy beach and stop. There was a single time that I traveled this exact trail with my two men in the lead. Henry was eight or nine years old. We landed at the airstrip early on a Saturday morning for a weekend of air camping. In the afternoon we hiked upriver to the beach to swim and fish. Ron must have been fooling with a fly rod, because Henry and I were alone. He took me down to the end of the beach where a great, flat slab of granite as big as a box trailer jutted into the water. Henry stood looking out, and then he turned to me. He took one big step backwards.

"Tell me when to stop," he said.

"Alright. But take smaller steps."

He put his left toes behind his right heel. "How about now?" he asked.

"You're fine," I said.

He measured another pace with his other foot. "Okay?" he asked.

I watched the rushing stream, its fast white water, and then I looked back at my son's feet. "Still a ways to go."

He smiled and stepped again. "I'm going."

It may seem astonishing that I did not feel a single bead of fear rising from my belly. Some might question my fitness as a mother for letting the game go on. I can only describe the security I felt at the time. Henry's gaze was on me straight as a clothesline. I spotted for him; he listened, and moved with great care. Our belief in each other was complete. The sense of trust I felt was as invulnerable as I have ever shared, stronger even than with bird dogs and airplane mechanics. "Don't worry," I told him, until his left heel dangled in space.

By the time I am below the ridge I cannot see it. I know I need to find a way up. The best I can detect is a game trail that zigzags up the hill, so I follow it. In a little while I am back in the trees, and although I can see where I want to go it takes me some time to reckon the right approach.

The game trail is gone, and I work through the brush, scratching my bare arms. The sun now is straight overhead, and I start to wish I'd brought some water for the trip, or at least dunked in the river before I started to climb.

After another half-hour and a few missteps I make it to a saddleback ridge above the crash site. It's too steep to descend without ropes, and I cannot see any evidence of the collision. But there on the ridge, farther out, are heavy stones that have been stacked into a cairn. I am surprised that no one spoke of it to me. I suppose, though, that Ron had enough friends who I haven't contacted since last autumn that this could pass untold.

The top rock has what looks like an "x" chipped into it. But I can see the two little extra marks angling from the bottom of one axis, making a tail. I lift the rock with its little flying petroglyph so I can trace the lines with my finger. A piece of metal is resting on a flat base beneath. Someone has fashioned a small capsule from two rifle shells crimped and fitted together. I lay the capstone at my feet and reach back up to pull the shells apart—a roll of paper slides out. Unfurled it reads, "Straighten up and fly right." It's pilot humor. For men who tend to live dead-serious lives, a fatal accident can rattle some of them badly enough to make nervous jokes. I read the note and it doesn't strike me as unbefitting. Someone made this trip, carried and placed these heavy stones, and scrawled out this anxious plea. It's a better tribute than I have so far managed.

ONE THING I am certain of is that I should not be in the air at this moment. At just after 3 P.M., I am in some of the worst chop of the day. The way the Cessna is bouncing around is proof enough of this.

I stayed on that ridge for another hour, meaning to say something to my men. I didn't come with anything prepared; I thought something would occur to me when I stood in that high, rocky place. It did not. I had soaring thoughts but a mouth full of cotton, maybe because I was so parched. By the time I made it back to the plane I was dizzy from my thirst.

Ron would be angry with me for flying. "It is foolhardiness to take such risks even for a good reason, and madness for no reason at all." I can hear him say this. Until this moment I have honored that concern. I have believed it to hold me up in the sky.

His own crash, I know, was not because of risk. We were in the air together that day, but in separate planes. I had four hunters and their gear with me and he had Henry and several hundred pounds of trophy elk. As I got to that spot in the canyon the cloud ceiling was starting to lower, but I did not radio to him. He was five minutes behind me and he would be able to care for himself. But evidently the clouds dropped and he did not turn to his instruments, not in time, and I think of this as a sense I must have dulled in him by my infidelity.

The insurance company settled the claim only a few weeks ago. I received a Notice of Benefits, still surprised Ron had not removed me as the beneficiary even after he knew. Maybe that's an odd concern, but I am inclined to view this inaction as a faith he did not break. Knowing this made it especially upsetting to hear in the weeks following the crash that the insurance investigators were pursuing a concern that it might have been the result of suicide, a despondency over our failed relationship. The claim was investigated for months, and I was deposed about my affair and the mental well being of my husband before I headed south. Eventually it was decided that the crash was not an intentional act, but an accidental death caused by a sudden shift in the weather. Even holding the insurance company's check, though, I knew I had stirred up the first of that blinding mist which ended up swallowing them both.

I swing across the canyon, trying to find the place where the aircraft can hold its loft the best. Both sides are bad, and I am left to fly the middle, which is where a pilot is taught never to be. It creates the greatest collision hazard, both with other aircraft and with surprises of terrain. In the middle, a pilot can move only marginally to either extreme. There is no room for a sharp maneuver in an emergency.

I finally reach the confluence of Bear Creek, which indicates my approach. I am landing at the Marbury Bar Ranch, a private holding in the Wilderness Area. It requires a blind approach at treetop level and, when the runway appears only five seconds before touchdown, a sharp right bank. This airstrip is only advisable for pilots who have made the landing multiple times as a passenger before attempting it on their own. The aircraft must be centerweighted properly, and constant attention must be paid to airspeed to avoid a stall. Even experienced pilots will find their nerve tested here as they dip their gear to the grass.

I WAIT IN the airplane until I see him approach. He's got an expression you could divide with a line from ear to ear: his mouth grins while his eyes frown. He moves with no great hurry from the little ranch compound.

The Marbury Bar is an old homestead from before the Wilderness Act, a tiny island of private property engulfed by the wide miles of canyonland. The ranch was donated to the state university, and for years it has been a center for wildlife research. That's what this man does—he tracks and studies mountain lions, alone out here for weeks at a stretch.

I knew him for a long time before I shared his bed. I can say with certainty that I never loved him or asked his love in return. But I required him for reasons I'm not sure I can explain. It was important that he was never a part of the aeronautic order, that imperative urge to keep airflow over the wings. He was a respite. For Ron, it was crucial that I pushed myself always to stay aloft. This man allowed me to come down. I think this is what I mean: I needed him for the comfort of the ground. I need him now.

When I meet him on the runway he clasps a hand behind my neck and pulls me to him. There is no kiss, only an embrace and then my chest starting to heave. The tears mash into his shirt.

Later, when I have calmed, and we are watching the clouds of Baetis hatches come out on the river as the light falls, I tell him I should use the radio.

I turn the dial to hear the hum and then wait to see if the channel is in use. There is nothing, so I lean into the microphone. "Cascade dispatch, come in please. Over."

After a few seconds, an electronic voice buzzes. "Cascade here. Over."

"Marbury Bar calling. Over."

There is a pause. "I read. Is that you, Wayva?"

"Yes. I'm checking in. Tell Chimp not to worry about his plane."

"Are you okay? Are you flying back tonight? Over."

I wait for several seconds. "Conditions are . . ." I don't know what I want to say. "Problems are nominal, but I have gone to ground. I am tied down for the night. Do you copy? I have landed. Over."

The fine crackle and whine of the radio waves leaping through all that air is soothing. I am at rest, and my voice can travel for me.

Sudden Death, Over Time

JOHN REMBER

John Rember is a fourth-generation Idahoan. Recurring themes in his writing include the meaning of place, the impact of tourism on the West, and the weirdness of everyday life.

His work includes short-story collections, a memoir, and numerous articles and columns in magazines and newspapers, including Travel and Leisure, Skiing, *and* Wildlife Conservation. *He is a longtime professor of writing, most recently at the Pacific University MFA program. He is Writer-at-Large at Albertson College of Idaho.*

Rember lives in the Sawtooth Valley of Central Idaho.

WE ARE GOING to build fence on my fifty-fourth birthday. We have fifty-four treated posts that Angel, my wife, ordered from the ranch-supply store in town two days ago. The posts are on the other end of the ranch, next to my mother's woodpile, which is complete and ready for winter. It's October. Any day now, a storm could drop a foot of snow and we would be done with fence and firewood for this year.

But today, under a warm blue sky, we will dig ten postholes along the highway, thirteen feet apart, plant posts in them, and nail three horizontal lines of poles to the posts. My birthday present to myself is a hundred and thirty feet of fence, or, put another way, three hundred inches of hole.

It's hard work. Boulders and gravel pass for our topsoil, and when I dig a posthole I have to loosen rock with a long steel bar before I can use my shovel. I'll work the bar into the gravel in a ten-inch circle. Then I'll shovel out the loose rock. Then I'll work the bar again.

It's dangerous work. At my age, I could overexert myself and have a heart attack. I've read the average age of death of ex-NFL players is fifty-three, and a steroid-induced heart attack gets most of them, although steroid-induced cancer gets some, too. I haven't ever taken steroids, but still I'm relieved that I've reached my fifty-fourth birthday without dying.

I suppose it goes without saying I haven't played in the NFL, either. I have an old girlfriend whose little brother was drafted by Detroit, but washed out of training camp with a torn groin muscle. He had quintuple bypass surgery last winter. I don't know if he took steroids, but heart disease runs in his family. He was a big guy and he'd let himself get huge.

Getting huge doesn't run in my family. We shrink and dry up, and heart disease often comes in second to what does get us.

My father had a stroke at eighty-two and spent a wordless month dying in an Elks' rehabilitation center two hundred miles from this place. He weighed a hundred and seven pounds when they carried him out to the cremation society's hearse. A heart attack is preferable to what he went through.

But it's my birthday. I'm in bed, leaning against a pillow, letting my eyes adjust to sunshine, waiting for coffee. Angel's baked a pumpkin pie for breakfast.

DUKE, THE GUY who delivered posts yesterday, also took Angel's order at the ranch-supply store. Angel told me he asked her whether she wanted blunts or sharps. She didn't know what he was talking about, so he asked her if she was going to dig postholes or drive posts.

"I don't dig post holes," she said. "My husband does." Angel's one of those women who works in the phrase "my husband" when she's talking to men she doesn't know. That sort of thing used to bother me, but then I got married.

So when Duke showed up with the posts he called Angel "that girl." I knew Duke from high school. He'd been on our football team but was not NFL-quality. He used to shove people around in the hallways, and beat up guys his girlfriends liked, but on the field he'd miss crucial blocks. Our team mostly lost when he was playing tackle. He'd gotten huge, too, since high school. I considered telling him if he wanted to lose weight he could help me dig postholes, but thought better of it. Duke's last name was Bottoms. He'd turned himself into an easygoing big guy, which is a career choice for a high school bully in a small ranching town if you've got a name like Bottoms. Another is to join the Army and not come back home until you're retired and then make everyone call you Major Bottoms, even after you're elected county commissioner or sheriff or something, although then you'd probably want to be called Sheriff

Bottoms. Duke didn't have it the worst in his family. He had a sister his parents had named Misty.

"Duke Bottoms," I said. He remembered me, but not well, probably because Angel and I have only lately moved back to my mother's place. And I didn't play football in high school, because I was just as skinny and short then as I am now. And I always had a job during practice. Duke never beat me up because none of his girlfriends had looked twice at me, even Wendy Winters, the cheerleader he had gone out with senior year, who used to borrow my notes before English exams.

Duke and I climbed up on his flatbed truck to unload the posts. From that altitude you could see most of the ranch.

"That girl helping you with the fence?" he asked me. Angel was out on the fence line, knocking down the old fence with a sledgehammer, pulling nails out of it with a crowbar, and putting the rotten poles and cross-bucks in the pickup.

When the pickup was full, she would unload it back near the wood-pile, where we would saw it up. It makes a hot, short fire, good for days when mornings are cold and afternoons warm with the sun shining through the windows.

"That girl," said Duke. "Teach her to dig postholes, she'd be a ten."

"I think she'd rather be a nine," I said.

I asked him if he'd married Wendy the cheerleader, thinking that if he had, her name could be Wendy Bottoms. He hadn't. He'd gone to our state university, had majored in biology, and had married his lab part-ner. "We decided to share petri dishes," said Duke. Then he said, "I came back home after I got my degree. Tried to get a wildlife job. You notice Fish and Game jobs get taken by people under five-foot-six? So I'm in posts and poles."

I told Duke most people used to be under five-foot-six.

He nodded. "That's right. Before vitamins." Then he said, "My wife feeds me any more vitamins, I'll have a heart attack."

I thought about telling him it probably wouldn't be the vitamins' fault if he fell over one day.

"I'll let you get to your fence," said Duke. "Get that girl a shovel." Then he said, "Where'd you find her, anyway?"

"She was my student," I said.

Duke didn't say anything, but he gave me a look I'd seen in high school. For a moment I could imagine him shoving me into a row of lockers. I counted the posts to make sure there were fifty-four. Duke had given us bigger posts than we had ordered, but bigger posts make better-looking fence.

I took Duke into the house so my mother could pay him. She was at the kitchen table, working at her checkbook to make sure that she had the money. She has eighty or ninety thousand to go before she has to worry, and then she has annuities she can draw on. My father started out poor but invested in stocks and real estate. When he died, my mother was destroyed by grief but well off. Angel helps her with her finances even when my mother comes home from a trip to the senior center with stories about children who take over their parents' money and put them in nursing homes where the staff abuses them until they die.

It's happening to a couple of her friends, because she's named names. One of those child-villains is Linda Loma, another girl I had a crush on all through high school, even if she wasn't a cheerleader. Linda's seized control of her mother's checkbook, her friends, her movements, her breathing, probably. That was the way Linda herself was supervised during high school, when she wasn't allowed to date and was put through a succession of math tutors and piano teachers, until her senior year, when she ran off with an auto mechanic down at the Ford garage who died in Vietnam, leaving her with a couple of kids to raise the hard way. Things come round. The old lady's lucky she's not taking piano lessons and learning calculus.

Angel tells my mother we're not going to put her in a nursing home. Angel walks with her every day. Since my mother quit driving, Angel drives her to the senior center once a week, to the hairdresser's, to the grocery store and to visit the friends she has left.

I introduced Duke and told my mother he needed a check for $457.50.

"That's plenty," she said.

"They'll last us fifty years," I told her.

My mother nodded and smiled. She liked the permanence of the posts, even at the price. When you get old you likely enjoy anything that moves some part of you into the future, even if it's just your checkbook.

"At least the labor's free," she said.

My mother likes saving money, even if it involves spending it. I replaced her foggy picture window earlier this fall by framing in three smaller windows in its place. The glass people had given her a bid of twenty-five hundred dollars, but the glass and lumber for the replacements only cost three-fifty. My mother was happy with her new view, which was unfogged and more to human scale. Human scale seems to be one of the things she's clued-in to, now that she's old. Duke and I looked out through the new windows and saw Angel still pounding apart the old fence.

"Good worker?" asked Duke.

"Good worker," I said.

"You got lucky," he said. He took his check, thanked my mother, said good-bye, got in his truck, and left. I told my mother I was going out to help Angel.

"How tall are you?" I asked Angel when I got close enough. She had put down the sledge and was trying to dig a posthole, but only had a scruffy little depression three inches into the gravel.

Angel looked at me. "Five-six and three quarters," she said. "Same as you."

"I was just thinking if you wore low heels, we could get you a job," I said. "Spawning fish in the hatchery or something."

"Yuck," she said. "What made you think of that?"

"Duke said you could get a job with the Fish and Game if you were short enough. He also said you would be a ten if I could teach you to dig postholes," I said. I looked at her. "You look good with a shovel. Sweaty helps, too."

She handed me the shovel. "I don't do sweaty," she said.

"Too late," I said.

so today i'm Fifty. Four. Fucking. Years. Old. I'm wondering how I explain this to people, and wondering if fifty-four is the average age of death of ex-NBA players. A few years ago I had a friend who was ninety-one. People would ask him his age, and he'd say ninety-fucking-one, and people would laugh. When he was ninety-two he was ninety-fucking-two, and then he died at ninety-fucking-three. After he died I started telling people I was fifty-fucking-two, but nobody ever laughed, because nobody worries about being fifty-two the way you worry about being ninety-one unless you've been in the NFL and done a lot of steroids.

I'm thinking this over when Angel brings me my coffee.

"Coffee fairy," she says. Coffee fairy, pie cook, wife, companion, tutor in situations requiring emotional intelligence: Angel does it all. On our next anniversary we will have been married ten years, which is a long time to spend with one person, especially given the close way we've run our marriage. In those ten years we've spent maybe a hundred days apart.

Angel hands me my cup. "How does it feel to know you'll never see fifty-three again?"

"I don't feel a day over fifty-two," I say.

"I'll inform the NFL," she says.

One of the reasons we're still married is we don't mind telling the same joke for a year or two, even if it's a Dying at Age Fifty-Three NFL Steroid Joke.

Now that I've made it to fifty-four, there's a kind of euphoria that comes with the joke, a happy cheating of fate, like Oedipus must have felt on the road to Thebes. It's possible to think that if one of the NFL teams needed a kicker, I could walk on and replace the guy who died last year at fifty-three.

Angel's being fifty-three is not something we joke about. When she's fifty-three I'll be seventy-three, and seventy-three doesn't sound like an age the NFL would be interested in, not even if I had a fan base of old guys who were seventy-three plus, the kind of fan base that would invite me—the oldest man in the NFL, pumped up on steroids—to tailgate parties *after* the game, when my team had lost, maybe even because I had missed a point after. But we would celebrate anyway because the group wisdom would be that death is worse than losing, and maybe losing would keep death at bay.

Would the NFL let me keep Death at Bay? I don't think so. Green Bay, maybe. Tampa Bay. But not Death at Bay.

Angel gets me out of bed by serving my pumpkin pie at the kitchen table instead of bed where I've asked for it. I think she knows if I act like most people act on their birthdays, no fence will get built and we'll have fifty-four posts stacked beside the woodpile all winter, where I'll worry about them and curse the frozen ground and they'll get in the way when I plow snow.

The pie is good. I finish two pieces. Then I put on my work clothes, grab the shovel and bar from the garage, and walk down to where I've marked the first hole.

It's easy. Occasionally there are pockets of loamy sand in the gravel that the river left behind ten thousand years ago, and the hole is in one of those pockets. The hole is a birthday gift, a blessing: an easy dig from a kindly universe.

When I was eight, my father made me dig postholes right on this fence line. We were replacing a rotten cross-buck fence built by the original homesteader of the property. There's a rhythm of fence building here—posts to cross-bucks to posts—that's apparent if you live long enough.

Now, even when I hit big boulders and gravel, I can dig a posthole in fifteen minutes. At age eight it took a couple of hours of intermittent bawling.

My father had worked as a young man digging holes for telephone poles. But instead of taking two weeks to build fence himself, he put me out on the fence line with a shovel for two summers. It could have been to keep me out of trouble. He could have thought it was character building, which it was, if he intended to produce a character deeply hostile to authority.

But what seemed endless at eight is a quick job at fifty-four. A hole needs to be dug. I dig it. Another needs to be dug—it's a chance to shine again. It's a wonder I didn't end up working in a cemetery.

But I still get angry with my father for putting an eight-year-old out on a gravel bar with a shovel and a heavy steel bar and telling him to dig holes until a distant dinnertime.

FROM WHERE I stand I can see bits of rotten wood marking the fence line. Untreated posts went into the holes I dug, because my father spent money on more land instead of on post-treat. So that fence, the one constructed at such an expense of child labor, rotted and fell down in fifteen years.

It *was* good exercise. Digging holes in the ground is an alternative to steroids, causing you to get leaner and stringier and shorter and tougher instead of making you tall and giving you giant male breasts and arterial plaques and absolute rage over the littlest things. I don't remember thinking that sort of thing when I was eight. When I was eight I probably would have taken steroids. I could have used the extra muscle, and rage would have been better than tears every time I started on a posthole.

As I am measuring for the second hole, I spot my mother hobbling out of her house toward me. She's not fast, but she's steady, and she reaches me when I'm a foot down. This hole is made out of rocks, and I've just dug down to a ten-inch boulder spanning the bottom of it.

"What are you doing?" she asks. It's a worrisome question. She has begun to suffer small strokes. They cause her to lose her memory, short-term and long-term. You can have the same conversation with her three times in ten minutes. After a day she's better and can remember, for example, the month she spent beside my father's deathbed. It's frightening because she lives alone in her house and heats with wood. You start thinking that maybe she shouldn't be, that it's time for the next step, and when you wonder what that might be, you think of a burning house.

"What are you doing?" she says again.

"Building fence," I say. "Posts this time."

"I thought the old one would outlast me," she says, "but I've outlasted it."

I'm relieved. She is hooked into the continuum of her life. The next thing she will say is that she has outlived all her friends, which she has, except for one or two that sometimes don't recognize her when Angel takes her visiting.

But that's not what she says. "Your father dug lots of postholes. He dug them all the way around this place. Back when we had horses."

I look at her. I don't remember my father digging holes, not at all. I only remember digging them myself. Then I remember building new cross-buck fence, and thirty years later, sawing it all up for firewood. And now more postholes.

There is no way I'd dug all those earlier postholes. Even three summers wouldn't have done it, not with my kicking and crying and foot-dragging. In this instance my mother is remembering things better than I am.

Then she says, "Your father would be helping you if he was still alive."

More truth. When my father was here, I couldn't work around the ranch without him helping me. He had worked in the woods and in construction, and had learned to love physical labor, and it occurred to me that sending me out to dig postholes at age eight had been, in his mind, a gift, in spite of my tears.

IT'S A RISK, because she might take me seriously, but I lean the shovel toward my mother and say, "Here. You can help."

She shakes her head and backs away a little bit. I check to see she's not going to trip over a rock.

"I would," she says. "But my arthritis would kill me."

"Digging postholes would be good for your arthritis," I say. "It's been good for mine."

"Do you have arthritis?" she asked. "You're not old enough for arthritis."

"I'm only thirty-three years younger than you," I say.

She digests this for a while. Then she says, "I never thought I'd be the only one alive."

I don't take it personally. She's talking about her generation, and it's a fear, not a fact, that she's expressing. She doesn't want to outlive anybody anymore, but she doesn't want to die, either. A couple of times this summer she's had panic attacks, which I recognized before Angel called 911.

She also has dreams, and in them her family who have died before her open their arms to her. She's told me a parent's worst fear is of outliving a child, but that's an abstract fear, one less real at night than being short of breath and feeling like the down comforter on your bed is crushing you. That's when Angel and I get calls, and we get up and go down and give her someone to talk to for a while. Then she tells us she can sleep and we go home and go to sleep ourselves.

My mother stands and watches me while I finish the posthole, and when I start on another she walks back toward her house. I'm relieved. Sometimes she comes out and watches me cut up firewood. I have to tell her to go to the house because I can't pay attention to her and the chainsaw at the same time.

"Go in the house, Mom," I say, "unless you want to watch me cut my foot off." It always hurts her feelings.

I am even more relieved when I see Angel walking toward me.

"Done yet?" she asks.

"Done in," I say, but I'm feeling pretty good.

"I'll go get the posts and poles," she says.

I nod, and she walks past me. A few minutes later I hear my mother's old pickup back up to the pile of poles we've cut over the summer, and then I hear the bang of wood on metal as Angel starts throwing them onto the pickup bed.

By the time Angel comes back with thirty poles and ten posts, I've finished five holes.

Angel scatters the posts and poles along the fence line, unloads a box of nails and the sledgehammer and chainsaw, and drives the pickup back to the woodpile. Then she goes to the house to get my mother, and the two of them get in my mother's car and they go toward town a mile to where there's a side road they can walk without getting run over by a semi. By the time Angel gets back I have all ten holes dug. It's lunchtime. Because it is my birthday, I'm going to have pumpkin pie.

IN THE MIDDLE of lunch the phone rings. Angel answers it. I grab my fourth piece of pie for the day. Dig holes all morning and you work up an appetite.

"They're fine," says Angel. "No. If they're too tall, we cut them off with the chainsaw. Or dig the holes deeper."

I look at her to see if the phone call is for me, but she shakes her head.

"Thanks. I'll let you know if that happens," she says. Then she says, "I'll tell him."

Angel puts down the phone. "That was Duke," she says. "He wanted to know if the posts were working out all right."

"Not really. He gave us all left-handed ones," I say. "Now we have to build the fence backward."

She ignores me. "He wanted to know if they were too tall," she says. "Also, he said if you ever decided to get rid of me, I should let him know."

"What did he say you were supposed to tell me?"

She smiles. "What you already know. That you're lucky to have me."

"If somebody's going to call up and hit on my wife, I wish they'd wait until after my birthday."

Angel walks around behind me and kisses me on the ear.

"He wasn't hitting on me. Anyway, he's *huge*."

"He was hitting on you. And he's married. Jesus. And he thinks his posts are too tall for me."

Normally I don't get worried about Angel being hit on. If it happens we go into a routine we call We're So Lucky:

"We've been together for fifteen years," I say. "Married for ten."

"And we're still in love," says Angel.

I say, "We never get bored with each other. I really like her body."

"And I really like his," says Angel. "Even if it is old and wrinkled."

"She was twelve when we met," I say.

"We're so lucky," we say together.

It usually discourages anybody, like Duke, who has checked out Angel and then checked out me and thought that she really does look like an angel and I look like a garden gnome.

"If I'm going to run off with anybody," says Angel, "it won't be anybody who will teach me to dig postholes."

Then she quits smiling and says, "But I'm not going to run off. Not until the fence is done."

"I'm so lucky," I say. And I mean it. Because the fence will never be done.

I SPEND A lot of time telling Angel she's pretty. When I do that she twists her mouth and rolls her eyes toward her nose and says, *"Pretty goofy."* She gets away with this because she's thirty-three. My birthday starts the half-year that I'm twenty-one years older than she is instead of twenty, and somewhere in my mind I must think that twenty is the absolute limit, because on my birthday I always look at her and suddenly understand my mind is being controlled by space aliens. I'm not here married to Angel, I'm really in the hold of a starship making the long trek back to Sirius where aliens will use my DNA to make their domesticated food animals tougher and stringier, which they like.

Angel and I met during my freshman composition class, which was the first class she took in college. We bonded like baby ducks do to whomever they see first after breaking out of the egg.

It was good that it was Angel I saw first and not Pamela Larson, the former Miss Idaho who was sitting beside her, back for her degree after five years in the beauty-pageant-and-modeling business. Pamela had been out of the egg for so long at that point she wasn't going to bond with anyone. The last time I heard about her she was stuck on the step in the twelve-step process where you try to make amends with the people you've hurt if it would do more good than harm, and she was stuck in it for a long time.

Two years after that first class Angel and I got together, and we had spent a year thinking it was all wrong and staying away from each other and being miserable. There were mutters about sexual predation, especially among some of the older faculty women, for whom no good thing was cause for joy. One of them took Angel aside and told her not to throw her life away, because she had a future as an academic ahead of her.

Fortunately, Angel did not want a future as an academic. And when my father died and we started selling his real estate I also didn't want a future as an academic, at least if that sort of thing is a tenured position where you've got fifty or sixty classes of freshman comp ahead of you, and where the photos in a twenty-year-old yearbook portray a youth wasted on comma splices. Where you totter into your old classrooms and read from a sheaf of yellowed notes until campus security once again leads you away from the podium.

I foresaw a lifetime of female colleagues glowering at me across committee-room tables. It was finally their faces that made me go back to the ranch. I admit I shouldn't have slept with so many of them before I met Angel.

ANGEL PUTS THE lunch dishes in the sink and gives them a quick rinse. Then she puts on her work gloves and tells me, "Ten down. Forty-four to go."

She could be talking years of marriage. I hope she is. But I think she's talking postholes. Most of the time I'm glad Angel is down-to-earth and literal. Not now. The phone call from Duke Bottoms has me feeling that awful high school I'm-a-geek-about-to-get-beat-up feeling. Right now if I had a syringe full of anabolic steroid I'd stick it in my thigh. One of the problems with leaving the academy and moving back to the place you were raised is that your self slides back to a time before it had tenure.

"I want you to know," I say, "I would never get rid of you."

Angel looks pained. "Are you still worrying about that phone call?"

"It's not good," I say, "to have somebody like Duke Bottoms look at your wife like she's a 4-H heifer."

"It's not good to mention your wife in the same sentence as '4-H heifer,'" she says.

Then she smiles. "Duke used to be young and strong and good-looking. Now he's old and weak and ugly. He can't figure out how it happened."

"What he can't figure out is how I ended up with you and I wasn't even on the football team." Saying this gives me satisfaction, but it ends when I realize what Angel said about Duke she could be saying about anybody Duke's age.

Then when we're walking down to the holes I've dug, Angel says, "Your mother says she doesn't want to see ninety. She says she didn't know that being old would be so hard and hurt so much."

"It's time she learned," I say.

"She says we really don't need to build this fence."

"I know," I say. "But she used to be the type of person who wanted the fences looking good. Anyway, we're not building the fence for her."

"She says what we could do for her is bring your father back."

"No we can't," I say. Even if we could, we wouldn't. It's hard to tell what he'd be like and what he'd say if he were back from wherever he is now. I don't think he would be happy, even to see my mother again, especially in her state of black-hole loneliness for him. It's tough enough when you're her son and she would sacrifice you just to have her husband back. It would be even tougher to be that husband. Even if I figured out a way to bring him back, I could never be sure it was my father, even if it looked like my father.

Angel has agreed to smother me with a pillow when I get weak enough for her to overpower me. That's because I've learned from my parents that there are worse things than death. I try to tell my mother that sixty years of happy married life is more than most people get, but she says all that happiness just makes the pain worse. I say Angel and I won't have sixty years together, to which she says nothing. There's no pity for the young in the hearts of the aged. That's probably why I can ask Angel to smother me with a pillow.

When we get to the postholes I tip a fence post into each one. Then Angel shovels gravel around each post while I go around and around it with the bar, tamping the gravel tight, making sure it's straight and solid. Then, with faith and trust, Angel holds the poles against the posts while I pound the nails in with the sledge. Then I trim things to human dimension with the chainsaw, and we're done for the day.

My arms are still pumped from lifting the bar and jamming its twenty pounds down into the gravel nine hundred or a thousand times. That slack skin that has begun to hang off the bottom of my arms—I've begun to notice it lately, in the mirror while I'm shaving—it's gone.

ANGEL WALKS BACK to our house while I throw the tools and the sawn-off ends of posts and poles into the pickup. Cleaning up a job at the end of the day is important. You never know when you'll get back to it.

I've got everything in when Duke Bottoms drives by. I wave at him but when he gets close he's looking straight down the highway. I wonder if he's wondering why my mother's paying for a new fence when all her horses are dead.

But he probably knows it's not her fence. It's Angel's and my fence. It's not for horses. It's for saying that this is our place. Inside these lines, we will stand together for a while.

This summer when cattle were being driven down the highway, they broke through the old fence on our end of the place, destroyed a new lawn we had put in, wrecked a rock retaining wall, and left shit all over our driveway. They were back on the highway before they got to my mother's place, but I started getting afraid for her lawn and flowers. They are among the last few things she tends to. They remind me that she was once a strong and nurturing woman. So we started rebuilding fence on her end of the place.

When I've parked the pickup, I walk on the highway to check on our work before I go on home. It looks good. But we're twelve hundred feet short of our driveway, and then there are the other three sides of the place.

After I get these first fifty-four posts planted, I'll order more. Duke will deliver them. With luck, Angel will be good at postholes by then, and will be out there with the shovel and bar when he shows up with his flatbed.

I wonder if Duke Bottoms did steroids. I wonder if I should have done steroids. Maybe I would have made the high school football team. Then maybe I would have done more steroids and played ball in college, and then maybe an NFL scout would have seen a game film, and—that's what happened to Lyle Alzado, who died of steroid-induced lymphoma of the brain at forty-fucking-two. At the end he was doing don't-do-steroids public service announcements featuring himself as what would happen if you did. At the end he couldn't walk without help.

The closest I ever got to being on steroids was before I met Angel. I got a cyst in my knee and went lame and hobbled around for two months refusing to see a doctor. It was a sign of mortality when I was thinking there still was time to train hard for five years and then maybe win some marathons.

The pain started making it hard to sleep. Finally I went to Dr. Klein-spritz, a retired team doctor for the Dallas Cowboys who was working a couple of days a week at a local clinic. If you went to him with a sore back, you got cortisone. A torn ligament, cortisone. Earache, cortisone.

Piles, thyroid problems, insomnia, existential dread: cortisone. There's a reason the Cowboys won those Super Bowls, and then fell apart.

Dr. Kleinspritz pulled out a huge syringe with a huge needle and stabbed it right into the cyst in my knee. He sucked out a teaspoon of what looked like mixed-fruit jelly and then he filled the cyst with cortisone and two weeks later the cyst was gone, I had no pain, and the knee's been fine ever since.

THE OCTOBER SUN is on the horizon when I walk into the house. I'm feeling good, maybe like you feel after running an interception back for a touchdown, and maybe after that touchdown won the game. Ten new panels of fence will do that to you. It's a warm evening, with no wind. Even though I know there's six feet of snow coming this winter, it feels like the warm days will never end.

Angel has taken a shower and is fixing a cheese and olive and cracker and smoked salmon tray. She's opened a bottle of red wine, which she tells me is good for my heart, and she says after I take a shower, she'll meet me on the deck. I agree to this program, even if it is my birthday and I can do anything I want.

I leave the shower, put on a clean T-shirt and fresh blue jeans, and a pair of sandals. Angel hands me a glass of wine and I walk out to where she's got the food sitting on a small table between a couple of low deck chairs. There's a sunset going on, and Angel has lined up fifty-four votive candles along all three sides of the deck rail and lit them. Their flames glow unwavering in the still air, and all together, they look like a short bright fence against the shadowed hills on the other side of the river. I'm not even going to think about blowing them out.

Just on the other side of the flames there are other shadows. There's Lyle Alzado, looking at me with sad public service announcement eyes. There's my father, who seems irritated that I'm resting before dinner rather than putting in more posts. My mother is there, too, but she's the age Angel is now. That's fifty-four years younger, and it may be coincidence, but it makes me see that the whole of my life is bracketed by two women.

Beyond my mother, there's Duke Bottoms in a football uniform, and some of his cheerleader girlfriends. There's a dozen grim ghosts in their academic robes.

None of them is really aware of Angel or me or each other. I wonder if they're alive or just memorial holographs, visible only in a soft crossfire of low light. But memories *are* alive—they must be, considering all the damage they do. It's probably good we can't see them all the time. It's probably good—for the sake of my birthday celebration—that Angel's staked out a small space and time in this world where I can sit untroubled by my past and my future, my birth and my death.

Dillinger in Hollywood

JOHN SAYLES

A 1972 graduate of Williams College, John Sayles, originally and still a novelist and writer of short stories, published his first novel before becoming a Hollywood screenwriter and actor. After making Return of the Secaucus Seven, *he struggled to finance other original films. A MacArthur Foundation Fellowship helped him secure a berth in the top level of American filmmakers, and he continues to write, direct, and edit his unique brand of intelligent, independent films.*

Sayles lives and works with Maggie Renzi in Hoboken, New Jersey, and upstate New York.

EVER HAVE ONE of those weeks where the TV is bust and there's steamed chicken for lunch three days in a row? It was one of those weeks, and Spurs Tatum starts in after Rec Therapy, before we could wheel them all out of the dayroom.

"Hoot Gibson held my horse," says Spurs. "I took falls for Randolph Scott. I hung from a wing in *The Perils of Pauline.* And Mr. Ford," he says, "Mr. Ford he always hired me on. You see a redskin blasted off a horse in one of Mr. Ford's pictures, like as not it's me. One-Take Tatum they called me, before the Spurs thing took."

We'd heard it all before, every time there was a Western or a combat picture on the TV, every time a patient come in with a broken hip or a busted rib, all through the last days when the Duke was dying in the news. Heard how Spurs had thought up most of the riding stunts they use today, how he'd been D. W. Griffith's drinking buddy, how he saved Tom Mix's life on the Sacramento River. It was hot and one of those weeks and we'd heard it all before, so I don't know if it was that or the beating he'd just taken at Parcheesi that made old Casey up and say how he used to be John Dillinger.

His chart said that Casey had been a driver on the Fox lot long enough to qualify for the Industry fund. I told him I hadn't realized he'd done any stand-in work.

"The bird who done the stand-in work," says Casey, "is the one they potted at the Biograph Theater. I used to be Johnnie Dillinger. In the flesh." He said the name with a hard g, like in *finger*, and didn't so much as blink.

Now we've had our delusions at the Home—your standard fading would-of-been actresses expecting their call from Mr. DeMille, a Tarzan whoop now and then during the full moon, and one old gent who goes around mouthing words without sound and overacting like he's on the silent picture screen. Generally it's some glorified notion of who they used to be. Up to this point Casey's only brag was he drove Joe DiMaggio to the airport when the Clipper was hitched to Monroe.

"If I remember right," says Spurs, giving me an eye that meant he thought the poor fella had slipped his tracks, "if I'm not too fuzzy on it, I believe that Mr. Dillinger, Public Enemy Number One, departed from our midst in the summer of thirty-four."

"You should live so long," says Casey.

NOW, I TRY to give a man the benefit of a doubt. With Spurs I can tell there's a grain of fact to his brags because I was in the wrangler game myself. I was riding broncs in Santa Barbara for their Old Spanish Days and this fella hires me to stunt for some rodeo picture with Gig Young in it. He says I take a nice fall.

The pay was greener than what I saw on the circuit, so I stuck in Hollywood. See, I could always *ride* the sumbitches, my problem came when it was time to get *off*. What I had was a new approach to tumbling from a horse. Whereas most folks out here bust their ass to get *into* pictures, I busted mine to get *out*. Some big damn gelding bucked me before I'd dug in, and I landed smack on my tailbone. The doctor says to me— I'm laying on my stomach trying to remember my middle name—the doctor comes in with the X-rays and he says, "I don't know how to tell you this, Son, but you're gonna have to learn to shit standing up."

If they'd known who I was, *Variety* would of headlined SON BISHOP SWAPS BRIDLE FOR BEDPAN. Horses and hospitals were all I knew. Over the years I'd spent more time in emergency rooms than Dr. Kildare. So it was hospitals, and pretty soon I drifted into the geriatric game. Your geriatrics and horses hold a lot in common—they're high-strung, they bite and kick sometimes, and they're none of them too big on bowel control. 'Course, if a geriatric steps on your foot it don't take a wood chisel to peel it off the floor.

It's a living.

So Spurs I can back sometimes, though I'm sure he didn't play such a starring role in the invention of the saddle. With Casey I had to bring it up at report.

"He thinks he's a dead gangster?" says Mrs. Goorwitz, who was the charge nurse that night.

"No, he thinks he's an old man in a Hollywood nursing home. He says he *used* to be John Dillinger."

"In another life?"

"Nope," I answered her, "in this one."

We had this reincarnated character in here once, claimed to have been all the even-numbered King Louies of France, from the second right up to Louie the Sixteen. I asked how he ended up an assistant prop man at Warner's and he said after all that commotion his spirit must of needed the rest.

"I thought he was shot," says Mrs. Goorwitz.

"At point-blank range," I tell her. "They couldn't of missed."

Mrs. Goorwitz was a bit untracked by the news. She hates anything out of its place, hates waves, and many's the geriatric she's hounded to death for holding a book overdue from the Home library. She pulled Casey's chart and studied it. "It says here his name is Casey Mullins."

"Well that's that, isn't it?"

"Confused behavior," says Mrs. Goorwitz, as she writes it into the report. "Inappropriate response. Watch carefully."

The only thing that gets watched carefully in this joint is the time-punch at two minutes till shift change, but I figured I might save Casey some headache.

"Maybe he's just lying," I tell her. "To work up a little attention."

"Did he say anything else?" She was on the scent now and threatening to go practice medicine on somebody any minute.

"Not a whole lot," I tell her. "But if we breathe a word to the Feds, he claims they'll find us off Santa Monica Pier with our little toes curled up."

"THIS BIRD JIMMY Lawrence, a very small-time character," says Casey, "he had this bum ticker. A rheumatic heart condition, congenital since birth. We dated the same girl once is how I got to know him. People start coming up to say, 'Jeez, you're the spittin' image of Johnnie Dillinger, you know that?' and this girl, this mutual friend, tells me and I get the idea."

After he let the Dillinger thing out, Casey got very talkative, like he had it stewing in him a long time and finally it blows out all at once. I'd be in his room tapping the catheter bags on these two vegematics, Kantor and Wise, and it would be just me listening, and this fella Roscoe Baggs, who was a midget. Roscoe was in *The Wizard of Oz* as a Munchkin and was a very deep thinker. He reads the kind of science-fiction books that don't have girls in loincloths on the cover.

"This girl has still got the yen for me," says Casey, "so she steers Lawrence to a doctor connection who tells him two months, maybe three, and it's the last roundup. The guy is demolished. So I make him this offer—I supply the dough to live it up his final days, and he supplies a body to throw to the authorities. You could buy Chicago cops by the job lot back then, so it was no big deal arranging the details. Hard times. Only two or three people had to know I was involved.

"Well, the poor chump didn't even know how to paint the town right. And he kept moaning that he wanted us to hold off till after the Series, onnaconna he followed the Cardinals. That was the year Ripper Collins and the Dean brothers tore up the league."

"Just like Spangler," says Roscoe. "Remember, he wanted to see a man walk on the moon? Held off his cancer till he saw it on television, and the next day he went downstairs."

Downstairs is where the morgue and the kitchen are located.

"One step for mankind," says Roscoe, "and checkout time for Spangler. You got to admire that kind of control."

"Another hoax," says Casey. "They staged the whole thing in a little studio up the coast. I know a guy in video."

I told Casey I'd read where Dillinger started to run when he saw the cops outside the picture show. And how his sister had identified the remains the next day.

"He turned chickenshit on me, Son. We hadn't told him the exact date, and there he is, coming out from the movies with a broad on each arm, and all of a sudden the party's over. What would you do, you were him? And as for Sis," says Casey, "she always done what she could to help me out.

"The day after the planting we send in a truck, dig the coffin out, pour concrete, and lay it back in. Anybody wants another peek at the stiff they got to drill a mine shaft."

It sounded reasonable, sort of. And when the shrink who comes through twice a year stopped to ask about his Dillinger fixation, Casey just told him to scram. Said if he wanted his brains scrambled he'd stick his head in the microwave.

I did some reading and everything he said checked out pretty close. Only I couldn't connect Casey with a guy who'd pull a stunt like that on the Lawrence fella. He was one of the nice ones, Casey—never bitched much even with his diabetes and his infected feet and his rotting kidneys and his finger curling up. A stand-up character.

The finger was curling up independent from the others on his right hand. His trigger finger, bent like he was about to squeeze off a round.

"It's like *The Tell-Tale Heart*," says Roscoe one day. I'm picking up dinner trays in the rooms, and Roscoe is working on four chocolate puddings. They had put one on Casey's tray by mistake and I didn't have time to spoon the other two down Kantor and Wise.

"The what?" asks Casey.

"It's a story. This guy kills an old man and stuffs him under the floorboards. When the police come to investigate he thinks he hears the old man's heart beating under the boards, and he cracks and gives himself away."

"So what's that got to do with my finger?"

"Maybe your finger is trying to blow the whistle on your life of crime. Psychosomatic."

"Oh." Casey mauled it over in his mind for a minute. "I get it. We had a guy in the can, kilt his wife. Poisoned her. At first everybody figured she'd just got sick and died, happened all the time in those days. But then he starts complaining to the cops about the neighborhood kids— says they're writing nasty stuff on the sidewalk in front of his place. OLD MAN WALSH CROAKED HIS WIFE WITH RAT BAIT—stuff like that. So the cops send a guy to check it out on his night rounds. The cop's passing by and out comes Walsh, sleepwalking, with a piece of chalk in his hand. Wrote his own ticket to the slammer, right there on the sidewalk, onnaconna he had a leaky conscience."

It had been bothering me, so I took the opening to ask. "Do you ever feel bad? About things you done back then?"

Casey shrugged and looked away from me and then looked back. "Nah," he says, "What am I, mental? This guy Walsh, he was AWOL."

AWOL is what we call the senile ones. Off base and not coming back.

"Hey, Roscoe," says Casey, "why'd this telltale character kill the old man in the first place?"

"Because this old man had a big eye. He wanted to kill the big eye."

Just then Spurs wheels in, looking to vulture a loose dessert.

"I wonder," says Casey, "what he would of done to a fat head?"

IT SEEMED TO make him feel better, talking about his life as Dillinger. Kept him up and alert even when his health took a big slide.

"Only reason I'm still percolating," he'd say, "is I still got my pride. They beat that into me on my first stretch."

I told him I'd never heard of beating pride into somebody.

"They beat on you one way or the other," he says. "The pride comes in how you stand up to it."

I went on the graveyard shift and after two o'clock check I'd go down to chew the fat with Casey. Roscoe slept like the dead and the two veggies were on automatic pilot, so it didn't make any difference how loud we were. Casey was a hurtin' cowboy, and his meds weren't up to knocking him out at night. We'd play cards by the light from the corridor sometimes or he'd cut up old scores for me. He told me about one where their advance man posed as a Hollywood location scout for a gangster movie. When they come out of the bank holding hostages the next day, sniping at the local shields, the townspeople just smiled and looked around for cameras.

He didn't have much to say on his years driving for Fox. He only hung on because of what he called the "fringe benefits," which mostly had to do with women.

"Used to be a disease with me," he'd say. "I'd go two days without a tumble and my eyeballs would start to swole up, my brains would start pushing out my ears. Shut me out for three days and I'd hump anything, just anything. Like some dope fiend."

When I asked how he'd dealt with that while he was in the slammer, he clammed up.

He was still able to wheel himself around a bit when Norma took up with him. Norma had bad veins and was in a chair herself. She'd been in the silents in her teens, getting rescued from fates worse than death. Her mother was ninety and shared a room with her. The old vulture just sat, deaf as a post, glaring at Norma for not being Mary Pickford. Norma had been one of the backgammon crowd till word spread that Casey thought he was John Dillinger. She studied him for a week, keeping her distance, eavesdropping on his sparring matches with Spurs Tatum, watching how he moved and how he talked. Then one day as the singalong is breaking up she wheels up beside him. Norma's voice had gone deeper and deeper with the years, and she filled in at bass on "What a Friend We Have in Jesus."

"All I do is dream of you," she sings to Casey, "the whole night through."

"That used to be my favorite song," he says.

"I know," says Norma.

It give me the fantods sometimes, the way they'd look at each other like they known one another forever. Norma had been one of those caught up by the press on Dillinger when he had his year in the headlines. A woman near thirty years old keeping a scrapbook. She had picked up some work as an extra after her silent days were over, but it never came to much. She still had a shoe box full of the postcards her mother had sent out every year to agents and flacks and producers—a grainy blowup of Norma in a toga or a buckskin shift or a French peasant outfit. Norma Nader in *Cimarron*. Norma Nader in *The Pride and the Passion*. Norma Nader in *The Greatest Story Ever Told*. They were the only credits she got in the talkies, those postcards, but her mother kept the heat on. I'd find Norma out in the corridor at night, wheels locked, watching the light coming out from her room.

"Is she in bed yet?" she'd ask, and I'd go down and peek in on Old Lady Nader.

"She's still awake, Norma."

"She always stood up till I come home, no matter what hour. I come in the door and it's not 'Where you been?' or 'Who'd you see?' but 'Any work today?' She had spies at all the studios so I could never lie about making rounds. Once I had an offer for a secretary job, good pay, steady, and I had to tell them 'Sorry, I got to be an actress.'"

Casey had his Dillinger routine down pretty well, but with Norma along he was unstoppable.

"Johnnie," she say, "you 'member that time in St. Paul they caught you in the alleyway?" or "Johnnie, remember how Nelson and Van Meter were always at each other's throats?" —just like she'd been there. And

Casey he'd nod and say he remembered or correct some little detail, reminding her like any old couple sharing memories.

I'd come on at eleven and they'd be in the dayroom with only the TV for light, Casey squirming in his chair, hurting, and Norma waiting for her mother to go to sleep, holding Casey's hand against the pain. We had another old pair like them, a couple old bachelors crazy for chess. One game could take them two–three days. Personally I'd rather watch paint dry.

Usually some time around one o'clock Norma would call and we'd wheel them back to their rooms. I'd park Casey by the window so he could watch the traffic on Cahuenga.

By the time I got back on the day shift, Casey needed a push when he wanted to get anywhere. He could still feed himself and hit the pee jug nine times out of ten, though we were checking his output to see what was left of his kidneys. This one morning we had square egg for breakfast, which is the powdered variety cooked up in cake pans and cut in little bars like brownies. If they don't get the coloring just right they'll come up greenish, and they wiggle on your fork just like Jell-O. Even the blind patients won't touch them. Usually our only taker is this character Mao, who we call after his resemblance to the late Chinese head Red. Mao is a mongoloid in his mid-thirties whose favorite dishes are square egg and thermometers. Already that morning a new candy striper had given him an oral instead of a rectal, and he'd chomped it clear in half. Now she was fluttering around looking for Mr. Hellman's other slipper.

"I looked in his stand and under his bed," she says to me, "and all I could find is the right one."

"He doesn't have a left one," I tell her.

"Why not?"

"He doesn't have a left leg."

"Oh." The candy stripers are good for morale, but they take a lot of looking after.

"Next time peek under the covers first."

"Well, I started to," she says, "but he was flipping his—you know—his *thing* at me."

"Don't you worry, honey," says Spurs Tatum. "Worst comes to worst I'd lay odds you could outrun the old goat."

"When they give us this shit in the state pen," says Casey, so's everybody in the dayroom could hear him, "we'd plaster the walls with it."

The candy striper waggles her finger at him. "If you don't care for your breakfast, Mr. Mullins, I'm sure somebody else would appreciate it."

"No dice," says Casey. "I want to see it put down the trash barrel where it can't do no harm. And the name's Dillinger."

"I'm sure you don't mind if somebody shares what you don't want. I mean, what are we here for?" Lately we've been getting candy stripers with a more Christian outlook.

"What we're *here* for," says Casey, "is to die. To die. And some of us," he says, looking to Spurs, "aren't doing much of a job of it."

Casey was on the rag that morning, with a bad case of the runs his new meds give him and a wobbling pile of square egg staring up at him. So when the candy striper reaches to give his portion over to Mao, Casey pushes his tray over onto the floor.

"You birds keep swallowin' this shit," he calls out to the others, "they'll keep sending it up."

Mao was well known for his oatmeal tossing. You'd get two spoonfuls down him, and he'd decide to chuck the whole bowl acrost the room. Or wing it straight up so big globs stuck to the ceiling. The old-timers liked to sit against the back wall of the dayroom afternoons and bet on which glob would loosen and fall first. So when Mao picked up on Casey and made like a catapult with his plate, there was chunks sent scattering clear to the Bingo tables.

"Food riot!" yells Roscoe, flicking egg off his fork, aiming for old oatmeal stains on the ceiling. "Every man for himself!" he yells, and then goes into "Ding-Dong, the Witch Is Dead."

I didn't think the old farts had it in them. It was like being inside a popcorn popper, yellow hunks of egg flying every which way, squishing, bouncing, coffee sloshing, toast frisbeeing, plates smashing, orange juice showering, while Mrs. Shapiro, stone blind and AWOL for years, is yelling, "Boys, don't fight! Don't fight, your father will get crazy!"

The rec therapist is a togetherness freak. They sing together, they make place mats together, they have oral history sessions together. So somebody starts throwing food the rest of them are bound to pitch in. When there was nothing left to toss, they calmed down. We decided to wheel them all back to their rooms before we cleaned out the dayroom.

"I'm hungry," says Spurs. "Crazy sumbitch made me lose my breakfast. Senile bastard."

"Shove it, cowboy," says Casey. "In my day we'd of used you for a toothpick."

"In *my* day we'd of stuck you in the bughouse. Dillinger my ass."

Casey didn't say a thing but Norma wheeled up between them, a big smear of grape jelly on her cheek.

"John Dillinger," she said, "was the only one in the whole lousy country was his own man, the only one that told them all to go hang and went his own way. Have some respect."

I NEVER LEARNED if she really thought he was Dillinger or if they just shared the same interest, like the chess players or the crowd that still reads the trade papers together. When Norma went AWOL it was like her mother called her in from the playground. She left us quick, fading in and out for two weeks till she gave up all the way and just sat in her chair in her room, staring back at her mother.

"I'm sorry," she'd say from time to time. No word on why or what for, just stare at Old Lady Nader and say, "I'm sorry."

Casey tried to pull her out of it at first. But it's like when we have a cardiac arrest and we pull the curtain around the bed—even if you're right in the room you can't see through to know what's happening.

"You remember me?" he'd say. "You remember about Johnnie Dillinger?"

Usually she'd just look at him blank. One time she said, "I seen a movie about him once."

For a while Casey would have us wheel him into Norma's room and he'd talk at her some, but she didn't know who he was. Finally it made him so low he stopped visiting. Acted like she'd gone downstairs.

"You lose your mind," he'd say, "the rest of you ain't worth spit."

Mrs. Goorwitz got on his case then and tried to locate relatives. None to be found. What with the way people move around out here, that's not so unusual. Casey's chart was nothing but a medical record starting in 1937. Next Mrs. Goorwitz loosed the social worker on him, Friendly Phil, who ought to be selling health food or real estate somewhere. Casey wasn't buying any.

"So what if I am crazy?" he'd say to Phil. "Delusional, schizo, whatever you wanna call it. I can't do squat one way or the other. What difference does it make if I was Dillinger or Norma was Pearl White or Roscoe was the King of Poland? You're all just a bag a bones in the end."

He went into a funk, Casey, after Norma faded—went into a silence that lasted a good month. Not even Spurs could get his goat enough to argue. He spent a good part of the day trying to keep himself clean.

"I'm on the cycle," he whispered to me one day. "I'm riding the down side."

The geriatric racket is a collection of cycles. Linen goes on beds, gets dirtied, down the chute, washed, dried, and back onto the beds. Patients are checked in downstairs, up to the beds, maintained awhile, and then down to the slabs with them. Casey even found a new cycle, a thing in the paper about scientists who had learned how to make cow flops back into cow food.

"I don't want to make accusations here," says Casey one day, pointing to his lunch, "but what does *that* look like to you?"

The day came when Casey lost his control, racked up six incontinents on the report in one week. His health was shot, but I tried to talk Mrs. Goorwitz out of it when she handed me the kit. He had a thing about it, Casey.

"A man that can't control his bowels," he'd say, "is not a man."

He knew what was up when I started to draw the curtain. Roscoe scowled at me from across the room and rolled over to face the wall. Kantor and Wise lay there like houseplants. It was midnight and they'd given Casey some heavy meds with his dinner. He looked at me like I'd come to snuff him with a pillow over the face. He was too weak to raise his arms, so I didn't have to put the restraints on.

"It has to be, Casey," I told him, "or else you'll be wettin' all over yourself."

I washed my hands with the soap from the kit.

"If they ask why I done it, the banks and all," he whispers, "tell them I was just bored. Just bored crapless."

I took the gloves out of their cellophane and managed to wriggle into them without touching my fingers to their outside. I washed Casey and laid the fenestrated sheet over so only his thing stuck through. If stories about Dillinger's size are true, Casey was qualified. The girls on the evening shift called it "the Snake." I swabbed the tip of it, unwrapped the catheter tube, and coated it with K-Y.

"You been white to me, Son," says Casey. "I don't put no blame on you."

"I'm sorry."

"Don't ever say that," says Casey. "Don't ever say you're sorry. Do it or don't do it but don't apologize."

I pushed the catheter tube down till it blocked at his sphincter, wiggled it, and it slipped past. It was the narrowest gauge, but still it's a surprise that you can fit one into a man. I stuck the syringe into the irrigation branch and shot the saline up till the bulb was inflated in his bladder. I gave a tug to see if it was anchored. Casey was crying, looking away from me. His eyes had gone fuzzy, the way fish eyes do after you beach them. I hooked the plastic tubing and the piss bag to the catheter.

"I used to be somebody," said Casey.

I HAD A long weekend, and when I came back on I didn't get a chance to talk with him. Mrs. Goorwitz said in report how he'd been moved to Intensive Care. On my first check I found him looking like the pictures of the Biograph shooting—blood everywhere, hard yellow light. Something had popped inside and he'd bled out the mouth. He had pulled the catheter out, bulb and all, and he was bleeding down there. We put sheets on the floor and rolled him sideways across the bed on his belly so he drained out onto them. It takes about half an hour or so.

I traced him back through the medical plan at Fox and ran into nothing but dead ends. Usually I forget about them once they go downstairs, but Casey had gotten his hooks in. There at Fox I found an old fella in custodial who remembered him.

"Always taking the limos for joyrides," he said. "It's a wonder he didn't get his ass fired."

I brought the subject up at the nurses' station one night—how maybe he could of been—and they asked me how much sleep I was getting. So I don't know one way or the other. Roscoe, he's sure, he's positive, but Roscoe also thinks our every move is being watched by aliens with oversized IQs. I figure if they're so smart they got better things to occupy their time.

One day I'm tube-feeding some vegomatic when out in the corridor I hear Spurs Tatum giving his brag to a couple of recent admissions that come in with their feet falling off.

"Hoot Gibson held my horse," says Spurs. "I took falls for Randy Scott. John Wayne blew me off a stagecoach. And once," he says, "I played Parcheesi with John Herbert Dillinger."

Preserves

ROBERT STUBBLEFIELD

Robert Stubblefield has published fiction and personal essays in Dreamers and Desperadoes: Contemporary Short Fiction of the American West, Hayden's Ferry Review, Left Bank, The Clackamas Literary Review, Cascadia Times, Oregon Humanities, Oregon Salmon: Essays on the State of the Fish at the Turn of the Millenium, *and* Open Spaces.

Recent awards include a Georges and Anne Borchardt scholarship from the Sewanee Writers' Conference and a Fishtrap Fellowship. He holds an MFA from the University of Montana.

NO HORSES AGAIN this morning. No dreams good or bad. Owings awakened slowly, the small bedroom taking shape around him, khakis folded over the footboard of the bed, black brogans with the toes stuck just under the siderail, and a blue chambray shirt hung from the nail on the door. In the winter the shirt would be wool flannel—otherwise the layout didn't change. Two narrow, rectangular windows faced north, and twin, overgrown lilac bushes spread against the wall, filtering and diffusing the morning light and providing all the privacy Owings could desire. He dressed and walked to the kitchen.

No horses, no urgency. On the best mornings Owings heard the horses stamping in the juniper pole corral, neighing and nickering, bluff charging each other and bolting across beaten earth, then standing stock-still, their endless, worldly patience and deep, liquid eyes transcending and paling all human understanding. Feed your animals before you feed yourself. That would have been Fred Owings's single, overriding rule, a family creed if the Owings held one. And Joe Owings missed that responsibility, mourned it over the long, fidgeting winters. He missed pitchforking the rye bundles over the peeled poles, the simple exchange and pure, animal gratitude as the horses settled and started munching hay.

His father warned him against falling for horses. They would nip you on the shoulder if you turned your back at an inopportune time, biting to the bone, holding and shaking, a long-toothed grip powerful enough to lift your feet from the ground. They would kick a man bent over a task, and depending where the sharp hoof struck, bruising deep with the thud of bone on flesh, or splitting with the clean crack of pine kindling an ulna or tibia. Scarring and costly. But old man Owings had been in no way resistant to the sentimental pull of the horses, the steadfast dependability of Dusty and Jug, the workhorses, the pride of being well-mounted on Flame, his handsome pinto saddlehorse. And Joe had admired the gentleness and earned authority Fred Owings exercised around the horses, the precise placement of hands when shoeing them, muscle and tendon flexed and defined, man and beast soaked or lathered in sweat.

Feeding animals built an appetite, and regardless of how humble the meal awaiting, how fruitless the daylong labor might ultimately prove, something had been accomplished. On a good morning Owings's waking motions recalled the gestures of hitching team to wagon, circling the fields hauling bundles of freshly cut rye hay in the summer, or traversing the timbered canyons for firewood in the fall, but on the best of days it was clear, cold winter, powder snow dry and coiling, sled runners slicing the surface crust as they crossed the plateau to feed the small cattle herd. And Owings was disappointed and grateful as the creaking sled runners, steaming horses, and crystalline light gave over to songbirds, intermittent passing cars, and the dim bedroom.

Seventy years gone and almost impossible to connect to a life where from his porch he watched passing semi-trailers laden with dairy-quality hay shipped hundreds of miles, or cattle on their way to slaughter half a continent away, to mornings consumed with shaving, preparing breakfast, solving puzzles on *Wheel of Fortune* and questioning the answers of *Jeopardy*, waiting for the noon news and his appetite to build enough to justify making a ham and cheese sandwich, cold in the summer, buttered and toasted in the winter.

The aroma of burning bacon, boiled coffee, and scorched eggs blended and sifted through the open screen of the kitchen window. Owings would eat his bachelor breakfast and go out to sit in his webbed lawnchair, then ease into conversation while watching Jimmy work. Joe hired Jimmy to paint the exterior of the weathered bungalow and would miss the company when the boy finished.

Owings rinsed the cast-iron skillet and the stream of water scattered to skittering droplets and hissing steam He washed the single plate and placed it in the drainboard basket. Jimmy momentarily picked up the pace when the screen door slammed to, stood straighter and moved briskly. It had been over fifty years since Joe Owings held the authority to shatter the pane of another's daydream. He had been uncomfortable with the command appointed him then and remained so with any now implied.

Jimmy painted in efficient strokes, hinging his wrist, brushing and re-brushing a two-foot swath. The weathered boards soaked up the paint, leaving the intended white on the clinging remnants of previous coats and the bare wood a dishwater gray. Jimmy worked the sunny side of the house in the morning and reserved the leafy, shaded north side for the afternoon. Joe hadn't suggested that to him, and thought it showed some initiative. He was a dreamy, decent boy.

Northern or southern exposure made all the difference in the dry mid-latitudes. Owings remembered harvesting huckleberries with his family from the northern slopes of the Blue Mountains. And harvesting it was—not recreational picking, although the traveling and camping was not without reward, but the purpose was undoubtedly the putting away of stores, huckleberries and applesauce the only fruit the family would have through winter and spring. The picking and canning orga-nized a campaign against the dull grains and boiled, stringy meat of winter—the last potatoes with eyes and mold cut out. Bright huckleber-ries rationed, served dappled with cream, fist-sized dumplings bobbing in tart berries and sweet syrup. Owings was eleven or twelve. The time before he remembered, then the war and everything after, but between a period when Owings recalled exactly the space he occupied in the world, the precise placement of sibling and parents, what they pushed against and pulled in.

Owings and his brother Frank were responsible for ferrying the pre-cious crop the twenty-odd miles from the mountain camp to the home-stead. There wasn't space in the wagon for the fruit-filled jars, the camping tents and bedrolls, the cast-iron kettle for boiling the jars. In a good year the Owings boys ferried two loads home; an average year re-quired a single trip.

The boys sat high on the plank seat, alternating holding the reins and hoping to meet someone on the dusty road so they could nod acknowl-

edgment, pull aside for passing, try on for size solemn manners mod-
eled after men they admired. And it wasn't the first trip or even the first
season Joe recalled. They'd already hard-earned their parents' trust.
Frank was a year older, but didn't exercise his unspoken authority over
Joe excepting the rarest occasions. They had proved their ability to pass
from the highlands to the mid, to deliver the precious cargo, canning
jars wrapped in burlap and carefully boxed, finally and carefully placing
glass containers on the rough-cut plank shelving of the root cellar.

The camping wasn't a hardship, and in many ways clean and convenient compared to daily life. They set camp close by the headwaters of
Potammus Creek and had cold, clear running water nearby. The mountains in early August were a mix of chilly, but frost-free mornings and
an endless succession of clear days. When the occasional thunderstorm
built the family gathered under the canvas tarp covering the cooking
area and played mumblety-peg, or just as often absently and fondly
watched rain dripping from the edges of the oiled canvas and hoped the
storm extended to the parched fields and grazing land surrounding the
homestead.

Joe and Frank counted the jars accumulating in the framed crate of
the wagon bed. The jars couldn't be stacked, so they spread in the single
layer with burlap packed between. And the evening came when the
wooden crate was full and six jars were left over.

The first frost of the season touched the tips of grasses and bushes
around the camp as they set out. Their father told them he would see
them tomorrow afternoon and their mother kissed Frank and then Joe,
following birth order as always. Frank kept a close rein on the team
for the first few miles. The horses sensed the direction and for whatever reason were attached to the dusty, hoofbeaten corral and picked up
the pace as they headed home. They descended the steep trail of the
streamside grade and the sky paled and brightened while the canyon
held the greenish shadow and chill of granite, thick conifers, and dense
snowmelt.

The day stretched before them and all was anticipation, but soon the
horses plodded to the dull cadence of heat, the road leveled and showed
evidence of travel, but the boys met no one and along with the horses
fell into the plodding, creaking, and swaying. See you late tomorrow afternoon, their father had said. A phrase containing encouragement,
love, and counsel a thousand words could not. Don't tarry, don't push

the horses, and Godspeed—all that and more clearly communicated in five words. Grasshoppers clattered from the dust as the boys settled onto the long plain eventually leading to the cabin. They had harvested the crops early because it was a dry summer following a dry spring, and the grasshoppers began stripping the forage, clipping any remaining greenery before it could grow or ripen.

The boys told stories and the horses again picked up the pace as they scented the homestead, the springwater captured in the watering trough. The stories included one of a bandit who watched the road from high on the rimrock and there were sufficient outcroppings, sagebrush, and stunted junipers to fuel the imagination. And Joe was at the reins and he'd read accounts of the Pony Express and the leap was not that far between a lone rider with a leather mail pouch and deadline and two boys with a rickety wagon and an aging, ill-matched team.

Joe lifted and shook the reins. Dusty and Jug leaped in response and Frank pulled the 30-30 from behind the seat, removed it from its leather scabbard and held off their pursuers. He didn't dare waste any of the precious ammunition, but pretended to shoot. It was heat, excitement— the horses lathered into a sweat, as grateful for exertion, motion, and speed as the boys. The rolling of the wheels, the clopping of the hooves and the creaking of the sideboards combined until Joe could hardly hear the mouthed cracks and ricochets from Frank's shooting. The homestead came into sight and instantly Joe pulled up the horses. A duststorm of their own making roiled over the horses and the boys as they descended back into responsibility.

Joe opened the corral gate as Frank unharnessed the horses. Dusty and Jug trotted toward the trough. And the boys, trained well, allowed the horses to drink their fill, waiting until they simultaneously lifted their heads and distractedly began picking at the remnants of the last feeding. Only then did the boys alternate filling the tin dipper from the trickling stream running into the trough. They cupped water in their palms, showered it over their sweaty, dust-stained faces, slapped the surface, and splashed each other's shirts damp.

They exited the corral and walked to the wagon and before they were within ten feet they heard dripping and saw syrup leaking between the cracks, the purplish stain spreading along the wood. Lost were forty-four Mason jars and countless, irretrievable hours of labor. They could have blamed the horses, the team could have shied from the buzzing of a coiled rattler, the clatter of a falling rock. But their father knew the horses, and more important, the boys knew themselves. The rough form of the lie was never put to the lathe.

Boys, boys, their father said. Through those words and their mother's pursed lips was all the labeling, lament, and admonition Joe and Frank could bear. They climbed the slope to the berry patch, gripping the bail of their buckets and avoiding catching their mother's eye as she bent back to the boiling kettle. It was one of only two deep regrets Owings held to this day.

Jimmy neared the extension of the bay window and Owings knew he feared standing on the narrow outcropping to paint the spot inaccessible from the ladder. Owings had watched Jimmy enough to notice the fear of heights. He hadn't made mention of the fact and was indeed looking forward to seeing how Jimmy would handle this. Joe didn't believe that anticipation cruel. It was likely standing on a ledge with quivering legs was only the beginning of the terrifying things a young man might be asked to do.

"Going to be hot today," Jimmy said as Joe arranged his chair. Joe smiled and thought it the innocuous greeting of an old soul rather than a thirteen-year-old boy. "Has the weather changed like people say?" Jimmy asked.

The mid-July heat was dull and lasting, wearing in endurance if not intensity. There had always been a hotter spell in the twenties or thirties or fifties depending on the age of the teller. "There are wet years and dry years and cold winters and open ones, but overall it's about the same," Joe said. The valley was truly a climate of extremes, but based on the portrait drawn by town elders the history had been one of record-breaking hot spells broken only by three-foot snowfalls. Owings had lived in the valley for most of seventy-five years and the weather hadn't changed.

"Everyone says it doesn't rain like it used to," Jimmy said. "My aunt says it's on account of the satellites."

"They said the same thing when I was a kid, but blamed airplanes. The thirties were the driest I've seen, all over the country. It was a long drought. They came before and they'll come again." Joe spat a stream of tobacco juice between his feet. "Same old bullshit from the same old bullshitters."

Jimmy dipped the brush in the tray and feathered long strokes along the grain of rough boards. He didn't interrupt and listened, and Joe wondered if that quiet attentiveness would serve the boy well later or only clutter his path. "My advice to you would be leave quick and come back slow, if at all," Joe said. "I came back here because it was the only place I'd ever been to come back to. Every year I thought I'd go somewhere else—look around some at least. But I got comfortable and the world kept turning. I ever tell you about the time I was in the motion pictures with Lana Turner?"

"No."

"You most likely don't even know who Lana Turner is, do you?"

"An actress. I know who she is."

"I have a picture there in the house. They rounded a bunch of us soldiers up as extras and dressed us in grass skirts and had us hold spears. We were supposed to be native islanders. Lana Turner is in the middle of the picture and I'm on one end."

"What's the name of the movie?"

"Can't even remember now. Fact is, I didn't end up in the movie after all. A guy from our company whistled at Lana when she walked by while we were standing in the chow line. They kicked us all off the set. That right there was the beginning and end of my acting."

"Did you ever talk to Lana Turner?"

"Never did. Lost my chance to be a star just because some smartass whistled."

Jimmy lifted the bucket and dumped the remainder of the gallon into the tray. "Were you out of the army then?"

Joe shifted the chewing tobacco from his left cheek to the right. "I was still in the army, but the war was over. There wasn't much to do. I was back and forth between the islands and Tokyo. The government tried to make farmers out of the islanders and recruited anyone who'd ever lived in the country to teach. I damn sure didn't know anything to tell those people. If they wanted a fish they caught it, and they picked just about everything else they wanted to eat. I couldn't see how plowing up their land and cutting down the trees was going to improve their lot. They had everything they needed until they got in the way of a war.

"I only saw one farmer while I was over there, and that was just before the end of the fighting. We were staked out on a hill and across the canyon a man stepped out from the trees and walked over behind a bush and dropped his pants. He was hidden from his own people, but in plain sight of us. No one else saw him. He finished his crap and walked halfway back to the trees, then stopped and turned into the wind and looked at the sky and checked the weather, the same way I'd seen my old man stand off our porch and do a thousand times. Only a farm boy would do that."

Crickets hummed from the dry, overgrown garden. The sound intensified, feigning the broadcast of an imminent shift, then faded to a low buzz. Joe said he wished he hadn't even noticed the soldier, or could have somehow watched him without anyone else noticing. "A couple of the other guys saw me staring across the canyon and started looking into the trees. It took them awhile to spot him there in the shadows. Then they started shooting at him just for the hell of it, not really sighting, but it wouldn't have mattered much if they had. It would have been a long shot for a sniper, but should have been well out of range for regular infantrymen. I raised my rifle to my shoulder, but I didn't fire. One of the bullets lobbed in there and dropped him."

"Did it kill him?"

"I don't know. A thirty-caliber round, and he dropped heavy. I've thought about that for a long time. He just stepped out to take a crap and check the air and got shot for no good reason. It didn't change a damn thing on either side, but it changed everything for his wife or mother, for anybody waiting on him back home."

Joe stood on wobbly legs, shook his head, and started shuffling around the house, then paused. "Lana Turner was from a mining town in northern Idaho. Far as I know, she hit Hollywood and never much looked back. I'll show you that picture tomorrow."

AT THE END of each day Jimmy placed the washed brushes and sealed paint cans away in the root cellar. He finished the paint tray and rinsed the brushes in the plastic bucket. The paint mixed and blended with the water until the color and consistency was that of skimmed milk. Owings watched. It was the first time in a long while he had spoken of combat, of random mortality. He thought the Lana Turner story hadn't really been much to tell a kid and most likely sounded like a lie. For a moment wished maybe he had at least been the one to whistle, or had said he had spoken to her, but the time to become a convincing liar was long past.

Jimmy swished the brushes in the bucket. "I'll put those away for

you," Owings said. "You better head on down to the river and cool off."
Jimmy thanked Owings and walked down the crumbling front walk and
out the gate. Joe carried the bucket containing the brushes in one hand
and the paint in the other and set them down at the cellar entrance. The
doors, constructed of rough-cut one-by-twelve-inch boards diagonally
braced with two-by-fours, lay at a forty-five-degree angle to the ground
and were of course heavier than Owings remembered. Cool, dense air
coiled like dark water around his ankles and then his knees as he descended the seven steps to the earthen floor. First dampness, followed
by mold.

Deeper yet, a ripe, lingering sweetness. Joe set down the buckets and
flexed his fingers. The bails had cut off circulation and stiffened his
hands. On the shelves he saw the dust-covered Mason jars containing
huckleberries, tart pie cherries, peaches, and applesauce canned by his
mother, dead all these years and known to townspeople only as Mrs.
Owings. It was difficult to remember himself as a son returning from
the war, difficult to picture his mother canning in the steaming heat of
that same town kitchen, all the while conjuring his return. After burying a husband, worrying over her sons for years, she sold the parcel that
to this day people referred to as the Owings place, left the high plains
for the small house in town, began cleaning houses and taking in laundry. For the first time it struck Joe that new life of indoor plumbing and
electric appliances might have tempered what he'd always viewed as a
bitter loss, might have seemed her rightful ease, a small measure of
sweet relief, tranquil and even luxurious compared to the hardscrabble
homestead.

Earlier that afternoon Joe told Jimmy about the Owings brothers' fortunes. "Among us we ended up with two purple hearts, no kids, and one
driver's license. Hard to imagine that." Hard to imagine. But Joe knew
the seductive danger of envisioning others in stasis while our fortunes
ebb and flow. The world moves—fruit dissolves to syrup, to simple sug-
ars, snakes curl sheltered from the scorching sun, shedding their skins in
blindness. Joe walked to the store to buy his fruit now, canned and la-
beled peaches, pears, and apricots that he stored under his bed. How
long ago had he stopped entering the root cellar? How could such
earnest efforts be forsaken? Joe Owings stood in the cellar, again flexed
his stiff fingers, and across the sunstruck plains grief seized one heart
and released another.

Stretched Toward Him Like a Dark Wake

GERONIMO TAGATAC

Geronimo Tagatac's father was from the Philippines, his mother was a Russian Jew, his stepmother is a Cajun from Happy Jack, Louisiana. He is one of six children. He has worked as a legislative consultant, university instructor, container ship cargo planner, dishwasher, fry cook, folk singer, computer system planner, roofer, and modern and jazz dancer. He has lived in a number of countries and has traveled extensively.

His short fiction has appeared in Writers Forum, The Northwest Review, Mississippi Mud, The River Oak Review, Alternatives Magazine, Orion Magazine, The Clackamas Literary Review, *and* The Chautauqua Literary Journal. *He is the recipient of an Oregon Literary Arts Fellowship and a Fishtrap Fellowship. A collection of his short stories,* The Weight of the Sun, *was published in 2006.*

He lives and writes in Salem, Oregon.

ON THE NIGHT of August 15, 1929, a heavyset man in a luminous, white linen suit stood and announced to the audience that anyone who could spend ten minutes in the ring with the heavyweight champion of the Philippines would be given one hundred dollars. Jacinto, with a few fistfights to his credit, was goaded into the ring by his friends. Twelve terrible minutes after the attendants had laced the gloves onto his hands, he climbed shakily back through the thick ropes, his seventeen-year-old cheeks bruised, his lips split and bleeding, and two of his left ribs cracked. He was nearly blinded by the blood in his eyes. In his dark hand, he held more money than he had ever seen in his life. Years later, he would shake his head at the craziness of what he had done.

He stayed in Manila for ten days, waiting for the bruises on his face to fade and the swelling to subside. Then he took the bus north to his family's hamlet, in Baay. He went back, one last time, to the smells of rice paddies, cane fields, and the bamboo groves of his boyhood. He spent a week saying good-bye to his parents, brothers and sisters, and aunts and uncles. The day before he left, there was a feast to commemorate the one-year anniversary of his grandfather's death. When the priest prayed aloud for his grandfather's soul, he heard his mother's voice among those of the older women, in soft refrain. After the sun had fallen beyond the soft fringe of the trees, he looked across the firelight into his father's eyes, and he knew by the iron stillness in the older man's face, that his father was mourning both the loss of his own father and the impending departure of his eldest son.

The next morning his father walked two miles with him to the north-south highway. They waited more than an hour in the rising heat for a two-wheeled horse cart to arrive. When it did, his father held his head between hands that were as hard as wood and kissed him on both cheeks. "Do not forget us when you are gone." Jacinto looked into his father's sharp face and deepset eyes. For the first time in his life, he began to understand, although imperfectly, what it was like to give up a part of himself in exchange for the promise of something over the horizon. In the brief seconds that remained, he realized that he must map the country of his father's face and voice, the feel of his hands, and the smell of his deep brown skin. And then he was in the bouncing cart, trying not to show his tears as he watched his father's form diminish into the shining apex of the road.

From Manila, Jacinto sailed east across the Pacific in the hold of a ship filled with men like himself, dreaming of returning to their villages one day, laden with gifts for their families, carrying enough money to buy land, to marry and have children. The men often stood together on the ship's deck, looking out at the circle of the horizon, where the blue sky met the green-blue sea. They sailed on and on, day after day. Beyond the slow rise and fall of the ship's hull, nothing seemed to move except the ship's wake, which was like a restless arrow, pointing the way back toward their homeland.

In the ten years that followed, Jacinto held jobs in a hundred places, washing dishes, harvesting asparagus, sugar beets, beans, and corn. He learned to fox-trot, to waltz, and to samba in the taxi-dance halls, at the edge of places like Sacramento and Stockton, where he paid the women a nickel for a dance and practiced his English on them. In all of those years, his only link with his homeland were the intermittent letters from his brothers and sisters. They came in faded white envelopes with stamps bearing the serious face of Jose Rizal, his country's national martyr. The postmarks were always months old. He would read and re-read the brittle pages filled with tight script, written in black ink. "Victorio's brother Antonio died in January." "Ophelia had another baby girl in March." "Marciano has gone to Laoag to find work." The letters always ended the same way. "We miss you very much, my dearest son. Please say that you will be coming home soon."

By the time he got the chauffer and houseboy's job, he was twenty-eight. He met Jean Glixman at a nightclub party. When first he looked into her gray eyes, he suddenly felt as though he had been floating through the years toward her without knowing it. They married a month later. No one in Jean's family attended the wedding. They had a son the following winter and, dreaming of raising the boy under high Western skies, they moved to a farm outside of Isleton, California. In the boy's fifth winter, his mother ran out into a rainstorm to pull her flapping sheets off of the clothesline, like a desperate sailor shortening the sails of his ship in the face of an oncoming gale. She died of pneumonia a month later. A week after Jean died, Jacinto received a letter from his brother in the Philippines. The postmark on the envelope was a six months old. He opened the letter and read the news of his father's death. He sat at the kitchen table for a long time, looking out at the dirt road that divided the world into two damp halves. And then he put his face into his rough hands and wept for the loss of his wife and his father.

Jacinto went back to the life of a migrant farmworker, taking his son with him. In the summer of 1947, they went southeast of the lifeless Salton Sea, to a large farm between Niland and Calipatria, in the dry, pale reaches of the Imperial Valley. It was miles off the highway, a place made possible only by irrigation. Jacinto labored alongside other Filipinos from Ilocos Norte, Batangas, and Samar. He worked six days a week, waist deep in the endless rows of deep green tomato plants, under the palest skies he had ever known. Whenever Jacinto looked across the green expanse of tomato plants, he remembered standing in the stern of the ship, somewhere between Manila and Honolulu, looking back at the deep water, churned white by the ship's propellers.

Once in a great while, a quick, soft breeze rippled the tops of the tomato plants. When that happened, all of the men would raise their heads in unison, as though they had each heard the same voice calling to them. And then they would bend their heads and backs toward the earth again. The nights in that place were so still that the only sound in the world seemed to be that of the large, green cooler on the side of the bunkhouse which could be heard a mile away. His son learned to play among the empty tomato crates, alongside irrigation ditches that bordered the endless rows of tomato plants. And he came to regard the other men as his uncles.

One morning, Jacinto's son told him that he had dreamed that he was standing in the middle of a field and did not know how he had gotten there because he could not see his footprints in the soil. On the following day, the boy said that he had had the same dream but that this time he had seen a man at the edge of the field watching him. Jacinto asked him who the man was. The boy replied, "An old, old man."

The next morning, the boy could not open his eyes. His eyelids had been sealed shut by a thin film of mucus which had dried in the night. Jacinto bathed his son's eyes with a damp, warm towel until he freed the eyelids. But when the boy tried to open his eyes, he could not bear the light. He told his father between sobs that the man in his dream had walked across the field to him and put his hands softly over his eyes. He said that the man's hands felt and smelled just like his father's.

Jacinto put the back of his hand on his son's forehead for a moment. "I'll take you to the doctor when I come home for lunch," he said.

"Pinkeye. In both eyes and as bad as I've seen it," the doctor said, after examining the boy. He did not bother with the medical term for the boy's ailment: severe, contagious conjunctivitis. He gave Jacinto a blue glass bottle of liquid, instructing him to bathe the boy's eyes with its contents once a day. Then he took a strip of white cloth and blindfolded the boy. "He should be better in a week." That evening, all of the uncles came by to see how Jacinto's son was. Cleto, the oldest of them, ran his dark, callused hands through the boy's black hair and made a clucking sound with his tongue.

Early the next morning, as Jacinto worked in the fields, he became aware of a sudden stillness among the other men, as though the very air had frozen. A faint movement at the end of his row caught his eye. It was his blindfolded son. The boy had somehow managed to find his way out of their shack and, in the semidarkness, feel his way down the half-mile of dirt track to the edge of the tomato field. In his blindness, his son had found the very row his father was working. One of the men behind Jacinto crossed himself and murmured, "Jesus y Maria."

At the end of the second week of his son's blindness, Jacinto went to old Cleto and asked him what he should do.

"Has someone in your family died?" the old man asked.

"My father."

"And when was that?"

"Two years ago."

"You had a feast one year after he died?"

"No. Who could I invite to such a feast? I had lost my wife and I had no money."

Cleto looked at the ground, shook his head. "Have you dreamed about your father?"

"No."

"What about your son?"

"He dreamed that a man touched his eyes."

"It is not good that you did not have a feast."

"Do you think that my father is angry with me?"

"The boy does not get better."

"Do you think that it will help to have a feast so late?"

"It cannot hurt," said Cleto, smiling.

The next day, Jacinto bought a pig. The men pooled their cash and sent one of their number into the nearest town to buy a fifty-pound bag of rice, cooking oil, garlic, vinegar, and the other things that they would need. From Cleto's small, carefully tended and watered vegetable patch, they got light green bittermellon and deep, purple eggplants.

The men killed and butchered Jacinto's pig early on Sunday and cooked all through the morning, making denuguan, adobo, pinakbet, and pansit. They made three large pots of snowy steamed rice. The boy, drawn by the sound of the men's voices and movements, wandered among them, his small hands before him, as though he could feel the sharp smells of cooking food. When they were done, the men went to bathe and put on clean clothes.

A Catholic priest, whom Cleto had invited from town, blessed the food and said prayers for the soul of Jacinto's father. Then he put his soft, white hands onto the boy's head and prayed for the return of his health and sight. Jacinto asked the priest to eat with them, and he accepted their food. Before he left, Jacinto gave him an envelope which contained ten one-dollar bills. Later that night, as the boy stood with the others around a fire, one of the men played old, sentimental songs on his mandolin, romantic melodies from the time when the Spanish ruled the Philippines, before the coming of the Americans. Several of the men raised their voices to sing about love and longing, young men's songs sung by men in their forties. Above them, the stars shone in the black, black sky reminding them of the restless nights of their youths.

Jacinto stood in fire's wavering light and told them the story of how, at the turn of the century, his father had joined the fighting against the Spanish and then the Americans. There had been a battle with the Americans near Bataac and the insurrectos, defeated, had scattered. His father, alone and exhausted, fell asleep beside a small stream. When he woke, he found a stone beneath his head. A clear, yellow stone with a tiny, coiled lizard imbedded in its heart. Thereafter, Jacinto's father had been able to set broken bones and extract bad teeth, neither of which he had been able to do before.

As he told this story, Jacinto saw that his son was standing very still with his blind face turned toward the sound of his voice, as though Jacinto's words were pushing their way into his skin.

The boy recovered in the following days and his eyes grew well enough so that, by the following Wednesday, he did not need his blindfold. The doctor said it was the eye wash that had done the trick. Jacinto said nothing, out of politeness and respect.

Sometimes the men saw Jacinto's son walking carefully along the edge of the field, his eyes closed and his hands before him, as though he were trying to find something that he had misplaced in the dark terrain of his blindness. One evening, at the end of the tomato picking season, just before sunset, Jacinto found his son standing in the middle of a freshly disked field. Jacinto watched the dusty red sun stretch the boy's shadow toward him like a dark wake. From where he stood, he saw that the boy was looking west, as though he were waiting for the arrival of someone who was just beyond the horizon's sharp edge.

Confession for Raymond Good Bird

MELANIE RAE THON

Melanie Rae Thon is the author of three novels and two story collections, including Sweet Hearts and First Body. Her fiction has been included in Best American Short Stories, O. Henry Prize Stories, and the Push-cart Prize. She has received grants from the National Endowment for the Arts, the Massachusetts Artist Foundation, the New York Foundation for the Arts, the Ohio Arts Council, the Utah Arts Council, and the Mrs. Giles Whiting Foundation.

Originally from Montana, she lives in migration between the Pacific Northwest and Salt Lake City, where she teaches at the University of Utah.

RAYMOND, I REMEMBER everything about the day: the heat, the rain, the cold wind after. I remember Danny was sick, bloated up like a toad and moaning on the cot, so I took the call alone, which never happens on TV, but can happen twice a week out on Rocky Boy Reservation.

The situation didn't sound extreme: one forty-four-year-old man down on the floor in his sister's kitchen. Drunk, I thought, heat and al-cohol, a bad combination. I was simple that way, prejudiced against my own people.

I figured I'd cool you down with rags and ice, take you to the river for a reservation baptism. It was Fourth of July, almost, people had been celebrating or mourning three days now. If things were worse than I thought, we'd have a rough ride, the rocky roads of Rocky Boy to the hospital in Havre where the medicine men use masks, but not the kind we know.

Doctors in town never appear as Owl or Coyote. They don't chant or smoke to heal your heart or sing the spirit back to your body. They carry drills and knives: they want to look inside; they need to open you. Doctors in green cut and cleave, suture and staple—they have miles of gauze to bind your wounds, respirators to help you breathe, electric paddles to jump you off the table.

If you swallow twenty-seven Darvocets with a pint of gin like Arla Blue Cloud, they pump your stomach dry, but they won't love you back to life—that's not part of the treaty. No hospital doctor ever pressed his ear to the flesh of Arla's womb to hear the bones of her lost children shatter.

Three months later, Arla chopped a hole in the ice and went down naked. In a dream, I'm swimming after her, and I can't breathe, and I'm so cold I'm cold forever, but I don't care because Arla Blue Cloud is quick as a pike and laughing like an otter; Arla is blue and green, beautiful as ice and water, and I think I can see—but I can't see—straight through her.

Nothing like that was going to happen to you and me, Ray. When I got the call from your sister Marilee, she didn't whisper, *No breath, no heartbeat.*

Danny Kite, my partner, my driver, tried to sit up, but his belly bulged with poison gas, something stuck deep in the bowel—roasted squirrel or kidney pie, blue cornbread and fried okra—something he ate two nights before, harmless once, and now gone rancid.

The woman on the phone, Marilee Dancy, older sister of Caleb and Raymond Good Bird, mother of Roshelle and grandmother of baby Jeanne, cousin of Thomas Kimmel, and granddaughter of Safiya Whirling Thunder said, *Six of us here, seven, counting Raymond.*

I told Danny plenty of people to help me lift the man, carry him to the bed, the river, the white station wagon we called our ambulance.

Whatever seemed right.

Whatever proved necessary.

I don't know why I didn't feel you, Ray, sticky as the sticky heat, already here, already gone, already breathing down my lungs, already deep inside me. I told Danny: *Sit, lie down, stay,* and like the sick little dog he was, Danny Kite obeyed me.

We're not real EMTs, not even *Woofers,* WFRs, Wilderness First Responders, but we did get a crash course, five hours one day in Missoula, three pink-skinned dummies to rescue and resuscitate, 1982, nine summers ago, the year we started fighting fires.

We go every year we can—Arizona, Utah, Idaho, Wyoming. *Summer vacation*, Danny says. Stomping flames and plowing firebreaks is good work for a hungry Indian. We don't throw firecrackers in the grass. We don't torch timber. We're hungry, yes, but not that crazy. We've seen our own forests blaze—Mount Sentinel, Lost Canyon. We're Chippewa-Cree, some cloudy mix with French and Oglala. We've been wandering half our lives, dazed and unemployed for a century. When the smoke signals rise, when the fire is somewhere else, we give thanks for strange mercies.

Back home on Rocky Boy, we run the ambulance, our magically re-built Falcon Futura. We answer anybody's call, any day, any hour. We come when the dispatcher in Havre won't answer, when there's no money and no insurance to ferry the half-dead in a real ambulance with trained medical technicians and a pulsing siren.

Maybe Nadine Hard Heart slips us two dollars for gas. Maybe her husband Kip who almost choked on a bone asks us to sit down, share their dinner: two little ducks, canned peas, a heap of instant mashed potatoes. Mostly we don't get paid, and it doesn't matter. Five terrified, not-so-hard-hearted children breathe their silent praise, and we feel lucky. Seven months later, one of those skinny kids appears at the door with three pounds of elk steak to sustain us on our journeys. Luisa Hard Heart's offering means her father survived, lived to hunt again, met the elk face to face high on a ridge in the Bear Paw Mountains. Now there's food to spare: this flesh, his flesh, our flesh, a miracle.

Danny and I don't keep track. It isn't necessary. We do this for us, all of us, our people, because we learned one day with pale dummies how to breathe into another man's body, how to slow the blood from a sev-ered artery, how to pump a child's heart with our hands, how to count and not stop and keep our faith, the old one. We don't have a choice: things you know but don't use eat you inside out, starved weasels biting hard, furious in your belly.

Saving you is saving me. It's not a good deed: it's my own body.

Looking at Danny rolling on the cot, I thought I'd have to resuscitate him before I helped you. *Stay*, I said. *Trust me*, I said, like a fool.

We were boys together, Danny Kite and me, one mother and one fa-ther between us. We'd rescued each other plenty of times. I rolled him home in a wheelbarrow the day he flew off Wendy Wissler's roof and broke his ankle. Six-year-old Danny pulled my head out of a pail the morning I passed out proving how long I could stay underwater. In a summer storm, we scrambled into the highest branches of a ponderosa pine to let the wind thrash us side to side, to spin, to heave, to be the storm, to think like wind and rain, to be that wild. Danny's father Earl had to climb the tree twice to save us.

Once January night, my father drank six shots of tequila and walked out into the snow barefoot and naked. He wanted to prove that the real world is beyond this one, that everything here is only a shadow, that fire could not scar and ice would not burn him. We found the man two days later, the blue shadow of him, and it was true: nothing before or after seemed real.

Danny's mother lived in Billings, in prison, sixteen years for forging a hundred-dollar check. Joella Kite wanted bourbon and cigarettes, a pink blouse embroidered with white daisies. She brought us banana cream pie and frozen Cool Whip, Orange Crush and spicy tortilla chips. I remember thinking nobody on Rocky Boy had ever been this happy.

Then Joella was gone, but between our houses, we had a whole family, and so it was: Danny Kite and I loved each other as brothers.

Trust me, I said when your sister Marilee called. Trust was all we had. Trust and luck and some kind of weird, hopeful vision.

My mother Pauline died of a toothache. *Abscess,* the doctor told us. *If she'd come to town in time, we could have taken the tooth, drained the hole, given her antibiotics.* I suppose he meant to comfort us with knowledge. In Pauline's little house on Rocky Boy, bacteria spilled into her blood and brain. My mother's feet and hands and ears turned black before Hector Slow Child found her. She said, *I don't think we'll make it. Please,* she said, *just lie down here beside me.*

Danny's father died of old age at forty-seven. Earl Kite drowned in his own bed, wheezing with emphysema, rattled by double pneumonia. *It's a good day,* he said. *I'm tired.* Joella Kite got out but went back and got out again and drove into a semi.

Now we were orphans.

Raymond, I see your face, a dark brown Chippewa face, pocked and pitted deep with holes like lava that bubbled up deep from the center of the earth to cool rough and ravaged on the surface. Raymond Good Bird, scarred by acne or disease, scorched like the earth itself, a face that revealed the suffering of a thousand homeless Indians or the aftermath of some spooky chemical explosion—like the trees of Vietnam, you'd erupted.

Yours was a face to love: without love, there was no way to look at you.

Marilee's kitchen steamed. Your sister had been simmering beans all day, frying bread and onions. She'd boiled up two sad, sorry, reservation chickens to shred the meat and make fajitas, a family feast to welcome you home, Raymond Good Bird, their soldier returned from the jungle war, then lost again, twenty-two years, working tugboats, hauling garbage, killing rats and roaches, grinding fat and flesh to stuff sausages, hosing hogs, plucking cherries, lying down drunk in the street and waking up half-frozen in jail—losing three toes, losing two fingers—Raymond found, Raymond recovered, Raymond come home at last only to lie down and die in the heat of your sister's kitchen.

You were skinny as a skinny chicken yourself, blistered from childhood and all the diseases of all our ancestors, wounded three times in the war, three times before, four times after it: firecracker, hand grenade, white boy's BB gun, brother's arrow—fishing knife, M-16, electric drill, broken bottle—shrapnel in the thigh, straight-edge razor across the belly.

Raymond Good Bird, cut up inside every hour of every day from the war you'd fought and the wars that killed you, sliced for forty-four years and sewed back together with invisible thread, invisible sinew of the last white buffalo.

You had no alcohol in your blood today, nothing to preserve you, only the homemade root beer you'd been drinking with your big sister Marilee and your blind, toothless grandmother Safiya. Your brother Caleb and cousin Thomas snuck nips out back and pretended nobody noticed, but you stayed straight to be with Marilee and your niece Roshelle. You stayed sober to hold Roshelle's baby Jeanne, eight months old and already speaking some secret language.

I see you eating chilies from a jar, ten green jalapenos and seven fiery orange habaneros. The buzz was quick but the burn lingered. Thomas and Caleb swallowed their peppers whole, a wild Raymond-Good-Bird-welcome-home contest.

You cradled wide-eyed, wonderful baby Jeanne against your wounded chest, and Roshelle, too beautiful for whiteman's words, Marilee's I've-come-to-break-your-heart daughter, gazed at you as if you were the child's long-lost beloved father.

Roshelle was just a baby herself the last time you saw her, round baby Roshelle two years old when you dressed up as a soldier boy and said good-bye forever. She kissed you on the mouth this morning and swore she remembered. She kissed you on each pitted cheek. *Uncle Ray.* She held you tight—scrawny, pocked you—and you felt whole and young, pressed up that way against her just-turned-into-a-woman, just-became-a-mother body.

Lovely, she was, your niece, long and lovely, smooth, as tall as you and much stronger, like Marilee before she swelled, soft and warm to touch like your mother Minnie before cancer curved her spine and turned her skin yellow.

In the light of Roshelle Dancy, in her body reflecting the morning light, *this* morning's light before the heat grew terrible, in the sweet golden light spilling through the worn-thin-as-gauze curtains, in the radiant love of Roshelle, your whole family came alive, the long-dead and unborn. All your wandering people filled the house and yard, and their voices surged, a song inside you.

That was morning, Ray, and now it was afternoon, getting on toward evening, and you rocked baby Jeanne to sleep, and you handed her back to her mother, and the silly boys came inside, not drunk, not quite, not really, and you swallowed jalapenos and habaneros, and the peppers made your head hum, and you said, *I need to sit down,* but you didn't make it.

You collapsed on the kitchen floor, and you stayed there till I found you. Now, in the thick glaze of afternoon, everything looked filthy. Bubbling beans and sizzling onions splattered; the smell of boiled chicken filled the house; orange cheese melted.

And it was hot, so hot, and I stood in the doorway, and I couldn't move: I didn't even try to help you. I've knelt over three dummies and twenty-seven real live human beings and thumped their chests to get their lungs heaving, but I saw you on the floor, and I saw something yellow above you in the terrible heat, a cloud of smoky yellow dust like the puff off a mushroom; I smelled something underneath the smell of boiled-to-smithereens chicken. Something a hundred times hotter than red chili dust seared my nostrils; and a voice that sounded like God's if

God had died with the Ghost Dancers, if God had been shoveled into a pit in the snow and buried, if God had lain dry in the dry earth for more than a century, *that* crackling voice said, *Too late, little brother.*

It could have been you, Ray, or the pinto pony at the window over the sink, or the little black dog with one white ear and one white paw that wouldn't stop yapping.

I think now it was the wind, the hot wind, the useless fan beating hot air into the hot kitchen. This voice from the whirlwind said, *Who are you?* And the voice inside my chest said, *You can't.* And the dry silence from your body said, *Don't bother.*

Maybe it's all an excuse, something I imagined after. I was scared, it's true. I don't know why you scared me.

I can still feel Roshelle's fist hammering my back, can still hear Marilee whisper, *Do something.* The frenzied dog ripped the cloth of my pants and sank her sharp teeth into my ankle, and the little spotted horse put her whole head through the open window by the sink, and I looked at the faces of all your people—Caleb, Marilee, Roshelle, Thomas, Jeanne, Safiya—and I thought if they loved you so much, why couldn't they save you?

Once upon a time you tried to come home, but you couldn't live in peace among us. Every dark-eyed boy was one you'd killed, every child a gook, every woman your enemy. A thin teenage mother at the grocery store in Havre propped her plump baby on one hip and stared at you with unmitigated rage or benevolent wonder, her look as impenetrable as the gaze of the wounded Vietnamese mother bleeding out, five holes: chest, thigh, belly. She held her child in one arm on one hip— yes, like this—and with miraculous grace, the tiny Vietnamese woman slit her son's throat, clean and deep through the vein: so he wouldn't starve when she died, so he couldn't be spared, so you would not shoot him.

Your platoon lost thirteen men in nine days to booby traps and sniper fire. You burned the first village you found, unnamed on your lieutenant's map, just a cluster of huts at a slow bend of the Cua Viet River. You shot the people as they ran. You killed their pigs and dogs and chickens. Later, you found three women and two boys bleeding into the water. You knew these people, five slender Cheyenne, cut breast to bowel and trampled at the banks of Washita, slaughtered to the joyful noise of bugles and gunfire. The ones whose thick blood swirled into the muddy Cua Viet were Pocatello's stunned Shoshone, five of the four hundred and forty-three slain at Bear River. These five were Nez Perce in flight, awakened to die, skulls crushed by the bootheels and gun butts of drunken soldiers at the Big Hole.

If you opened their bodies, would you find your last word, a curse spit out and long forgotten? What did it matter? You fired. Their blood spilled. You witnessed. You'd murdered them all: brothers, sisters, ancestors, grandchildren.

You didn't want forgiveness. You wanted the wounded Vietnamese mother to take you in her arms as her own child—to comfort, and kill you.

For twenty-two years you lived without faith, without love or the hope of it. *Bozeman, Coeur d'Alene, Walla Walla, Wenatchee.* You thought if you moved fast enough the dead might lose your scent and stop following.

You dangled sixty feet in the air, washing windows, downtown Boise. You met yourself face to face, the blue-skinned man hanging in dark glass, flesh pocked by soap and water. You hauled thirty-seven dead sheep down a hillside west of Helena. They'd died as one, skulls fractured by lightning, the head of each sheep resting tenderly on the rump of another. They were filthy now, their gray wool rain-soaked, their shocked bodies bloated. Flies swarmed you and them. Crows and hawks and kestrels circled. You lifted them by their broken legs, you and two Colombian men who called themselves Jesús and Eduardo, who jabbered as they worked, quick Spanish words muffled by bandannas. You tore your own rag from your mouth and nose to be with the dead, to know their smell, to breathe their bodies. The Colombian brothers laughed when they heard you choking. *Estúpido.* Even then you didn't hide your face. You heaved the pitiful animals into the bed of the rancher's truck. You saw that each face was distinct, with a certain space between the eyes, a soft curve of the mouth, a singular tilt of nose and forehead. Each one of them—and you, and Jesús, and Eduardo—secretly made, silently beloved. Why were you whole? Why were they shattered?

You left that night. *Issaquah, Butte, Aberdeen, Seattle.* You slept in the woods, in a cardboard box, in a barn with a whiteman's cow, in a bed of leaves under a freeway. You dove in Dumpsters for bruised fruit, half-eaten buffalo wings, cold biscuits and gravy. You snatched three perfect blue eggs from the nest of a robin. The birds woke you for a hundred nights, beaks sharp as barbs in your lungs and liver. You stole corn from pigs and a gnawed bone from an old wolfhound. He rose on his crippled hips to tug his chain, too sick and slow to nip you. A goat gave you her milk, and for this offering, you praised her.

North of Spokane, you walked up a dirt road to a weather-wracked farmhouse. You meant to ask for work mucking stalls in exchange for one meal. Nobody answered your knock, but you touched the doorknob and it turned. You breathed, and the door opened. The sweet smell of cherries sucked you inside, pulled you in a dream down a long passage to a sun-dazzled kitchen.

There it was, all for you, a cherry pie with a lattice crust, cooling on the table. In the freezer, a half gallon tub of vanilla ice cream waited—untouched, perfectly white, unbelievably creamy.

You thought, *Just one piece or maybe a quarter.* The pie vanished. Who could blame you? You tried to stop, but you couldn't do it. In your swollen stomach, seven scoops of ice cream swirled.

Your head throbbed. You felt hot and cold at the same time, stunned by bliss and suddenly so tired. You staggered to the living room, but the couch was old, too short, too lumpy. Somehow you gathered the strength to climb the stairs. You opened three doors before you found the room you wanted, cool and dark with a wide bed and a down comforter.

You were afraid to sleep, but a voice that was your own voice gone mad and mocking said, *Why stop now? Why resist this last pleasure?* You knew you might die in this bed, victim of your own delight and a farmer's righteous fury. You woke to a woman's voice, insistent and gentle. *Mister, you best get up now, go down those stairs and keep walking.* She was white-haired, but not old—thin, but not frail. A farmer's wife, yes, without the farmer. The widow cradled an unraised rifle. She was kind: she wanted you to go, but she didn't want to scare you.

That night it rained and you slept in a child's tree house. You crept out hours before dawn. If the boy came with his BB gun, he'd aim for your right eye and kill you.

Raymond Good Bird, twenty-two years gone. You walked close to death every hour, but somehow you survived, and then one day you came home to rest, and I let you die in your sister's kitchen.

Yesterday, Thomas said he wouldn't believe you were home till he touched you with his own hands. But he didn't touch: seeing was enough, too much in fact—Thomas wouldn't look you in the eye. *The light,* he said, *I can't do it.* Late last night, in the shelter of darkness, your delicate, almost pretty cousin Thomas picked you up, lifted you a foot off the ground and held you high to dance you in a circle dance. Your grandmother felt your face and skull, traced your chest and ribs to see you whole with her fingertips. Long after, when the others had fallen asleep on the couch and floor and single bed, your big brother pulled you close and breathed you in. Caleb, like a mother and a father now: wide shoulders, soft breasts. You were twenty-two years lost again. Rocking in his arms, you thought, *I'm him.*

Now you lay on the floor, and I heard you say, *Let the dead stay dead.*

Your brother and sister rolled you onto a wool blanket. These two, and blind Safiya, and doubting Thomas lifted you by four corners. You swung in their grip, a man in a hammock. Roshelle cradled baby Jeanne to follow behind you.

Marilee's turquoise Catalina sat on cement blocks in the yard, its rusted engine propped against a stump, its hood torn off, crumpled in some junkyard. Sunflowers and thistle grew high and wild in all its open spaces. Your people slid you, most beloved one, into the back of my white Falcon. Roshelle gave the baby to Thomas so that she could lie down with you, *Uncle Ray,* close, and hold you tight, *my love,* and keep you from rolling.

I resisted no one. Caleb took my keys and left me to walk, seven miles. What did he care? Your people drove you to town, the dead man, the wounded-ten-times, the resurrected-and-returned-home and now dead-for-true Raymond Good Bird. They delivered you to the hospital in Havre, as if some man of faith might call you out of the cave of yourself, punch a hole in your vein or throat, split your chest and work his miracle—as if some scrubbed nurse might forget her latex gloves, just this once, and lay her naked hands on your heart to close these last wounds, the wounds that saved, the wounds that healed you.

By then the rain had started, soft at first and still hot, more like dust than water falling, then hard and cold until the whole sky filled, a wailing, weeping rain of river.

I stood in your sister's yard, *estúpido,* cut by icy rain, jolted each time a drop hit me. At least you didn't die alone, foolish as our fathers, mine playing Crazy Horse in the snow, yours failing to jump a freight train east of Fargo. I didn't want to die today, another frozen Indian. I pictured my wife Delilah at our doorway, face blown open by the storm, long hair loose and dangerous, a tangled net whipping around her. I conjured Lulu, thin and dark, already too wise, strange and silent, old at seven. I heard tinkling Kristabelle, just three, our child of joy who burst into the world laughing.

That laughter fell from the sky, arrows of rain, sharp enough to pierce me. I dreamed myself home and safe, though I knew I didn't deserve it.

The wind spun, as if it wanted to speak, as if it were trying to become a person. I hoped to make it to Hector Slow Child's house, prayed that the man who loved my mother might let me sleep in his bed for a few hours, but I was barely a mile up the road, stung by rain, already staggering. I thought I'd fall, die here in a rut, drown in three inches of water.

God roared behind me. In a rush of breath, *his* breath, two angels thundered out of the storm, Luc Falling Bear and Leroy Enneas, my saviors, Luc driving Leroy's once-shiny-green-and-now-mostly-gray Torino. They didn't know yet what I'd failed to do, how I refused to kneel, refused even to try to help you. They didn't sense I was a ghost, gone like you, a dead man walking. They'd been drinking rum and Mountain Dew all day. To Luc and Leroy, I was still visible.

They were thoughtful drunks: I tried to slip in back, but they cried *no* in unison. They wanted me up front, soaked and shivering between them. They offered rum, straight from the bottle. I don't remember anything on earth for which I ever felt more grateful.

They ate corn chips with extra salt. *To stay thirsty,* Luc said. *You think drinking all day is easy?*

They were polite, the way Indians are polite. They didn't ask where I'd been or wonder aloud why I was walking. They didn't make jokes about my ambulance. They didn't mention my father.

They waited for me to speak or not speak. They lived on reservation time. They had forever.

I couldn't go home. Lulu and Kristabelle would grab my legs to pull me down on all fours and ride me like a pony. Delilah would say, *Let him go. Your father's cold and tired.* But somehow I'd find the strength to carry them, *my sweethearts, my darlings.* I'd buck and whinny. I'd be myself again, whole, Jimi Shay Don't Walk, father, husband, wet mustang. I wasn't ready for that much love. I thought the weight of it, of them, might crush me.

I must have said, *Drop me at Danny's,* because suddenly I was there, trembling in my brother's doorway. Without Luc and Leroy close, my skin hardly held my bones together. There he was, Danny the betrayed who didn't know it, Danny Boy curled up like a baby, smiling in his sleep, soothed by the sound of rain, back inside his mother's body.

Danny Kite was his thin self again, and I could smell the stink coming from the toilet, his bowels clean at last, the dam burst wide open. My Danny woke all sweet and groggy. He said, *Sorry, brother,* and, *how did it go?* And I said, *Fine, everything's fine.* I said, *Everything happened just the way it was supposed to happen.*

Let him sleep in peace, I thought. *Let the story find him.*

There are stories I like to tell, things I believe though I can't prove them. Sometimes I think Hector Slow Child is my real father, that he came to my mother as starlight falling through an open window, a constellation broken on her bed, the Great Bear, the White Buffalo.

My wife tells another story, how her mother died with Delilah inside her. Nona Windy Boy skidded on ice, side-swiped Martin Cendesie's truck and rolled fifty feet down a gully. *Brain dead,* the doctor told her husband Joseph. *Fractured ribs—fractured feet, femurs, pelvis. No hope,* he whispered, *fractured skull, massive hemorrhage.*

Somehow Delilah lived. Delilah, unborn, rocked herself to sleep in a windy cradle. The doctor stood amazed, listening to her heart beat. Softly he said, *We should take the baby now while we can save her.*

Joseph saw tiny flecks of his wife's blood spattered on the young man's glasses. Joseph said, *Let the child stay inside as long as her mother wants her.*

Nona's mother and Auntie Bea chanted thirteen days and thirteen nights without ceasing. I tell you now: on the fourteenth day, Nona Windy Boy breathed again, no respirator. She lived thirty-four more days, and the child came in her own time of her own will, and the mother with her own breath released her.

Delilah says, *I'm my father's bitter miracle.*

Delilah says, *My mother turned herself into a trout and swam down into her own womb and swallowed me and kept me safe for seven weeks until I got too big to hold and then my mother writhed three times and spit me out to live in the world without her.*

Nona never opened one eye to see her child. Auntie Bea swore she laughed when the baby howled, but the nurse who witnessed said, *The poor woman was finally choking.*

Tonight, when I lie in Delilah's arms, when we lie entwined, her long arms and long legs wrapped around me, when I tell her our story in the dark, the story of Raymond Good Bird and Jimi Shay Don't Walk, my wife will say, *Not everybody wants to be saved. Not everybody can bear it.*

Raymond, three months ago you took a real job, the first you wanted to keep, as a janitor, a custodian at Lewis & Clark Elementary School in Missoula. The urinals set to a child's height, the little desks, the low mirrors, the windows decorated with butterflies and birds broke your heart, and you let them. You wanted to hurt, and the hurt was love, and love roared back into you. You stole children's drawings from the walls and took them home to your motel, the River's Edge, a rundown dive where you paid by the week to live among prostitutes and addicts, where you shared bread and beans with bewildered half-bloods.

A little girl named Tania colored a family of bright angels—mother, father, sister, brother—even the purple dog had a halo. Max and Arturo drew a house on fire and a galaxy exploding. Coral painted a child in a garden where red tulips grew taller than she was. Darnell Lasiloo saw seventeen Appaloosas from the sky, as if he were God, as if he were White Bird in flight over the Bear Paws. The spotted horses lay on their sides, all sixty-eight legs splayed, all sixty-eight legs visible. The ponies seemed to float along a trail of tears beside a winding river. You taped the pictures to your walls and door and mirror. So many children alive to love! The miracle was endless. The dead whispered through the radiators. *Don't forget us.* They wished you no harm. They were hungry, like the rest of us. You saved six dollars the first week and nineteen the week after. You thought someday soon you'd send all your extra money and a child's vision home to Roshelle and your sister.

One night in a whiteman's bar, a half-Kootenai, half-Mexican woman danced you across the room, and you thought this was the end of hope, your last possibility. She asked you to come home with her, to her trailer up a rutted road north of Evaro. She was twenty-seven years older and fifty pounds heavier than you, but still, in your eyes, beautiful. You refused. Refused even to kiss, though her mouth looked soft as a girl's mouth. Her face was scarred, it's true, pocked as yours, but her lips bloomed, full and ready. *No, please.* You thought if you kissed her once, you'd never stop kissing.

Fear made you unkind, and for this you were sorry.

The heads of elk curving out from the walls, the bighorn sheep, the pronghorn antelopes all watched you drink your beer and crack your nuts and keep your silence. The big Kootenai woman, Magdalena Avalos, drifted away to dance alone, and then to spin with a one-armed man by the jukebox. Three whitemen in the booth behind you bragged about the ducks they'd slaughtered last autumn. The creatures made a terrifying sound, mallards and pintails hissing and chewing. The first three shots cleared a path: dozens lay strewn, wounded and dying. The others rose, a jabbering cloud. The men fired again, three more shots, and then another three—that was all it took—the sky opened. They stood stupid in a rain of ducks, stunned by a storm of feathers. A hundred and eight birds dropped dead between them. They laughed now, remembering the crime, ninety-nine ducks past the limit. The men spent all day gutting and plucking.

You tried to be Tonto, one of those two-syllable wooden Indians, but your thoughts roared, and the men must have heard them. You looked into the eyes of the auburn bear whose head and skin hung from the ceiling, and you meant to whisper only to him, but your heart betrayed you.

Father, you cried, *Father, forgive them.*

Then you laughed a wild Indian laugh and you whooped one last wild whoop and the three white hunters lifted you high and danced you out into the alley, not in a tender way, not soft like Magdalena. They pushed you to your knees. They wanted you to be sorry.

You were sorry: for the ducks and the elk and the bear and the children, for the sheep on the hill and a black man in Florida, electrocuted twice because the first time the chair sparked and fizzled, and he didn't die: only his hair and slippers caught fire. His picture in the paper last week looked so familiar, so much like you, you taped it on your mirror, beneath the bright angel family.

The men wanted you to pray, and you wanted this too, wanted to believe in a god that hears, and comes, and loves in mercy. Your pants were torn, your knees scraped, your palms full of grit and bloody. You felt the first kick and the second, and the blow to the back of your head, and you closed your eyes, and the god who answers in mysterious ways spared you all joy and pain, all desire, all language.

You woke in the moonlight, facedown on the rocks by the Bitterroot River. They must have dumped you here, and you thought, *This is fine,* and you saw ponies swimming and a dog with a halo. When you woke again, Magdalena Avalos and her one-armed friend Gideon Daro were rolling you up in a tarp and carrying you to her Chevy. They were strong, these two, despite age and afflictions. Gideon had a story like yours, an arm of his own left back in the jungle.

In her trailer, in her bed, Magdalena splinted your broken fingers with sticks and bandaged your slashed belly with rags torn from a child's Superman pajamas. *Try not to move,* she said. *You're leaking.*

Twenty-two years you'd waited for this. You loved your own precious life. You couldn't help it. You wanted to stay alive—one more hour, one more day—to lie here like this while a woman who wasn't afraid touched you.

When you were strong enough to kiss, you kissed. When you could dance, you danced Magdalena Avalos out under the stars. She wore a heavy shawl, sewn with acorns and shells and juniper berries. It opened and closed, violet and green, one great wing whirling around you. It sang with its thousand bells, this shawl with a voice like no other. You fell in the tall grass. You thought you had fallen forever.

But Magdalena wouldn't let you stay. She said, *If you have a home go home. If anybody wants to love you, let them.*

Twenty-two years, and then you were home, holding baby Jeanne in your sister's kitchen. Blessed was the God who hears, who had kept you alive and sustained you and delivered you whole to this moment. Blessed was Roshelle's kiss full and wet on your sweet mouth in the soft light of morning. Blessed was the child you held, the child reborn, the one come to save you.

Your people thought you'd stay for days and years to come.

The living, the left behind, the bereft think of all the days unlived—tomorrow and tomorrow. But you thought only of today, each holy moment. Blessed was this God who belonged to no one, who was the spark in all things, in everyone, everywhere. Blessed was this life, not held, not in you alone, not contained in one body: *this* life, *this* God, moving here as breath, as light, as love between you.

The wounded Vietnamese mother took you in her arms at last, Raymond Good Bird, her own, her most beloved child. Blessed was the mother of God. You and she knew only comfort.

Bid Farewell to Her Many Horses

LUIS ALBERTO URREA

Luis Alberto Urrea, 2005 Pulitzer Prize finalist for nonfiction, is a prolific writer who uses his dual-culture life experiences to explore greater themes of love, loss, and triumph.

Born in Tijuana, Mexico, to a Mexican father and an American mother, Urrea has authored eleven books. He won the Lannan Literary Award in 2004, and has been a recipient of the Christopher Award. Urrea also won a 1999 American Book Award and was voted into the Latino Literature Hall of Fame. His book of short stories, Six Kinds of Sky, was named the 2002 small-press Book of the Year in fiction by ForeWord Magazine. He has also won a Western States Book Award in poetry and was in the 1996 Best American Poetry collection.

Urrea lives with his family in Naperville, Illinois, where he is a professor of creative writing at the University of Illinois–Chicago.

THE INDIANS WEREN'T talking to me. At Gabe's food store, they looked away from me when I bought a soda. There were three of them in there, plus Gabe's wife. Just to tweak them, I popped the lid right there and chugged it. Obviously, word had gotten around the res. They knew why I'd come, but they didn't know what to think of it. I felt bad enough. Their anger only made it worse.

Out in the light, I felt eyes watching me. The perfect smell of South Dakota was all over the street—I could fly in that air, fat with miles of prairie and storm clouds rushing from Nebraska to Iowa. I hunched up my shoulders. White boys visiting Pine Ridge can't help but remember all those cowboy movies. You listen for a whistling arrow, prepare for the mortal *thwack* when the shaft nails you between the shoulder blades. Well, at least this white boy does. I probably had it coming.

I'd married one of the local girls. Her family didn't want her to marry me. They didn't want her to marry any white man. But we were wild for each other. We ran off to Deadwood, to a small chapel near the casinos. The minister was a Brule Sioux. She was Oglala. We took our honeymoon in the Black Hills—*Paha Sapa*, she told me, the center of the world. We stayed in a small motel below Mt. Rushmore. We bought those T-shirts that show four huge bare asses and say: "Rear View Mt. Rushmore." We laughed. Everything was funny.

Then the usual tough years. We went to California, both of us trying college. She tried writing to her family, but they were fighting mad. Our few visits back to the reservation were grim. I thought I was lonesome, but what happened to her heart out in California was a terror to see. I'd catch her looking up at the rattling palm trees sometimes, this look of sorrow on her face that almost looked like rapture.

And she couldn't get out of the bottle. They blamed me. I started to believe it, too. I'd fooled her away from her people, her world. Empty bottles, hidden at first beneath the sink, behind the apartment, clanked in the trash basket. She was quiet, as old-time Indian women are, and she wore a long braid in the old way. When she crashed the car, they say the braid was caught in the glass of the window. I don't know—I couldn't bear to look at the body. I sent her home on a train. It took me two days to drive out after her, and now I was burying my wife in the little graveyard near Our Lady of the Sioux. The headstone was already made. It said: "Joni Her Many Horses, Daughter, Sister. We Will Miss You. 1960–1990." They left my name off entirely.

DON HER MANY horses was Joni's oldest brother. Back in high school, when our teams played the Indians from Red Cloud, Don was a monster on the basketball courts. The way things were in those days, though, Indian boys didn't get too many victories. Even when they won. It was easy—the refs called them foul, or ejected them from the games for the least infraction. If they did win, they'd get their asses kicked after the game if we could find them . . . if there were more of us than them.

I made the mistake once of cracking wise to Don on the court. After one spectacular drive to the basket—when Don seemed to be floating over our heads for an impossible distance, then drove the ball down through the hoop so it caught no net, just streaked and hit the floor like a rock—I sidled up to him. I did what all us whites did in those days, dreaming of ourselves in Technicolor cowboy hats, our ideas as fixed as

Mt. Rushmore, made sick in our hearts whenever we saw an Indian smile, certain somehow his smile took something away from our own souls.

"Hey, Chief," I said. "You got-um heap good medicine, huh? Y—"

Bang.

I was gone from the world.

When I came to in the shower room, it was like drifting out of deep purple water flecked with chips of fire. They brushed my skin as I surfaced. A million sweaty and hysterical dudes were glaring down at me. "Bobby!" they were shouting. "Bobby!" Don Her Many Horses was in jail, charged with aggravated assault. There had been trouble with the Indian kids, both teams slugging it out on the court. Cops had come in, sticks swinging. I listened to them babbling all about it as I stood in the shower, letting the water claw into my back and scalp. My left eye was tender as cube steak, and I could tell it was turning black.

"Shit," I said to no one in particular, "that brave sure can pack a punch!"

We all laughed and said the standard anti-Indian things you say. But I knew I was wrong. Here Don had made a spectacular play and I'd gone and opened my big ignorant mouth. I don't know that it changed my life. Maybe a little bit. I didn't turn all religious or anything over it.

DON HER MANY horses wasn't much interested in me at that point. He was slumped on the cot in his cell, nursing a collection of welts and eggs coming up all over his forehead. He had a rusty-bloody old rag soaked from the tin sink and held over one eye. I watched the water drops fall and hit the knee of his jeans. They shone bright for a second then sank in, spreading a color like grape juice as the denim darkened.

"Hi," I said.

"Fuck you, Bobby."

I ducked my head.

"Listen," I said. "I want to apologize for what happened."

He looked up at me. That eye was about swollen shut.

"Apologize, huh?" he said. He smiled a little. "All right. Go ahead."

"Sorry."

He stared at me with his one black eye. He didn't talk. That's one thing that drives you crazy with the Indians. Sometimes they just don't say anything. You don't know if they're thinking or laughing at you or what.

"I'm . . . ," I said, "sorry. You know. About that wisecrack. And now you're in jail."

"Yeah, I can see that," he said.

Another pause.

"You got any chew?" he said.

I dug my tin of Copenhagen out of my back pocket and tossed it to him. Those boys, when they're not smoking, they're chewing. The women, too. Joni always had a little plug of peppermint tobacco pinched into her lip. I gave it up after high school. Don does it to this day.

I was thinking about leaving when he spoke: "You know what?" he said. "Next time I see you, I might have to take me a scalp. I might skin you, too. Brain-tan your hide and have me a new pelt to paint my winter count on. Hang your balls from my war lance. 'Course, everybody'd have to get up *real close* to see 'em."

There was nothing to say to that, so I left. I could hear his back-of-the-throat little laugh skittering around behind me as I walked down the hall. Damned Indians.

THE RESERVATION MEDICAL examiner was taking care of Joni. I couldn't even look at the building as I drove by. I hooked south, out of Pine Ridge Village, heading toward White Clay, Nebraska. A couple of the guys driving around recognized me. Yellowhorse waved, one of the Red Clouds nodded imperiously at me, raising one hand as he coasted by in his old Ford pickup. They were burning a small pile of tires outside of town; the smoke rose like a mourning veil torn by wind. It angled away, fading to a haze that reached all the way out to the edge of the Badlands. The grass looked like Marilyn Monroe's hair. Horses swept through it like combs.

I was listening to KILI, "The Voice of the Lakota Nation." They were playing a twenty-megaton dirge by Metallica. It was followed by some Sioux music—the Porcupine Singers. If I listened long enough, they'd probably toss in some jazz and three Johnny Cash songs. There were supposed to be announcements of Joni's burial on there, but I never did hear any. I pulled up at the gate of the Her Many Horses spread. Don was walking a mottled gray horse in slow circles in front of their house. He ran his hand along the horse's flank; its skin jumped at his touch. It was limping. He glanced up at me and turned back to the horse.

I dropped the section of barbed wire fence that served as a gate and drove through.

"Close the gate!" Don hollered.

"I know, I know," I muttered to myself. Six dogs and four young horses headed for the opening, but I beat them to it. The horses veered away, suddenly innocent and fascinated by the sage plants beside the drive. The dogs charged me, then collapsed in the dirt, wagging their tails.

I drove up to Don, shut off the engine, and got out.

"She's sick," he said.

The old horse looked like rain clouds. I recognized her. They called her Stormy.

"That's Joni's old horse," I said.

Stormy put her giant old face next to Don's. He rubbed her long white upper lip. "That's okay," he murmured. "That's okay now."

"I'm sorry, Don," I said. "I did my best."

"Stormy's dyin'," he said. He had this disconcerting way of ignoring what I said. "I've been feeding her this medicine they give me down in Rapid. But them vets don't know shit about horses. You know it? She's got these tumors." He stroked Stormy's side. I saw that she was bloated, her abdomen distended like a barrel behind her ribs. "Now we got to kill her."

Stormy snorted.

"Go on now," he said to her. "Go ahead." She limped away.

"Them mother-effers."

"Don?" I said. "I'm sorry. About Joni. I mean, I'm sorry about Stormy too. But, what I mean . . ."

One of the dogs nosed my crotch.

"Stop it," said Don. "I got a trailer pulled around back. You sleep there. Got food if you're hungry."

He lit a cigarette and walked away.

NIGHT ON THE reservation is like night nowhere else. They say flying saucers visit the Sioux lands. Flying saucers and ghosts. When you're out there, there's a blackness that's deeper than black. The stars look like spilled sugar. You can hear the grass sometimes like water. Like somebody whispering. And the weird sounds of the night animals. Anything could happen. You get scared, and it's for a reason that hides behind the other reasons—behind the silence, and the coyotes, and the dogs barking, and the eerie voice of the owl. It's that *this is not your land. This is their land.*

And you don't belong. A thousand slaughtered warriors ride around your camp, and you think it's the breeze. And they wonder why you're there.

I had the sleeping bag pulled over my head. It smelled like dust. My wife was lying five miles away, her breasts already dense as leather in death, her eyelashes intertwined, the perfect brown tunnels of her eyes sealed, the path within already forgotten. "Joni," I said. "Joni. Joni."

I MET HER at night. Off the reservation, there are small joints scattered all along the roads. You can go in there for ice cream or burgers or beer. Lots of them sell Indian art and beads to the tourists, and a bunch of them still won't let an Indian in the door. The reservation folks knew which stores wanted them and which didn't.

We were in one that didn't. Six of the footballers from our school were in there with me. It was one of those dull nights. Red Cloud School had won the football game. They'd all been going down to see that *Little Big Man* movie, and they were all turned on. They were crazy-wild. Nobody could catch them.

Franklin Standing Bear's car broke down. He came walking up to the place from the road to Hot Springs. I watched him through the window, materializing out of the blackness. He paused in the parking lot, looking at us. His glasses glittered in the lights. I nudged one of the boys and pointed with my chin.

"Gaw-damn," he said.

We left our spoons sinking into our sundaes and gawked.

Franklin came in the door and dodged his head.

"More balls 'n brains," one of the football boys said.

Franklin went to the register and asked to use the phone. Sonny, the owner, had served in Korea with Franklin's dad, so he let him use the phone. But he told him he'd best get moving as soon as he was through.

We hustled out to the lot and waited for him, all jittery with crazy heat.

Franklin came out and our quarterback called, "Hey, boy!"

He put his hands up in front of him and said, "Not looking for trouble."

"You calling me a troublemaker?" the footballer asked.

"Look," Franklin said, "my car's busted down. That's all."

"You Indian boys did pretty good tonight," said the tight end. He looked like a chimp in the half light. All beady glittery eyes, stupid with lust. Jeez, this is how it begins, I thought.

"I don't know nothing about it," said Franklin. "I was over to Rose-bud." He was drifting away.

"Rosebud," the first footballer said. "What kind of a faggot name is that, Standing Bear? You Indians all faggots or what? That why you got them ponytails?"

Franklin had a frozen smile on his face. He could see a freight train coming and he couldn't get out of its way.

"Let's go inside," I said. I tugged on the tight end's sleeve. "C'mon," I said.

Franklin Standing Bear spit on the ground.

"You know what?" he said. "You're just a bunch of low-life shit-lipped pud-pulling cow fuckers. I'm about fed up with your bullshit, so come on cowboys! Fuck it! *Hoka hey!*"

Oh man, I thought, he's doing his war cry. It was a good day to die. Franklin was in full-on warrior mode now.

The footballer grunted and charged at him. Franklin leaped about three feet high and kicked him precisely in the mouth. Franklin's glasses flew one way; blood and teeth flew the other. The footballer fell back, squealing, rolling on the blacktop with his fingers in his mouth. They closed in on Franklin, but he broke for the road. All our bootheels sounded like three horses crossing a highway. I didn't know what the hell I was doing. I was just running.

Two sets of headlights rounded the curve, and Franklin dodged between them. Indians poured out at us, like they were flying out of the light. One of them was Joni. She cornered me, waving a tire iron in my face. God, she was beautiful. She looked like a wolf; her small perfect teeth were bared, the muscles in her arms tight with rage. She was wearing a small choker. The cold had made her nipples stand up. She hissed and cussed at me. In her cowboy boots, she was taller than I was. I was sure she was going to knock my head loose. The sound of massacre was all around us. Don appeared beside Joni, grinning. He was panting from the fighting, flushed and sweaty.

"Well, well," he said. "It's the Indian lover." He turned to Joni. "This here is a big Indian lover. Isn't that right, Bobby?"

Joni stopped waving the iron at me.

"Hey," said Don. "You come out here to *apologize?*"

There was a scattered rubble of white boys all over the road.

"I don't know," I said.

"You don't know," Joni taunted.

"I don't know." I was looking around.

"Looks like you picked the wrong place to be," she said. "That's for damn sure."

But they didn't do anything about it. We walked over to Don's car—a ferocious orange Chevy Impala—and Don drove us back to the edge of the lot and put me out. "Forgive us," he said in the phoniest arch-sounding accent, "if we shan't stop in for tea." They burned rubber. They were doing those manic *yip-yip* war cries as they sped away. I thought Joni waved good-bye, but I couldn't be sure.

We met again at a movie theater, by accident. I finally got down to see *Little Big Man*, and damned if I didn't wish I was a Sioux warrior. Somebody in the balcony kept pelting me with popcorn, though, but every time I turned around, there was nobody there. I finally jumped out of my seat and glared up there. Joni was laughing down at me. I blushed. After that, I kept thinking of the massacre at the Indian village—I kept thinking of a soldier shooting Joni in the back as she ran. It made me sick inside. I couldn't get the picture out of my mind. I was Dustin Hoffman, and I watched Joni run and die, run and die, in slow motion, extreme close up. The next time we saw each other, we were on.

MORNING. HORSES. THEY walked in patient circles around the trailer, snorting as they went past the screened window, trying to get a whiff of me without letting me know they were inspecting. Today was the burial. I got up, dragged on my jeans and a T-shirt, and stepped out. They trotted away with their ears bent back and their tails lifted. I went in the house quietly, but Don was already up, sitting at the table drinking coffee. He gestured to a skillet with three eggs and some bacon fried up. "Toast," he said, nodding to a stack of bread slices on a saucer before him. Silent, I got my breakfast and sat across from him. We stared at each other as I ate. Don's boy, Snake, was asleep on the couch, facedown. Elinore Her Many Horses could be heard taking a shower. I was through eating. "Thanks," I said. "Put them dishes in the sink, hey?" he said. I did it. Then I waited my turn for the shower. Then it was time to go. I drove in my truck alone.

BETWEEN BREAKFAST AND packing to leave, I can't remember the day. As soon as I saw the coffin, I was hit in the ribs, like a shovel swung by a batter. I kept focusing on breathing, dragging in air and letting it out slowly. My memory of everything else is a vague gray hum. I know that one of the Catholic Brothers from Red Cloud School led the service, and somebody played piano. I can't remember anybody's face, just the thought: breathe-breathe-breathe. Then we were standing on the steps of the church like a real family, and I shook hands with a faceless crowd. I didn't cry.

At the graveyard, I stood behind Don, about three paces, and watched the grass waver in the breeze. And afterward, I stopped at Red Cloud's grave to pay my respects to the old chief. Some Oglalas had left him tobacco ties, little sacred bundles in all the colors of the four directions. I asked him to take care of my woman out there, where she was new and maybe lost. I asked him to take her into his lodge and protect her until I could come for her. That's all I remember.

I ROLLED DON'S sleeping bag carefully, taking pains to leave the little trailer neat. It was already late afternoon. We'd sat around inside, sipping coffee, murmuring. The television was on, turned down low. Snake stared at MTV, never looking up. Elinore sat beside me on the couch, and she periodically got up and fetched me cookies or more coffee, though I didn't ask for any. After tending to the sleeping bag, I stuffed my jeans into a small bag, and stepped outside and headed across Don's pasture, away from the trailers to the dark hump of the sweat lodge he'd built near a small stand of cottonwoods. I walked down to the stream that cuts through Don's eighty acres. There was one spot, one small, white-gravel pool where Joni and I made love.

It was perfectly matched to my memory, like a photo pinned inside my skull. I remembered every detail, even the giggling terror that Don, or their old man, Wilmer, would catch us at it. I stood there watching the wasps sip water at the edge of the pool, where the gravel gave way to mud. I half expected to see the double-seashell imprint of her bottom on the shore. Dragonflies tapped the water. I'd moved in her, minnows between our legs, tickling us. Bubbles came out of her body and ran over my sides.

There were tiny smears of black hair in her armpits. Her nipples were small and dark as nuts. She hardly had any hair on her body. Afterwards, as we lounged in the water, chewing leaves of spearmint that grew on the banks, she played with the hair on my chest. She scratched it: I could hear her nails scraping. I leaned up on one elbow, watching my seed rise from her and drift. It looked like a pearl column of smoke.

"Bobby."

I jumped. I looked around, feeling caught.

It was Don. He had a rifle on one shoulder. He was leading Stormy. They were dark against the sky. Huge.

"I . . . ," I said. "I guess I saw a ghost."

Don nodded.

Stormy brushed flies away from her sides with lazy smacks of her tail.

"Wanna come?" he said, gesturing at the horse with his head.

I clambered up the bank and followed him. You could hear bees working the alfalfa and the sweetgrass. Stormy's limping gait played on the ground like a drumbeat. Don stared at the ground as we walked. She wheezed, the sound pitifully hollow and weak.

"Stormy thinks we're having fun," he said.

Her ears still turned to each sound. She watched a dove burst out of a small bush and fly away. She dipped her head at tall grasses, though she couldn't eat anymore. I noticed her legs trembling.

We took her over a small hillock, out of sight of the house and the other horses. "All right now," Don murmured. He worked the bit out of her mouth and pulled off the bridle. She worked her long yellow-brown teeth. She stared off.

Don cranked a round into the chamber. The lever sounded cool and final as it slid home.

"I tried," I said. He didn't look at me. "Whatever I did wrong, I loved your sister."

Don petted Stormy.

"I know it," he said. "Shit. I guess we all know it."

He raised the gun and fired into her head, behind her left ear. It was a sharp little *crack*, like a dry branch snapping. I jumped. She jerked her head straight up and fell. Her legs just vanished. Don had to dance out of her way when she dropped. The whole thing was unbelievable, some kind of trick. One of her hooves twitched; she groaned; then it was done. The silence was like a curtain in a play. You couldn't even see any blood. Don was standing there, the smoking rifle loose in his grip. I looked up at him—his eyes were closed, his head went back, and he began to sing.

He began to sing, quietly at first, but it grew louder as he went. Long mysterious Sioux sounds, Indian words that could have been going out to God, or to Stormy, or to Joni, there was no way of knowing. But his voice rose, became a haunted sound, a cry from someplace else. I wanted to join him. I wanted to sing, to cry my pain and loss to Him—to the Grandfather, to the one she'd called *Wakan Tanka*. But I had no song, I had no prayer. I felt so small beside the voice of Don Her Many Horses.

I closed my eyes and stood with him. The good horse-smell still rose from Stormy. And he sang. I started to sob, it just tore out of me. I thought I might fall down, but his hand gripped my upper arm to steady me. The wind sighed around us, and there were crows. Don kept singing, but he had slowed, enunciating carefully, and I realized he wanted me to follow. My voice was weak, at first, tentative, but I repeated the sounds. He waited until I grew strong in my song.

We sang for a long time, together. We sang until dark. We sang until I thought we would never find our way home.

Hearts

RICHARD S. WHEELER

Recipient of the 2001 Owen Wister Award for Lifetime Achievement in Western Literature, Richard S. Wheeler is a five-time Spur Award–winning author with more than fifty titles published about the American frontier. He has also been a mentor to many other popular Western writers.

A former newspaper and book editor, Wheeler lives in Livingston, Montana.

LAURA DUVALL HAD expected every man in Tombstone to wear a sidearm, but that was not what she discovered as the Wells Fargo agent opened the door of her coach. She did not see a holstered weapon. At least not at first.

She had choked on the golden dust all the way from Benson, along with the fumes emanating from seven overheated males jammed onto the sticky leather seats. She knew the Arizona heat would torment her, and had prepared for it as best she could with a dress of white muslin that filtered air through her gauzy camisole and petticoat.

It was her turn to step out, and as she did so she spotted a familiar face in the shadow of the awning over the boardwalk. John Behan, sheriff of Tombstone. She knew him but he didn't know her. She would have known him even without the polished steel circlet on his chest. She had studied numerous tintypes of him and had read lengthy reports describing him. One thing he always did was meet the stage.

And now he was lounging casually in the shadow, out of the fierce Arizona sun this May day of 1881. She stepped into the dust of Allen Street and let the faint breeze begin to erase the sweat that had darkened the armpits of her white dress. Behan's attention was entirely upon her. She did that to certain men. She was not particularly beautiful, but striking, with bold chestnut hair now largely concealed under her broad-brimmed white straw hat. She turned her back to Behan, a deliberate gesture fraught with messages. The Jehu and Wells Fargo agent were unloading the boot, where her two items of luggage nestled.

Duvall was not her real name, but she used it with some success in her field, where French names opened doors. It had been the name of her lover, Jean Duvall. The late Jean Duvall, but few people knew that, either. Before that she had been married to a dull army lieutenant, Jason Keogh, but he had divorced her . . . for adultery.

She bent her thoughts away from that. Her two pieces of luggage descended to the dirt of the street. One was a routine pebbled black leather portmanteau; the other an oblong case that always aroused curiosity. It held the oilcloth faro layout, the faro box, casekeeper, numerous unopened decks of plain-backed cards, and several chip trays.

She eyed the luggage, knowing she would need a porter, and that's when Behan glided in.

"Help you, ma'am?"

The sheriff stood before her, darkly Irish, of medium height, a man with knowing eyes and a face full of question marks and lust.

"Why, you're the sheriff. Perhaps you can recommend a hotel."

His gaze surveyed her and she understood that he was not merely assessing the obvious costliness of her attire. He had instantly discovered the thing she tried so hard to conceal, the thing that only a connoisseur of women would unearth. Not even her high-necked and prim dress could conceal her one vulnerability from eyes such as his. He had known nothing about her, but suddenly knew everything.

That figured. Sheriff Behan was a Democrat. Laura Duvall had formulated an iron law of life: Republican gents were bad lovers but were good at business, while Democrat males knew everything there is to know about pleasing a woman but couldn't do anything else with their feckless lives. John Behan was a case in point. She knew that in five minutes he would turn her to pudding, and that he was dangerous, and that she must avoid him and get on with her mission.

"The Cosmopolitan Hotel, I think. It would be suitable for a lady of your sort."

"Thank you. You may take my bags there," she said, faintly enjoying the imperial command.

"And whom do I have the honor of welcoming to town?"

"Laura Duvall," she said.

His eyes registered nothing.

"I am Sheriff Behan, at your service," he said.

"No doubt about it," she said.

He plucked up her bags, obviously curious about the oblong one. "What do you do?" he asked.

"Gamble."

"A lady gambler. Well, I know a few parlors where you'd be welcome."

"I rarely am unwelcome."

He steered her into the hotel, which stood only a few doors away, and waited while she negotiated a room.

"You're in luck," he said. "Usually it's full. It's not the cheapest place in town, either."

He was fishing. She smiled.

"Thank you, Mr. Behan. I'm sure we'll be running into each other soon."

Behan stood there, trying to prolong the meeting, but finally smiled and retreated into the heat.

The clerk helped her to her second-floor room.

Her expense money from William was adequate, but it wouldn't allow her to stay in this sort of quarters for long unless she got very lucky. The Pinkertons did not pay their agents well. He had sent her here to find out what she could about the rampant lawlessness in Cochise County. He had wanted a detailed telegraphic report in a fortnight, if possible. They had worked out a code and an address that would keep the report and its recipient entirely private.

Somebody wanted to untie the Gordian knots of Cochise County, but William refused to tell her who his client was.

"It's best if you don't know. Keep an open mind. Look at all sides. Use your charms."

She knew what he had meant.

"Each side is pointing fingers at the other. All we know is that rustling is rampant; murder so commonplace that it is scarcely noted in the local papers; and Wells Fargo coaches carrying bullion from the silver mines are robbed so frequently that the losses for the insurers, Wells Fargo, and the mines, are rocketing. Death is in the air down there."

"It's Wells Fargo, then."

"I'm not at liberty to say, and don't assume anything. I will tell you one thing: Wells Fargo already has a private agent in Tombstone."

And that was all she could get out of him.

This would be rather easy. She would report to William in a fortnight, maybe less. Women had their ways. William had alluded to that without ever saying it or asking her to employ her charms. Damned puritan hypocrite. She already knew the cast of characters, thanks to some elaborate preparation in the Chicago offices of the Pinkerton Detective Agency. All she needed was to start some pillow talk.

She doffed her muslin dress, poured water from the pitcher into the bowl, and gave herself a spitbath. The tepid water felt like heaven. Twenty minutes later she was ready for Tombstone. With luck, she might have her game going before nightfall.

Odd how she already liked the town even before examining it closely. It had the effrontery to put on cosmopolitan airs, even if it had mushroomed out of desert wastes in barely three years. It was all veneer, like the flocked bloodred wallpaper that hid the rude planks of this ramshackle building. It was a gaudy fake of a burg, and reminded her of herself.

She liked Johnny Behan, and wished she didn't. What sort of man met the arriving coaches just to womanize? She liked to be womanized, and that was the trouble. The Pinkertons didn't know that.

Like most Arizona towns, this one slumbered through the midday heat. Tonight it would come alive and kill a few more people. She didn't like daylight anyway. But she would have to brave the sun now, and try to set herself up.

She finished her ablutions, dabbed lilac between her breasts, and headed into the blistering heat. Her objective was the Oriental, less than a block away, the best saloon and gambling emporium in Tombstone, and the locus of high rollers. Wyatt Earp had a piece of the action there. Lou Rickabough, Dick Clark, and Bill Harris ran the gambling operation, and had given Earp a quarter interest mainly to protect the place. The other side, the Cowboys and Behan, were scheming to shut it down.

Earp was a Republican, damn him. He wouldn't know the first thing about women, and worse, wouldn't care.

She walked through the open double doors and into gloom. Her first impression of the Oriental was one of ornate melancholia. A gorgeous mahogany and white marble bar dominated one side. Light from the front doors faded swiftly, and to the rear, where the solemn gambling tables lay, the darkness was pervasive. But she could make out a handsome blue and gold Brussels carpet, and extravagant glass chandeliers

above. At night it would be different, but by day, the Oriental was as for-
lorn as a cemetery. The place was almost empty, which was what she expected midafternoon of a weekday.

The rank odor of smelly armpits told her men were about somewhere
in there. She made out assorted bodies once her eyes adjusted. Only one
table was operating, a faro outfit with a small dim lamp burning above
it. It had no customers.

But closer at hand, at a marble bar table, sat several dead-faced men
she identified at once, again from assorted tintypes she had scrutinized.
Wyatt Earp and Morgan. Lou Rickabough. Dapper Luke Short, looking
like a Manhattan swell but far more deadly. They were sipping fizzy
phosphates.

Good.

"You looking for something, ma'am?" The sepulchral voice emanated
from the mustachioed bartender she knew to be Frank Leslie, an enig-
matic gunman. Was it the faint redolence of burnt gunpowder that
stamped the Oriental as the most memorable sporting palace she had
ever been in?

"Yes, the owners of the gambling concession."

The bartender nodded her toward the sole occupied table.

Rickabough stood.

"You come to reform Tombstone, ma'am?"

"I deal."

"No women," said Wyatt Earp.

She stared at the Illinois man. Big, slim, blond, ice-blue eyes, and a
gaze that would frost a windowpane. He stared back, his eyes measuring her for God knows what. Probably a black enameled coffin. He was
not visibly heeled. Her pulse quickened. What was it about him?

"That's a little quick," she said. "I bring trade."

"Women are trouble."

She turned to portly, graying Rickabough, one of the owning partners.
"I'm Laura Duvall. I'll improve your trade. Do you want profits or not?"

Earp remained quiet this time.

"We don't need anyone, Miss Duvall."

"Mrs."

"Ah, yes, but recently widowed. New Orleans, right?"

She nodded.

"Aw, Wyatt, we need some action," said Morgan, admiring her with a bedroom stare. He oozed youthful enthusiasm and she wondered how long he let his cautious older brother dominate him.

"We've some safety concerns," Rickabough said. "If Mr. Earp is not inclined to let you run a table, then I'll have to acquiesce, as much as I'd be inclined to try out so comely a lady."

She didn't dislike him.

Wyatt continued to stare. "No women in here, but I'll buy you sarsaparilla," he said. "Then you'll take your trade elsewhere."

Rickabough looked unhappy but said no more.

"I made a temperance oath. No lips that touch sarsaparilla will ever touch mine. You sure you won't change your mind?"

Morgan snickered.

Wyatt never answered, but turned to the others. They had been discussing the recent perforation of some tinhorn called Charlie Storms by Luke Short, and returned to it. The perfume of gunpowder was what seduced Earps. They never noticed the cologne between her breasts.

She stood on one foot and then the other, but the employment interview had terminated. That damned Wyatt Earp.

No women.

She hurried out. The dead heat slapped her. She headed across Fourth Street and plunged into the Crystal Palace, and found it better lit from side windows. It boasted a made-in-France brass and porcelain chandelier, chased brass spittoons and a gaudy cherrywood bar with a fat lady, naked save for a diaphanous something or other crawling over her thick thighs, gazing down from a gilt frame.

She approached the keep, a mustachioed bald spaniel with popeyes.

"Who runs the games?"

"We don't serve women," the keep said.

"I said who runs the games? I deal."

"Forget it. He don't allow women behind the tables. You want to play, that's okay. You want to deal, you go down the street."

"I'll come back and ask him tonight."

The keep shrugged.

What the hell. Tombstone was a man's world.

She knew better than to try Jim Earp's Sampling Room, so she headed along Allen to the Alhambra, and got the same story. No distaff dealers. They once let Poker Annie play a high stakes game for fifty-one hours, but she was so ugly no one got into a fight, the keep explained.

She did no better at the Occidental. In fact, worse. The slick-haired tinhorn told her to set up shop in the sporting district. She could run a game there.

"I may be a sporting lady," she said, "but not on my back. I deal sitting up."

"You can sport with me sitting up," he said.

She was used to it.

They were all as bad as the Earps. Tombstone had no room for women. For the first time since she arrived, she began to fret about her mission. Her employer wanted facts. If she couldn't siphon them off the gaming tables, she would have to think of something else. But what?

She hiked back to the Cosmopolitan, wanting to lick her wounds and think. Bill Pinkerton had given her a couple of small jobs, but this was her first big one, and she didn't want to disappoint him.

She had known the Pinkertons for years. Family friends. She had grown up in flossy circles on Chicago's north shore, the daughter of a Great Lakes steamboat magnate. She had been given everything a young lady could want, and had made her debut to introduce her to polite society and potential husbands.

But she wasn't made for polite society. They had called her brazen and reckless back then, and several swain backed out of marriages at the eleventh hour. She couldn't help it. She had no intention of being the mistress of some dull brickpile on Lake Michigan full of whining children.

So much happened, so fast, that she could barely remember the whirligig. She had gotten herself disinherited after one wild episode, married an Army captain during one of her occasional respectable interludes, found herself divorced and in bed with a New Orleans gambler, and learned the trade only to have him succumb to a lead pill that erupted from a rival's derringer. Then she was on her own, and that was when William Pinkerton, who knew her well and had kept track, recruited her.

"Laura," he said, "you're perfect for us. At home in any situation. At home in a mansion or a yacht, at home in a casino, at home with the demimonde. At home with any sort of man."

The latter had been said delicately. Her conquests were legend. She had permitted herself a wry smile. Sleuthing would be entertaining, and being entertained was more important than money, except when she had none. She planned to give Bill Pinkerton about a hundred times his money's worth.

Her treatment at the Oriental rankled. If Wyatt Earp had the slightest understanding of the ways of the world, he would have shown her some respect. From her very first glance she had known she would do anything, be anything, for Wyatt Earp, and she loathed herself for it.

She knew that the worse he treated her, the harder she would try to seduce him. She knew all about him. He had stolen some theatrical tramp named Josie Marcus from Sheriff Behan, and that was one of the reasons Tombstone smouldered. A Juliet was usually at the bottom of gang wars, and Tombstone was about to be torn apart by one.

She intended to knock Wyatt Earp down a few pegs, and maybe the way to do it was already at hand. She had caught the eye of the sheriff, and that was an ace of hearts.

Much to her surprise, Sheriff Behan was sitting there in the small lobby. He rose smoothly as she entered.

"Ah, it's Mrs. Duvall. How did it go?"

"I think you already know."

He smiled. The man was as smooth as baby flesh. "Lawmen do hear things," he said. "It seems our sporting establishments have no room for a lady."

"A woman, you mean. Whether I'm a lady is debatable."

"A lady," he said. "It's a man's town, all right. How did matters proceed at the Oriental?"

"Mr. Wyatt B. S. Earp would have no part of me."

"How do you know his middle initials?"

"I live in the sporting world."

He smiled again. Butter lips, she thought. "Perhaps you are better off not working there."

"Why?"

"Oh, the Earps are not appreciated in some quarters."

"Your quarters."

He smiled once again. He was the smilingest sheriff she had ever met.

"You have something against him," she said. Like an actress named Josie.

His smile retreated for a moment. "I will help you if you wish."

"Maybe."

"Come along. I'll talk with certain friends at the Crystal Palace. I'll tell them that a woman dealer is good for trade. You'll suck the players right out of Rickabough's place, a looker like you. What shall I offer? You run your own table and they get a quarter of your take? That's the usual."

She nodded. The man had been around.

It took only moments. Behan talked to the proprietor, a man named Frank, and Frank talked to her, and she nodded, and she was invited to set up her table in a place that reminded her of a New Orleans mortuary.

"Give the Oriental a little competition," Frank said.

"There you are, Mrs. Duvall. A table and a living. You may thank me by letting me take you to dinner at the Maison Dore. Fine food, best this side of San Francisco."

She agreed. Behan didn't waste a minute.

"You gonna start tonight?" Frank asked.

"Don't copper the bet," she replied.

The gaudy french restaurant astonished her. Johnny Behan astonished her too. It would cost him a week's salary to feed her there. Plainly, wearing the badge was a lucrative business.

She waited until they were knife-deep in filets mignons before opening up certain lines of inquiry.

"I don't think I like Wyatt Earp," she said.

"So I heard."

"Then you already know the story. We don't want women, he said, and that was it. I was dealt out."

"That's what I heard."

"You have funnels for ears. Come on, Johnny Behan, tell me who runs Tombstone."

He smiled again, as if life were a secret.

They drifted through four courses, but not until the chocolate mousse did Sheriff Behan pitch the deal.

"You need protection," he said. "Single woman. I'll make sure you're unharmed and free to run your game for one quarter of the take . . ."

She smiled and awaited the rest. A man like Behan would give her options.

Two spoonfuls of mousse later he offered her the rest.

"Of course, you could always live with me."

"Pay you your quarter? And pay that Frank his quarter? And pay

Cochise County and Tombstone taxes for my table? That's another quarter. So I keep about a quarter of my winnings? That'd break the bank. The odds are no good."

"I am very skilled at what I do," he said softly.

She turned into pudding.

"I will decide after looking at your rooms and I hear the rest of your offer."

He nodded.

He led her through dead desert dusk to Toughnut Street, where he maintained a small shiplap-sided cottage with spindle gingerbread. That was luxury in a boomtown like Tombstone. Within she discovered lace curtains on each window, doilies strewn promiscuously over the horsehair furniture, a bathing closet with a clawfoot tub, sink and running water, and an unused dead kitchen with a zinc sink. The bedroom contained a single four-poster marital bed with a bedpan under it. A privy stood at the rear corner of the lot.

"Well?"

"Where is my bed?"

"You get me in the bargain."

She laughed, not unhappily. "I don't sell myself."

"My cut for protecting you is one fourth—unless you move in. You move in and there's no game table taxes, either. You keep everything except for Frank's cut."

Damn him. Damn him. He had ferreted her out and he was right. "All right, I'll try it. We'll see. Don't count on anything. Move my stuff from the hotel. I'm going to deal tonight, and after that, I'll be here."

He wasn't going to see her in this room again until two or three in the morning.

"I will do that," he said.

She had her table running by nine. A crowd gathered to buck the tiger—and have a gander. She invited the gander with a decollete neckline. The players stood three deep, and she was reaping a fat profit as she pulled the turns out of the faro box. At times she saw Behan gazing her way. At other times she discovered various Earps, especially Wyatt, peering dead-eyed at her and her spectacular trade. The gents from the Oriental didn't look a bit happy.

A shrewd jowly player, probably another tinhorn, kept doubling on his losses until she pointed at the sign saying there was a twenty-five-dollar limit, and then he got angry and began baiting her. Behan materialized out of nowhere.

"You heard the lady," he said.

The player turned and found himself staring at the steel circlet. He withdrew fifteen one-dollar blue chips, leaving twenty-five, and won on a coppered seven. He was still behind, but picked up his money and retreated, still under Behan's steady gaze.

Laura Duvall sighed.

In the dead of the night she discovered the sheriff was as much a killer in bed as a lady's man, and that was going to ruin her judgment, damn Democrat Johnny Behan all to hell.

That's how it went. But she learned nothing of consequence, except the names of those who came to visit Sheriff Behan. Whatever they said, they said far from her ears. Even so, the events of the next weeks bore out what information the Pinkertons already had: Behan's associates were the "Cowboys," as the mob of reckless outlaws from the adjoining ranches were called. The Clanton boys, the Laury boys, John Ringo, Curly Bill Brocius, a dozen more hard and murderous men. They all smiled politely at her, if she happened to be around, and led the sheriff off into the dusty streets. Behan spent a lot of time talking in a dead whisper to Harry Wood, editor of *The Nugget*, the Democrat paper that loudly defended them and Sheriff Behan, and assailed the Earps and Doc Holliday.

It dawned on her that the odds were staggering. The Earp brothers, and Holliday, and maybe a couple others, against a dizzying mob of fifty or sixty, every one of them skilled with deadly weapons, full of brag, and without even the tatters of conscience.

Boozy Harry Wood made every effort to lay the blame for ongoing holdups, stagecoach robberies, rustling, and mayhem at the door of the Earps, while Mayor John Clum's Republican *Epitaph* returned the fire, but less effectually. The Cowboys spent their ill-gotten loot liberally, and made friends everywhere, especially in the cathouses.

She heard talk of murder, revenge, triumph.

So they were going to kill the Earps and throw Holliday's emaciated corpse to the dogs. It was all coming clear. There were badges enough all around: the Earps had a deputy federal marshal badge and a city marshal badge. The Cowboys had a sheriff's badge. Legal murder.

The novelty of a woman faro dealer drew a lusty crowd every night.

As word got around the moribund outlying ranches, players drifted to the Crystal Palace and stood three deep at her table, waiting for the chance to play. That pleased her. She was bleeding trade from the Oriental, and making Wyatt Earp rue his words. A striking lady with a low neckline drew more players than some grease-haired tinhorn with soiled cuffs and tobacco-stained teeth.

Johnny Behan hovered around in the background, his meaty presence discouraging the toughs from trying to snatch her bank or cheat her or bully her with fake grievances. No sooner had a fortnight passed than the Crystal Palace was the hottest gambling emporium in Tombstone, every night a wake. She opened at three in the afternoon and rarely closed up before two in the morning, and the afternoons were her only slow moments.

That's when a woman named Kate drifted in and began playing during the sunlit afternoons when no one else was around. Laura liked her looks. Kate had a magnificent nose, thin and long and prominent, curved like a raptor's beak, an eagle nose, a noble nose that made her look royal. She spoke with a subtle accent that Laura discovered was Hungarian.

"I am John Henry Holliday's lover," Kate said one afternoon. "I have come to tell you things."

"Tell me?" Something froze in Laura. Had she been uncovered?

"I will tell you for my own reasons, even if you are Johnny Behan's woman."

"Why tell me anything? Keep your own counsel. If it's anything against Johnny, I don't want to hear it."

"Johnny is a famous lover. Not like the Earps."

Kate played a chip on a king, and Laura drew a turn. The king lost.

"Don't ever got hooked up with the Earps," she said. "At least not Wyatt. He uses women and throws them out."

"I have no intention. And why don't you talk about something else?"

"Because Wyatt is looking at you. He comes over here and watches you and thinks you don't notice."

"Mostly I don't. I keep my eyes on the board. You can't run a faro game any other way."

"What Johnny Behan has, Wyatt wants. He stole his Josie from Behan and kicked out his poor drunken Mattie. Now he's going to steal you."

Laura smiled. "Is this what you came to warn me about?"

"Yes. And not to believe a word, not one word, that Johnny Behan says about Doc or any of them."

Kate peered about sharply, afraid she had been overheard. She put five chips on the eight and coppered it. Laura drew a king and a four and adjusted the cases. Kate let her bet ride.

"Come to me if you want to know anything," Kate said. "I know everything."

Laura's caution welled up again. "About what?"

"About anything."

Laura yawned, drew a seven and six, and shuffled the deck, pulled the soda and hock and laid them faceup under the deck, and placed it in the faro box. Then she adjusted the cases and awaited Kate's play.

Laura kept her curiosity in check. "The only thing that interests me is my game," she said.

"Not Johnny?"

"It's cheaper than the Cosmopolitan—and paying the cut he wanted."

"So is Doc's room."

They laughed.

"What's Doc like?" Laura asked.

"A Southern gentleman, fragile, sad, quick-tempered and self-obsessed because consumption is killing him. He uses me. But I love him and always have. Is that strange?"

"No, not strange. Is he solvent?"

"Almost always. Cards are a living. He can't practice dentistry any-more. Not consumptive. But when he's broke, that's what he does until he's got a new stake."

"Why do the Cowboys say he robbed a stagecoach?"

"He's too sick to rob a child of candy. I beg of you, don't listen to Johnny Behan."

"Why does Johnny Behan say it, then?"

"Because Wyatt Earp stole that slut actress from him, and Doc is a friend of the Earps."

Laura smiled and cleaned Kate's five chips off the board. She had drawn a pair of eights, and all ties went to the house.

Kate sighed, and vanished toward the blind-bright doorway and the Crystal Palace went dead.

With a little encouragement, Doc Holliday's woman would divulge much of what Laura needed to know.

The next day Wyatt Earp sat down at her table, hulking over it as if he owned it. He had obviously waited for the moment when no other players were around. He exuded a faint malice, and she found herself loathing him. He bought a stack of dollar chips, laid one on the deuce, and coppered it.

She shuffled the deck, pulled the soda and hock, and stuffed it into the faro box. The first turn produced a seven and two. She pulled the chip off the table.

"You're costing us business," he said.

"That's good to know."

"What would it take to get you to leave?"

"I'm happy where I am."

If she had disliked him before, she hated him now. The man was a cool, assessing bully.

"You're Behan's lady."

She reddened slightly. "You're wrong on both counts."

He ignored it. "You're Behan's spy. Everything said at this table siphons into his big Irish ears, along with all your winnings."

"I'm glad you think so," she said. "And if I am, what's it to you? Here's Laura Duvall, setting up shop in the Crystal Palace because Wyatt Earp didn't want her in the Oriental. Here's Duvall, ending up with Sheriff Behan because Wyatt Earp wouldn't let her make an honest living in Tombstone. I tried every saloon in town and they all said no, and now I know why. Virgil made threats."

"You'd better be on the next stage out of town."

"I knew I was going to despise you. Play, dammit. Only players sit at my table."

"It doesn't matter to me what women think."

"Oh? Is that so? What I think is that Sheriff Behan's a crook. He lives pretty high on a sheriff salary, and I can't say I admire the gang he runs with. The only thing good about him is his way with women. He's a Democrat, and Democrats know how to pleasure ladies. I've yet to meet a Republican who was any good at it. He's a better man than you."

That sure as hell froze Deputy U.S. Marshal Earp to his stool.

"Still want me to leave?"

"Yes."

"Just try it."

He grinned suddenly and unexpectedly. "Maybe I will."

"You're a sonofabitch, Wyatt Earp."

Earp drifted into silence. A poxed cowboy, actually one of Behan's crowd, settled down, bought some chips, and began playing.

"I'll cash these," said Earp. "Cowshit's pretty thick around here."

She gave him eleven dollars.

That's how it stood. She was about to be booted out of Tombstone before she could finish her task. William Pinkerton was getting impatient. He'd spent a lot to put her in place, and she hadn't given him one snippet of information. The coded wires grew tart.

In the month she'd spent in Tombstone, it had all become clear enough. The Earps were brutes and greedy, but basically law-abiding and supported by the town's merchants. The Cowboys were flat-out bad men, itchy with the trigger finger, crooks, grafters, rustlers, stagecoach robbers, and ferocious executioners who didn't hesitate to rob and kill people in lonely places. The Cowboys were more fun. Behan milked the county of all that it was worth, and raked off a percentage of the gang's take, in exchange for "protection."

One other thing was obvious: the Earps, and their handful were outnumbered about ten to one, and weren't long for this world. Every time Laura spotted Wyatt or Morgan or Virgil Earp, she knew she was observing a dead man. Any day, something would set off the whole thing, and the Earp brothers would occupy permanent addresses on Boot Hill.

Young Morgan Earp played her game now and then, mostly to look down her neck, but Virgil never sat down and Wyatt played only to see who was buying her chips. She never saw the Earp women and wouldn't have recognized them if they had walked in. Wyatt Earp fascinated her, and stirred something morbid in her belly she couldn't name. He used women, Kate had told her, and there was something in Laura willing to be used. He drew women to him but would be a lousy lover. That was his paradox. It really didn't matter. Sometime, unless the Earps packed up, they would be lying cold and pickled in that glass-walled hearse that paraded down Allen Street a couple times a week.

She encountered Doc Holliday only once or twice, and knew that he wasn't long for the world, either. Death lay in his gaze, and if consumption didn't take him soon, he would try to hasten the matter by provoking a quarrel of his own. But she could see why her friend Kate, with the big nose, put such store in him. That frail, tragic honor-bound man was like a bird with a broken wing.

Then the kid, Morgan, quit playing at her table, and then Virgil began nabbing patrons of the Crystal Palace for public drunkenness and fining them eleven dollars. Then they announced a cockamamy new rule: no women in saloons. Laura knew it was aimed dead square at her, and it was because she was cleaning up. She had taken half the trade away from the Oriental, and the Earps finally decided to do something about it.

"You're my protector, so do something," she said to Johnny.

"I don't enforce city ordinances, Laura. I can't. I'm a county officer. It's up to Virgil Earp."

"So tell the Earps to get the hell out of the way."

He stared at her, and she realized he was dead afraid of them. Johnny the Protector wasn't protecting her.

"Guess I'll move on," she said. "Frank says I got to pack up the game and never come back to the Palace."

"No, stay."

"It's called whoring."

"What is?"

"My favors for your support. No thanks. I've got better things to do. I like the action."

"Suit yourself."

That was dead-hearted Johnny Behan, for you.

She packed up her rig at the Crystal Palace, paid Frank his quarter of the last night's deadfall, and stepped across the clay of Fifth Street and into the Oriental.

"You're not supposed to be in here," said Bill Harris.

"I won't be long. Where's the iceberg?"

"The who?"

"Wyatt."

"Taking lunch at his brother's saloon."

That meant crossing Allen Street, which she did, managing not to dip her hem in manure.

He was in there.

"Don't tell me I can't be in here, damn you."

He shrugged. Virgil, off in a corner, started to get up.

"I'll deal for you in the Oriental," she said. "Quit putting women out of saloons and I'll earn you more money than you ever saw before."

For once, that damned Wyatt Earp smiled. She didn't know how it was possible because he lacked the proper facial muscles.

"No. You should get out of here."

"Why?"

Earp peered about. A pair of rummies sat at the far end of the bar, talking to each other. He turned his back to them and lowered his voice.

"Because William wants you to."

She froze. "What are you talking about?"

"You stayed too long. They want the report. You should have wired it two weeks ago."

"You don't make any sense," she said, fearing that he made all too much sense.

"William Pinkerton asked us to boot you out of Tombstone."

"Wyatt Earp, you think you know something but you don't."

"You did a good job. Got right in bed with the Democrats."

She reddened.

"Miss Duvall, sweetheart, did you imagine that Republican President Garfield, would hire the Republican Pinkertons, to look into some political rivalry in the Territory without knowing in advance which side to support? Did you think they were going to turn their backs on the Republican Earps?"

She absorbed that. "I was working for the Garfield Administration?"

"You sure were. They'd heard that Tombstone was getting a bit frolicsome, and the president thought to run in the army or something. But first they needed facts. They turned to your Chicago friends to get them."

"And?"

"William sent you hither."

"And?"

"Instructed us to make sure you set up in the right shop. The Oriental isn't the right place. We hardly see a Cowboy in there. So we had to nudge you a little. Push you into the arms of Johnny Behan. Get you a table in a Cowboy hangout. Get you out of Tombstone when you overstayed."

"And?"

"It worked fine. Go wire your report. You know exactly who's rustling and robbing and killing around here. William's going to be pleased with it. Then catch the next train East."

It angered her. William Pinkerton had set up the whole deal. The president would get a report he could put to good use.

"You look unhappy . . . Jimmy, give her a sarsaparilla."

"The hell with you, Wyatt Earp," she said.

He laughed. "Have a drink."

"It was a sham. The whole thing was a sham. William sent me down here for nothing."

"No, for something. He could truthfully tell the president he had an operative here and she had laid the troubles to the Cowboys."

She had never been angrier. Swiftly, she came to some decisions. That swine William Pinkerton wouldn't get a report from her. Not one damned word. In fact he would never see her again. And she wasn't returning to Chicago. She'd head for Leadville and set up her game. The big play in Tombstone had supplied her with a fat bank, two thousand dollars. She'd take on the high rollers up in Colorado, and enjoy it. Johnny Behan, crook and grafter that he was, had treated her with ten times more respect.

She smiled suddenly. "You've gone one thing wrong, Wyatt. I've been in bed with Republicans."